LEARNING AND USING
GEOGRAPHIC INFORMATION SYSTEMS:

ARCGIS EDITION

LEARNING AND USING
GEOGRAPHIC INFORMATION SYSTEMS:
ARCGIS EDITION

Wilpen L. Gorr
*H. John Heinz III School of Public Policy and Management
at Carnegie Mellon University*

Kristen S. Kurland
*H. John Heinz III School of Public Policy and Management
and the School of Architecture at Carnegie Mellon University*

THOMSON
™
COURSE TECHNOLOGY

Australia • Canada • Mexico • Singapore • Spain • United Kingdom • United States

THOMSON

COURSE TECHNOLOGY

Learning and Using Geographic Information Systems: ArcGIS Edition

by Wilpen L. Gorr and Kristen S. Kurland

Acquisitions Editor
Maureen Martin

Senior Product Manager
Alyssa Pratt

Development Editor
Lynne Raughley

Marketing Manager
Penelope Crosby

Content Project Manager
Danielle Chouhan

Editorial Assistant
Erin Kennedy

Print Buyer
Julio Esperas

Compositor
GEX Publishing Services

Copy Editor
Mark Goodin

Proofreader
Karen Annett

Indexer
Rich Carlson

ISBN-13: 978-1-4188-3558-7
ISBN-10: 1-4188-3588-7

TABLE OF CONTENTS

Geographic information systems (GIS) is an amazing technology that fascinates and engages students. GIS maps have a dazzling array of purposes:

- Street maps create delivery routes, provide driving directions for the public and emergency vehicles, aid planning public transportation routes and schedules, and even pinpoint the location of fire hydrants and manhole covers.

- Maps that show geographic features help planners identify wetlands that need protection, areas at risk for flooding, and neighborhoods near or downwind from pollution sources.

- Population profile maps provide demographic analysis. At the neighborhood level, this data can reveal residents' ages, gender, ethnic background, income, educational attainment, transportation modes, and occupation. Such maps can help retailers determine the location and size of new stores—or which customers to target for increased business. Similarly, city planners can use such maps when planning public facilities.

- Crime maps show recent criminal activity in neighborhoods, identify locations' criminal history, and highlight "at risk" areas. Every major city's police department has crime analysts that produce daily and monthly crime maps for uniformed police, detectives, and top management.

- Maps that track long-haul trucks using global-positioning-system receivers can show where trucks are at any point time, how fast they are traveling, and provide directions to the nearest loads for return trips. The same technology can track emergency medical service, stolen, and military vehicles.

GIS maps are built layer by layer. A typical city might have more than 100 map layers, each showing a different feature type. A municipality's map layers can be combined with map layers from other sources to provide endless combinations of data that profile people, the land, infrastructure, and the built environment.

Extraordinary Free Resources

This textbook would be impossible without great GIS software and digital maps. The good news: (1) Great GIS materials are available, (2) this book shows students how to locate and use those resources, and (3) the digital maps are *free*!

The world's leading vendor of GIS, the Environmental Studies Research Institute (ESRI), produces a wide range of GIS software packages including *ArcGIS Desktop*™ that we use throughout this book. ArcGIS is software for use on a Windows 2000 or XP computer. It is available in many schools, colleges, and universities through educational site licenses. In addition, a 60-day trial version is available, and so is a one-year educational version for a nominal price. See the Appendix for details on obtaining site licenses and individual copies of ArcGIS.

Tax dollars are at work in this textbook: The Federal government used them to create digital maps for the entire United States and many spatially-referenced data sets, such as the decennial census, that can be mapped. These maps and data are free and easily downloaded from the Internet for your own city or community. In addition, many states, cities, and counties have created their own maps, which are often free for downloading.

A Unique Approach

There is no doubt that GIS is an exciting technology and career field. Unfortunately, the obstacle to entering this field is that it has a very steep learning curve—it is very hard to get a start in GIS. This textbook, however, flattens out the learning curve and makes it easy to teach, learn, and use GIS at an introductory level. We have been teaching GIS for more than 15 years to a wide range of students, including high school juniors and seniors, GIS practitioners, undergraduates, master-degree students, and Ph.D. candidates. *Learning and Using Geographic Information Systems* brings together all the good ideas and approaches to introducing this subject that we have discovered.

Learning and Using Geographic Information Systems provides a one-stop, complete educational solution for an introduction to GIS. It has both the instructional text students need to learn GIS's underlying principles, concepts, and knowledge, **plus** step-by-step tutorials for hands-on use of ArcGIS. This arrangement, with instructional text at the beginning of each chapter followed by computer tutorials, solves several problems. For instructors, it coordinates readings and tutorials for a good flow of study and computer lab work. For students, it means that they must buy only one book, and there is no waste in what they read—it all "bakes bread." Furthermore, the tutorials are time efficient because students already know the underlying concepts for use before turning their computer on. This means that the tutorial portions of this book have no background reading to slow down computer learning.

This textbook's only prerequisite is basic computer literacy, including the ability to locate and open files, use a file-compression program to unzip compressed files, and create simple word-processing and presentation documents. Some experience with spreadsheet software is desirable but not essential: We provide step-by-step instructions for the tasks to be carried out on Microsoft Excel and PowerPoint.

To the Student

ArcGIS requires a 1 GHz PC-Intel processor, minimum 512 MB RAM, and 765 MB of free disk space for a typical Windows XP computer installation. You will need an additional 1.23 GB of free space for installation of data files and for working through tutorials and exercises.

We want you to be able to work smoothly and quickly through the book's computer tutorials. At the same time, you need practice to internalize computer instructions. It is critically important, therefore, that you do the Practice exercises that are interspersed throughout the tutorials. They make you pause long enough to rethink and reuse what you just learned—and that really helps you start make the material your own. In many cases, you must complete these exercises to be able to continue tutorials.

To the Instructor

Instructors can use this textbook for a semester-long GIS course or for a module in an information technology (IT) course or other field of study. It can also be used for a short, stand-alone course on GIS. For IT courses, GIS makes an attractive extension to spreadsheet or database skills: It attaches the graphic features of maps to spreadsheet and database tables. For substantive coursework areas courses, such as geography, environmental science, public policy, or sociology, GIS is an invaluable tool for student projects.

Chapters 1 and 2, 1–3, or 1–4 make a nice short course, workshop, or course module that spans two weeks to a month at the pace of regular classes. Chapters 1–4, with exercises assigned, make a more complete introduction that can be covered in approximately three to four weeks. Adding the remaining chapters, which provide more advanced GIS capabilities, project management skills, and an independent project, can easily fill a semester course.

Supplemental Materials

This book is accompanied by the following materials:

- *Electronic Instructor's Manual*: The Instructor's Manual assists in class preparation by providing suggestions and strategies for teaching the text, chapter outlines, technical notes, quick quizzes, discussion topics, and key terms.

- *Solutions Manual*: The Solutions Manual contains answers to end-of-chapter questions and exercises.

- *Sample Syllabi and Course Outline*: The Sample syllabi and course outlines are provided as a foundation to begin planning and organizing your course.

- *ExamView Test Bank*: ExamView allows instructors to create and administer printed, computer (LAN-based), and Internet exams. The Test Bank includes an array of questions that correspond to the topics covered in this text, enabling students to generate detailed study guides that include page references for further review. The computer-based and Internet testing components allow students to take exams at their computers, and also save the instructor time by grading each exam automatically. The Test Bank is also available in Blackboard and WebCT versions posted online at *www.course.com*.

- *PowerPoint Presentations*: Microsoft PowerPoint slides for each chapter are included as a teaching aid for classroom presentation, to make available to students on the network for chapter review, or to be printed for classroom distribution. Instructors can add their own slides for additional topics they introduce to the class.

- *Figure Files*: Figure and table files from each chapter are provided for your use in the classroom.

- *Data Files*: Data Files, containing all of the data necessary for steps within the chapters are provided in the data CD-ROM that comes with this book, through the Thomson Course Technology Web site at *www.course.com*, and on the Instructor's Resources CD-ROM.

Book Organization

The goal of this book is to give students the knowledge and skills to do analytic mapping and provide information to shed light on issues in their own communities. To help students meet this goal, we use an actual project from our community as an example throughout the book. The project, the Swimming Pool Case Study, provides a real-world backdrop against which students can learn the principles of GIS.

The Case Study

The Swimming Pool Case Study is examined in each chapter. Its purpose was to provide information to help city officials in Pittsburgh, Pennsylvania, determine which public swimming pools to keep open. Prior to our consultation, city officials had closed half of the city's 32 pools because of city budget problems. In the future, the city will close four more pools. A GIS was needed to determine which subset of pools best serve the needs of Pittsburgh's youth population, some of whom, in the absence of summer recreation, are at risk for delinquent behavior. Students will begin working on this project in Chapters 1–8 and then complete their analysis in a project provided in Chapter 9.

Chapter Features

Instructional text: Each chapter begins with a section for students to read before turning on their computer. The text presents key concepts and methodologies that are supported by examples.

Step-by-step tutorials: To build students' GIS skills, we have students work through short sequences of steps on their computer. Most blocks of work contain 8 to 10 steps. Screen captures illustrate parts of steps that are difficult or lengthy to explain in text.

Practice activities: Series of hands-on tutorial steps are periodically interrupted by Practice exercises. These brief activities have students repeat the steps they've just completed, but for slightly different situations. This additional practice moves students toward independent work and helps them to internalize the concepts and skills they've practiced.

Summary: Each chapter concludes with a summary of the chapter's content.

Key terms: Key terms are highlighted and explained within the instructional text. For easy reference, the chapter's key terms are listed and defined after the Summary.

Short-answer questions: To help students absorb the reading materials, each chapter has short-answer questions that make students probe the principles and concepts presented. Some questions have specific answers that can be found in the instructional text; others require students to extend their knowledge by predicting outcomes and making hypotheses.

Exercises: Each chapter contains hands-on exercises that require some independent thinking on the student's part. In Chapter 9, students can choose one (or more) of four projects to complete: the Swimming Pool Case Study; a project related to Chapter 9's two examples, using the chapter examples as templates; or a completely new project based on the student's own interests.

References: Each chapter concludes with a list of references, both print and electronic, that the student might wish to consult for further study.

A brief summary of each chapter's content follows.

Summary of Chapter Content

Chapter 1, Introducing GIS: The instructional text defines GIS, explains its unique capabilities, discusses the fundamental nature of digital map layers, introduces map infrastructure (base maps and data) available from the Federal government, and introduces the Swimming Pool Case Study. The tutorial section has the student explore an existing ArcGIS map document, to gain familiarity with the user interface, plus has the student use two GIS Web sites. The first Web site, the Greenwood County, South Carolina GIS, has GIS functionality for using detailed maps and data on all land parcels and supporting infrastructure in the county. The second Web site, San Francisco's Prospector, has advanced spatial-analysis functions that support economic development by making it easy for businesses to find and analyze buildings or sites for new businesses.

Chapter 2, Navigating GIS: The instructional text covers fundamental knowledge of latitude and longitude coordinates, map scales, and map projections. The tutorial has students open a finished map document that we built for the Swimming Pool Case Study. Students use the GIS to zoom and pan the map, turn layers off and on, set threshold scales to automatically turn layers on and off as they change map scale, measure distances, and project map layers to common flat representations.

Chapter 3, Getting Information from a GIS: The instructional text covers vector maps and file formats, feature attribute tables of vector maps and their data dictionaries, raster maps and file formats, attribute queries including simple and compound logical conditions, and spatial selection of mapped features using buffers. The tutorial has students open a second map composition for the Swimming Pool Case Study. Students use the map to select graphic features and records directly, through a data-attribute query builder; and spatially, using circular buffers.

Chapter 4, Designing Maps: The reading material covers graphic-design principles, including graphic hierarchy; explains various properties of color and devices for choosing colors; explains how to construct numeric-variable categories needed in mapping data; provides guidelines for symbolizing graphic features on maps; and provides guidelines for designing maps for different audiences. The tutorial guides students to build their own swimming-pool map composition from base-map layers. They use ArcGIS to symbolize boundaries and other context layers, symbolize the swimming-pool layer by using unique symbols, symbolize a color-coded map layer, symbolize a point layer with size-graduated symbols, and finally build stand-alone map compositions called map layouts.

Chapter 5, Finding GIS Resources: The instructional text summarizes two key Web sites for obtaining free map layers and associated data. The text also points the student to several other sources for map resources. Included is an introduction to database concepts including primary keys and table joins. The tutorial guides students to visit the Web sites, download materials, prepare them for use, and then use them in ArcGIS.

Chapter 6, Building A GIS Study Area: The instructional text provides an introduction to issues in creating study areas by extracting geographic subsets of map layers or by appending adjacent map layers. In addition students learn how to create administrative polygons by dissolving boundaries of census or other base map polygons for use in study areas. The tutorial has students use several spatial processing tools to create study areas, including scripts that are available from ArcGIS Help. Finally, students learn how to create macros for automating interactive steps using ArcGIS ModelBuilder.

Chapter 7, Geocoding Your Data: This chapter's text covers formats for recording street addresses in databases, TIGER street centerline map layers for use as a reference in mapping street addresses, and ArcGIS algorithms for sophisticated matching of street address data to TIGER streets for creating new point map layers. Students use ArcGIS to build address locators and then geocode address data in batch and interactive modes.

Chapter 8, *Digitizing Map Features:* This chapter's text introduces control networks of benchmarks and GPS technology used in creating maps. It also covers various topics related to digitizing graphic features including tablet and heads-up digitizing. Students use ArcCatalog to create new shapefiles and then digitize and edit vector features using a raster map as a reference.

Chapter 9, *Working on GIS Projects:* This chapter's text introduces project management techniques including a project life cycle and deliverables abridged for use in small GIS projects. Included are a project proposal, process log, folder and file structure, and report. The chapter includes two completed projects, with all inputs and deliverables available from the book's data CD—one on public transportation and the other on air pollution. The exercises of this chapter are project assignments. The first two projects have the student replicate and extend the solved projects in their own county. The third project has advanced spatial analysis of additional data for the Swimming Pool Case Study. Finally the fourth project is open-ended, but following the format of the two solved projects.

Appendix: Installing the LearningAndUsingGIS Data Files and Obtaining the ArcGIS, ArcView Software: The appendix has instructions for copying the data folders and files necessary to complete the tutorials and exercises to the student's computer. It also has pointers to Web sites for obtaining educational site licenses and individual copies of the ArcGIS, ArcView software.

ACKNOWLEDGEMENTS

We are profoundly grateful for the expert help, guidance, and work provided by Thomson Course Technology editors and staff on this book: Mac Mendelsohn, Maureen Martin, Eunice Yeates, Alyssa Pratt, and Danielle Chouhan. We're also grateful to the copyeditor, Mark Goodin, and the proofreader, Karen Annett. A special thanks is due to Lynne Raughley, development editor, whose contributions to this book have been invaluable.

We also thank many others: Duane Asheley, Director of Pittsburgh's CitiParks Department, who provided the data and photographs used throughout this book and is our client for the Swimming Pool Case Study. He commissioned our GIS study, provided much valuable information on the problem and its solution, and provided funding for data input. Thomson Course Technology helped pay for the early demonstration-phase of pool data input, for which we are very grateful. In addition, Bradley Barnell kindly gave us permission to use the Greenwood County, South Carolina, GIS Web site; and Erich Seamon gave us permission to use the San Francisco Prospector GIS Web site. Matt Smith of *www. HomeTownLocator.com* gave us permission to use data on schools and Karen Florini of Environmental Defense gave us permission to use pollution data from *Scorecard.org*. We have learned much about teaching GIS from our students over the years, especially from those at Carnegie Mellon's Heinz School of Public Policy and from high school students enrolled in our InfoLink program (see *www.heinz.cmu.edu/infolink*). We thank them all.

CHAPTER **1**

INTRODUCING GIS

LEARNING OBJECTIVES

In this chapter, you will:

- Survey GIS and its unique capabilities
- Explore the basics of digital map layers
- Learn about map infrastructure
- Gain an overview of the Swimming Pool Case Study
- Get an overview of the ArcMap and ArcCatalog user interfaces
- Use your browser to navigate maps in a Web GIS site
- Use your browser to conduct analysis on a Web GIS site

So, you're new to this?

INTRODUCTION

If you have ever used maps to find places, you know that they work pretty well. The actual streets are

shown, and they lead you to the retail store, lake, or whatever it is that you are seeking. Similarly, sailors

use nautical charts to avoid hitting reefs, and travelers use maps to find points of interest in strange lands.

For many purposes, such information needs are met even better using a **geographic information system (GIS)**, a computer-based, dynamic mapping system.

MapQuest is a commonly used GIS. If you have not previously used the MapQuest Web site, go to *www.mapquest.com*, click the Get Directions button, type your address as the starting address, type the address of the White House (1600 Pennsylvania Avenue NW, Washington, D.C.) as the ending address, and click Get Directions. How many legs, door to door, does it take to travel from your house to the White House? One of the authors can make the trip in 20 legs from his house.

Place-to-place directions are an example of **reference mapping**. GISs also include a second kind of map use—**analytical mapping** (which is mostly what you will learn about in this textbook). This second kind of mapping requires you to collect digital maps and data for the purpose at hand, create your own map compositions, and use a GIS and its unique information-retrieval capabilities to help answer questions that involve locations. For example, the case study that runs throughout this textbook is about helping the director of Pittsburgh's CitiParks Department decide which public swimming pools to keep open. Recently, Pittsburgh had to close 16 of its 32 public swimming pools because of budget problems, and in the future it will close four more. Did the city choose the right 16 pools to close? Which additional pools should it close? It takes an analytic GIS to answer such questions.

A GIS is a tool. To use it well, you must first learn certain principles and concepts. Then, you need to gain experience using a GIS package. In this book, you will use **ArcGIS Desktop GIS**, the world's leading GIS software, to put your new knowledge to work. ArcGIS is a product of ESRI, a privately held firm based in Redlands, California.

This chapter introduces some of the unique capabilities of GIS and the fundamentals of digital map layers. The chapter also provides an overview of the Swimming Pool Case Study. In the tutorial portion of this chapter, you will see GIS in action in two ways—(1) using ArcGIS and data files installed on your PC and (2) using your Web browser and ESRI's **ArcIMS** (Arc Internet map server) package running remotely on Web servers.

For an introduction to ArcGIS, you will open a finished **map document** to become familiar with ArcGIS's user interface. A map document is a computer file created by you using ArcGIS that displays a map and provides access to tools for modifying and using the map. In this chapter, you will review ArcGIS's two major components: **ArcMap**, which is where you build and use map documents, and **ArcCatalog**, which is a special utility program for GIS that is analogous to My Computer and Windows Explorer.

Finally, to expand your GIS horizons, you will use two sophisticated Web-based GISs that were built using ArcIMS and that run on remote Web servers. Although you will not learn how to build ArcIMS Web sites, just using these finished sites will give you a quick overview of the richness of map layers available today and the power of GIS to provide unique and valuable information. You will navigate through maps and retrieve incredibly detailed and rich information about properties in Greenwood, South Carolina; then, you will analyze commercial properties for lease, sale, or rent in San Francisco. Your market analyses in San Francisco will take minutes to complete using the GIS, but it would take weeks without the GIS. We have included screen shots from both Web sites, just in case you do not have Internet access or the Web sites are not available. If you do have Internet access, you should carry out the tutorial steps for those Web sites.

Definition of GIS

This brings us to the question: What exactly is a GIS? Clarke (2003) makes the point that there is no single, good definition of GIS; there are many. We define a GIS as *a computer-based, dynamic mapping system with spatial data-processing and querying capabilities*. Let's analyze each part of this definition:

- *Computer-based*: Clearly, GIS is a computer technology. You will be using ArcGIS Desktop GIS on your desktop or notebook computer.
- *Dynamic mapping system*: A GIS is not a static map, but a dynamic system that you control. A GIS allows you to compose and view your own maps; change colors, symbols, and labeling as you desire; zoom in to get details; turn layers of the map on or off; get recorded data by clicking on mapped features; and so forth.
- *Spatial data-processing and querying capabilities*: You can put points on the map from scratch, such as the Pittsburgh swimming pools. You can also conduct data queries; for example, you might find and highlight all the residences of people who intended to use a certain pool when they sign up for pool passes. In addition, you can conduct spatial queries, such as having ArcGIS add up the number of youths living within a 1-mile radius of any pool.

Unique Capabilities of GIS

Information systems are tools that provide answers to the questions who, what, when, where, why, and how. Until the advent of GIS, however, there was no good way for an information system to answer the question *where* for many important uses. It is true that any information system can store street addresses, such as 4800 Forbes Ave, Pittsburgh, PA 15213 (our university address), and, thus, in a limited way answers *where*.

What if, however, your information needs are more sophisticated? For example, students enrolled in any Pittsburgh university can register and take a limited number of classes at any other Pittsburgh university. Suppose that several Pittsburgh universities want to combine their separate shuttle bus services so students living off campus can get from their housing to any number of universities—and travel between universities. How would you go about designing shuttle bus routes? The relative locations of student residences, universities, and the street network would all come into play. You would need an analytical map with those features. (In the past our students worked on this problem in a project using a GIS.)

An important and unique capability of a GIS is that it represents locations in ways that we can process on a computer. To do this, a GIS stores the coordinates of **graphic features**, such as points and lines, for use in displaying maps, showing their relative positions on the Earth's surface, calculating distances, and so forth. Instead of storing all graphic features for a map in a single folder or file, a GIS stores related graphic features in separate collections of files called **map layers**. For example, swimming pools, residences of pool users, streets, city boundaries, and so on are different map layers. An advantage of this arrangement is that map layers can be reused easily and assembled into any number of map documents. What we commonly refer to as a *map* in a GIS or on paper is actually a map **document**—several map layers symbolized and arranged in specific ways with all settings stored in a file. Viewed in another way, a map document is the final product of map design and GIS work. It provides reference information and supports analysis for the purpose at hand, such as deciding which public swimming pools to close in Pittsburgh.

Figure 1-1 is an ArcMap map document window that shows some map layers from the Swimming Pool Case Study and some features of the GIS interface. First, the left panel of the map document window, which is called the map **table of contents**, shows the map layers included in the map document and how they are symbolized. Map layers draw from the bottom up in the table of contents, so large areas that have color fill must be on the bottom and smaller areas or points and lines on top. You can turn layers on and off by clicking the check boxes to the left of the layer names in the table of contents: You can see that the top seven layers are on, but the three additional layers visible in the table of contents are turned off. There are even more layers in the table of contents; to see them you would have to scroll down. The map, while including all of Allegheny County, Pennsylvania, is zoomed in to an area containing the City of Pittsburgh. The **map extent** is the rectangle bordering the visible map.

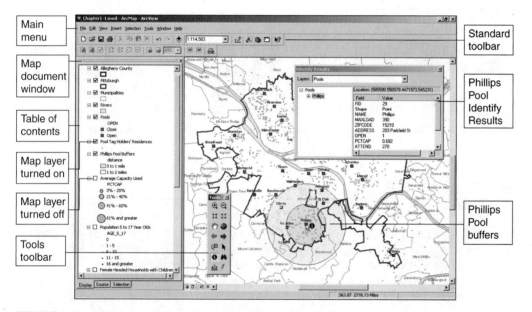

FIGURE 1-1   ArcMap map with buffers, selection, and Identify Results

Notice the Main menu and Standard toolbar in Figure 1-1, which have many frequently used menu items and tools. Also, the Tools toolbar is visible. It has several tools for using the map and its underlying data records. For example, in Figure 1-1 we used the Identify tool to click the blue square point marker for the Phillips swimming pool, which opens the Identify Results window with a listing of attributes for Phillips: The pool has a maximum capacity of 390 swimmers, is in zip code 15210, has a mailing address of 203 Parkfield St., is open to the public (signified by a value of 1), and uses 69.2 percent of its capacity with an average of 270 swimmers per day. Making such linkages between graphics on the computer screen and corresponding data records is a very powerful feature of GIS, one that you will use in many ways for analysis.

An advanced kind of GIS tool creates **buffers** for **proximity analysis**. Buffers are areas around graphic features of a specified radius. Point buffers are circular, as the 1- and 2-mile buffers shown in Figure 1-1 for the Phillips Pool. Proximity analysis provides information about what features are near other features. For example, we used the 1- to 2-mile ring of the Phillips buffers to select all pool-tag holders' residence points, shown in the yellow selection color in Figure 1-1. To use any Pittsburgh public pool, residents had to sign up and obtain a pool tag. By selecting pool-tag-holder residences on the map, we easily obtained the statistics seen in Figure 1-2: There are 289 households within 1 to 2 miles of Phillips Pool with an average of about 5.5 pool tag holders per household and a total of 1599 pool tag holders.

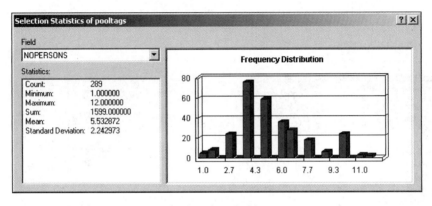

FIGURE 1-2   Statistics for selected pool tag holders

MAP LAYERS

All the map layers that you saw in Figure 1-1 are **vector-based map layers**; that is, they are based on geographic locations, called **points**, that have x- and y-coordinates. A second kind of map layer is a **raster map**, a checkerboard of small squares each with a solid color fill. Most of the graphic features in maps that have analytic value are vector based, like the pools example, because this type of map layer has data records. Let's take a closer look at the two kinds of map layers.

Vector-Based Map Layers

Vector-based maps have point, **line**, and **polygon** features. As previously noted, a point has x- and y-coordinates. A **line** has starting and ending points and may have additional shape vertices (points) in between for bends in the line. Lines in an urban street network are generally one block long and share end points to form a connected **street network**. Figure 1-3 is a portion of the map in Figure 1-1 zoomed in to Phillips Pool, with streets turned on. A **polygon** has three or more lines joined to form a closed area. In maps, polygons generally share lines with adjacent polygons in a way that partitions a large area into smaller areas. Note that we have used points for swimming pools, lines for street centerlines, and a polygon for Pittsburgh's boundary (which is not visible in Figure 1-3).

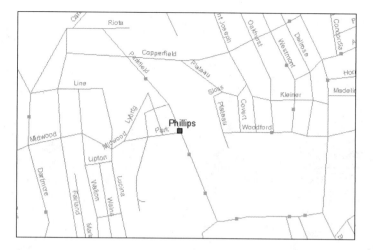

FIGURE 1-3   Street network in vicinity of Phillips Pool

A vector map can display points, lines, and polygons, but a vector map *layer* has only one vector type: point, line, or polygon. Also, by convention and because of the practicality of needing a different set of attributes for each layer, each vector layer is homogeneous in terms of features. For example, the pools is a separate point layer as is the residences of pool users. The Pools layer has an attributes for the name and address of the pool, and the layer for residences of pool users has the number of pool tag holders at the address and the name of the preferred pool of the household—different attributes for each layer.

A **feature attribute table** stores whatever characteristics we desire, and the characteristics are available for point, line, or polygon map layers. An **attribute** is a column of data with a name, such as MAXLOAD, and a data type, such as numeric or text. Each graphic feature, like a swimming pool, has its own record, or row, in its feature attribute table. Figure 1-4 symbolizes two points, a line, and a polygon with color, line type, outlines, and color fill for graphic features that might appear on a map. You do not have to individually paint each graphic feature in a GIS map. Instead, you use a GIS's automated method of symbolizing vector features based on data values.

For example, in Figures 1-1 and 1-3, we used a solid blue square point marker of a certain size for open pools, and a red point marker for closed pools. The GIS uses the *1* and *0* values for the OPEN attribute from the feature attribute table, as shown in Figure 1-4, to draw the finished map. Any pool with the value *1* in the OPEN column gets the blue symbol, and so on. In the same way, some lines might get solid line types and others dashed lines, as shown in Figure 1-4, depending on the values of an attribute. Finally, the outline color and width and color fill of polygons are similarly the result of an attribute—perhaps land use categories, such as residential, commercial, and industrial.

A final note on vector-based maps: As you might have gathered, vector-based maps are not stored images that are merely retrieved and displayed. Your computer draws and symbolizes vector maps on the fly, from scratch, every time you display them in your GIS.

Vector Graphic Features

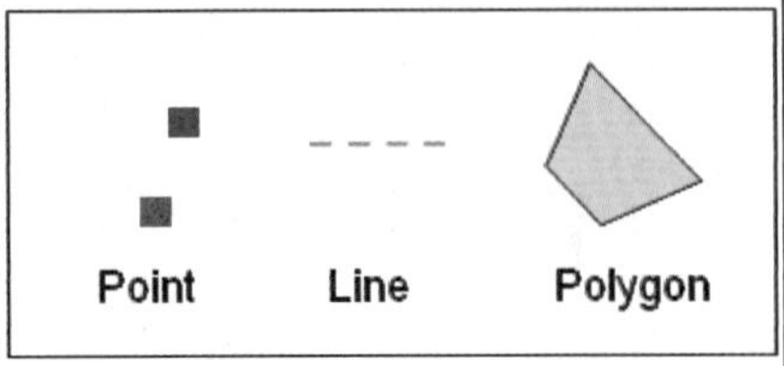

Point   Line   Polygon

Feature Attribute Table

POOL	CAPACITY	OPEN
Phillips	390	1
Leslie	615	0

FIGURE 1-4   Vector map feature types and attribute table

Raster Maps

A raster map, by contrast, is a stored electronic image or picture taken as an aerial photograph or satellite image. The electronic image is composed of a rectangular array of square cells, called **pixels**, with a number in each cell representing the solid color fill of that cell. When zoomed out far enough, the rendered array is a picture, and none of the individual pixels are distinguishable because they are so small. Figure 1-5 is an example of a raster map zoomed in to an individual building, a church. The second and third panels show the church spire zoomed in farther and farther until the pixels are evident.

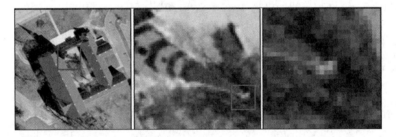

FIGURE 1-5   Raster map progressively zoomed in

A raster map is more than a picture, however, because it also has the same coordinates as do vector maps; otherwise, the two types of map layers would not plot together. For the most part, raster maps provide detailed spatial context for vector maps. The vector land parcels carry the data on property attributes, and the raster map provides a realistic picture. Many vector maps for physical features begin with aerial photographs that are digitized by tracing over the photos using software (such as in ArcMap) to create vector layers for street curbs, parking lots, building outlines, and so forth.

Classification of Map Layers

So far, we have a classification of map layers based on the underlying representation of graphic features: vector or raster. Another classification is by the kind of real-world features portrayed:

- *Physical features*: This kind of map layer shows the boundaries of bodies of water, continents, street curbs, parking lots, buildings, and so on. These are features that you could see from an airplane. Generally, physical features are the only map layers that have a raster image representation. Most other layers are vector based. Map layers such as street curbs and parking lots are digitized from raster images.
- *Political features*: This kind of map layer displays the boundaries of countries, provinces or states, counties, and cities. Of course, such features are invisible unless some physical features happen to be used as boundaries.
- *Legal features*: For the most part, these map layers show the boundaries of deeded land parcels owned by individuals, companies, or the government. Again, these tend to be invisible.
- *Statistical features*: These map layers show boundaries used by the U.S. Census Bureau and other agencies to report tabulations such as the population census. Included are polygon map layers such as **census tracts**—polygons used as the primary reporting areas of census variables such as population—and traffic analysis zones.
- *Administrative features*: These map layers are polygons designed by governments or companies to assign responsibilities to people who perform work by geographic territory. Examples include zip codes for delivery of the mail, school districts for delivery of public education services, and police car beats for assigning patrol areas to police cars.

MAP INFRASTRUCTURE

The work of building most information systems starts from scratch. For example, designers build databases using information collected from their company or agency. To build a GIS, however, you must begin with existing national and local government map layer infrastructures. We downloaded most of the map layers used in the swimming pool case—streets, municipal boundaries, city blocks, rivers, and the county boundary—for free from government sources, and we could not have built the GIS without them. Then, we built a few unique layers based on street addresses and the streets layer, namely, the swimming pool and pool-user-residence point layers.

TIGER/Line Maps

A major federal government map infrastructure is known as the **TIGER/Line maps** (Topologically Integrated Geographic Encoding and Referencing system). These vector-based maps were created to help the Census Bureau take the census every 10 years, but the maps have found many more uses by organizations and individuals across the country.

Free TIGER/line maps are available by county for all of the United States and its territories. There are many different layers, but some of the most useful ones include street centerlines, rivers and lakes, states, counties, cities, and census tracts. Chapter 5 covers the TIGER/Line maps in more detail; you will download some of these maps from the Census and ESRI Web sites.

FIPS Codes

When using political or statistical polygon layers, you must have a unique identification value, or code, for each polygon. The U.S. federal government has codes for every such polygon in the world in its **Federal Information Processing Standards (FIPS) codes**. For example, every country and state or province has a code. For the United States, the country code is *US*, and for Pennsylvania the state code is *42*. Political and statistical areas were designed to be **coterminous**, or to share boundaries and partition areas into smaller divisions. This allows FIPS codes to be **hierarchical**, or to be subdivided into smaller areas. The next smallest division under *state* is *county*. Allegheny County in Pennsylvania has FIPS code *003*, but to uniquely identify Allegheny County among all of the state/province subdivisions throughout the world, we have to put all of the pieces together: *US42003*. For a reference on FIPS codes, see *www.census.gov/geo/www/fips/fips.html*.

Census Data

In addition to map layers, you need data to attach, or join to, map layers for analysis. One of the most useful kinds of data for GIS is population statistics from the U.S. Census. This data is tabulated for all political and statistical areas, from census blocks up through the entire country, and they are freely downloadable. In Chapter 2, you will see the population map of 5- to 17-year-old youths by block compared to swimming pool locations in Pittsburgh. The population data is from the 2000 Census. In Chapter 5, you will learn more about the census and downloading census data from the Internet.

Yellow Pages Listings

Another important kind of data is locations and attributes of commercial land, such as retail stores, supermarkets, and so forth. You can download data from free sources, such as *www.smartpages.com*, that have telephone book yellow pages listings, but you will need to do some work in Microsoft Excel and ArcGIS to preprocess the data and get map coordinates for them (see Chapter 7). Many public libraries have CDs from Reference USA (see *www.referenceusa.com*) that already include map coordinates for yellow pages listings, so you can obtain ready-to-use data on a storage device from the CDs.

SWIMMING POOL CASE STUDY

Our purpose in writing this book is to teach you how to work on GIS projects that answer important questions. Chapter 9 provides a follow-up project on the Swimming Pool Case Study, plus three projects you can work on using maps for the geographic area of your choice, but you can also find additional projects in your community or area of interest. Whether you are using this textbook's projects or developing your own, you should learn to consider the "big picture" and what is needed and what is important. This section steps back from the details of GIS and examines the big picture for the Swimming Pool Case Study.

Costs and Benefits of Public Swimming Pools

Pittsburgh, Pennsylvania, has had a declining population for some time. That trend might reverse, but many city services were designed for a larger population than Pittsburgh has now, including its 32 public swimming pools. The city's budget crisis has forced the closing of many public facilities that the city perhaps no longer needs or can justify on a cost-and-benefit basis.

What are the benefits of swimming pools? The benefits are enormous for the city's youth and especially for those living in poverty. Swimming pools have many health and social benefits and are fun. They keep kids off of streets, out of trouble, and under the watchful eyes of parents, guardians, and swimming pool staff. Suppose that out of the 50,000-plus pool tag holders who use Pittsburgh pools, one child is averted from a life of crime each year because of being at the pool instead of hanging out on the street. How much would this save society?

The leading authority on such benefits is Cohen (1998), from whom we learn that that the value of saving a person from a lifetime of crime is approximately $1.3 to $1.5 million. Included are cost savings (or monetary equivalents) to victims (71 percent of the savings), the criminal justice system (24 percent of the savings), and foregone earnings of the criminal (5 percent of the savings). Roughly $1.3 to $1.5 million is how much it costs to operate all 32 pools per year! What do you think? Does it seem worthwhile to keep pools open? We think so. Nevertheless, regardless of benefits, city officials had to close pools and halt many other services to avoid bankrupting the city.

Criteria for Closing Swimming Pools

That leaves us with the question of which pools should be closed and which left open. There are many criteria for such a decision. Some criteria, such as the condition and age of the pools, do not depend on GIS. Other criteria depend on location and GIS. One criterion is equity; for example, it would be unfair to keep pools open in the wealthier parts of the city and close them in the poor areas. Other location-based criteria are based on efficiency, such as which pools draw the most youths and use the largest percentages of their rated capacities. Still other criteria attempt to maximize the number of residents with good access to pools. Finally, a political criterion is spatial in nature: Each council representative in Pittsburgh city government wants her or his constituencies, who are in polygon areas called wards, to have good access to swimming pools.

The goal in the Swimming Pool Case Study is to develop or estimate a set of location-based performance measures for all 32 pools that can inform the decisions on closings. The tutorials and exercises of Chapters 2 through 8 get a good start on this analysis. A project in Chapter 9 has you pull all of these chapters' Swimming Pool Case Study materials together and extend them with additional data that we provide to wrap up the case study.

INTRODUCTION TO ARCGIS

It is time for you to begin using GIS. The following activities assume that ArcGIS is installed on your computer and that you have installed this textbook's data files (see the appendix) to C:\LearningAndUsingGIS\. If you installed the files on another drive or path, just make the appropriate adjustment to our instructions when browsing for files—everything will still work properly.

You will open the map document shown in Figure 1-1 in ArcMap, and use some of the menu items and tools available in that package. Then, you will open ArcCatalog to see the file structure, utilities, and preview capabilities there. Finally, you will examine map layer properties using ArcMap, and that will complete your first experience with ArcGIS. Then, you can go on to see some advanced GIS map layers and functionality on the Internet.

Open the Chapter1-1.mxd Map Document

1. On your computer's desktop, click **Start**, click **All Programs**, click **ArcGIS**, and click **ArcMap**.
2. In the ArcMap window, click the **An existing map** option button, and double-click **Browse for maps** in the panel below the option button.
3. In the Open window, browse to your **LearningAndUsingGIS** folder *(most likely in C:\LearningAndUsingGIS)*, and double-click **Chapter1-1.mxd**. See Figure 1-6. *(The Chapter1-1.mxd map document window opens in ArcMap.)*

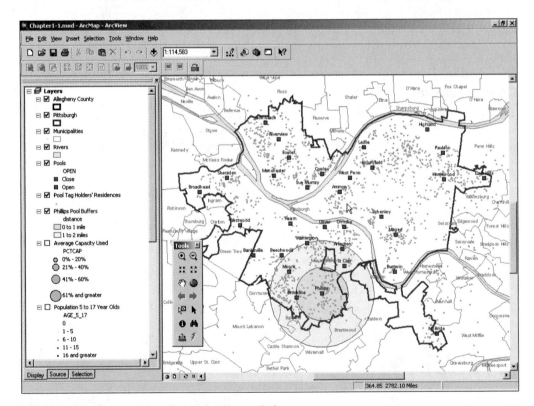

FIGURE 1-6   Chapter1-1.mxd map document window

1. In the table of contents, click the **Pittsburgh** check box to turn that layer off. *(Notice that the thick, black outline of Pittsburgh disappears or is off.)*
2. Click the same **Pittsburgh** check box again to turn that layer back on.
3. Turn off the **Phillips Pool Buffers** layer and turn on the **Average Capacity Used** layer. See Figure 1-7. *(Pools that use roughly half or more of their capacity in a day are considered efficient. Now you can see which of the open pools are efficient and inefficient.)*

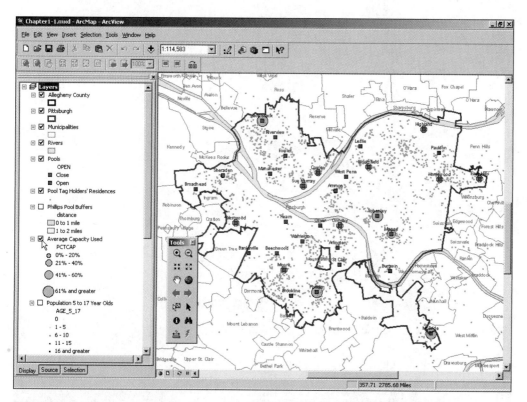

FIGURE 1-7   Chapter1-1.mxd map document window with Buffers off and Average Capacity Used on

4. In the table of contents, click the text label **Average Capacity Used**, hold your mouse button down, drag upward in the table of contents until ArcMap draws a horizontal black line between the Pools and Rivers layers, and release. *(Now Average Capacity Used draws on top of the open pools, obscuring their point markers.)*
5. Reverse this process by clicking the **Undo** button ↰ . *(Alternatively, you could have dragged the Average Capacity Used layer back down below the Phillips Pool Buffers layer. Very often you will find more than one way of accomplishing a task.)*

6. On the Standard toolbar, click the **Add Data** button ✦, and in the resulting Add Data window, browse to your C:\LearningAndUsingGIS\Maps\ folder, double-click the MapsPools folder, double-click the **zipcodes.shp** map layer in the large panel, and click **OK** to dismiss the warning message (see Figure 1-8). *(The table of contents has the zip codes added with a random color fill on top, thus obscuring other layers. Instead of working with zip codes and getting it to work well in the map document, you will just remove it next.)*

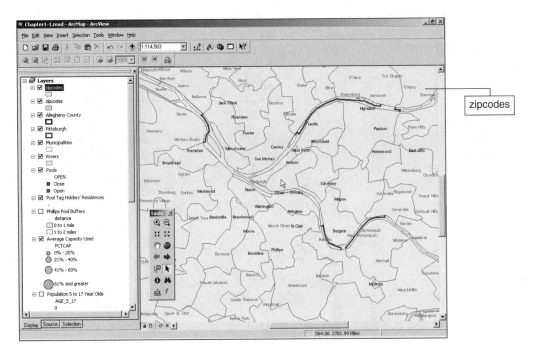

FIGURE 1-8   Chapter1-1.mxd map document window with zip codes added

7. In the table of contents, right-click the **zipcodes** text label and click **Remove**.

1. If the Tools toolbar is not visible, click **View**, **Toolbars**, scroll down, and click **Tools**.
2. On the Tools toolbar, click the **Full Extent** button ⬤ . See Figure 1-9. *(The map zooms out to the largest area possible to view with the given map layers—in this case all of Allegheny County, Pennsylvania, which contains the city of Pittsburgh. Notice that you are zoomed out too far for the Pools and Pool Tag Holders' Residences layers to make any sense. In Chapter 2, you will learn how to have ArcMap automatically turn map layers on and off at the appropriate zoom levels.)*

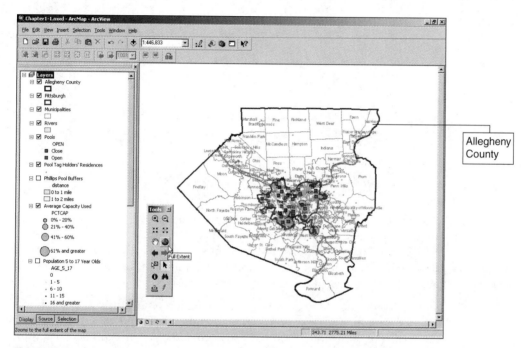

FIGURE 1-9   Chapter1-1.mxd map document window zoomed to full extent

3. On the Tools toolbar, click the **Go Back To Previous Extent** button ⬅ . *(You are back to where you started from, with Pittsburgh zoomed in.)*
4. On the main menu, click **View** and click **Layout View**. See Figure 1-10. *(We built a simple map layout, shown in Figure 1-10, which is a stand-alone map suitable for including in a Microsoft Word document, a Microsoft Power-Point presentation, or a Web site. You can export the layout easily as an image file for any of these purposes.)*
5. Click **View** and click **Data View**.

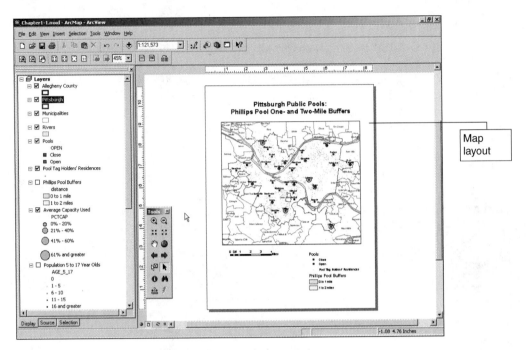

FIGURE 1-10   Chapter1-1.mxd map document in Layout view

Use ArcCatalog

ArcCatalog has many utilities for importing and exporting map layers between various file formats, renaming map layers, copying map layers, and so on. These utilities are essential for setting up and maintaining map layers at the file level because of the complexity of map layers, as you will learn in later chapters. For now, you will just take a brief look at Arc-Catalog, without doing much except using its preview properties.

1. On the Standard toolbar, click the **ArcCatalog** button. *(ArcCatalog is a separate computer application. Leave ArcMap open. Sometimes, to accomplish work in ArcCatalog, you have to save and close ArcMap because your PC detects a conflict in control between ArcMap and ArcCatalog over a map layer or table. Then, you reopen ArcMap from ArcCatalog, when finished working on the files.)*

2. In the file-tree panel on the left of the ArcCatalog window, click the expander boxes (with plus signs) to the left of C:\LearningAndUsingGIS and MapsPools, and click **MapsPools**. See Figure 1-11. *(The last action places the contents of the Maps folder in the right panel of ArcCatalog, where you can get valuable information on them, as will be done next.)*

3. In the right panel, click **Pools**, click the **Preview** tab, and, if not already selected, click the list arrow in the **Preview** field, and click **Geography**. See Figure 1-12. *(ArcCatalog provides a quick map of the pools points. Notice that the lower-right edge of the ArcCatalog window displays two numbers, -79.9632 and 40.4394. These are the longitude and latitude of the tip of the*

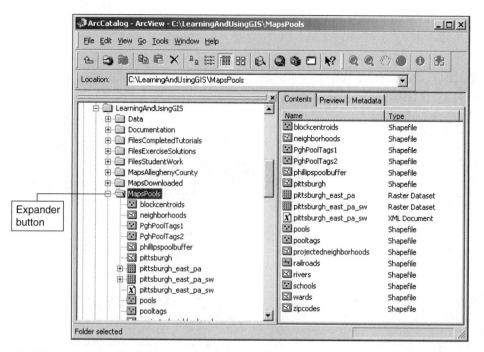

Expander button

FIGURE 1-11   MapsPools folder and files tree as viewed in ArcCatalog

cursor's pointer in the pools coordinates. You will learn more about coordinates in Chapter 2.)

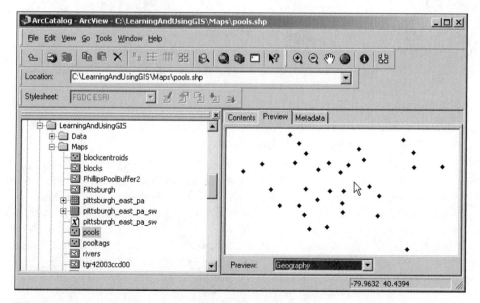

FIGURE 1-12   ArcCatalog with a preview of Pools Geography

4. In the Preview field, click **Table**. See Figure 1-13. *(ArcCatalog gives you a preview of the Pools attribute table, with one row of data, or record, per pool.)*

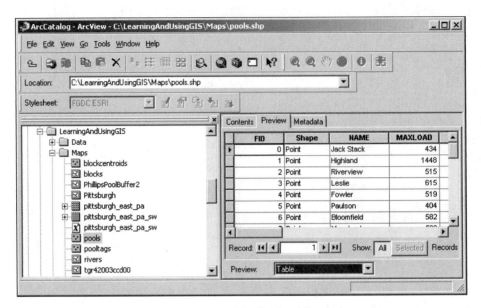

FIGURE 1-13 ArcCatalog with a preview of the Pools table

PRACTICE 1-2

Try getting previews of other layers. Pay particular attention to attribute tables and the data available for different layers. Comprehensive documentation on these layers is in Chapter 3. When finished, close ArcCatalog. ArcMap should still be open. If not, open it and *Chapter1-1.mxd.*

View Layer Properties in ArcMap

Each map layer has many properties that you can set or change using the Layer Properties window. Next, you look at some of the Pools layer properties.

1. In the table of contents in ArcMap, right-click **Pools**, click **Properties**, and in the Layer Properties window click the **General** tab. See Figure 1-14. *(Here is where you can change the name of the layer and, as you will see in Chapter 2, set this layer up to turn on and off automatically, depending on how zoomed in or out you are.)*
2. In the Layer Properties window, click the **Source** tab. See Figure 1-15. *(This tab provides information on the map layer—its extent or bounding coordinates, its file type and path on your computer, and its coordinate system.)*

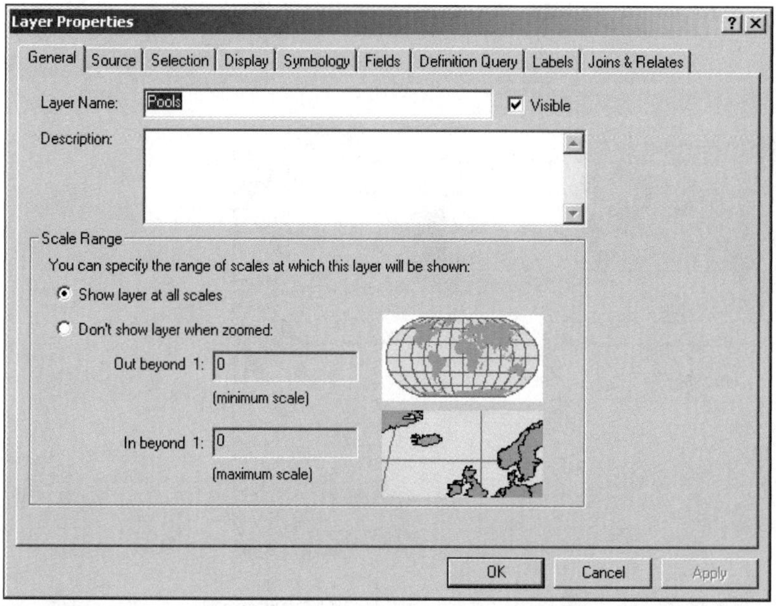

Layer Properties ? X

General | Source | Selection | Display | Symbology | Fields | Definition Query | Labels | Joins & Relates |

Layer Name: Pools   ☑ Visible

Description:

─ Scale Range ─────────────────────────────────
You can specify the range of scales at which this layer will be shown:

⦿ Show layer at all scales

○ Don't show layer when zoomed:

    Out beyond 1: [0
         (minimum scale)

    In beyond 1: [0
         (maximum scale)

        OK   Cancel   Apply

FIGURE 1-14   General properties of Pools

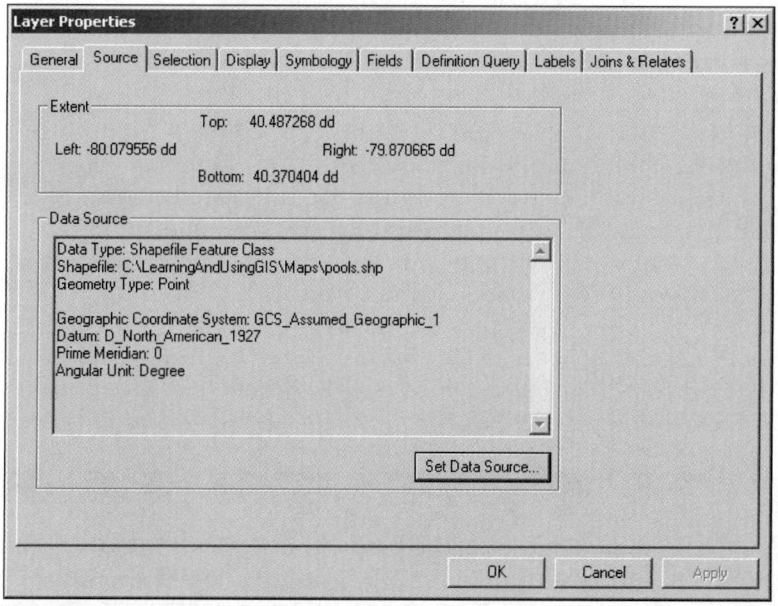

Layer Properties ? X

General | Source | Selection | Display | Symbology | Fields | Definition Query | Labels | Joins & Relates |

─ Extent ─────────────────────────────────
               Top: 40.487268 dd

Left: -80.079556 dd   Right: -79.870665 dd

          Bottom: 40.370404 dd

─ Data Source ─────────────────────────────────
Data Type: Shapefile Feature Class
Shapefile: C:\LearningAndUsingGIS\Maps\pools.shp
Geometry Type: Point

Geographic Coordinate System: GCS_Assumed_Geographic_1
Datum: D_North_American_1927
Prime Meridian: 0
Angular Unit: Degree

                    Set Data Source...

        OK   Cancel   Apply

FIGURE 1-15   Source properties of Pools

3. In the Layer Properties window, click the **Symbology** tab. See Figure 1-16. *(Here is where you have many options for symbolizing a map layer. We symbolized Pools with the Unique Values option that assigns a different symbol for each value of the Open attribute. There are only two: 0 for closed and 1 for open.)*

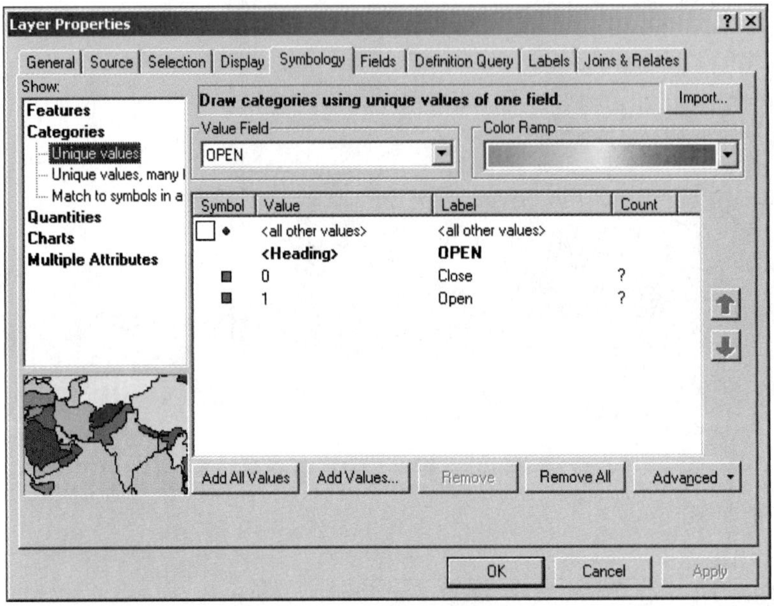

FIGURE 1-16 Symbology properties of Pools

4. In the Layer Properties window, click the **Fields** tab. See Figure 1-17. *(This tab provides metadata on the attributes of the Pools layer—the data types and lengths. If you click a check box off for an attribute, it is not displayed when viewing the map layer's attribute table. You can also type an alias, or self-describing label for an attribute, if an attribute has a cryptic name. ArcMap uses the alias instead of the name in various places.)*

5. In the Layer Properties window, click the **Labels** tab. See Figure 1-18. *(This last tab that you examine for now lets you label a graphic feature, such as the pools, with a Pools attribute. Here we labeled Pools with the attribute NAME. You see that there is a check box to turn labeling off and on.)*

PRACTICE 1-3

Use the Fields tab to turn off the first two attributes of Pools—FID and SHAPE. These are attributes needed by ArcMap but are of no value for the GIS user to see at this point. Right-click Pools in the table of contents and click Open Attribute Table. Notice that the FID and SHAPE attributes are not displayed. When finished, close the attribute table and exit *Chapter1-1.mxd* without saving.

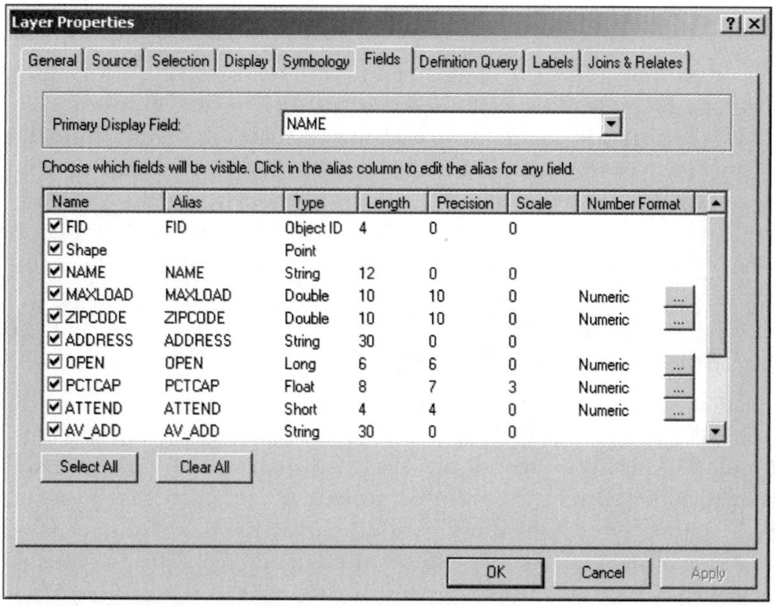

FIGURE 1-17   Fields properties of Pools

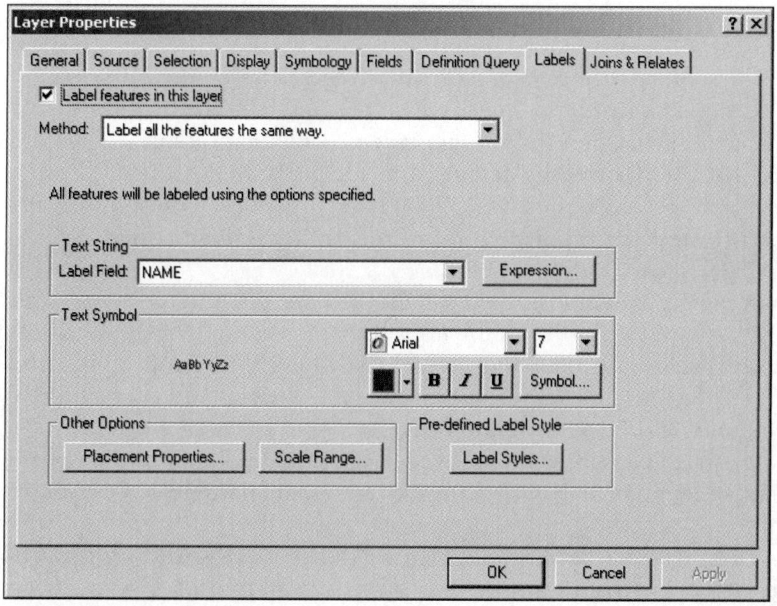

FIGURE 1-18   Labels properties of Pools

GIS EXAMPLES ON THE WEB

If you have an Internet connection, follow the upcoming tutorial steps. If not, or if for some reason the Web sites will not open, read through the steps and look at the figures that show pages from the Web site. You will use map navigation and some advanced GIS tools and will see some amazing local-government map infrastructure. Local governments contract to build their own aerial photographs, digitize their own land parcel maps, collect their own real property data, digitize their own utility lines and pipes, and maintain their own database of licensed businesses—all of which you will see and use. Both Web sites also use census data, which plays a critical role in the second Web site.

Greenwood County, South Carolina, Web GIS Site

Greenwood, South Carolina, has a great cadastral GIS. The term **cadastral**, or cadastre, refers to data that establishes boundaries and ownership of land parcels. County governments maintain such data because they record the legal documents of ownership and deeds, and they collect the majority of local government taxes, the property tax, based on assessed property value. County employees must assess the market value of properties from time to time for levying property taxes, which can be a difficult task. The county government wants property owners to be able to look up the assessed values of properties comparable to their own.

Next, let's explore this site.

Open the Web Site

1. Open a Web browser such as Microsoft Internet Explorer or Mozilla Firefox. (*Note: Commands may differ depending on the Web browser.*)
2. Click **File** and click **Open** (*or an equivalent command*), type **http://165.166.39.5/giswebsite/default.htm**, and click **OK**.
3. In the disclaimer window, click **OK**. (*These steps produce a map of the county with several map layers visible for this scale, which is about 1 inch = 6.0 miles on one particular monitor.*)
4. Hover your mouse pointer over the far-right (far east) point in the county. See Figure 1-19. (*On the lower left of the browser window, you get a readout of the map coordinates for the point. We get (34.13058° N, 81.86716° W), and yours should be close to that. These are degrees latitude and longitude, which you will learn about in Chapter 2.*)
5. Click, hold, drag, and release the right edge of the map window to the right to make more room for the map, but leave the Legend button visible at the top right.
6. Click the **Legend** button Legend . See Figure 1-20. (*You can see the yellow area denoting the city of Greenwood, where you will zoom in next, by dragging the rectangle shown in Figure 1-20.*)

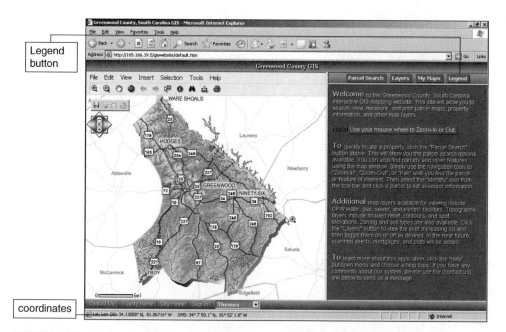

FIGURE 1-19   Greenwood County, South Carolina, home page

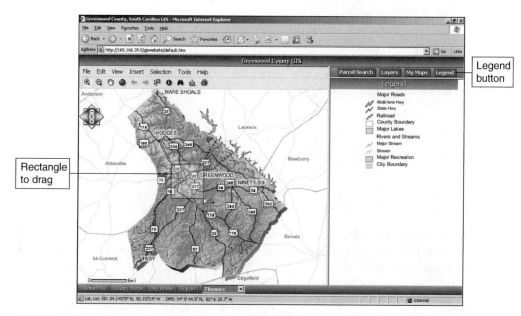

FIGURE 1-20   Home page with legend and rectangle to drag next

Zoom in to the City of Greenwood

1. By default, the Zoom In tool 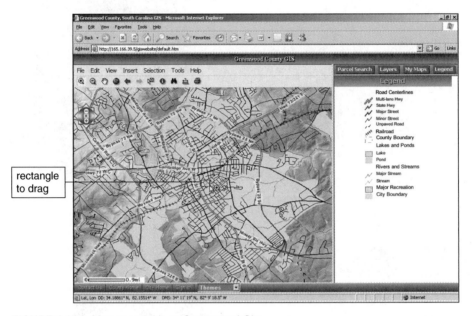 is selected, so use it to drag a rectangle around the yellow Greenwood City area, as shown in Figure 1-20, to zoom in to the map. See Figure 1-21. *(If you want to try again with the zoom-in step, click the Go Back To Previous Extent button ◄ ; do not use your browser's Back button. The map has threshold scales that turn layers on and off, depending on the current map scale. At a scale of 1 inch = 1.1 miles, more street and stream layers are on.)*

rectangle to drag

FIGURE 1-21   Map zoomed in to Greenwood City

2. Drag another zoom-in rectangle, as shown in Figure 1-21. See Figure 1-22. *(This zooms the map in to a single block. The white land parcel outlines and aerial photo are visible. You should see Magnolia Park in the center of your map.)*

Identify a Real Property Record Accessed

1. Click the **Identify** tool ⓘ on the top horizontal menu.
2. Click inside the parcel of the **County Bank Offices** *(see Figure 1-22, where we positioned the Identify tool for this step)*. See Figure 1-23. *(The right panel displays data from the corresponding real property data record. You can see that the property was built in 1988 and has an appraised value of $899,100, among other pieces of information.)*
3. Zoom in to the **County Bank Offices** land parcel, and click the **Layers** button **Layers**.

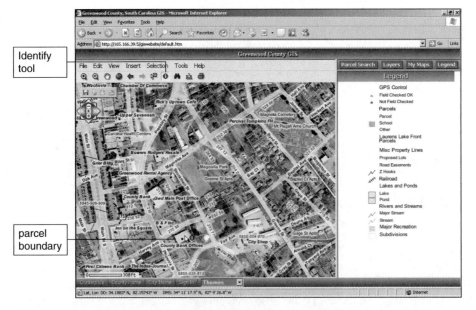

FIGURE 1-22   Map zoomed in to city blocks

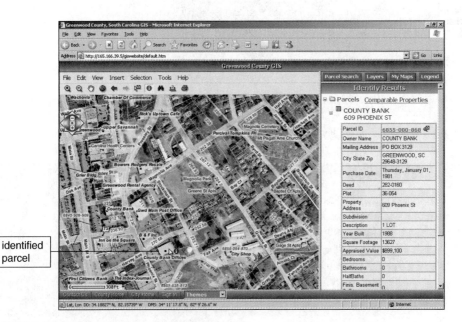

FIGURE 1-23   Map with land parcel identified

4.   Click the **expander** box next to the Utilities folder icon, and click all of the available utility layers (GMD Sanitary Sewer, GMD Sewer Manholes, and so on). See Figure 1-24.

5. Click the **Refresh** Map button at the bottom of the layers panel. *(When you change the map composition or anything about the map, the map server computer in Greenwood has to redraw the map, take a .jpeg format picture of the map, and then send it to your browser. The Refresh button initiates this process.)*

6. Click the **Legend** button Legend so you can interpret the utilities. *(Greenwood County is clearly in the twenty-first century with this great map infrastructure and Web GIS site. Notice the water tower in the upper right of the map.)*

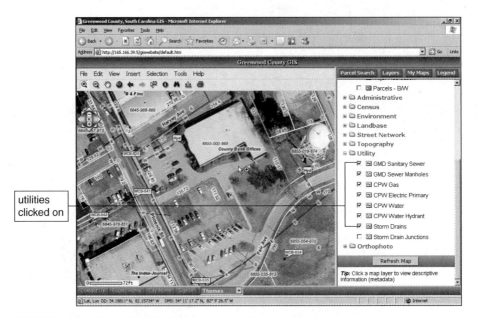

FIGURE 1-24 Map with utility layers turned on

PRACTICE 1-4

- Use the Identify tool to extract a few more real property records.
- Use the Measure Distance and Area tool to get the perimeter and area of the County Bank Office's land parcel.
- Use the Pan tool (white-gloved hand icon) to drag the map around.
- Zoom in a few times, first to a single land parcel and then to a parked car, until the pixels of the aerial photo are visible.
- Close your browser when you are done.

The San Francisco Prospector Web GIS Site

Cities attempt to attract new businesses and industry to generate more jobs, attract more residents, increase the tax base, and so on. This is called economic development. San Francisco's Prospector is an economic development Web site using an ArcIMS application program written and sold by a company called GIS Planning. It has valuable and advanced GIS query capabilities to find and evaluate land and buildings for new businesses. Prospector is an incredible technology and a remarkable resource for San Francisco.

Open the Web Site

1. Open a Web browser, such as Internet Explorer, Netscape, or Mozilla. *(Note: Commands my differ depending on the Web browser.)*
2. Click **File**, click **Open** or a similar command, type **http://www.ci.sf.ca.us /site/sfprospector_index.asp**, and click **OK**.
3. Click the **Search for Available Commercial Sites & Buildings** link. See Figure 1-25. *(This brings up the map of San Francisco and a form in the right panel. In the next few steps, you will enter information in to this form.)*

data entries and selections

FIGURE 1-25   San Francisco Prospector starting map

Query Retail Properties for Lease

1. In the right panel, click the **Type** field list arrow, and then click **Retail**. *(See the previous figure for form entries.)*
2. In the **Minimum Size field**, type **10000**, and in the **Maximum Size field** type **20000**.
3. Click the **properties for lease** check box.
4. Click the **Search** button. See Figure 1-26. *(You will get different results than we have here, so you will have to translate this discussion to match your own results. When we ran this query, there were only two properties available. If you do not find any properties, increase your maximum size from 20000 to*

50000 and try again. You can see that our map zoomed in automatically to the two properties.)

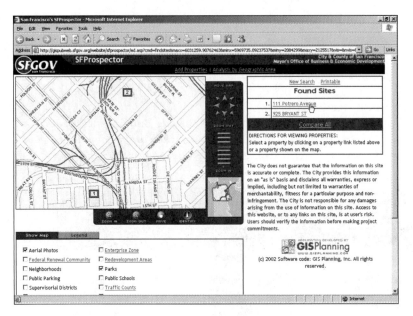

FIGURE 1-26   Map zoomed in to available properties

5. Under Found Properties, click the first property link. See Figure 1-27. *(Ours is 111 Potrero Avenue, but yours might be different. The map zooms in again, this time to an aerial photo with the building that has the available space. In the right panel is information about the property and who to contact for leasing information. You can see that the lease rate is $1.25 per square foot per year.)*

Conduct a Demographic Analysis

1. At the top of the right panel, click the **Demographics** tab. *(The new panel is set up to calculate and report demographics for the population living within 1 mile of the property for lease. You can change the report to one of two other types, Consumer Expenditures or Business and Workforce, but leave the selections as is.)*
2. Click the **Calculate** button. See Figure 1-28. *(The map zooms in to an area to accommodate the resulting circular buffer with a 1-mile radius, and the right panel displays demographics for the buffer.)*
3. Scroll down to see all of the information. *(There are age and race distributions, household income and net worth distributions, employment by industry and occupation, unemployment, number of households, educational attainment, and household size distribution. Amazing! It would take an analyst days to get the same information using non-GIS methods.)*

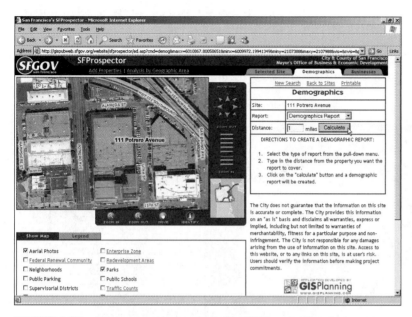

FIGURE 1-27 Map zoomed in to selected building

Demographics tab

FIGURE 1-28 Map with 1-mile buffer for demographics

Get a Business Report

1. At the top of the right panel, click the **Businesses** tab. *(This form is set up to find businesses within a quarter mile of the selected property. Keep that setting.)*

2. Click the **Calculate** button. See Figure 1-29. *(This time the Web site retrieves all businesses within a quarter mile. Suppose that we want to open a restaurant at the selected site.)*

FIGURE 1-29 Map with quarter-mile buffer for businesses

3. In the right panel, scroll down to the **Retail Trade** heading, and click the **EATING AND DRINKING PLACES** link. See Figure 1-30. *(The result is a narrowed list of points on the map and links to them in the right panel. This is the competition for our new restaurant.)*

PRACTICE 1-5

- Click some other layers of interest to you, and click Display to refresh the map.
- Click the Demographics tab, and try out the Consumer Expenditures and Business and Workforce reports. Change the distance, but do not make it larger than 2 miles or less than 0.25 miles.
- Perform a new search for a property with characteristics of your own choosing.
- When finished, close your browser.

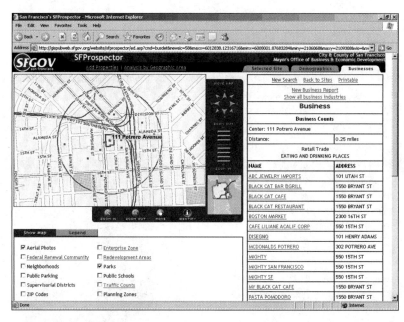

FIGURE 1-30 Map with quarter-mile buffer for eating and drinking places

Chapter 1 Summary

Paper maps are mostly used for reference—to find points of interest, routes, and so forth. Reference mapping is enhanced by a geographic information system (GIS). Another kind of mapping, analytic mapping, is used for analysis. The user assembles the map layers and data needed for the problem at hand, builds a corresponding GIS, and then uses the dynamic maps and tools of GIS to answer questions. In most cases, the cost of paper-based analytic mapping is prohibitive, but analytic mapping is relatively low cost, easy, and flexible using a GIS.

A GIS is a computer-based system that includes location coordinates for mapped features and has unique spatial processing and querying capabilities. There are many location-based questions that are impossible for textual databases to answer, but those questions are commonly answered with a GIS. One example is "How many youths, aged 5- to 17-years-old, live within 2 miles of Phillips Pool?" Locations, saved as coordinates, are necessary to answer this question, along with a program that can calculate distances. Those features and capabilities are available in a GIS.

A GIS's unique capabilities include a linkage between mapped features and database records, the ability to easily symbolize maps and to add layers to a map composition, to turn layers on and off as needed, to integrate drawn maps and images (such as aerial photos), and the ability to analyze features near other features.

GIS map layers include vector-based maps and raster maps. Vector-based maps are drawings composed of map layers having either points, lines, or polygons. A GIS easily symbolizes maps, giving such line features as line types, widths, and colors; giving point markers shapes, sizes, and colors; and giving polygons line outlines and color fill. A GIS uses the data attributes attached to each graphic feature to automatically symbolize maps.

Raster maps are images that a GIS stores and retrieves for viewing. Examples are aerial photographs and satellite images. In addition to the image file, a raster map also includes geographic coordinate data so the map can be displayed in its proper location. Map layers are also classified by type of real-world feature represented: physical, political, legal, statistical, or administrative.

A GIS depends on national and local map infrastructures. TIGER/Line maps are a key source of maps from the U.S. government. These free maps depict many of the real-world features of the United States and its possessions. Perhaps most important for analytical mapping are streets, census tracts, and political boundaries. To establish uniformity in naming and retrieving map data, the U.S. government has created identification codes (FIPS codes) for most political and statistical boundaries around the world. Other useful map layers and related data are provided by the U.S. Census Bureau, Yellow Pages listings, and many other sources.

In this chapter, you used a map document, which we prepared using ArcGIS's ArcMap, showing Pittsburgh's swimming pools and many other map layers. You saw how layers can be turned on and off and moved to change their drawing order, how you can zoom out and back in, that a map composition has data and layout views, and that you can view and modify map layer properties. You used a separate computer application provided in ArcGIS, called ArcCatalog, that provides many unique utility programs for working with map layers.

Finally, you examined two Web-based GISs to complete your introduction to GIS. ESRI's ArcIMS is the Web GIS server software implementing both Web sites. The Greenwood, South Carolina, Web site provides a good user interface for viewing detailed map layers of the kind that local governments create—deeded land parcels with attached property data, utility lines, and very detailed aerial photographs. The San Francisco Web site provides real-time databases of commercial properties available for new businesses to lease or buy, along with analytical capabilities to obtain demographic and business information within the vicinities of available properties.

Key Terms

Analytical mapping   A type of map that requires you to collect digital maps and data, create your own map compositions, and use a GIS and its unique information-retrieval capabilities to help understand behavior or make decisions in regard to locations. An example is the GIS constructed for the Swimming Pool Case Study of this textbook, whose purpose is to provide information to help decide which public swimming pools to close.

ArcCatalog   A software utility program and supporting component of ArcGIS Desktop GIS. It has interactive functionality for importing and transforming map layers to and from a variety of formats; copying, moving, and deleting map layers and data tables; previewing map layer graphics and attributes; and building macros using a graphical user interface.

ArcGIS Desktop GIS   A type of GIS software produced by ESRI that runs on a PC. Available in the ArcGIS family are three increasingly more advanced GIS packages: ArcView, ArcEditor, and ArcInfo. Most GIS users have ArcView, while relatively fewer users have ArcEditor or ArcInfo. ArcView is a full-featured GIS and meets most users' needs, and ArcEditor and ArcInfo add specialized tools to ArcView, such as for certain kinds of editing and digitizing of map layers. Although we wrote this book for ArcView, you can also use it with ArcEditor or ArcInfo.

ArcIMS (Arc Internet map server)   The GIS software produced by ESRI for building and deploying interactive GISs on the Web. Most implementations of ArcIMS have all GIS processing performed on remote Web servers and send simple HTML pages to your Web browser. Each interaction with a map in your browser results in the Web server generating and sending you a new map image file.

ArcMap   A software application program and major component of ArcGIS Desktop GIS. It has interactive functionality for creating, modifying, and using map documents. You can add or delete map layers, symbolize and label map layers, edit the attribute data or graphic features of map layers, display and navigate maps by zooming and panning, query maps using attribute and spatial queries, and conduct advanced spatial analyses.

Attribute   A characteristic of an entity, such as a map layer, that is represented as a column of data in a table. Attributes, also known as variables and data elements, have data types such as text or numeric.

Buffer   An area surrounding a graphic feature on a map defined by a specified radius. For example, a 1-mile buffer of a point is a circle whose center is the point and has a 1-mile radius. The buffer of a rectangle is the area extending away from the rectangle for a distance up to the specified radius and is a rectangle with rounded corners. The buffer of a straight line segment is a long thin rectangle with circular ends, containing the line.

Cadastral   A term that refers to data or maps that have the purpose of identifying the boundaries and owners of deeded land parcels.

Census tracts The polygon boundaries that divide up all of the United States into homogeneous neighborhoods of approximately 4000 population each. Census tracts use street, river and streams, and railroad centerlines plus many other kinds of lines for boundaries. The Census Bureau reports data tabulations from the decennial census by tract. Census tracts are coterminous with the smaller census block groups and blocks as well as the larger municipalities, counties, and states.

Coterminous A term that refers to polygons that share boundaries and partition areas into smaller areas. For example, counties are made up of census tracts, and states are made up of counties. States, counties, and census tracts are coterminous.

Feature attribute table A table attached to the graphic features of a vector map layer. Every point, line, or polygon of a vector map layer has a record in that layer's feature attribute table.

Federal Information Processing Standards (FIPS) codes A set of codes provided by the federal government for identifying political and statistical areas around the world. For example, the FIPS code for Allegheny County, Pennsylvania, is US42003, in which the code for Pennsylvania is 42 and that for Allegheny County is 003.

Geographic information system (GIS) A computer-based, dynamic mapping system with spatial data-processing and querying capabilities.

Graphic feature An element of a map that is visible on the computer screen or when printed out. For vector maps, a graphic feature is a point, line, or polygon that has been symbolized.

Hierarchical A top-down organization with finer subdivisions at each layer. In GIS, we use *hierarchical* to refer to a classification and coding of coterminous areas that partition countries into states or provinces, states into counties, and so forth. FIPS codes are hierarchical.

Line An element of a line vector map. A line has two end points with geographic coordinates that locate the line on the Earth's surface. They are connected with a line graphic and symbolized with a line type, width, and color.

Map document A single data file, with the *.mxd* file extension, that points to and uses a collection of map layers symbolized and arranged in ArcGIS for a specific purpose. A map document generally uses many map layers but does not make copies of them and save them in its file. Instead, a map document uses them wherever they are stored on your computer or network. A map document is the end product of map design and GIS work.

Map extent The rectangular window on the world provided by a GIS displaying a map. It is defined by its lower-left and upper-right coordinates on the displayed map.

Map layers The separate, related files in which a GIS stores related graphic features. Map layers are arranged and combined to create map compositions, also called maps.

Pixel A square area from a rectangular array of such squares that make up a digital image. Each pixel has a stored number that represents the solid color fill of the pixel.

Point An element of a point vector map. A point has geographic coordinates locating it on the Earth's surface and is displayed using a point marker graphic that has shape, area, and color.

Polygon An element of a polygon vector map. A polygon is three or more lines joined together to form a closed boundary and area. The points that make up the lines of the polygon have geographic coordinates, locating the polygon on the Earth's surface. Polygons generally share lines with neighboring polygons to partition larger areas. They are symbolized with an outline and color fill or a pattern.

Proximity analysis The study of map features near to other map features, which is often carried out using buffers. For example, such an analysis might determine the number of 5- to 17-year-old youths living with 1 mile of each public swimming pool in Pittsburgh.

Raster map   An image file, such as for an aerial photograph, that also has geographic coordinates locating it on the Earth's surface.

Reference mapping   The common type of map used for travel or in atlases. Its primary use is to provide information through visual examination.

Street network   A set of street centerline segments that share end points to make up a connected network of streets in an area. Connectivity is the property that allows specialized computer programs to find shortest routes between two addresses.

Table of contents   A panel in a GIS map window that lists all map layers available for viewing and analysis. It includes values, symbols, colors, and line types used to symbolize map layers displayed in sample graphic elements.

TIGER/Line maps   Vector-based map layers provided by the United States Census Bureau that serve as a primary source of base maps for the United States and its possessions. TIGER stands for Topologically Integrated Geographic Encoding and Referencing system.

Vector-based map layers   Maps layers made up of points, lines, and polygons that have geographic coordinates and corresponding feature attribute tables. Such maps have no lines that are real curves, but are made up of all straight-line elements, albeit with many of them very short in length to give the appearance of curves.

Short-Answer Questions

1. When you are using a GIS, explain what happens to vector and raster maps as you zoom in closer and closer.

2. Explain the difference between reference maps and analytical maps. Why is it easy to find good paper reference maps, and why do you need a GIS for analytical maps?

3. How does a vector GIS represent a circular shape or oval, such as an outdoor ice skating rink or a football stadium?

4. Do raster maps have feature attribute tables? Why or why not?

5. Map layers draw from the bottom up as listed in the left layer panel (or table of contents) of ArcMap (and most other GIS packages). See Figure 1-1. Suppose that you had the following three layers: (1) swimming pools; (2) zip code areas color coded to display the number of residents using swimming pools (0 to 499 are white, 500 to 999 are light gray, 1000 to 2000 are medium gray, 2000 and higher are dark gray); and (3) street centerlines. Which order would be best from bottom to top? Why?

6. Suppose that you have a point vector-based map layer for schools in your city, and the feature attribute table for this layer has an attribute called Type with these values: Public, Private, and Parochial. What would be a good way to symbolize the schools? Explain how symbolization works.

7. Imagine a one-street city that has its population in three various-sized clusters along a straight line. One cluster is at either end and the third is in the center. Each cluster has its residents spread out along the street but is fairly far away from the nearest other cluster. Geographers have established that demand for goods or services declines inversely with the distance that a person must travel to make purchases. If you could locate only one swimming pool for the city, where would you best locate it? Two swimming pools? Three? Explain your rationale.

8. When creating administrative areas, it is a good idea to use census tracts as building blocks and to make each administrative area one or more contiguous census tracts. Pittsburgh's police patrol districts (areas assigned a patrol car) are designed in this way. There are 42 patrol districts and 139 census tracts, so each patrol district has 3 to 4 tracts. Why are such patrol districts valuable for top police management? Assume that crime rates are roughly proportional to population levels, that the goal for designing patrol districts is to equalize work load, and that police need to study crime patterns relative to such population characteristics as income and age distributions.

9. Greenwood County, South Carolina, has a service called "comparables" that it sells to realtors. If you subscribe to the service, you can log in, type the address of a property for sale in Greenwood County, and the system finds similar properties that recently were sold. It provides the list of such properties and their selling price. Realtors use such information to determine the asking price of the property for sale. How do you suppose that the comparables computer program works? List the steps it must use.

10. San Francisco's Prospector Web site is able to use census data for areas within a user-specified distance of a property that is available for lease or sale. Suppose that the census data is attached to a point file for the centers of city blocks. How do you suppose Prospector calculates the census statistics? List the steps it must use.

Exercises

1. **Find Your House on a Map.** In this exercise, you will use the TerraServer Web site, supported by the U.S. Geological Survey, to find your house on a map. If you cannot find your house, then look for another address, such as that of your school.

   a. Create a Word document and save it as **C:\LearningAndUsingGIS\FilesExerciseSolutions\MyHouse<YourName>.doc**, where you substitute your actual name or other identifier for <YourName>.

   b. Open your Web browser and go to *http://terraserver-usa.com/*.

   c. Type your address, and save the resultant images of the topographic map and aerial photograph by right-clicking each image and saving it to your desktop with the names *MyHouseAerial.bmp* and *MyHouseTopo.bmp*.

   d. At the top of your Word document, type the title Maps of My House. Include your name. Click Insert, click Picture, click From File, browse to find one of your images, and insert it in the Word document. Do the same with the other image. Add some text describing some features of the maps; for example, describe something about your neighborhood from the map that you did not previously know.

   e. Save your Word document. If you have an instructor, turn this document in as instructed.

2. **Use the MapQuest Web Site to Study Routing.** In this exercise, you will study the routing capabilities of the *www.mapquest.com* Web site and find any bad directions. You can use your home address as the starting point, or another address, such as that of your school. Select three destination addresses in your own neighborhood. Look the addresses up in a telephone book or use *www.smartpages.com*.

a. Create a Word document called **C:\LearningAndUsingGIS\FilesExerciseSolutions\Directions<YourName>.doc**, where you substitute your actual name or other identifier for <YourName>. At the top of your document, type the title MapQuest Routes from My House. Include your name. List the three destination addresses that you are using.

b. Open your Web browser, go to *www.mapquest.com*, and click the Get Directions button on the home page.

c. Type a starting address and one of the three destination locations as the ending address. Click the Get Directions button.

d. Save a map image of each route. Right-click the image and click Copy. In your Word document, right-click the insertion point at the desired location for the directions, and then click Paste.

e. Comment on each of the sets of directions in your Word document. Do they look like the best route? Is there a better route? Are there any mistakes, such as sending you down the wrong direction on a one-way street?

f. Save your Word document. If you have an instructor, turn your Word document in as instructed.

3. **Explore the National Geographic Map Machine.** In this exercise, you will explore many interesting maps of your choice.

a. Create a Word document called **C:\LearningAndUsingGIS\FilesExerciseSolutions\MapMachine<YourName>.doc**, where you substitute your actual name or other identifier for <YourName>. Type the title MapMachine Maps.

b. Choose a map that interests you from the Web site *http://plasma.nationalgeographic.com/mapmachine/search.html*. Type the name of the map in your Word document.

c. Zoom in to an area of interest, and copy the screen by right-clicking the map and saving it to your desktop with the name **MyMap1.bmp**. In Word, click the insertion point below your map title, click Insert, click Picture, browse to find one of your images, and insert it in the Word document.

d. Write a short paragraph on interesting map features.

e. Repeat the preceding steps for another map of interest.

f. Save your Word document. If you have an instructor, turn the Word document in as instructed.

4. **Benchmark a GIS Web Site.** In this exercise, you will use benchmarking to identify organizations that have good practices, study the good practices, and write a report on them to influence others. Benchmarking is a process that designers use to get good ideas from existing facilities, organizations, systems, or policies.

a. Select an ArcIMS Web site from *www.esri.com/software/internetmaps/visit_sites.html* that you find interesting and that has at least one advanced GIS function and one unique data set. Do not choose San Francisco Prospector or a similar economic development site with the same Web application program. Also, do not choose the Greenwood, South Carolina Web site.

b.   Identify a unique GIS capability used on the Web site, such as finding an address, zooming in with layers turning on and off automatically, calculating statistics using buffers, selecting map features using data queries, and so forth.

c.   Create a Word document called **C:\LearningAndUsingGIS\FilesExerciseSolutions\ Benchmark<YourName>.doc**, where you substitute your actual name or other identifier for <YourName>. Include a title at the top that reads Benchmark Study of http:// TheSiteURL. Include your name. Write a paragraph describing the purpose of the Web site.

d.   Describe the inputs to the unique GIS capability, such as any special databases or layers used and any inputs required of the user.

e.   Describe the output of the unique GIS capability. Print the output by right-clicking your screen and saving the file to your desktop or elsewhere with a name such as Screenprint1.bmp.

f.   Give each unique GIS capability a title, include your descriptions of inputs and outputs, and include the images of the Web pages you saved. Click Insert, click Picture, click From File, browse to find one of your images, and then paste it in the Word document.

g.   Save your Word document. If you have an instructor, turn the Word document in as instructed.

References

Clarke, K. C. *Getting Started with Geographic Information Systems*, 4th Ed., Prentice Hall, Upper Saddle River, New Jersey, 2003, pp. 2–6.

Cohen, Mark E. "The Monetary Value of Saving a High-Risk Youth," *Journal of Quantitative Criminology*, 1998, Vol. 14, No. 1.

U.S. Census Bureau, TIGER/Line maps: Internet URL: http://www.census.gov/geo/www/tiger/ index.html (accessed March 25, 2005).

NAVIGATING GIS

LEARNING OBJECTIVES

In this chapter, you will:

- Learn how features are located on maps using coordinate systems
- Learn the role of geographic scale on map detail
- Learn about projecting the spherical world onto flat maps
- Work with map layers in ArcGIS
- Change map scale and move around in an ArcGIS document
- Measure map features
- Use ArcGIS to change map projections

Everybody, into the pool!

INTRODUCTION

The most important information maps provide is location. Where is something positioned? Is it on a major

street with good access? Is there a barrier to accessing it, such as a river? Is it in a certain area? Where are

similar things positioned? What or who is near it? These are some of the questions that maps can answer.

Where you are sitting right now has two unique numbers, **latitude** and **longitude**, that pinpoint your location precisely on the surface of Earth. In this chapter, you will learn some useful facts about latitude and longitude coordinates and the **geographic coordinate system** that they define. You will also learn about map scale, which refers to the relative size, or proportion, that the map bears to the actual area that it represents. In essence, it shows how far above Earth you appear to be when looking at a map, zoomed in or out. The closer you are, the more detail you see. Finally, you will learn about map projections, making flat maps from the nearly spherical Earth. There are at least 100 ways to project maps, and ArcGIS uses many of them. Sometimes, which projection you choose makes a big difference, so we give you some guidelines.

After you learn basic concepts and facts about map navigation, you will open an ArcGIS map document, similar to *Chapter1-1.mxd*, that has a map composition for the Swimming Pool Case Study. Then, you will start navigating the map, zooming in and out, to get information. You will also work with several map projections for a new, simple map document that you will build.

MAP NAVIGATION

Your location on a map in a GIS is determined by the **map extent**, a rectangle on Earth corresponding to the boundaries of your map (whether on a computer screen or a printed map). Map extent is defined by two pairs of map coordinates, opposite ends of the corresponding rectangle such as the lower-left and upper-right corners of the rectangle. The **full extent** of the map is the maximum extent for the map layers in your GIS. For example, for TIGER maps it is often a rectangle that encloses a county boundary because these maps are prepared for counties. The portion of the map that you're currently zoomed in to on your computer screen is called the **current extent**.

Changing map extent is a form of **map navigation**, which is the process of changing the view of all or part of a map document. The underlying structure for map navigation and the maps themselves is their coordinate system. In actuality, the Earth is nearly a sphere, a **spheroid**, and, therefore, we need a coordinate system for locating points on a spheroid. However, the maps that you view on your computer screen or on paper are flat and, thus, use a corresponding flat coordinate system. How do coordinates on a spheroid work? How do you transform coordinates on a spheroid to coordinates on flat surfaces? You will learn about these and related issues in the remainder of this chapter.

Geographic Coordinates

Planet Earth appears to be a sphere, but it is very slightly flattened at the poles and bulged out at the equator, making it a spheroid. While Earth was forming, the centrifugal force of the planet spinning on its axis threw out a little more mass at the equator at the expense of the poles. However, it is only about 77 miles shorter to go around the world passing through the poles than it is taking the 22,770-mile route around the equator (Clarke, 2003, p. 37), not much of a shortcut. Nevertheless, here is the question we need to confront: How do you locate points on a spheroid?

The answer is not the usual **rectangular coordinates** as used for locating an intersection on a flat sheet of graph paper or a flat map. On graph paper, the point (-80, 40) is 80 linear units measured to the left of the vertical y-axis and 40 units measured up from the horizontal x-axis (see Figure 2-1). On the globe, the point (-80, 40) is 80° (80 degrees) west longitude and 40° north latitude—roughly our hometown of Pittsburgh, Pennsylvania. Latitude and longitude are **geographic coordinates** (or **spherical coordinates**), angles of *rotation* of a radius anchored at Earth's center. One simple way to make latitude and longitude coordinates precise is to allow for decimal degrees; for example, the far-western tip of Pittsburgh's central business district has decimal degree coordinates of (-80.013297°, 40.442206°).

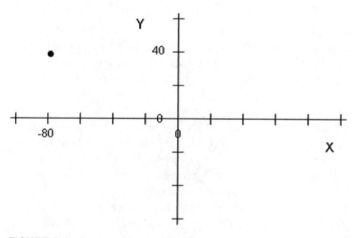

FIGURE 2-1   Rectangular coordinates

Figure 2-2 illustrates this measurement system (Demers, 2005, p. 28). A **great circle** is a circle on the surface of the world that has the radius of the world. A **meridian** is a great circle that passes through the poles. The **prime meridian** is the meridian that passes through Greenwich, England. It is the line of 0° longitude, because of historical reasons and by agreement (it is not a natural reference line). This circle establishes the reference point for measurements east and west on the globe. In the opposite direction, the natural reference circle for north and south measurements is the equator, which is at 0° latitude.

So, the (0, 0) point on the globe is the intersection of the prime meridian, proceeding south from Greenwich, with the equator. To get Pittsburgh's coordinates, we rotate the

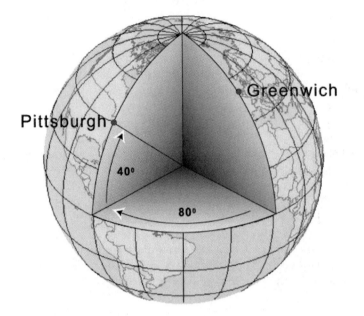

FIGURE 2-2 Latitude and longitude on the globe

radius seen in Figure 2-2 through an angle of 80° longitude to the west along the equator, and then rotate 40° north along the meridian passing through 80° west longitude.

Figure 2-3 plots latitude and longitude (geographic) coordinates of the world as if they were rectangular coordinates. This is a misuse of geographic coordinates, but serves to illustrate the range of coordinate values. Longitude can range from -180° to 0° to 180° for a total of 360° when measured around the equator. Latitude can range from 0° at the equator up to 90° at the North Pole and from 0° down to -90° at the South Pole. The lines of constant latitude circling east to west around the globe are called **parallels** because they are parallel to each other, as you can see in Figure 2-2. So, if you are looking at a map on a GIS, which gives you readouts of map coordinates wherever your mouse pointer is hovering on a map, you can recognize geographical coordinates of latitude and longitude because they range between -180° to 180° in the first position (longitude), and -90° to 90° in the second position (latitude).

A degree of longitude, measured west to east between two meridians, is longest in miles (when straightened) at the equator. As we move north or south from the equator, this length decreases until approaching the poles, where longitude's length disappears. Pittsburgh, at 40° north latitude, is a midlatitude area. Whereas a degree is 63 miles long on the equator, it is roughly half this in Pittsburgh. Sometimes, we display maps with their geographic coordinates on a flat computer screen, as shown in Figure 2-3. This is not the intention nor purpose of geographic coordinates, so such maps are distorted in the north-south direction, and more so nearer the poles. You will see this when you project maps for this chapter's tutorial.

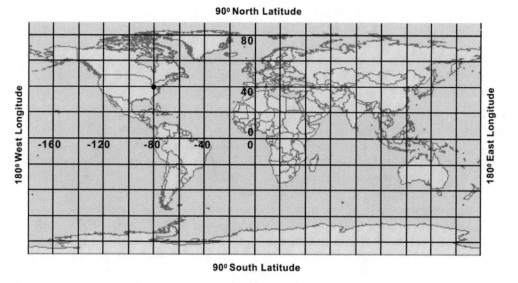

FIGURE 2-3   Latitude and longitude on a flat sheet

Map Scale

To understand map scale, consider this analogy: Model trains come in different scales. *N* is the smallest scale with a ratio of 1:160, meaning that 1 inch of model train is equivalent to 160 inches of real train. The largest model trains are G scale, with a ratio of 1:23. G-scale model trains are larger than N-scale trains. For example, if a real train is as long as a football field, 300 feet, then a G-scale model train is 300/23 = 13 feet long, but an N-scale model train is 300/160 = 1 foot 10 inches long. Model train manufacturers can place a lot of realistic detail on a G-scale model train because there is a lot of room to do so, but there is less detail on an N-scale model train.

Map scale is analogous to that for model trains, except that the ratios need to be much more extreme to get sufficient reduction for maps. **Large-scale** maps, like the G-scale train, are relatively large, and **small-scale** maps are relatively small. Many people find these terms confusing. To make the terms *large scale* and *small scale* concrete, suppose that you have a paper map of Lake Erie. A large-scale map having a scale of 1:50,000 to 1:10,000 makes the lake look large because it is so big on paper. By contrast, a small-scale map, with for example, a map scale of 1:250,000 to 1:1,000,000, makes the lake look small because it appears smaller on paper (Rosenberg, 2005).

A **map scale ratio** with the numeral *1* as its numerator, such as 1:24,000, is called a **representative fraction** by **cartographers** (map makers). Its beauty is that it is dimensionless, so that you can use it with any linear measurement unit, such as feet, meters, or miles. For example, 1 inch on the map is 24,000 inches on the ground. It is possible to use two different linear measurement units, in which case the same scale is called a **verbal scale**. For example, 1 inch on the map is 2000 feet on the ground (divide 12 inches per foot into 24,000 inches to get the 2000 feet). The graphic representation of map scale, the **graphic scale**, places a line on the map with ground distances marked, such as 10 miles, 20 miles, and so on (Demers, 2005, p. 50).

Maps are created at different scales. For a fixed area on the ground, like a park, a small-scale map will have less detail than a large-scale map—in fact, the park could be a point on a small-scale map and a polygon on a large-scale map. Most of the maps that you download for free have scales appropriate for your use.

Map Projections

As you learned in Chapter 1, the five main types of features represented on maps are physical, political, legal, statistical, and administrative. You can locate features on the globe in many different ways: surveying methods, aerial photography, **Global Positioning System (GPS)** receivers, and so forth. GPS uses a constellation of satellites to determine the position and velocity (if moving relative to Earth) of any GPS receiver on or above the Earth. How do cartographers transform geographical coordinates into flat coordinates so we get good representations of Earth on our flat computer screens and paper maps?

If you have ever cut a hollow rubber ball in half and tried to flatten one of the halves on a tabletop, you know what the problem is. Some parts of the ball must stretch and others must shrink. This causes distortion on the ball's surface, or variations in scale, but only for large areas of the ball, such as an entire half. Any small area, relative to itself, has no significant variation in scale. Similarly, for small areas on Earth and large-scale maps—such as a city, county, or even a state—there is not much distortion. For example, the major projections used by local governments and the U.S. military, **State Plane** and **Universal Transverse Mercator (UTM)**, have no detectable distortion. For small-scale maps of the world or a continent, however, there is much distortion.

A **map projection** is a mathematical transformation that behaves as if it were projecting features of the world onto one of three surfaces: a plane, cone, or cylinder. See Figure 2-4 (Muehrcke, 1986). Planes are used for projecting the areas around the North and South Poles, as if the plane were touching one of the poles. For a cone, it is as if the cone were sitting on the Earth, with its point above one of the poles. The projection has no distortion where the cone touches Earth and more distortion the further from the circle that touches. Depending on how pointed or shallow the cone is determines where it touches the Earth for one hemisphere. For the cylinder, it is as if the Earth were inside the cylinder, touching at the equator. There are similar distortions for the cylinder, but it can only touch at a great circle. Sometimes, the cone or cylinder is rotated 90°, resulting in **transverse projections**. Sometimes, the cone or cylinder pierce through and reemerge through the surface of the Earth, resulting in **secant projections**.

Suppose that we are using a conic projection with the cone touching the 40° north parallel that goes through Pittsburgh. A main street in Pittsburgh is Grant Street. If we are mapping the location of a manhole (sewer line access point) in the 100 block of Grant Street, imagine a light source at the center of the Earth shining up through that manhole and onto the cone. We place a dot for the manhole where the point of light shines on the cone. When we've finished projecting all the manholes in Pittsburgh, using the same approach, we cut the cone from edge to point, unroll it, and flatten it to get the projected map.

Here are a few guidelines for map projections:

- *Get latitude/longitude base maps*: **Base maps** are those provided by governments or commercial firms in digital form for use in a GIS. If possible, get base map layers in unprojected, geographic coordinates of latitude and longitude.

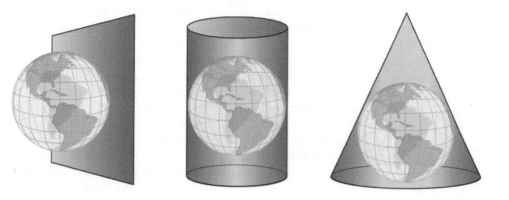

FIGURE 2-4 Map projections

You can always project these on any flat projection surface, a capability of ArcGIS. Generally, you also can transform from projected coordinates back to geographic coordinates.

- *Troubleshoot map layers that do not appear*: If map layers from two different sources for the same area do not all appear when you put them in ArcGIS (or nothing appears), it is because one of them is missing **spatial reference data**, information on which projection and specific parameters of the projection are used to create a map layer's coordinates. If you know the projection of a map layer, you can use ArcCatalog to add a map layer's spatial reference data. If you do not know the projection of a map layer, trial and error with popular projections can help you discover the projection.

- *Use State Plane or UTM projections for local areas*: For UTM, you have to look up the zone for your area (for example, see Morton, 2005, for UTM and see Mentor Software, Inc., 2005, for State Plane codes). When you project a map using either of these projections, you must supply the proper code as an input parameter. You also have to specify the **geoid**, or specific shape assumed for the world, generally either NAD 27 or NAD 83. For analytic mapping, it does not matter which you choose as long as you are consistent. UTM is a more modern projection. It uses metric system measurements and applies to the entire world. State Plane projections are widely used by U.S. local governments and are defined only for Alaska and the lower 48 states.

- *Use the Robinson projection for the entire world unless you have a better option*: Many projections of the world have enormous distortions. The Robinson projection is most accurate at the midlatitudes in both the Northern and Southern Hemispheres where most people live. *National Geographic Magazine* often uses this projection.

- *Use conformal projections to preserve shape and direction*: For maps that depict areas the size of a continent or larger and that preserve local shape and direction, good projections are the Lambert Conformal conic and Mercator projections. **Conformal projections** are easy to recognize because their projected lines of latitude and longitude intersect at right angles (Clarke, 2003, pp. 41, 42). Conformal projections distort areas. You can either preserve accurate shape or accurate area, but not both in map projections. Equivalent projections are better for analytic mapping, and are discussed next.

- *Use equal area or equivalent projections to preserve area*: For maps that depict areas the size of a continent or larger and that preserve area measurements, use **equivalent projections**, such as the Albers equal area or Lambert's equal area projections. Often when doing analytical mapping, it is necessary to use population or other densities, calculated as the number of persons or other entities per unit area. Then, an equivalent projection is needed to avoid projection-caused variations in areas and, therefore, in densities. General reference and educational maps often use equal area projections (Demers, 2005).

ARCGIS FOR MAP NAVIGATION

Now you will work in ArcGIS on the concepts you learned in the previous sections. To get started, you will start ArcMap and open the *Chapter2-1.mdx* map document. Note that a map document file does not store copies of map layers, but rather points to their locations on disk and uses them where they are stored. Hence, generally it is important not to rename or move folders that contain map layers after corresponding map documents are built. ArcMap can, however, store **relative paths** for the files used in a map document. Relative paths allow you to move the folder containing all map layers and your map document, including subfolders, to a different location on your hard drive and the map document will still function correctly.

Open the Chapter2-1.mdx Map Document

1. On your PC computer's desktop, click **Start**, click **All Programs**, click **ArcGIS**, and click **ArcMap**.
2. In the ArcMap window, click the **An existing map** option button and double-click **Browse for maps** in the panel below the option button.
3. In the Open window, browse to your **LearningAndUsingGIS** folder and double-click **Chapter2-1.mxd**. See Figure 2-5. *(The Chapter2-1.mxd map document window opens in ArcMap showing Allegheny County and its municipalities. The rectangle around Allegheny County is the one we want you to drag with your cursor in the following "Create Spatial Bookmarks" section.)*
4. If the Tools toolbar is not visible in ArcMap, on the main menu click **View**, click **Toolbars**, scroll down in the resulting menu, and click **Tools**. *(Before moving on, we'll have you check to make sure that the map document uses relative paths.)*
5. On the main menu, click **File**, click **Map Properties**.
6. In the resulting *Chapter2-1.mxd* Properties window, click the **Data Source Options** button.
7. In the resulting Data Source options window, verify that the **Store relative path names** option button is on. *(If not, click it on. Thus, you can have the LearningAndUsingGIS folder—which has all files and subfolders of this*

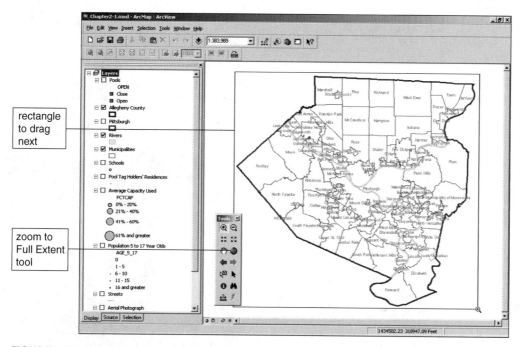

rectangle to drag next

zoom to Full Extent tool

FIGURE 2-5 ArcMap window with Chapter2-1.mxd map document open

book's GIS—installed anywhere on your hard drive and corresponding map documents will function correctly.)

8. Click **OK**, and click **Cancel** again.

Create Spatial Bookmarks

A GIS enables you to zoom in to particular areas for close-up views. Sometimes, you'll want to save a zoomed-in map extent for easy reuse later. ArcMap allows you to create spatial bookmarks, or bookmarks for short, for that purpose.

1. On the Tools toolbar, click the **Zoom In** tool 🔍. Starting on the upper left, drag the rectangle shown in Figure 2-5, and release your mouse button. See Figure 2-6. (If you have any problems, click the Full Extent tool ⬤ on the Tools toolbar to start over. The map gets larger, maximizing use of your map window.)

2. On the main menu, click **View**, click **Bookmarks**, and click **Create**.

3. In the resulting Spatial Bookmark window, type **Allegheny County** and click **OK**. (That creates a spatial bookmark that you can use in the future and in the next step to get this fully maximized view of the county again by making a simple selection.)

4. On the Tools toolbar, click the **Full Extent** tool ⬤. (This returns you to the initial view of the county.)

5. Click **View**, click **Bookmarks**, and click **Allegheny County**.

6. In the table of contents, click the **Pittsburgh** map layer on.

larger
county
map

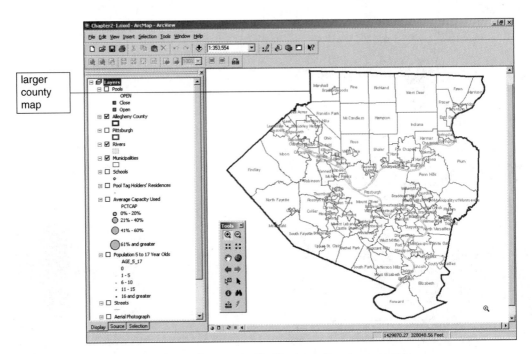

FIGURE 2-6 Chapter2-1.mxd map document with Allegheny County zoomed in

7. In the table of contents, right-click **Pittsburgh**, and in the resulting shortcut menu, click **Zoom to Layer**. (*That makes Pittsburgh's boundary centered and nearly filling the current map extent.*)
8. Repeat Steps 2 and 3 to create a bookmark for Pittsburgh. (*Suppose you want to delete a bookmark. Then you need the next step.*)
9. Click **View**, click **Bookmarks**, and click **Manage**.
10. In the resulting Spatial Bookmarks window, click **Pittsburgh**, click **Remove**, and click **Close**.

PRACTICE 2-1

Re-create the Pittsburgh bookmark. Repeat the preceding steps to create bookmarks for the aerial photo and topo map, with those names respectively. When finished, use the Pittsburgh bookmark to zoom back to Pittsburgh and turn off the aerial photo and topo map layers.

Use Zooming Tools

A GIS enables you to zoom in to particular areas for close-up views.

1. If you are not zoomed to the Pittsburgh bookmark, do so now.
2. Turn on the following layers, relevant to Pittsburgh and the current scale: **Pools** and **Population 5 to 17 Year Olds**. See Figure 2-7. (*Now you can see which*

pools have nearby populations of the target population of youths. Notice that Figure 2-7 indicates the current scale for our computer monitor size, 1:115,828 inches. Your scale might be different, depending on your monitor size.)

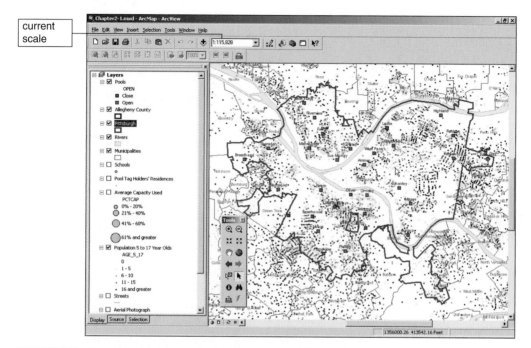

FIGURE 2-7 Chapter2-1.mxd map document zoomed to Pittsburgh

3. On the Tools toolbar, click the **Fixed Zoom In** tool. See Figure 2-8. *(The view is still centered on Pittsburgh but is zoomed in a fixed step size. You could keep clicking this tool to zoom in to the center of Pittsburgh further, but don't do so now.)*

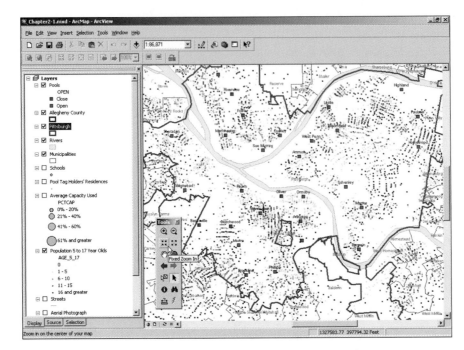

FIGURE 2-8   Chapter2-1.mxd map document after one fixed zoom in

4. Click the **Fixed Zoom Out** tool . (*This reverses the process, but not exactly back to where you started.*)

5. Use the **Pittsburgh** bookmark to get back to the starting place exactly. (*Suppose that you would like to zoom in to a specific scale, such as 1:24,000. You will do that next.*)

6. In the scale field on the Standard toolbar, type in **1:24,000** and press **Enter**. See Figure 2-9. (*The map stays centered on Pittsburgh and zooms in to a scale of 1:24,000, a common scale used in large-scale maps. At this scale, it is useful to have the Streets map layer turned on.*)

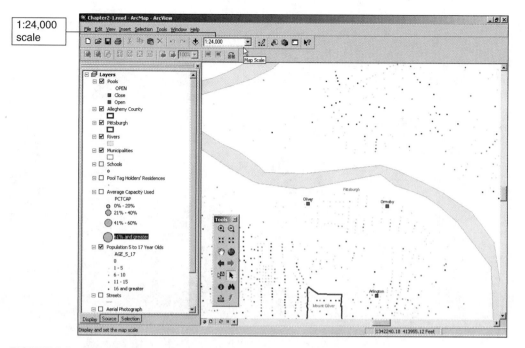

FIGURE 2-9 Chapter2-1.mxd map document zoomed to 1:24,000 scale

7. In the table of contents, turn the **Streets** map layer on, and drag the **Rivers** map layer to just below Streets. *(With Rivers moved below Streets, you can see the bridge centerlines.)*
8. On the Tools toolbar, click the **Go Back To Previous Extent** tool ⬅. *(This is a very handy tool when doing a lot of map exploration.)*

Use More Zooming Tools

There is a feature of ArcMap called the Overview window that helps you determine where you are, when zoomed in. It uses the bottom layer in the table of contents as the reference layer. We want you to use Municipalities for this purpose, so in the following steps you make a copy of that layer and place it at the bottom of the table of contents as a "trick." Otherwise, you have to reset the reference layer to Municipalities every time you open the Overview window.

1. If you are not zoomed to the Pittsburgh bookmark, do so now.
2. In the table of contents, right-click **Municipalities** and click **Copy**.
3. On the main menu, click **Edit** and click **Paste**. *(That action places a second copy of the Municipalities layer just below the Pools layer.)*
4. Drag the new copy of **Municipalities** to the bottom of the table of contents and turn it off.
5. Click **Window** and click **Overview**. See Figure 2-10. *(Now you see the current extent in reference to the entire county and municipalities. Mount Oliver, indicated in Figure 2-10, is where you will zoom to next.)*

Navigating GIS

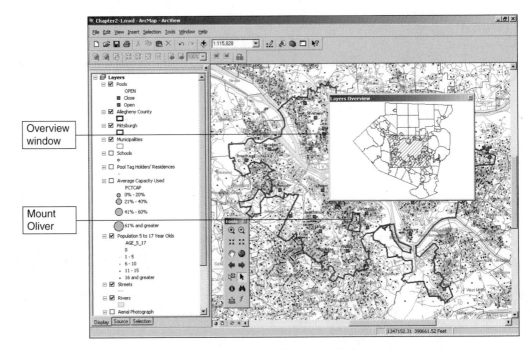

FIGURE 2-10 Chapter2-1.mxd map document with Overview window

Overview window

Mount Oliver

6. On the Tools toolbar, click the **Zoom In** tool ⊕, and drag a rectangle around **Mount Oliver**. See Figure 2-11. *(Notice how the Overview window has changed to show that you are now zoomed in to Mount Oliver.)*

7. On the Tools toolbar, click the **Pan** tool ✋, click **Mount Oliver**, hold down your mouse button, drag about two or three inches to the right, and release. *(Your map shifts, or pans, to the right and your Overview window is updated.)*

8. Close the Overview window.

PRACTICE 2-2

Use zooming tools to create three bookmarks for Pittsburgh: (1) Northside of Pittsburgh (the portion of Pittsburgh that has the closed Fowler Pool and is bounded by rivers, (2) Central Pittsburgh (the portion of Pittsburgh that has the open Schenley Pool and is bounded by rivers, and (3) South Pittsburgh (the rest of the city). When finished, zoom back to the Pittsburgh bookmark.

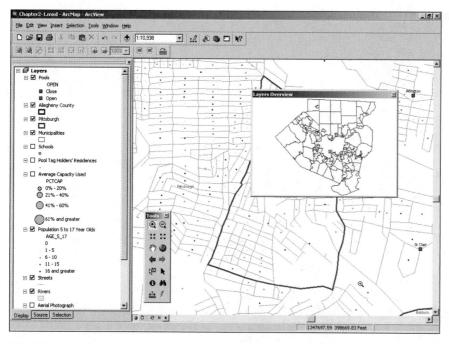

FIGURE 2-11 Chapter2-1.mxd map document zoomed to Mount Oliver

Add and Symbolize a Map Layer

Your next objective is to use a feature in ArcMap that automatically turns map layers on and off, when zooming in and out. First, however, you will learn how to add a new layer to your map document, Pittsburgh neighborhoods, that is helpful to turn on when zoomed to the Pittsburgh bookmark or further in.

1. Use your Pittsburgh bookmark to zoom to the whole city.
2. On the Standard toolbar, click the **Add Data** tool ✛, browse to **C:\LearningAndUsingGIS\MapsPools**, and double-click **neighborhoods.shp**. *(This action adds the Neighborhoods map layer to your map document.)*
3. In the table of contents, right-click **neighborhoods**, and click **Properties**.
4. In the resulting Layer Properties window, click the **General** tab, and capitalize the **Neighborhoods** layer name.
5. Click the **Symbology** tab, click the **left** button in the Symbol section, in the resulting Symbol Selector window, click the **Hollow** color swatch in the left panel, click **OK**, and click **OK** again. Turn off the Streets and Population 5 to 17 Year Olds layers. See Figure 2-12.

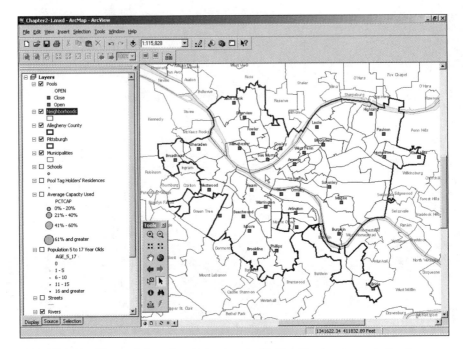

FIGURE 2-12   Chapter2-1.mxd map document with Neighborhoods symbolized

Create Minimum Visible Scale Ranges

Now, you are ready to automate turning the Neighborhoods layer on when zoomed in to Pittsburgh or further, using the layer's minimum visible range property. Then, neighborhoods are only displayed when zoomed in further than the Pittsburgh bookmark. We would like neighborhoods to appear, however, when using the Pittsburgh bookmark, exactly at its scale. To trick ArcMap and make the bookmark work as desired, you will add one to the denominator of the map scale when setting the minimum visible range for neighborhoods. Then, the Pittsburgh bookmark will take you one foot beyond the minimum visible range for neighborhoods, and neighborhoods will turn on.

1. On the Standard toolbar, modify the map scale to make its denominator one increment larger, and press **Enter**. *(On our monitor, the scale was 1:115,828, so we made it 1:115,829.)*

2. In the table of contents, right-click **Neighborhoods**, click **Visible Scale Range**, and click **Set Minimum Scale**. *(This terminology is confusing because the closer zoomed in you are, the larger the scale. If you want to turn on a map layer when zoomed in far enough, you set a minimum scale. If you want to turn a layer off when zoomed in far enough, you set a maximum scale.)*

3. Use your **Allegheny County** bookmark to see that neighborhoods disappear when zoomed to a smaller map scale *(which is 1:353,554 for our monitor)*, and then use your **Pittsburgh** bookmark to see that neighborhoods appear *(because the Pittsburgh scale is a tiny bit larger than the visible minimum).*

Turn on the Population 5 to 17 Year Olds and Streets map layers.

- Set a minimum visible range for Population 5 to 17 Year Olds at the Pittsburgh scale, as you did for the Neighborhoods layer.
- Use your Central Pittsburgh bookmark to zoom to that part of the city (if you do not have this bookmark, go back to Practice 2-2 and create it). Set a minimum visible range for Streets (no trick needed).
- Try out your new visible range by using the Allegheny County and Pittsburgh bookmarks and by zooming in to an area smaller than Central Pittsburgh.

Use the Find Tool

We want you to zoom in to a particular Pittsburgh neighborhood, Highland Park, and set a visible range there, but of course you do not know where Highland Park is. This is no problem, because ArcMap has a Find tool, which you will use next.

1. On the Tools toolbar, click the **Find tool** 🔍.
2. In the resulting Find window, type **Highland Park** in the Find field, click the list arrow in the **In** field, click **Neighborhoods**, and click **Find**.
3. In the resulting bottom panel of the Find window, right-click the **Highland Park** row, and click **Flash Feature** to see where that neighborhood is on the map.
4. Again, right-click the **Highland Park** row, click **Zoom to feature(s)**, and close the Find window. *(The map zooms in to the Highland Park neighborhood of Pittsburgh.)*

Create a Maximum Visible Scale Range

The Population 5 to 17 Year Olds layer is best used when zoomed in to reasonably large areas. When zoomed in far, such as to the neighborhood level, it is a good idea to turn this map layer off.

1. In the table of contents, right-click **Population 5 to 17 Year Olds**, click **Visible Range**, and click **Set Maximum Scale**. *(This layers turns off at this scale and further zoomed in.)*
2. On the Tools toolbar, click the **Fixed Zoom Out** tool ⬚. *(The Population 5 to 17 Year Olds layer turns back on.)*
3. On the Tools toolbar, click the **Go Back To Previous Extent** tool ⬅. *(That puts the map back to the Highland Park scale.)*

Create a Visible Scale Range for Labels

At the current scale, you are zoomed in far enough that labels for street names would be useful. You can set a minimum range scale on the labels to turn them on.

1. Right-click **Streets** and click **Properties**.
2. In the resulting Layer Properties window, click the **Labels** tab, click the **Label features in this layer** check box, and click the **Scale Range** button.

3. In the resulting Scale Range window, click the **Don't show labels when zoomed** option button, type the **Highland Park** scale *(from your scale readout on the Standard toolbar)* into the **Out beyond** field *(our monitor's scale is 1:16,753 so we typed 16753)*, click **OK**, and click **OK** again. See Figure 2-13. *(The street labels turn on.)*

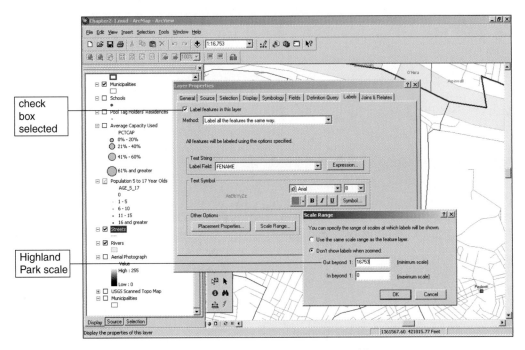

check box selected

Highland Park scale

FIGURE 2-13 Property settings to turn street labels on when zoomed in

4. On the Standard toolbar, click the **Fixed Zoom Out** tool. *(The labels turn off, but the streets stay on.)*
5. On the Tools toolbar, click the **Go Back To Previous Extent** tool to get back to the Highland Park neighborhood. *(The street labels turn on again.)*

Use the Magnification Window

ArcMap has a neat tool that lets you slide a Magnification window around the map to see zoomed-in views. If there are visible scale ranges turning detailed layers on for the scale of the Magnification window, they function to show you more detail.

1. Use your **Allegheny County** bookmark.
2. On the main menu, click **Window** and click **Magnifier**. See Figure 2-14. *(The Magnification window opens.)*
3. Click, hold, and drag the top of the resulting Magnification window to Pittsburgh's point where the two large rivers *(the Allegheny to the north and Monongahela to the south)* join to form the Ohio River. See Figure 2-15. *(The*

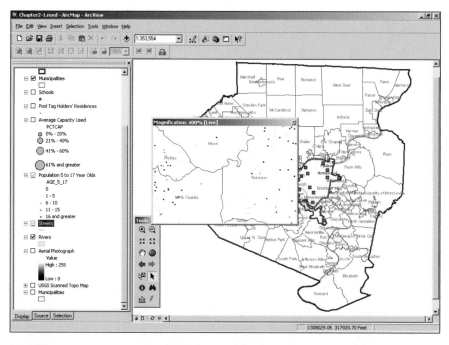

FIGURE 2-14 Chapter2-1.mxd map document with Magnification window

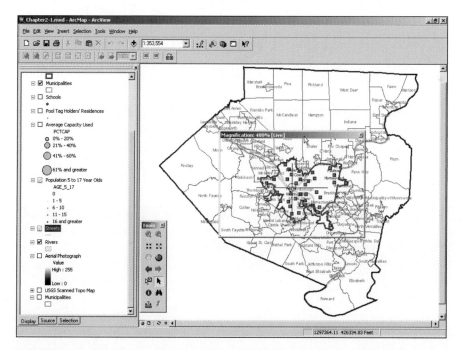

FIGURE 2-15 Chapter2-1.mxd map document with Magnification window and crosshairs

Navigating GIS

window switches to the current map scale of Allegheny County with crosshairs for picking a point to zoom in to.)

4. Release the Magnification window. See Figure 2-16. *(The window zooms in to Pittsburgh's point at a magnification level of 400 percent.)*

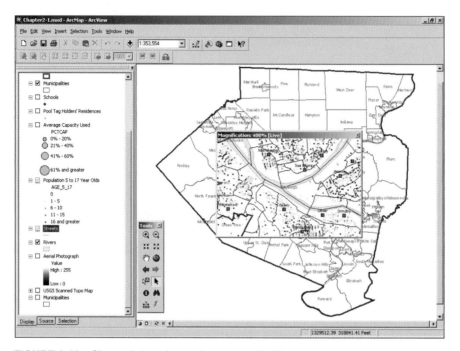

FIGURE 2-16   Chapter2-1.mxd map document with Magnification window zoomed in to Pittsburgh's point

5. Right-click the top of the Magnification window, and click **Properties**.
6. In the resulting Magnifier Properties window, click the **list arrow** for the zoom percentage, click **800%**, and click **OK**. See Figure 2-17. *(The magnifier should be zoomed in far enough so that your streets turn on.)*
7. Close the Magnification window.

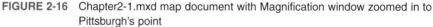

PRACTICE 2-4

Use the Magnification window to explore areas around some pools. Experiment with Magnifier tool settings and properties.

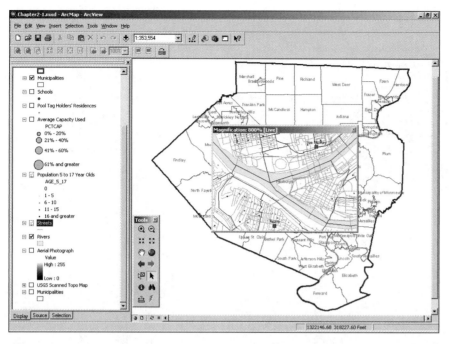

FIGURE 2-17   Chapter2-1.mxd map document with Magnification window zoomed 800%

Use the Measure Tool

Next, you will use the Measure tool to measure features on the map. Later in this tutorial, you will learn how we set the coordinate units of the map *Chapter2-1.mxd* document to be feet. Given that ArcMap "knows" that the map units are feet, you can set the properties of the Measure tool to have a readout in any practical unit, such as miles or kilometers.

1. On the main menu, click **View**, and click **Data Frame Properties**.
2. In the resulting Data Frame Properties window, click the **General** tab. *(Notice in the Units panel that the map units are Feet and that you cannot change them.)*
3. In the Units panel of the General tab, click the **list arrow** for Display, click **Miles**, and click **OK**. *(The result is that the Measure tool now gives measurements in miles.)*
4. On the Tools toolbar, click the **Measure** tool ⬚.
5. Click the **extreme west point** of Allegheny County, move your cursor straight to the right, double-click the **right side of the county**, and notice the segment and total width of the county. See Figure 2-18. *(The width is nearly 35 miles. Next, you will estimate the perimeter of the county.)*
6. Again, click the **extreme west point** of the county, and then click a **series of points** approximately along the perimeter of the county, finishing with a double-click back at the starting point. See Figure 2-19. *(If you click too quickly along the edge, you might generate a double-click by mistake, so*

be careful not to go too quickly. As you go along clicking, the readout at the lower left of the map window provides both the length of the most recent segment measured and the running total of all segments. The perimeter is approximately 125 miles.)

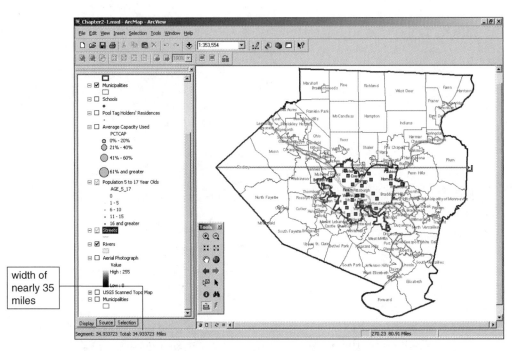

width of nearly 35 miles

FIGURE 2-18   Measuring the width of Allegheny County

PRACTICE 2-5

Use the Measure tool to measure the width of Pittsburgh and its perimeter. Be very approximate in measuring the perimeter. You should get about 12 miles for the width and about 60 miles for the perimeter.

Use the Identify Tool

This is the last navigation tool that you will learn about in this section. With the Identify tool, you can read the attribute data records for any feature in any map layer.

1. Use your Pittsburgh bookmark.
2. On the Tools toolbar, click the **Identify** tool $\bullet$.
3. In the resulting Identify Results window, click the **Layers** list arrow, and click **Pools**.
4. Click **Highland Pool** in the upper right of Pittsburgh. See Figure 2-20. *(The results for the Highland Pool record are reported where you can see that its*

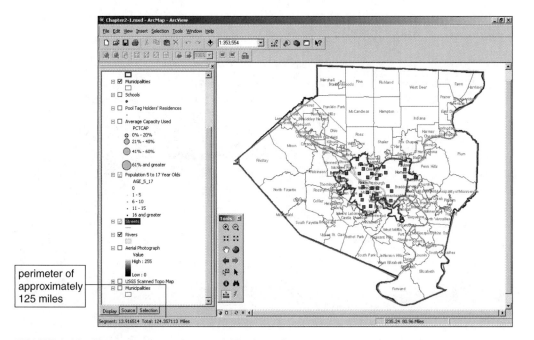

perimeter of approximately 125 miles

FIGURE 2-19 Measuring the perimeter of Allegheny County

capacity, MAXLOAD, is 1448 persons and that its average number of visitors per day when open is 556.)

5. In the Identify Results window, click the **Layers** list arrow and click **Neighborhoods**.

6. Click on or near **Highland Pool**. (This time, you get Identify Results for the Highland Park neighborhood polygon. The only attribute for the neighborhoods layer is NAME, which has the value Highland Park.)

7. Close the **Identify Results** window.

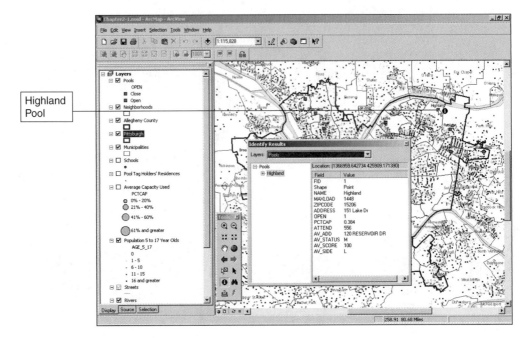

Highland
Pool

FIGURE 2-20 Identify Results for Highland Pool

ARCGIS FOR MAP PROJECTION

ArcGIS has comprehensive and sophisticated capacities to handle map projections. You can use ArcCatalog to assign spatial reference data to each map layer, if not already included. Then, even if map layers are in different projections and coordinate systems, ArcMap will reproject them automatically to your map document's coordinate system. This allows you to integrate map layers from many different sources and in different projections into your map documents and choose the best projection for the problem at hand.

Set Layer Spatial Reference Data

Here, you will change the data frame's coordinate system in the *Chapter2-1.mxd* map document. The result is that ArcMap reprojects all map layers to whatever projection you chose. Note for your future work: When creating a new map document, if you do not explicitly assign spatial reference data to a data frame, ArcMap uses the coordinate system of the first map layer that you add to the document.

63

1. Use your **Allegheny County** bookmark.
2. At the top of the table of contents, right-click **Layers**, and click **Properties**.
3. In the resulting Data Frames window, click the **Coordinate System** tab.
4. In the bottom panel of the Coordinate System tab, click the following expander boxes or icons: **Predefined, Geographic Coordinate Systems, North America,** and **North American Datum 1983**.
5. Click **OK** and click **Yes**. See Figure 2-21. *(This results in your map being displayed with latitude and longitude coordinates and, therefore, with much distortion, flattening the map out. This is not a good choice, but illustrates how you can set the data frame coordinates.)*

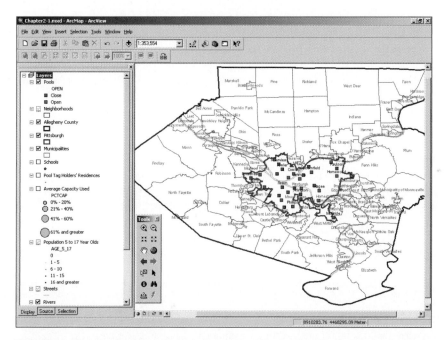

FIGURE 2-21   Chapter2-1.mxd map document with geographic coordinate system

- Repeat Steps 2–5, except in Step 4 use the UTM projection. Click expander boxes or icons for Predefined, Projected Coordinate Systems, UTM, NAD 1983, and NAD 1983 UTM Zone 17N.
- Repeat Steps 2–5 to get back to the original frame projection of State Plane. Click expander boxes or icons for Predefined, Projected Coordinate Systems, State Plane, NAD 1983 (Feet), and NAD 1983 StatePlane Pennsylvania South FIPS 3702 (Feet).

Set Map Layer Spatial Reference Data

In the following steps, you will examine the spatial reference data of some of the map layers making up *Chapter2-1.mxd*. You will see that there are map layers with different coordinate systems.

1. On the Standard toolbar, click the **ArcCatalog** tool 🔥.
2. In the left panel of the resulting ArcCatalog window, click **expander buttons** (if necessary) for **C:** and **LearningAndUsingGIS\MapsPools**. *(Those actions expose the shapefiles of the MapsPools folder.)*
3. Under MapsPools, right-click **blockcentroids**, and click **Properties**.
4. In the resulting Shapefile Properties window, click the **Fields** tab and click the **Geometry** cell of the second row and second column. See Figure 2-22. *(This action exposes a new panel at the bottom of the Shapefile Properties window. In the new panel, you can see that the Spatial Reference for blockcentroids is GCS_Assumed_Geographic. Although blockcentroids was never assigned a spatial reference, ArcGIS examined its map feature coordinates and deduced that they are latitude and longitude.)*
5. Click **Cancel**.
6. In the left panel of the ArcCatalog window under MapsPools, right-click **Pittsburgh_east_pa_sw** *(the raster map layer for the aerial photograph)*, and click **Properties**.
7. In the resulting raster data set properties window, scroll down to the Spatial Reference section to see that the raster map is in state **UTM** coordinates.
8. Click **Cancel**.

- Repeat Steps 2–4 for schools under MapsPools. We obtained this map layer from the Pittsburgh City Planning Department, whose staff projected the map layer to State Plane coordinates.
- Repeat Steps 2–4 for wards under MapsPools. You see that there is no spatial reference for this layer, which leads to a problem covered in the following sections.

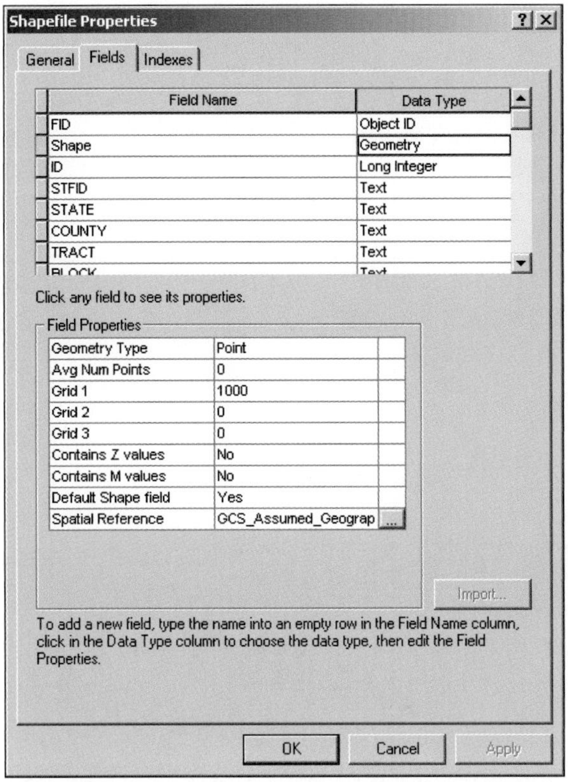

Shapefile Properties

General | Fields | Indexes

Field Name	Data Type
FID	Object ID
Shape	Geometry
ID	Long Integer
STFID	Text
STATE	Text
COUNTY	Text
TRACT	Text
BLOCK	Text

Click any field to see its properties.

Field Properties

Geometry Type	Point
Avg Num Points	0
Grid 1	1000
Grid 2	0
Grid 3	0
Contains Z values	No
Contains M values	No
Default Shape field	Yes
Spatial Reference	GCS_Assumed_Geograp

Import...

To add a new field, type the name into an empty row in the Field Name column, click in the Data Type column to choose the data type, then edit the Field Properties.

OK | Cancel | Apply

FIGURE 2-22   Shapefile Properties for the blockcentroids map layer

See Effects of Missing Map Layer Spatial Reference Data

If a map layer is missing its spatial reference—which is common when map layers are obtained from external sources—then you might not be able to successfully add the map layer to your map document. If the map layer has a different projection than that of your frame, the map will not appear because it will not overlay the existing map layers. Wards is projected to UTM coordinates but is missing its spatial reference data, the file, *wards. prj*. (Be sure that you completed the second part of Practice 2-6 to reset the frame in *Chapter2-1.mxd* to the State Plane projection.)

1. In ArcMap on the Standard toolbar, click the **Add Data** tool ✚.
2. In the resulting Add Data window, browse to your MapsPools folder and double-click **wards.shp**. *(ArcMap adds wards to your project, but the map layer does not appear. It is out there someplace, as you will see next.)*
3. On the Tools toolbar, click the **Full Extent** tool ◉. See Figure 2-23. *(The wards are on the map, but in the wrong place. You will correct this problem by adding the correct spatial reference for wards.)*

Navigating GIS

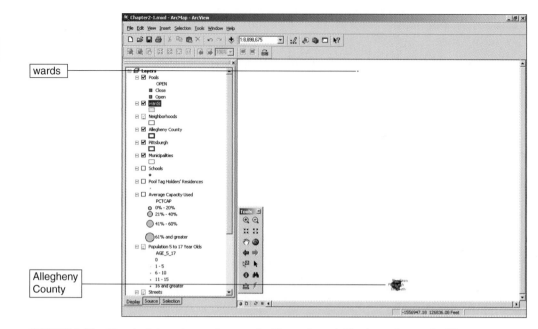

wards

Allegheny County

FIGURE 2-23   Chapter2-1.mxd map document with wards and Allegheny County in different projections

Add Missing Map Layer Spatial Reference

1. Close **ArcMap** and save changes. *(If you do not close ArcMap, you cannot make the following changes in ArcCatalog because ArcMap would still have control of the Wards file.)*
2. In ArcCatalog in the left panel under MapsPools, right-click **wards**, and click **Properties**.
3. In the resulting Shapefile Properties window, click the **Geometry** cell of the second row and second column.
4. In the resulting bottom panel of the Shapefile Properties window, click the **Builder** button ⬚.
5. In the resulting Spatial Reference Properties window with the Coordinate System tab selected, click the **Select** button.
6. In the resulting Browse for Coordinate System window, double-click the following icons: **Projected Coordinate Systems, UTM, NAD 1983**, and **NAD 1983 UTM Zone 17N.prj**.
7. Click **Add**, click **OK**, and click **OK** again.
8. On ArcCatalog's Standard toolbar, click the **Launch ArcMap** tool 🔍, and open **Chapter2-1.mxd**.
9. Use your **Allegheny County** bookmark. See Figure 2-24. *(ArcMap opens with wards successfully reprojected to State Plane and displayed in Pittsburgh.)*

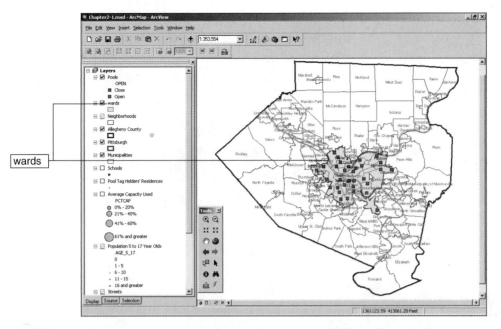

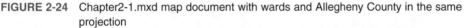

FIGURE 2-24 Chapter2-1.mxd map document with wards and Allegheny County in the same projection

From the MapsPools folder, add railroads to *Chapter2-1.mxd*. This shapefile is in UTM coordinates, NAD 1983, Zone 17N, but is missing its spatial reference data (*railroads.prj*). Add the missing spatial reference data.

Create a World Map Document

1. In ArcMap, click **File** and click **New**.
2. In the New window, double-click **Blank Document**. *(If prompted to save changes in* Chapter2-1.mxd, *do so. A new blank map document opens.)*
3. On the Tools toolbar, click the **Add Data** tool ✛.
4. In the resulting Add Data window, browse to **C:\LearningAndUsingGIS\ MapsWorld**, and add the **countries** and **latlong30** map layers.
5. Right-click **latlong30** and click **Properties**.
6. In the Layer Properties window, click the **Symbology** tab, click the **left** button in the Symbol panel, click **Hollow**, click **OK**, and click **OK** again.
7. If latlong30 is not above countries in the table of contents, drag it up so that it is. See Figure 2-25. *(The map document's frame has the same coordinate system as the first map layer added—latitude and longitude geographic coordinates. Note: The color fill for countries in your map document may not match that in Figure 2-25 because ArcMap chooses random colors by default.)*
8. Click **File** and click **Save**.

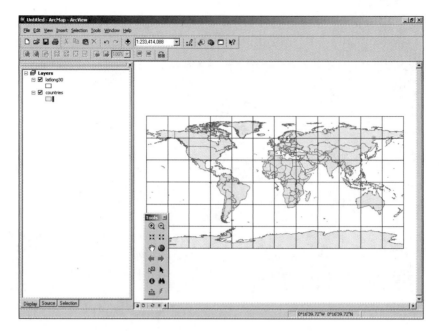

FIGURE 2-25　Map document with countries of the world in latitude and longitude coordinates

9. In the resulting Save As window, if necessary browse to **C:\LearningAndUsingGIS\MapsWorld]**, type the filename **Chapter2-2.mxd**, and click **Save**.

Set World Map Projections

1. In the table of contents, right-click **Layers**, and click **Properties**.
2. In the resulting Data Frame Properties window, click the **Coordinate System** tab.
3. In the bottom panel of the Coordinate System tab window, click the following expander buttons or icons: **Predefined**, **Projected Coordinate Systems**, **World**, **Robinson (world)**, and then click **OK**. See Figure 2-26. *(The resulting Robinson projection is quite pleasing.)*

PRACTICE 2-9

Repeat Steps 1–3, but instead of the Robinson projection try Equidistant Cylindrical (world), Mercator (world), and The World from Space projections. Notice that you can click the Modify button for the last projection (which really isn't a projection) and change the latitude or longitude of the center of the view. Try changing the longitude of the center to 0 (the prime meridian). When finished, save your map document and close ArcMap.

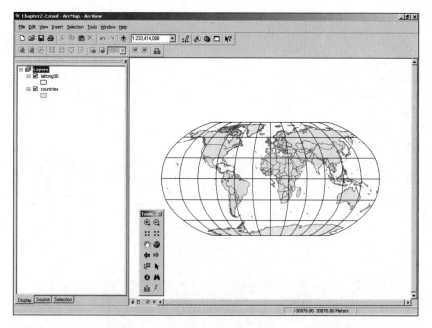

FIGURE 2-26   Chapter2-2.mxd map document with the Robinson projection

Chapter 2 Summary

Geographic coordinates locate features on the Earth's surface. These coordinates are angles of rotation of the Earth's radius, measured east or west from the prime meridian, which goes through Greenwich, England (longitude), and north or south from the equator (latitude). Longitude ranges from -180° to 180° , and latitude ranges from -90° (South Pole) to 90° (North Pole). Common rectangular coordinates, such as on graph paper, are based on straight-line distances, rather than angles of rotation.

Map navigation refers to methods of changing the current extent in a GIS. The current extent is the rectangle framing a map composition on the computer screen and is denoted by the map coordinates of its lower-left and upper-right corners. A GIS user can navigate by zooming in, zooming out, and panning, or dragging, the map in any direction.

Map scale is the reduction in length of features on the Earth's surface so that they can fit on a map. Map scale is often stated as a representative ratio; for example, 1:24,000 means that 1 inch on the map is equivalent to 24,000 inches on the ground. Lake Erie on a small-scale map (such as 1:1,000,000) is smaller than on a large-scale map (such as 1:10,000).

Features on Earth, located with latitude and longitude coordinates, can be projected onto flat maps by any one of several mathematical transformations. Projected maps have rectangular coordinates. A point on Earth, such as the western tip of Allegheny County, has unique latitude and longitude coordinates, but it has different projected coordinates for every individual projection. Therefore, map layers for the same area will not appear in a GIS if they have different projections.

ArcMap uses map document files that it can display and process. A map document has one or more map layers symbolized to be part of a map composition. Map layers draw from the bottom up in ArcMap's layer panel, so it is necessary to place map layers with large features that have color fill on the bottom so they do not cover up other features.

You can use ArcMap to navigate a map, to zoom in to areas of interest, and to investigate detailed map layers. After zooming in, you can pan or move the map within the view window. When you find a zoomed-in area that you would like to revisit later, you can create a spatial bookmark.

ArcMap has the Measurement tool for measuring lengths and estimating areas. It is always a good idea to check map layers and units by measuring some feature having known dimensions, such as the width of the United States.

An ArcMap user can project base maps on the fly from practically any projection to the projection that you choose for your map document. It is important that our map layers have spatial reference data that allows ArcMap to automatically project maps to match the projection of the map document.

Key Terms

Base maps   Map layers available from governments or GIS vendors that provide an infrastructure, or costly-but-shared resources, for GIS applications. These map layers commonly include street centerlines, boundaries (political, legal, administrative, and physical), and so forth.

Cartographers   People who design maps using associated principles and standards. Historically, cartographers were among the earliest graphic designers, and many of the graphic principles in use today derive from map making.

Conformal projections   A kind of map projection that preserves shape and direction in local areas, at the expense of distorting area.

Current extent   The map extent at any moment in a GIS. It is the current window on a map composition.

Equivalent projections   A kind of projection that preserves area on maps. These projections show all polygon features with their correct areas as calculated from map measurements and scale, but at the expense of distorting shape and direction.

Full extent   The rectangle that encloses an entire map composition. Maps are usually available for specific locations, such as a country, state, or smaller area. Each such map has its own full extent.

Geographic coordinate system   Latitude and longitude coordinates that locate points on Earth. They represent angles of rotation of Earth's radius along the equator and a meridian. Coordinates in this system are called geographic or spherical coordinates because they represent points on the approximately spherical world.

Geoid   A mathematical representation of the shape of Earth, often an ellipsoid that is nearly spherical. The user of a GIS must choose which geoid to use when projecting maps. It is important to be consistent when projecting multiple map layers for the same map composition, but which geoid you use matters little for analytic mapping.

Global Positioning System (GPS)   A constellation of satellites that triangulate location and velocity (if they are moving) of points on Earth with GPS receivers. Positional accuracy within a meter or less is commonly available.

Graphic scale   A horizontal line on a map with tick marks for corresponding ground distances, such as 1 mile, 2 miles, and so on.

Great circle   A circle on the Earth's surface that has the Earth's radius and, thus, is of the largest possible size. A great circle's plane includes the Earth's center.

Large scale   A reduction of features on Earth's surface for mapping that results in relatively large sizes on the map. Large-scale maps are zoomed in so the user sees only a relatively small area, but in much detail.

Latitude   The number of degrees rotation of a point on Earth north or south from the equator and along a meridian. A point on the equator has 0° latitude, the North Pole has 90° latitude, and the South Pole has -90° latitude.

Longitude   The number degrees rotation east or west of the prime meridian of a point on Earth along the point's parallel.

Map extent   A rectangle in map coordinates corresponding to boundaries on your computer screen's map or a printed map.

Map navigation   The methods or processes for changing map extent on a GIS. Map extent behaves like a window on the world that can be made larger, smaller, and moved around to change your view.

Map projection   A mathematical transformation for creating flat maps in rectangular coordinates from geographic coordinates (latitude and longitude) on the spherical world.

Map scale ratio   Two numbers that represent the reduction in size of a real-world object to a reduced-size mode, drawing, or other representation. Examples for the same level of reduction are 1 to 1000 or 20 to 20,000, which correspond to a thousand-fold reduction.

Measurement tool   A GIS tool for measuring straight-line distances in a map composition.

Meridian   A great circle that passes through Earth's North and South Poles.

Parallels   Circles of latitude on a globe. They define planes that are parallel to one another.

Prime meridian   The meridian that passes through Greenwich, England. It is the line of 0° longitude as measured east or west from it.

Rectangular coordinates   Common coordinates as seen on regular graph paper that can be used to measure distances.

Relative paths   A method of referring to folder and file locations relative to a specific location on a computer storage device. For an ArcGIS map document, relative paths refer to locations relative to that of the map document, at the same level, up the folder tree to a higher folder, or down. A relative path only includes a portion of the full pathname.

Representative fraction   Expression of map scale as a dimensionless ratio such as 1:24,000, meaning that a unit length on the map is equivalent to 24,000 of the same units on the ground. The units can be any linear measurement, such as inches, centimeters, and so on.

Secant projection   A projection of world features onto a cone or cylinder that pierces the world.

Small scale   A reduction of features on the Earth's surface for mapping that results in relatively small sizes on the map. Small-scale maps are zoomed out so that the user sees relatively large areas, but not in much detail.

Spatial reference data   Data included as part of a map layer that identifies the map layers coordinate system. Included are the projection name, map distance units, and any parameters used in the projection.

Spherical coordinates   Coordinates that locate points on any sphere, using angles of rotation for position. These are also known as *geographic coordinates*.

Spheroid   A three-dimensional shape that is an ellipse in cross-section. The Earth is a spheroid because the radius around the equator is slightly larger than the radius around the poles.

State Plane   A collection of map projections for use by local governments in Alaska and the contiguous 48 states.

Transverse projections   A projection in which the projection surface, a cone or cylinder, is rotated so that its central axis is running east-west, as opposed to the usual north-south.

Universal Transverse Mercator   A collection of map projections for use in small- to medium-scale regions of the world, based on the metric system.

Verbal scale   A map scale ratio that uses two different linear measurement units; for example, 1 inch equals 2000 feet.

Short-Answer Questions

1. How are geographic coordinates different from rectangular coordinates? What distortion do you expect for northern Canada when plotting geographic coordinates on graph paper?

2. Two sets of geographic coordinates are (180°, 0°) and (-180°, 0°). What do these two points have in common, and why?

3. Express the representative scale 1:10,000 as a verbal scale in inches to feet.

4. Explain how threshold scales are useful to GIS map designers and users.

5. Express the verbal scale 1 inch = 1 mile as a representative scale.

6. What are the major trade-offs in distortions for projections of the continental United States or another similarly large area of the world (for example, you can have one aspect accurate at the expense of the other)?

7. What is a spheroid, and why is Earth better represented as a spheroid instead of a sphere?

8. What is the difference between panning and zooming?

9. What is different about zip code boundaries from other sets of boundaries, such as municipalities?

10. In a GIS, what is *map extent*?

Exercises

1. **Getting Information on Pools and Areas.** Decisions in local governments, such as which pools are kept open, are often made by or influenced by politicians who represent areas, such as wards. A sensitive issue is which wards do or do not have swimming pools and whether the pools are open or closed. In this exercise, you'll provide some relevant information for the Northside area of Pittsburgh.

    a. Start a new Microsoft Word document and save it as **Exercise2-1<YourName>.doc**, where you substitute your name for <YourName>. Save the document in a private location such as a jump drive, a folder on a local area network, or on your hard drive if you are working on your own computer.

    b. At the top of the document, type the title Exercise 2-1, followed by your name and date. On a new line, type Wards and after it click Table, click Insert Table, and create a table with eight rows and three columns. In the first row, in different columns, type Ward, Pool, and Open?. If you want, you can drag borders of rows and columns to resize the table.

    c. In your C:\LearningAndUsingGIS\ folder, open *Chapter2-1.mxd* and save it as **Exercise 2-1.mxd**. Make sure that the Pools and Wards layers are turned on, as well as other layers that you think are relevant. Symbolize Wards to have a hollow color fill and red border. Label Wards with the WARD attribute. Work only with the seven wards in the Northside of Pittsburgh bookmark that are north of the major rivers.

    d. Using your map, fill in the table. If a ward has more than one pool, list all pools of the ward in one cell separated by commas. Use *Yes* or *No* for values of Open? If there is more than one pool in a ward, list *Yes* and *No* as appropriate, separated by commas.

    e. In ArcMap, click File, click Export Map, and export a *.jpeg* map image to your desktop called *NorthsideWards.jpg*. In your Word document, click Insert, click Picture, click From File, browse to your desktop, and insert *NorthsideWards.jpg* below the table. Right-click the map image in your Word document, click Borders and Shading, click the Box button, and then click OK. The resulting boundary makes your map look more professional.

2. **Getting Information on Swimming Pools and Nearby Schools.** Schools sometimes have events at public pools in Pittsburgh. In this exercise, you will provide profiles and maps for two pools—Phillips and Jack Stack—and nearby schools.

    a. Start a new Word document, and save it as **Exercise2-2<YourName>.doc** where you substitute your name for <YourName>. Save the document in a private location such as a jump drive, a folder on a local area network, or on your hard drive if you are working on your own computer.

b. At the top of the document, type the title Exercise 2-2, followed by your name and date. On a new line, type Jack Stack Pool and after it click Table, click Insert Table, and create a table with four rows and three columns. In the first row, in different columns, type School, Distance, and Enrollment. If you want, you can drag borders of rows and columns to resize the table.

c. In your C:\LearningAndUsingGIS\ folder, open *Chapter2-1.mxd* and save it as **Exercise 2-2.mxd**. Turn on only the following layers: Pools, Schools, and Streets. Turn on labeling for Schools.

d. Zoom in to the area surrounding Jack Stack Pool until streets and street names are on and you can see the nearest three or more schools. Using the street network and Measurement tool with measurements in miles, determine the three nearest schools, and fill in the information for the table.

e. In ArcMap, click File, click Export Map, and export a *.jpeg* map image to your desktop called *JackStack.jpg*. In your Word document, click Insert, click Picture, click From File, browse to your desktop, and insert *JackStack.jpg* below the table. Right-click the map image in your Word document, click Borders and Shading, click the Box button, and click OK. The resulting boundary makes your map look more professional.

f. Go to a new line in your Word document and type Phillips Pool and repeat Steps b–e. In Step e, name your image **Phillips.jpg**.

3. **Build a World GIS.** In this exercise, you will practice adding map layers to a new map document, making document paths relative, setting the map document's projection, carrying out simple symbolization of layers, setting bookmarks, and setting visible scale ranges. Your map will have countries and cities of the world, with latitude and longitude lines.

a. Start ArcMap, create a new map document called **Exercise 2.3<YourName>.mxd**, and save it in the C:\LearningAndUsingGIS\ folder. Substitute your name for <YourName>. Set up your map document to use relative paths.

b. Use the Robinson map projection for the map document's frame.

c. Add all of the map layers in the GIS\MapsWorld\ folder: countries, cities, and latlong30.

d. Symbolize latlong30 to have a hollow color fill, and pick a neutral color for the countries color fill.

e. Create bookmarks for the continents North America, South America, Europe, Asia, and Australia. Also create bookmarks for India and any other two countries of your choice.

f. Set a visible scale range for cities to turn on when zoomed to the largest continent. Set a visible scale range for a city label when zoomed into India or further.

4. **Build a United States GIS.** In this exercise, you will practice adding map layers to a new map document, making document paths relative, setting the map document's projection, carrying out simple symbolization of layers, setting bookmarks, and setting visible scale ranges. Your map will have states, counties, cities, hospitals, and water features.

a. Start ArcMap, create a new map document called **Exercise 2.4<YourName>.mxd**, and save it in the C:\LearningAndUsingGIS\ folder. Substitute your name for <YourName>. Set up your map document to use relative paths.

b. Add the following map layers in the C:\LearningAndUsingGIS\MapsUSA\ folder: states, cities, counties, and airports.

c. Use a predefined projected coordinate system of continental, North America, and North America Albers Equal Area Conic.

d. Add all of the map layers in the C:\LearningAndUsingGIS\MapsWorld\ folder: countries, cities, and latlong30.

e. Symbolize states and counties to have a hollow color fill. Make the outline for states have a 1.5-width line. Give cities and states different colored point markers. Giver water a light blue color fill.

f. Create a bookmark for the lower 48 states, and one for Texas, Rhode Island, and any other additional state of your choice.

g. Set a visible scale range for counties to turn on when zoomed into Texas. Set a visible scale range for cities, hospitals, water, and labels for counties to turn on when zoomed into Rhode Island or further.

h. Label states and cities.

References

Clarke, K. C. *Getting Started with Geographic Information Systems*, 4th ed. Upper Saddle River: Prentice Hall, 2003.

Complete Electric Toy Train Sets. Internet URL: http://www.discounttrainsonline.com/electric-toy-train-sets.html (accessed February 19, 2005).

Demers, M. N. *Fundamentals of Geographic Information Systems*, 3rd ed. Hoboken: Wiley, 2002.

Mentor Software, Inc., State Place Codes. Internet URL: http://www.mentorsoftwareinc.com/resource/stplane.htm (accessed February 21, 2005).

Morton, A. UTM Grid Zones of the World. Internet URL: http://www.dmap.co.uk/utmworld.htm (accessed February 21, 2005).

Muehrcke, P. C. *Map Use: Reading, Analysis, and Interpretations*, 2nd ed. Madison: JP Publications, 1986.

Rosenberg, M. Map Scale. Internet URL: http://geography.about.com/cs/maps/a/mapscale.htm (accessed February 19, 2005).

CHAPTER **3**

GETTING INFORMATION FROM A GIS

LEARNING OBJECTIVES

In this chapter, you will:

- Get an introduction to vector and raster map file formats
- Learn how data records are attached to map graphics in feature attribute tables
- Learn about database attribute queries, which locate records and map features
- Learn about spatial queries, which select map features and data records by location
- Create feature attribute queries in ArcGIS
- Create location queries in ArcGIS
- Build buffers and make spatial queries in ArcGIS

Into the deep end of the pool!

INTRODUCTION

After completing Chapter 2, you should be able to navigate in ArcGIS and obtain some information from it. You can learn a lot by just navigating a map, studying patterns in graphic features, and reading attribute data of graphic features, but you can obtain deeper-level information by running queries on one or more map layers of a map document. A **query** is a means of selecting records and graphic features from one or more map layers in a map composition that meet specific criteria. This is an example query: *Select all pool-tag-holder residences within one-half mile of open swimming pools.* The criteria here are (1) a distance of one-half mile or less and (2) swimming pools that are open. The query yields two things: a list of all pool-tag-holder residences meeting the criteria *and* corresponding point markers in a special selection color that distinguish those residences from nonselected residences.

To extract information from an information system, you must understand that system's underlying data. In this chapter, you will begin by learning more about vector and raster map formats. In Chapter 1, you learned that vector maps are made up of point, line, and polygon graphic features and that each graphic feature has an attached data record with one or more attributes. In this chapter, you will learn about the various file formats for vector maps, about data types for attribute data, and about data dictionaries, which are essential for querying graphic features using attribute values. You will also learn more about raster maps and file formats for digital images.

Anybody who uses computers is already familiar with using attribute data for making queries. For example, when you are searching for a book or other item at a site such as *www.amazon.com*, you begin by clicking a category from a drop-down menu, such as "Books" or "Electronics." The Web site uses your selected criterion value to navigate to a new Web page and show you some useful information for a next step, including recently published books or sale items that match your previous purchases. You will learn how to do this kind of data searching or querying in general, and how to apply it to GIS in particular. ArcGIS uses the industry-standard Structured Query Language (SQL).

GIS has the unique ability to use locations and distances for record and graphic feature selection. You can simply study a map and select the features you want to analyze with a GIS tool designed for this purpose. ArcGIS has built-in capabilities to analyze data and produce statistics; however, you can also export attributes from features selected and displayed in a special color on the map, for further analysis in Microsoft Excel or other software package.

An important kind of spatial query is **proximity analysis**—finding out what is near certain graphic features on a map, such as swimming pools. Are there many 5- to 17-year-old youths living near a pool? If so, that would make it a good pool location. GIS uses buffers as one approach to making spatial queries.

After you've mastered these concepts, you will use ArcGIS in this chapter's tutorial to start an analysis of the Swimming Pool Case Study. You will answer some of the same questions asked by the director of Pittsburgh's Citiparks Department.

MAP FORMATS

To extract information from ArcGIS, you need an in-depth understanding of digital maps and how they represent data. In this section, you will build on what you learned in Chapter 1 about the two kinds of map layers, vector and raster.

Vector-Based Maps

The workhorses of analytical GIS are vector-based map layers. Besides their graphic features, they also have rich attribute tables that provide much of the text and numerical information that analysts seek. In contrast, raster maps' main GIS function is to provide rich visual information as a background for vector-based maps.

Vector maps have several alternative computer file formats. Some common ones originated by ESRI are as follows:

- *ArcView* **Shapefile**: This is a simple and widely used format. Each shapefile map layer has three or more files, all with the same filename, but with different file extensions. For example, the Pools shapefile has seven files: *pools.shp* stores the pools' point, graphic-feature coordinates; *pools.dbf* stores each pool's attribute table; *pools.prj* stores data on the coordinate system or projection of the pools' features; *pools.shp.xml* stores additional documentation on the pools map layer; and the remaining files (*pools.sbn*, *pools.sbx*, and *pools.shx*) have various indices to expedite processing.

- **Personal geodatabase**: This is a modern computer map format, using the Microsoft Access relational database package. A **relational database** stores data in a collection of related rectangular tables. You can store all of the vector and raster map layers of a GIS into a single Access database. Then each map layer is called a feature class.

- *ArcInfo* **Coverage**: This is an obsolete format that has a folder for each map layer and about 12 or more files (with filenames such as *arc*, *tol*, *pat.dbf*, *lab*, and so forth) within the folder. In coverage format, the Pools layer would have a folder named *Pools* containing its files. Many of the files in a coverage have the purpose of speeding up advanced GIS processing, which was more necessary years ago when computers had less capacity and speed than they do now.

- *ArcInfo* **E00 export format**: This is a single file that includes all of the data files of a coverage for easy export and interchange of map files. You need a utility program to transform E00 export files into a coverage before you can use them in a GIS.

ArcGIS can input and transform all of the preceding map formats plus several others. In addition, ArcGIS can display an **event theme**, which is a data table that includes map coordinates for points, such as latitude and longitude or projected coordinates.

In this book, you will work mainly with shapefiles, simply because of their widespread availability. Each attribute of a shapefile's feature attribute table can be one of several data types. Some of the common data types are as follows:

- **Text** *(or String) data*: Such as names, addresses, and so on
- **Date**: Dates such as 12/31/2007
- **Integer**: Numbers without decimal places such as 100 or 213
- **Decimal** *(or Real)*: Numbers with decimal places such as 3.141592
- **Boolean**: One of two values, such as true or false and 1 or 0

Table 3-1 is a data dictionary for the Pools GIS. A **data dictionary** documents attribute tables, listing all of the attributes and their definitions and data types. There is no practical limit to the number of attributes that can be included in attribute tables. Sometimes, you need to modify, add, or delete attributes. For example, we used ArcGIS to create the PCTCAP attribute in Table 3-1 (percent of pool maximum capacity used on average) by dividing ATTEND04 by MAXLOAD and then multiplying the result by 100. Note that to keep Table 3-1 from getting too long, for some map layers we only defined attributes used in this book.

TABLE 3-1 Data dictionary for Pools GIS

Map layer	Attribute name	Attribute definition or map layer description	Attribute data type or layer type
BlockCentroids		**24,283 center points of census blocks in Allegheny County**	Point
	STFID	Unique census ID of each block	Integer
	AGE_5_17	Population of 5- to 17-year-olds	Integer
	FHH_CHILD	Number of female-headed households with children	Integer
County		**Boundary of Allegheny County**	Polygon
	FIPSSTCO	FIPS code for state (42) and county (003)	Integer
	STATE	State name	Text
	COUNTY	County name	Text
MinorCivilDivisions		**130 minor civil divisions (cities, towns, boroughs)**	Polygon
	COUNTY	FIPS code for state and county	Integer
	MCD2000	FIPS code for municipality	Integer
	NAME	Name of minor civil division	Text
Neighborhoods		**Boundaries of Pittsburgh's 89 neighborhoods**	
	NEIGHBORHOOD	Name of neighborhood	Text
Pittsburgh		**Minor civil division of Pittsburgh**	Polygon
	COUNTY	FIPS code for state and county	Text
	MCD2000	FIPS code for municipality	Text

TABLE 3-1   Data dictionary for Pools GIS (continued)

Map layer	Attribute name	Attribute definition or map layer description	Attribute data type or layer type
	NAME	Name of minor civil division	Text
Pools		**32 public swimming pools in Pittsburgh**	Point
	NAME	Swimming pool name	Text
	ADDRESS	Street address	Text
	ZIPCODE	5-digit zip code	Integer
	OPEN	Whether or not the pool was open in 2004: 1 = open, 0 = closed	Boolean
	MAXLOAD	Maximum pool capacity in terms of number of swimmers	Integer
	ATTEND04	Average daily attendance in summer 2004	Integer
	PCTCAP	100 x ATTEND04/ MAXLOAD	Decimal
PhillipsPoolBuffer		**1- and 2-mile radius pool buffers for Phillips Pool**	Polygon
	DISTANCE	Radius of buffer (1 and 2 miles)	Decimal
PoolTags		**Random sample of 2680 pool-tag-holder residences**	Point
	TAGNO	Serial number on pool tag	Integer
	POOL	Pool that the pool tag holder intended to use when they obtained the pool tag	Text
	NOPERSONS	Number of persons with pool tags at the residence	Integer
RailRoads		**Railroad tracks**	Line
	FENAME	Name of the railroad	Text

TABLE 3-1 Data dictionary for Pools GIS (continued)

Map layer	Attribute name	Attribute definition or map layer description	Attribute data type or layer type
Rivers		**Rivers**	Polygon
	LANDNAME	River name	Text
Schools		**Schools in Pittsburgh**	
	NAME	Name of the school	Text
	TYPE	Type (H = high school, E = elementary, M = middle, S = special)	Text
	STATUS	Open or closed	Text
	ADDRESS	Street address	Text
	DISTRICT	Text	Text
	ENROLLMENT	Student enrollment	Integer
	EMPLOYMENT	Staff and teacher employment level	Integer
Streets		**65,535 TIGER/LINE 2000 street centerline segments in Allegheny County**	Line
	LENGTH	Length of street segment (m)	Decimal
	FEDIRP	Street direction prefix (N, E, S, W)	Text
	FENAME	Street name	Text
	FETYPE	Street type (St, Ave, Rd, etc.)	Text
	DEDIRS	Street direction suffix (N, E, S, W)	Text
	CFCC	Census code for street type	Text
	FRADDL	House number at the start of the block on the left	Integer

TABLE 3-1 Data dictionary for Pools GIS (continued)

Map layer	Attribute name	Attribute definition or map layer description	Attribute data type or layer type
	TOADDL	House number at the end of the block on the left	Integer
	FRADDR	House number at the start of the block on the right	Integer
	TOADDR	House number at the end of the block on the right	Integer
	ZIPL	5-digit zip code on the left side of the street	Integer
	ZIPR	5-digit zip code on the right side of the street	Integer
Wards		**Political wards**	Polygon
	WARD	Ward number	Integer
	SQMILES	Area (square miles)	Decimal
ZipCodes		**117 5-digit zip code boundaries**	Polygon
	NAME	5-digit zip code	Text
	ZIPCODE	5-digit zip code	Integer

Raster Maps

In Chapter 1, you learned that raster maps are digital images that have map coordinates, and that a digital image is a rectangular array of pixels (short for *picture elements*). When considered as a mathematical object, a digital image is a rectangular array, or grid, of numbers. Each number signifies a unique color. The maximum size number that can be stored in each grid cell determines **color depth,** or the number of colors possible. Each storage location in a computer's memory is a **bit**, an on/off location. One character on your keyboard requires 8 bits, called a **byte**, of storage. Typically, black-and-white images use 8 bits (1 byte) per pixel, and color images use 24 bits (3 bytes) per pixel (Koren, 2005).

A digital image has many possible file formats, many of which use **file compression**, a method for making files smaller to reduce storage requirements and speed up transmission across networks. Some common image file formats are as follows (Koren, 2005):

- *TIFF (Tagged Image File Format)*: This has *.tif* as its file extension. It yields very high-quality images and is commonly used in publishing. Its file sizes are large because it is uncompressed.

- **GIF (Graphic Interchange Format)**: This has *.gif* as its file extension. It is at the opposite end of the spectrum from TIFF format images with lower color depth and much file compression. It is ideal for schematic drawings that have relatively large areas with solid color fill and few color variations. Its advantage is that it has small file sizes.

- **JPEG (Joint Photographic Experts Group)**: This has *.jpg* as its file extension. It is the most widely used format for photographs and other images that have a lot of color variations. You can specify compression levels; the greater the level of compression, the greater the loss of picture detail.

Unlike other images, raster maps have map coordinates referenced in accompanying world files (ESRI, 2005). The world file for the raster map *pittsburgh_east_pa_sw.tif*—used in the Pools GIS—is *pittsburgh_east_pa_sw.tfw*, where the *.tfw* extension signifies that it is a world file for a *.tif* image. Table 3-2 displays the contents of this world file. Line 1 denotes that each pixel is 1 meter on a side (because the map units of the UTM projected coordinates of the raster map are in meters, and the image has 1-meter pixels). Lines 2–4 are of no importance to us. Lines 5 and 6 are the x- and y-coordinates of the upper-left corner of the image in projected coordinates. If you set the display units to be meters and hover over the upper-left corner of the image in ArcGIS, you can read the coordinates in Table 3-2.

TABLE 3-2 World file for *pittsburgh_east_pa_sw.tif*

Line	Example values from *pittsburgh_east_pa_sw.tfw*
Line 1: x-dimension of a pixel in map units	1
Line 2: rotation parameter	0
Line 3: rotation parameter	0
Line 4: NEGATIVE of y-dimension of a pixel in map units	-1
Line 5: x-coordinate of center of upper-left pixel	584510
Line 6: y-coordinate of center of upper-left pixel	4477170

The following are a few additional notes on raster map images:

- Raster maps can portray only one attribute—a color for a picture, a decimal number for an elevation, a code for land use, or other value.
- Raster map files are enormous. The black-and-white aerial photo for one small portion of Pittsburgh, *pittsburgh_east_pa_sw.tif*, is 44.8 MB. This is more than half of the total size of the LearningAndUsingGIS GIS!
- Technicians **digitize** aerial photographs to create vector-based map layers for physical features. Using a process similar to the measurement work you did

in Chapter 2 (clicking along the boundary of Pittsburgh to estimate its perimeter), technicians or automated line-following software trace out street curbs, parking lots, building rooftops, and so on, and put them in vector format.

- Satellite remote sensing yields images outside the visible range, but they are given **false colors** so we can see them. Every material, type of plant, and so forth has a signature reflection of electromagnetic radiation and, thus, can be identified (Wall, 2005).

GIS QUERIES

The partnership between database tables and vector-based graphics in a GIS is very powerful. Each vector-graphic feature on a map has a data record and vice versa. These two kinds of data are linked in a GIS: You can select records from a feature attribute table by using query criteria and this action automatically highlights the corresponding graphic features. The opposite is true as well: You can select graphic features on a GIS map, directly using your mouse or indirectly using shapes such as circular buffers, to automatically select corresponding data records. These capabilities are not available in standard information systems and are unique to GIS.

Attribute Queries

To select all the Pittsburgh swimming pools that were closed in summer 2004 from the Pools feature attribute table, you use the following query criterion: ("OPEN" = 0). This criterion says: *Select all pool records with attribute named Open that have their value equal to 0.* Another example is ("PCTCAP" >=.5), meaning: *Select all records with average percent capacity used in summer 2004 that equals or exceeds 50 percent.* This query yields the four pools out of 32 that had good average attendance relative to capacity.

Each example given is a **simple query criterion**, or simple condition, that makes up a portion of an SQL command and has the general form (<data attribute><logical operator><value>). For attributes in shapefiles, enclose attribute names in double quotes. For values, use numerals without any special characters, but include single quotes around text and date values for shapefiles. For example, a text-value criterion is ("NAME" ='Riverview') and a date-value criterion is ("DELIVERYDATE" >= '06/25/2006'). Query data attributes are not case sensitive in ArcGIS, thus NAME and DATE could be written Name, name, Date, date, or any other combination of uppercase and lowercase letters. We use all capital letters in our queries to be consistent with the data dictionary in Table 3-1. In contrast, query values *are* case sensitive in ArcGIS, so *a* is different from *A*.

Table 3-3 lists several logical operators you can use in query criteria, along with their meanings and examples. Most are self-explanatory; however, the like operator is a bit complicated. It compares text attributes to text values where the text values include the (*) or (?) **wildcard** characters. The (*) symbol stands for zero, one, or more characters of any kind. So, for example, the simple query criterion ("NAME" like 'We*') selects any pools with names starting with the letters *We*, including West Penn and Westwood. Another example is ("NAME" like '*r*'), which finds any name that contains at least one *r*, regardless of its location. The names *Riverview, Sue Murray, Fowler,* and others meet this criterion. The (?) wildcard is similar, except it stands for any single character.

TABLE 3-3 Logical operators for query criteria

Logical operator	Meaning	Examples
=	Equal to	(`"OPEN"=0`) retrieves closed pools (`"NAME"='McBride'`) retrieves McBride Pool
<	Less than	(`"PCTCAP"<0.5`) retrieves pools using less than 50% capacity (`"NAME"<'McBride'`) retrieves pools before McBride alphabetically
>	Greater than	(`"PCTCAP">0.5`) retrieves pools using greater than 50% capacity (`"NAME">'McBride'`) retrieves pools after McBride alphabetically
<=	Less than or equal to	(`"PCTCAP"<=0.5`) retrieves pools using less than or equal to 50% capacity (`"NAME"<='McBride'`) retrieves McBride and pools before it alphabetically
>=	Greater than or equal to	(`"PCTCAP">=0.5`) retrieves pools using greater than or equal to 50% capacity (`"NAME">='McBride'`) retrieves McBride and pools after it alphabetically
<>	Not equal to	(`"NAME"<>'McBride'`) retrieves all pools except McBride
like	Wild-card query with text value including the (*) wildcard	(`"NAME" like 'We*'`) retrieves all pools with names starting with *We*, such as West Penn and Westwood

For queries with text data type attributes, results of queries depend on the order in which text values sort. Suppose you have a text attribute named ODDSANDENDS with four values: the numbers 7 and *223* and the words *zebra* and *apple*. If you sort ODDSANDENDS in ascending order, the result is numbers in order analogous to alphabetical order and then words alphabetically: *223*, 7, *apple*, and *zebra*. In this case, the number of digits in a number—its magnitude—does not determine sort order; instead, the number with the smallest first digit on the left is first, and if there are any ties, they are broken using the second digit and so forth. So, the query criterion (`"ODDSANDENDS" >= '300'`) yields 7, *apple*, and *zebra*. The criterion (`"ODDSANDENDS" >= 'lion'`) yields *zebra*.

A **compound query criterion** or a compound condition combines two or more simple queries with the **logical connectives** AND or OR. For example, (`"OPEN" = 0`) AND (`"MAXLOAD" > 500`) selects records that satisfy both simple criteria simultaneously. The result is a closed pool AND it has capacity greater than 500. The open pools and the small-capacity pools are excluded. The connector AND is restrictive.

The connector OR is inclusive: `("OPEN" = 0) OR ("MAXLOAD" > 500)` selects any pool that satisfies either condition—or both. It selects any pool that is open or that has large capacity, *or* any pool that is both open and has large capacity. The OR connector for two simple conditions selects the same number or more records than an AND connector for the same two simple conditions.

Spatial Queries

Instead of using the values of attributes to select records, a **spatial query** uses location on the map to select spatial features and their records. Direct spatial queries depend on your ability to see what you want to select on a displayed map layer. For example, you can select graphic features by dragging a rectangle around them. You can use other mapped features for selection. For example, you can select all the blockcentroids for 5- to 17-year-old youths that lie within the municipality of Mount Oliver. See Figure 3-1.

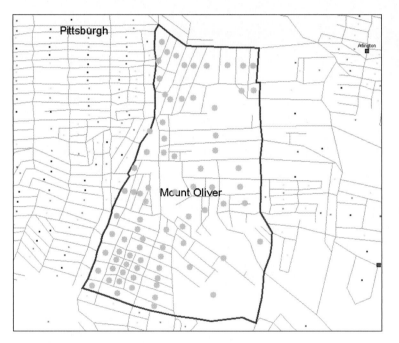

FIGURE 3-1   Selection of blockcentroids using the Mount Oliver polygon

An indirect spatial query method uses buffers to select features. See Figure 3-2. For example, the general question might be this: How many 5- to 17-year-olds live near each swimming pool? With buffers, you translate this question as: *How many youths live within a circular buffer with a 1-mile radius around each swimming pool?* Pools with large numbers of youths living nearby are better located, in most cases, than those with smaller numbers of youths. Buffers can be made for line features too, for example: *How many 5- to 17-year-old youths live within one-tenth mile of a bus route that has a pool as one of its stops?* Perhaps the better-located pools are on bus routes that pass through residential neighborhoods. Lastly, as you might have suspected, you can make buffers for polygons, for example: *How many pool tag holders live outside of Pittsburgh, but within 1 mile of the border?* Pittsburgh would like surrounding municipalities to help pay for the pools that their residents use.

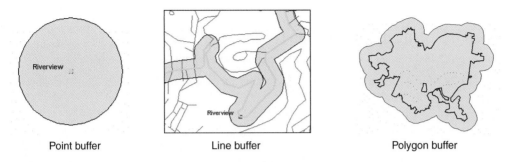

| Point buffer | Line buffer | Polygon buffer |

FIGURE 3-2   Examples of point, line, and polygon buffers

Notes on the Swimming Pool Case

In this chapter's tutorial, you will use ArcGIS to see queries at work. The map composition used in the tutorial has some familiar map layers, including PoolTags.shp. This a random sample of 2680 pool-tag-holders' residences out of 56,162 that had street address data for a recent year. We selected data and input them from scanned paper forms and typed them into an Excel file, as if we were pulling them randomly out of a hat. Then, using the address data, we placed residence points on the map using geocoding, a process that you will learn in Chapter 7. Although the resulting sample size is small, it nevertheless represents the spatial patterns of the entire population because of the random selection process.

A random sample has some nice features, besides keeping the data-entry cost low for us. For example, if you find that there are 100 sampled pool-tag-holders' residences in a specific geographic area, you can scale this number up to get a reasonable estimate of the actual population of pool-tag-holders' residences in the same area. You can use the factor of the total population divided by the sample size: 56,162/2680, which is approximately 21. Thus, the 100 sampled residences represent approximately 2100 (= 21 * 100) total residences with pool tags in the same area. In the exercises, you will make this adjustment to counts of sampled pool tag data in areas; namely, you will multiply by 21.

Our interest is in youths 5 to 17 years old, so you need to make a second adjustment to eliminate persons younger than 5 and older than 17 from sampled pool tags. Approximately 47 percent of pool tag holders are aged 5 to 17 years old; therefore, you must adjust estimates of pool tag holders by multiplying by 0.47.

A final note before we begin. The PoolTags.shp map layer represents the *intentions* of youth and their parents or guardians to use swimming pools. Pool tags were free during the summer for which the data was collected, but in previous years they had cost $60 for a family of four. So perhaps people obtained pool tags but did not use them. To investisgate pool use, we have data on pool visits by tag holder, data that you will use in a project in Chapter 9.

ARCGIS QUERIES

ArcMap and its ArcToolbox provide much functionality for querying maps. Generally, there are several ways to accomplish the same query task. Some ways are simple and quick and others are sophisticated but also more powerful. Depending on the task at hand, you can choose a simple or a sophisticated approach—whichever gives you the results in the shortest time.

Open the Chapter 3-1.mdx Map Document

To begin, you will start ArcMap, open a map document, and change a few settings.

1. On your computer's desktop, click **Start**, click **All Programs**, click **ArcGIS**, and click **ArcMap**.
2. In the ArcMap window, click the **An existing map** option button, and double-click **Browse for maps** in the panel below the option button.
3. In the Open window, browse to your **LearningAndUsingGIS** folder and double-click **Chapter3-1.mxd**. See Figure 3-3. *(The* Chapter3-1.mxd *map document window opens in ArcMap showing familiar map layers. One new map layer is Population 5 to 17 Year Olds by Tract. Census tracts have approximately 4000 population and are homogeneous neighborhoods. The same data by blockcentroid, which we used earlier, is still available in this map document.)*
4. On the main menu, click **View**, click **Bookmarks**, and click **Pittsburgh**. *(The map zooms in to Pittsburgh.)*

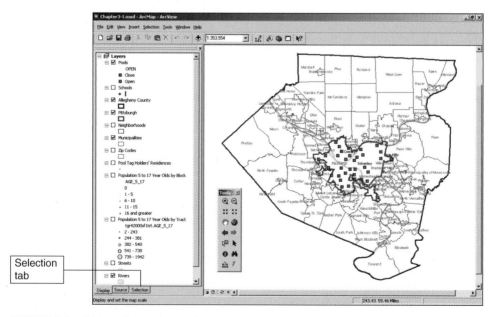

FIGURE 3-3   Chapter3-1.mxd map document

Make Selection Options

You can control the behavior of selection tools by setting options. First, you need to be able to control which map layers are selectable when using the map.

1. At the bottom of the table of contents, click the **Selection** tab. See Figure 3-3. *(At present, all 11 map layers are selectable. Generally, you only want one layer selectable at a time. Rather than clicking off 10 layers here, you can use a simpler way, which we will show you next.)*
2. At the bottom of the table of contents, click the **Display** tab.
3. In the table of contents, right-click **Pools**, click **Selection**, and click **Make This The Only Selectable Layer**. *(When you use the Select Features tool, only features in the Pools layer will be selected.)*
4. On the main menu, click **Selection**, and then click **Options**. See Figure 3-4. *(This window has additional options for fine-tuning the selection process.)*

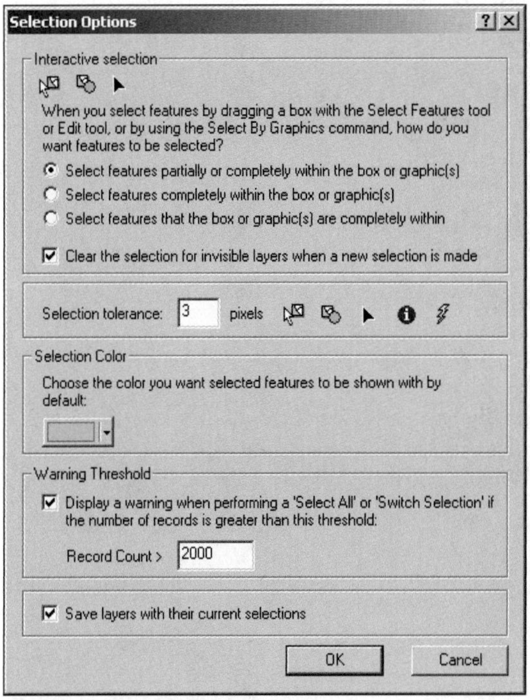

FIGURE 3-4   Selection options

5. Click **Cancel**.

Use the Select Features Tool

The Select Features tool enables you to select features on the map by clicking individual features or by dragging a rectangle around them.

1. If the Tools toolbar is not visible, click **View** on the main menu, click **Toolbars**, and then click **Tools**.
2. On the Tools toolbar, click the **Select Features** tool 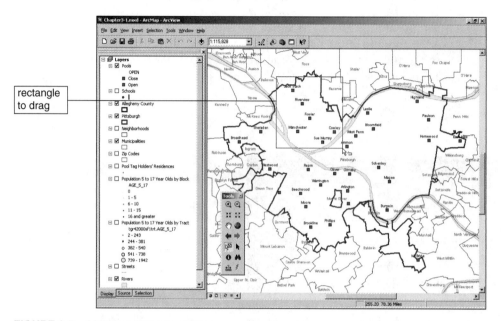.

1. If the Tools toolbar is not visible, click **View** on the main menu, click **Toolbars**, and then click **Tools**.
2. On the Tools toolbar, click the **Select Features** tool.
3. Click, hold, and drag the rectangle shown in Figure 3-5 to select the pools on the north side of Pittsburgh.

rectangle to drag

FIGURE 3-5   Making a feature selection

4. Release your mouse button. See Figure 3-6. *(The six pools on the north side of Pittsburgh get the selection icon to indicate that they are selected.)*

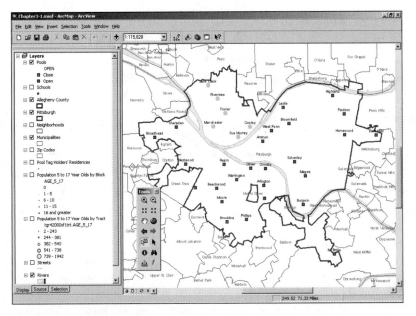

FIGURE 3-6   Selected pools

5. In the table of contents, right-click **Pools** and click **Open Attribute Table**. See Figure 3-7. *(The Attributes of Pools table opens with six selected rows in the selection color.)*

column
heading

FID	Shape	NAME	MAXLOAD	ZIPCODE	ADDRESS	OPEN	PCTCAP	ATTEND
0	Point	Jack Stack	434	15212	600 Brighton Woods Rd	1	0.615	267
1	Point	Highland	1448	15206	151 Lake Dr	1	0.384	556
2	Point	Riverview	515	15214	400 Riverview Dr	0	0	0
3	Point	Leslie	615	15201	4600 Butler St	0	0	0
4	Point	Fowler	519	15214	2438 Wilson Ave	0	0	0
5	Point	Paulson	404	15206	1300 Paulson Ave	0	0	0
6	Point	Bloomfield	582	15224	400 Ella St	1	0.376	219
7	Point	Manchester	502	15233	1258 Columbus Ave	0	0	0
8	Point	Cowley	387	15212	1200 Goettman St	1	0.292	113
9	Point	Sheraden	566	15204	1071 Adon St	1	0.152	86
10	Point	West Penn	345	15219	450 30th St	0	0	0
11	Point	Homewood	455	15208	540 N Lang Ave	1	0.303	138

Record: 1   Show: All Selected   Records (6 out of 32 Selected.)   Options ▾

FIGURE 3-7   Attributes of Pools table with selected records

6. In the resulting Attributes of Pools window, right-click the **gray column heading** of the MAXLOAD column *(see Figure 3-7)*, and click **Statistics**. See Figure 3-8. *(You can see several statistics for the selected pools, including the minimum capacity of 387, the maximum capacity of 700, and the mean capacity of 509.)*

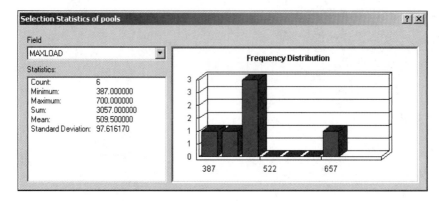

FIGURE 3-8   Selection statistics for pools

7. Close the **Selection Statistics** of pools window.
8. On the right-side bottom of the Attributes of Pools window, click the **Options** button and click **Switch Selection**. *(The 26 pools that were unselected before are now selected and the six selected pools from before are now unselected.)*
9. Repeat Step 6 to get statistics for all pools except those on the north side of Pittsburgh, and close the **Selection Statistics** of pools window after you have examined the results. *(You can see that the range of capacities is much larger, but the mean is about the same, slightly less than 500 at 494.)*
10. Close the **Attributes of Pools** window; on the main menu, click **Selection** and click **Clear Selected Features**.

PRACTICE 3-1

Select pools on the south side of Pittsburgh—all the pools south or below the main rivers. Get the mean capacity of those pools versus the rest of Pittsburgh. (*Hint:* If you need to make more than one selection with the selection tool, hold down the Shift key while making your selections.)

Select Records

Another simple way to select features is directly in attribute tables. You will do this using the Pools attribute table to select and highlight small pools (with capacity less than or equal to 300 persons) on the map.

1. On the main menu, click **Selection,** and then click **Clear Selected Features**.
2. In the table of contents, right-click **Pools** and click **Open Attribute Table**.
3. In the resulting Attributes of Pools window, right-click the **MAXLOAD** column heading, and click **Sort Ascending**. See Figure 3-9. *(ArcMap sorts all of the rows of data by MAXLOAD, in ascending order. You can see that the smallest pool is McBride, with a capacity of only 54. Next, you'll select all rows with MAXLOAD values of 300 or smaller.)*

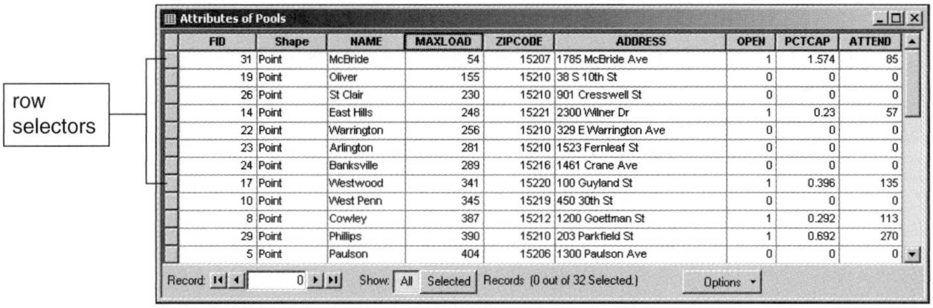

FID	Shape	NAME	MAXLOAD	ZIPCODE	ADDRESS	OPEN	PCTCAP	ATTEND
31	Point	McBride	54	15207	1785 McBride Ave	1	1.574	85
19	Point	Oliver	155	15210	38 S 10th St	0	0	0
26	Point	St Clair	230	15210	901 Cresswell St	0	0	0
14	Point	East Hills	248	15221	2300 Wilner Dr	1	0.23	57
22	Point	Warrington	256	15210	329 E Warrington Ave	0	0	0
23	Point	Arlington	281	15210	1523 Fernleaf St	0	0	0
24	Point	Banksville	289	15216	1461 Crane Ave	0	0	0
17	Point	Westwood	341	15220	100 Guyland St	1	0.396	135
10	Point	West Penn	345	15219	450 30th St	0	0	0
8	Point	Cowley	387	15212	1200 Goettman St	1	0.292	113
29	Point	Phillips	390	15210	203 Parkfield St	1	0.692	270
5	Point	Paulson	404	15206	1300 Paulson Ave	0	0	0

FIGURE 3-9 Attributes of Pools sorted by MAXLOAD

4. In the Attributes of Pools window, click and hold down your mouse button on the row selector of the first row *(see Figure 3-9)*, slide down seven rows through the Banksville row, and release. See Figure 3-10. *(That action selects all of the first seven rows.)*

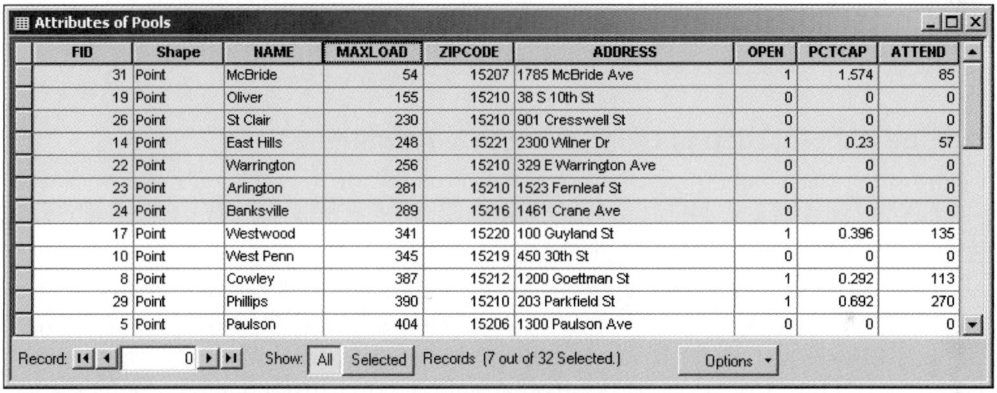

FID	Shape	NAME	MAXLOAD	ZIPCODE	ADDRESS	OPEN	PCTCAP	ATTEND
31	Point	McBride	54	15207	1785 McBride Ave	1	1.574	85
19	Point	Oliver	155	15210	38 S 10th St	0	0	0
26	Point	St Clair	230	15210	901 Cresswell St	0	0	0
14	Point	East Hills	248	15221	2300 Wilner Dr	1	0.23	57
22	Point	Warrington	256	15210	329 E Warrington Ave	0	0	0
23	Point	Arlington	281	15210	1523 Fernleaf St	0	0	0
24	Point	Banksville	289	15216	1461 Crane Ave	0	0	0
17	Point	Westwood	341	15220	100 Guyland St	1	0.396	135
10	Point	West Penn	345	15219	450 30th St	0	0	0
8	Point	Cowley	387	15212	1200 Goettman St	1	0.292	113
29	Point	Phillips	390	15210	203 Parkfield St	1	0.692	270
5	Point	Paulson	404	15206	1300 Paulson Ave	0	0	0

FIGURE 3-10 Attributes of Pools with small pools selected

5. Close the **Attributes of Pools** window, and examine the map. See Figure 3-11. *(You can see that the south side of Pittsburgh has the majority of small pools, six out of seven.)*
6. On the main menu, click **Selection,** and then click **Clear Selected Features**.

PRACTICE 3-2

Use the Pools attribute table to select all pools with average attendance of 200 or higher. Turn on the Population 5 to 17 Year Olds by Block layer. Are heavily used pools in areas with high densities of youths? When finished, clear all selections, but leave the Population 5 to 17 Year Old by Block layer on.

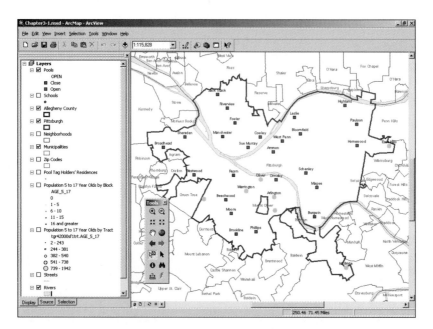

FIGURE 3-11   Pools selected with capacity of 300 or less

Execute Simple Queries Using Select By Attributes

A more sophisticated and powerful way to select records is to build and execute query criteria. ArcMap has a well-designed user interface for this purpose. At first, you will use it to replicate the small pools selection as a query.

1. On the main menu, click **Selection,** and then click **Select By Attributes**.
2. In the Select By Attributes window, make sure that **Pools** is selected as the layer and **Create a new selection** is selected as the method.
3. In the large panel listing attributes of the Pools attribute table, double-click **"MAXLOAD"**, click the **<=** button, and type **300** after the <= sign in the bottom panel. See Figure 3-12. *(Those selections result in a complete SQL select statement: SELECT * FROM pools WHERE "MAXLOAD" <=300 seen in Figure 3-12.)*
4. Click **OK**. *(The same seven pools as in Figure 3-11 are selected.)*
5. On the main menu, click **Selection,** and then click **Clear Selected Features**.
6. On the main menu, click **Selection**, and then click **Select By Attributes**. *(You can see that the Select By Attributes window remembers your select query command. Next, you will save the select command permanently as a file for reuse. That capacity is valuable for complex queries that you want to reuse from time to time, and perhaps modify as needed.)*
7. In the resulting Select By Attributes window, click the **Save** button, browse to the **C:\LearningAndUsingGIS\FilesStudentWork** folder, type **SmallPools.exp** in the File name field, and click **Save**.
8. In the Select By Attributes window, click the **Clear** button.

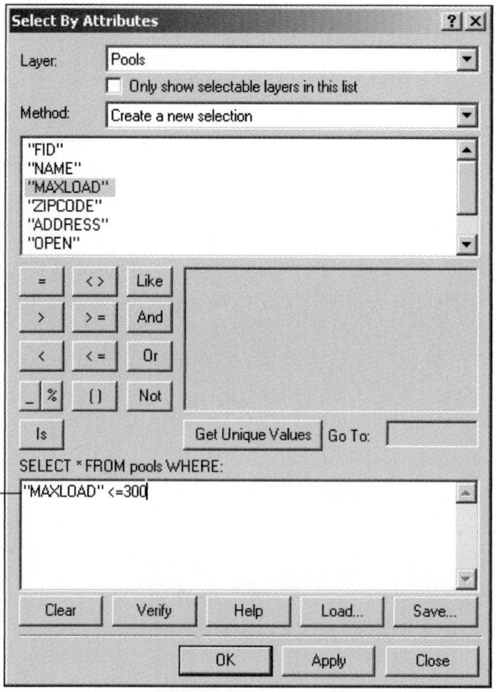

FIGURE 3-12   Select By Attributes window with query for small pools

9. Click the **Load** button, and in the resulting Open window double-click
    SmallPools.exp. *(This action reloads your query expression into the Select
    By Attributes window.)*

10. In the bottom select panel, change the 300 to **400**, and click **OK**. *(Now you
    have several more pools selected, those with capacity 400 or less. The last
    few steps simulate reusing and modifying a saved query—a valuable
    capability for repetitive work.)*

PRACTICE 3-3

Build and execute a query for average percent of capacity used, PCTCAP, that is 0.5 or
greater. Officials consider 50 percent or greater as efficient use of pools. Save the query
as EfficientPools.

Execute More Simple Queries Using Select By Attributes

The Select By Attributes interface has a helpful feature that finds potential values for you
to use in query criterion. The best use of that feature is to get a list of all code values for
an attribute, which you can then use by double-clicking a value, instead of typing.

1. On the main menu, click **Selection**, and then click **Clear Selected Features**.
2. Turn on the **Schools** map layer.
3. Right-click **Schools** and click **Label Features** to toggle labels off.
4. On the main menu, click **Selection**, and then click **Select By Attributes**.
5. In the Select By Attributes window, click the **Clear** button, click the **list arrow** in the Layer field, and click **Schools**. In the panel with school attribute names, scroll down and double-click **"DISTRICT"**, click the **=** button, and click the **Get Unique Values** button. *(DISTRICT has code values for type of school: 'City of Pittsburg' for public schools, 'Pittsburgh Diocese' for catholic schools, and 'Private School' for private schools. You can conveniently look up such values and enter them by clicking.)*
6. In the panel with unique values, double-click the first value, **"City of Pittsburg"**. See Figure 3-13. *(This places the code value into the query expression.)*

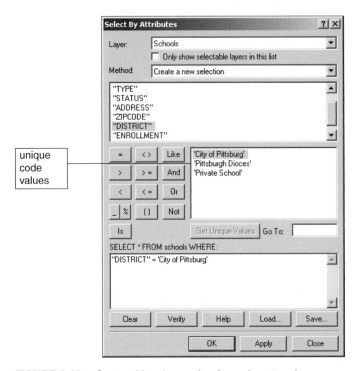

FIGURE 3-13 Query with unique value for code entered

7. Click **OK**. See Figure 3-14, where we have turned off the Population 5 to 17 Year Old by Block layer. *(This selects all public schools.)*

PRACTICE 3-4

Build and execute a query for private schools. In which part of the city are they concentrated?

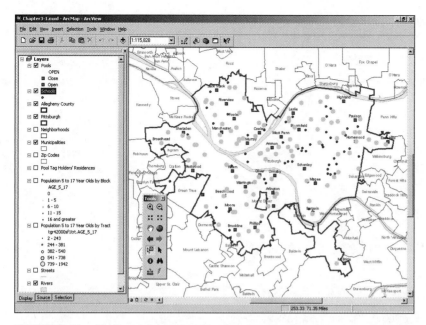

FIGURE 3-14   Public schools selected using a code value

Execute Select By Attributes AND Compound Queries

The strength of SQL queries becomes apparent in cases where there are two or more simple criteria that must be combined to yield compound criteria. The first such case that you will handle is for selecting pools that have a small average percentage of capacity used. If you do not include a criterion for open pools, you would include closed pools in the selection, which have the value "0" percent of capacity used in the Pools attribute table.

1. Turn off the **Schools** map layer.
2. On the main menu, click **Selection**, and then click **Clear Selected Features**.
3. On the main menu, click **Selection**, and then click **Select By Attributes**.
4. In the Select By Attributes window, click the **Clear** button, click the **list arrow** in the Layer field and click **Pools**.
5. In the panel with pool attribute names, scroll down and double-click **"OPEN"**, click the **=** button, click the **Get Unique Values** button, and double-click the **1** in the list of unique values. *(Those actions complete the first of two simple query criteria: "OPEN" = 1 for open schools.)*
6. Click the **And** button, scroll down in the list of pool attributes, double-click **"PCTCAP"**, click the **<** button, click the **Get Unique Values** button, and double-click the **0.303** value from the list of unique values. See Figure 3-15.
7. Click **OK**. See Figure 3-16. *(You can see all of the open, underused pools. Three are near the central business district of Pittsburgh, formed by the triangle where the three rivers join. Two are outlying pools.)*

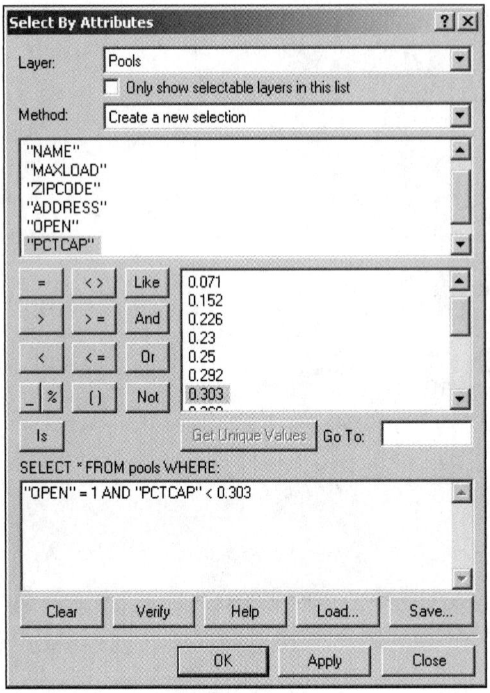

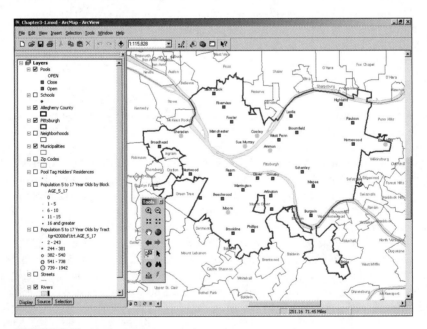

FIGURE 3-15   Compound criteria with AND connective

FIGURE 3-16   Underused open pools

PRACTICE 3-5

Build and execute a query for large-capacity pools, 500 or more persons, that are closed.
Where are these pools located?

101

Execute Select By Attributes OR Compound Queries

You have built compound queries using the AND connective for simple queries. Next, you build a compound query using the OR connective. You will select all pools lying in the 15203, 15210, or 15226 zip codes.

1. On the main menu, click **Selection**, and then click **Clear Selected Features**.
2. On the main menu, click **Selection**, and then click **Select By Attributes**.
3. In the Select By Attributes window, click the **Clear** button; in the list of pool attributes double-click **"ZIPCODE"**, click the **=** button, click the **Get Unique Values** button, and double-click the **15203** value in the list of unique values.
4. Click the **Or** button, and repeat parts of Step 3 to add "ZIPCODE" = 15210.
5. Click the **Or** button, and repeat parts of Step 3 to add "ZIPCODE" = 15226. See Figure 3-17.

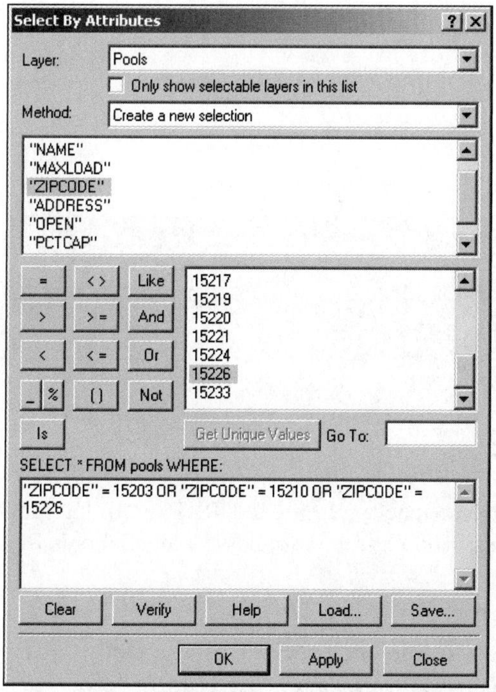

FIGURE 3-17   Compound criteria with OR connectives

6. Click **OK** and turn on the **Zip Codes** layer. See Figure 3-18. *(This is a nice transition to the next topic, selection by location. You will select the same point features using the Zip Codes boundary map, instead of the values in the pools table.)*

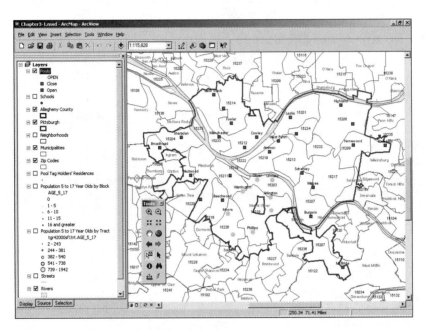

FIGURE 3-18   Pools selected by zip code

Execute Select Points by Location Queries

The next set of queries uses the powerful location capacity unique to GIS. Even though the Schools layer does not have a zip code attribute, you can, nevertheless, select schools by zip code using the Zip Codes map layer.

1. Turn on the **Schools** map layer.
2. Right-click **Zip Codes**, click **Selection**, and click **Make This The Only Selectable Layer**. *(This action restricts what the Select Features tool can select but does not affect Select By Location, which you will use to select schools next.)*
3. On the main menu, click **Selection**, and then click **Clear Selected Features**.

4. Click the **Select Features** tool 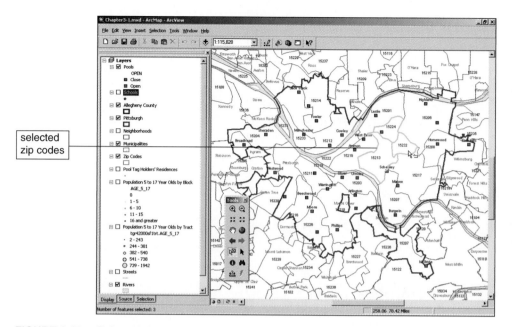, hold down your **Shift** key, and click inside the **polygons** for zip codes **15213**, **15224**, and **15232** to select them. See Figure 3-19, where we have turned off the Schools layer.

FIGURE 3-19   Selected zip code polygons

5. On the main menu, click **Selection**, and then click **Select By Location**.
6. In the resulting Select By Location window, in the I want to field make sure that **select features from** is selected in the following layer(s) field, click the **check box for Schools**, make sure that **Intersect** is selected, click the **list arrow** in the last field, and click **Zip Codes**. See Figure 3-20. (*Note that the Use selected features check box is clicked automatically, which is what we want.*)

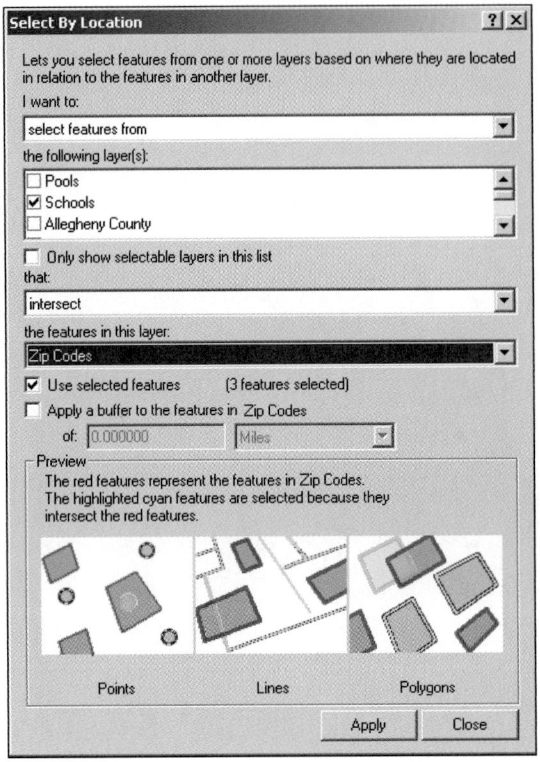

FIGURE 3-20 Parameters for select schools by location

> 7. Click **Apply** and **Close**. See Figure 3-21 where the Schools layers is turned on.

PRACTICE 3-7

Build and execute a query to select schools in the 15207, 15208, and 15217 zip codes.

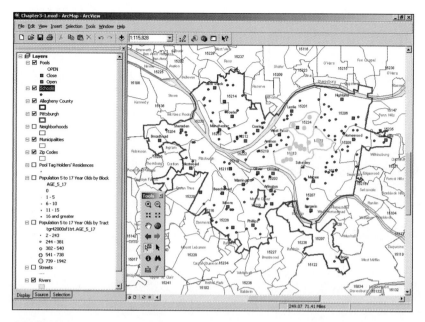

FIGURE 3-21 Schools selected by zip code

Execute Select Polygons by Location Queries

Zip code boundaries are administrative areas designed to efficiently deliver the mail. As such, they do not follow other polygon layers such as political boundaries, but cross over them. Suppose that you want to select all zip codes that are completely within Pittsburgh. There is an option for that kind of selection by location.

1. Set up the map: Turn off the **Schools** map layer; on the main menu, click **Selection**, and then click **Clear Selected Features**; right-click **Municipalities**, click **Selection**, and click **Make This The Only Selectable Layer**.
2. Click the **Select Features** tool, and click anywhere inside of Pittsburgh.
3. On the main menu, click **Selection**, and then click **Select By Location**.
4. In the resulting Select By Location window, in **the following layer(s) field** click off **Schools** and click **Zip Codes**, click the **list arrow** in the field that has the value Intersect and click **are completely within**; click the **list arrow** in **the features in this layer** field and click **Municipalities**. See Figure 3-22.
5. Click **Apply** and **Close**.
6. In the table of contents, right-click **Municipalities**, click **Selection**, and then click **Clear Selected Features**. See Figure 3-23. (*Now you can see the selected zip codes that are entirely within Pittsburgh. The rest of Pittsburgh's zip codes cross its boundary and so are not selected.*)

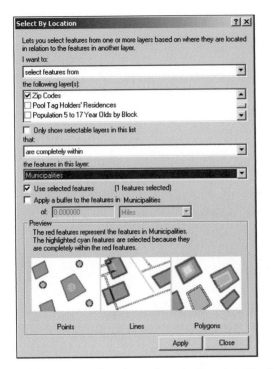

FIGURE 3-22   Parameters for selecting zip codes by location

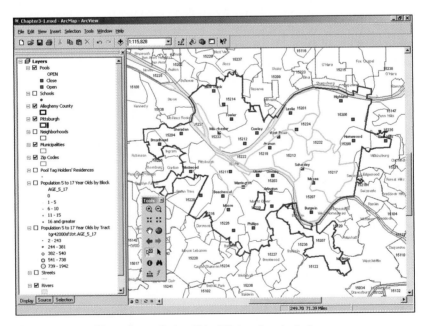

FIGURE 3-23   Zip codes entirely within Pittsburgh selected

PRACTICE 3-8

Build and execute a query to select streets that intersect Mount Oliver. (*Hint:* Be sure to turn off Zip Codes in the Select By Location list of layers to select from and turn on Streets.) Zoom in to your selection by right-clicking Streets, clicking Selection, and clicking Zoom to Selected Features. Notice that some street segments cross over Mount Oliver's boundary. When finished, turn off Streets and use the Pittsburgh bookmark.

Build a Square Graphic

If you have to travel by streets in an urban area and if the streets are laid out in a square pattern, the Manhattan metric is a good surrogate for actual travel distance. To get from point A to B on the street network, we assume that the traveler moves along the sides of right angles in a shortest path, not the hypotenuses. With a little bit of work, sketching with a pencil and paper, you can see that to select an area with an approximate travel distance x, you need a square with side length = $1.414x$, where 1.414 is the square root of 2, rotated $90°$ around the street network. For example, for a travel distance of 1 mile in feet (5280), you need a square with sides 7466 feet long.

1. Set up the map: Use the **NorthSide Pittsburgh** bookmark; turn off **Zip Codes** and turn on **Streets**; click **View**, click **Data Frame Properties**, click the **General** tab, change the Display units to **Feet**, and click **OK**.
2. Place your cursor over **Fowler Pool** and note its coordinates: 1,338,710, 421,455.
3. On the main menu, click **View**, click **Toolbars**, and click **Draw**. *(That turns on the Draw toolbar.)*
4. On the Draw toolbar, click the **New Rectangle** tool. See Figure 3-24.
5. Drag a **rectangle** on the map and release. See Figure 3-24. *(Any size rectangle will work. You'll change its size and other properties next.)*
6. Double-click the **new rectangle**.
7. In the resulting Properties window, click the **Symbol** tab, click the **Fill Color** list arrow, click **No Color**, and click **Apply**.
8. Click the **Size and Position** tab, type **7644** in the **Width** and **Height** fields, type **1338710** and **421455** in the X and Y Position fields, and click the **central anchor point** icon. See Figure 3-25.
9. Click **OK**. See Figure 3-26. *(Now you have a square with its center on Fowler Pool.)*

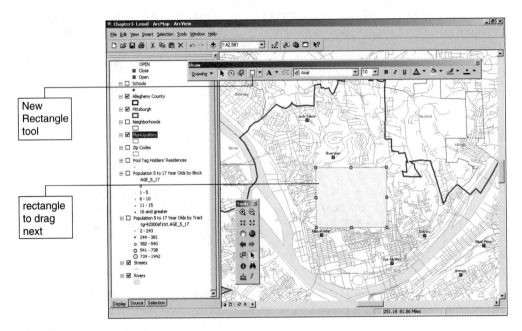

New Rectangle tool

rectangle to drag next

FIGURE 3-24 Draw toolbar

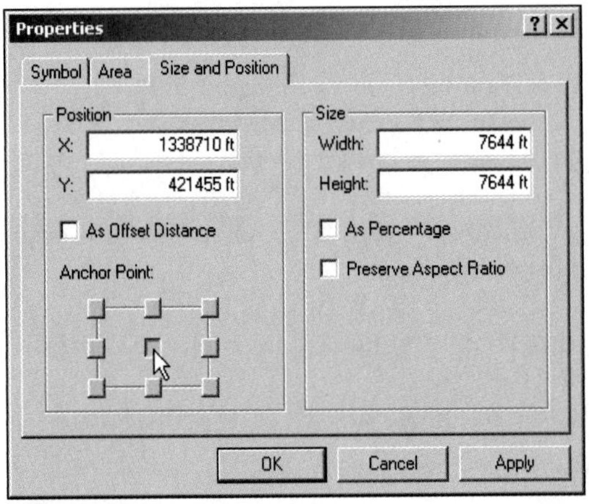

FIGURE 3-25 Rectangle size and position properties

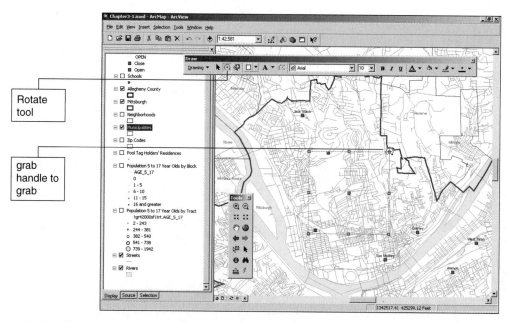

FIGURE 3-26   Finished rectangle graphic

10.   On the Draw toolbar, click the **Rotate** tool, click, hold, and drag the **upper-right grab handle** of the rectangle, and rotate about 80°. See Figure 2-27.

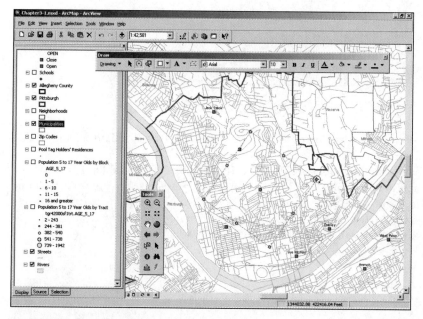

FIGURE 3-27   Rotated rectangle

Select Points by Graphic

Now you can select features using the rectangle graphic.

1. Set up the map: Turn on the **Pool Tag Holders' Residences** layer and in the table of contents, right-click **Pool Tag Holders' Residences**, click **Selection**, and click **Make This The Only Selectable Layer**.
2. Click **Selection**, and then click **Select By Graphics**. See Figure 3-28. *(Now you have all pool-tag-holders' residences within approximately a 1-mile travel distance of Fowler Pool. Let's get the total number of tag holders in that distance next.)*

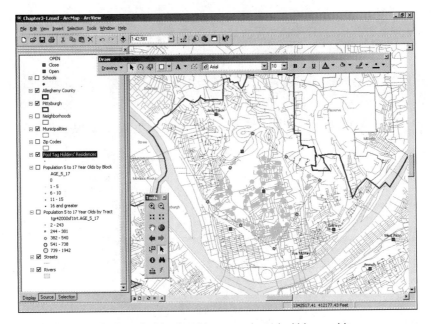

FIGURE 3-28　Pool-tag-holders' residences selected within graphic

3. In the table of contents, right-click **Pool Tag Holders' Residences**, and click **Open Attribute Table**.
4. In the resulting Attributes of Pool Tag Holders' Residences table, right-click the **column heading for NOPERSONS**, and click **Statistics**. See Figure 3-29. *(You can see from the Sum statistic that 669 sampled tag holders live within approximately a 1-mile travel distance of Fowler Pool.)*
5. Close the **Selection Statistics** and **Attributes** windows.

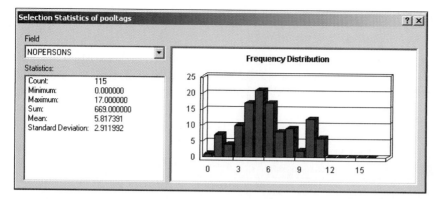

FIGURE 3-29   Statistics on pool tag holders living within 1-mile travel distance of Fowler Pool

111

PRACTICE 3-9

Get coordinates for Jack Stack Pool, relocate the rectangle graphic to center on that pool, and get the number of pool tag holders living within a 1-mile travel distance of that pool. When finished, close the Draw toolbar, clear all selections, and delete the rectangle graphic by clicking its edge and pressing Delete.

Buffer Points

The Selection by Location interface has a feature to use buffers of features to select other features. You'll use that capacity to select points next.

1.   Set up the map: Turn off **Streets**; use your **Pittsburgh bookmark**; in the table of contents, right-click **Pools**, click **Selection**, and click **Make This The Only Selectable Layer**.
2.   Click the **Select Features** tool ⬚, hold down the **Shift** key, and select the three open pools on the north side of Pittsburgh (Jack Stack, Sue Murray, and Cowely).
3.   On the main menu, click **Selection**, and then click **Select By Location**.
4.   In the resulting Select By Location window, in **the following layer(s)** field make sure that all layers are turned off except **Pool Tag Holders' Residences**, which you turn on. Make sure that **intersect** is selected, click the **list arrow** in **the features in this layer** field and click **Pools**. Then, click the **check box** for **Apply a buffer to the features in Pools**, and set the buffer distance to **1 mile**. See Figure 3-30.
5.   Click **Apply** and click **Close**. *(You can see the diameter roughly in the selection.)*

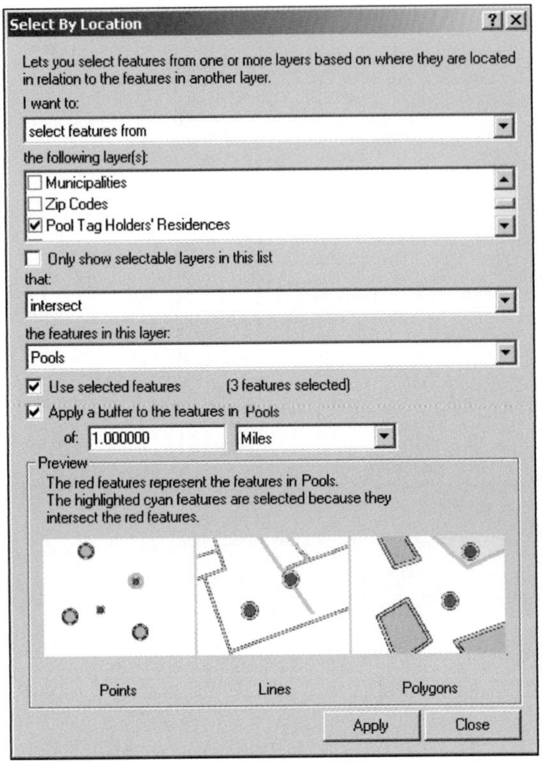

FIGURE 3-30   Parameters for pool buffers

PRACTICE 3-10

Make Municipalities the only selectable layer, select Pittsburgh, use a 1-mile buffer of Pittsburgh, and select all pool tag holders within a 1-mile buffer of Pittsburgh. You should find 2207 residences out of a total of 2,680 are in the buffer.

Buffer Map Layers

Besides selecting map features using a buffer distance from other map features, you can use ArcGIS to build permanent buffer layers. Buffer layers can be reused for proximity analyses and to display buffer results. ArcGIS builds buffer layers in the coordinate system of individual map layers, instead of in your map document's data frame coordinates, leading to possible distortions in buffer shapes. For example, the Pools map layer has latitude/longitude geographic coordinates, and circular buffers in latitude/longitude coordinates plot as ellipses in rectilinear coordinates such as State Plane (the coordinates of *Chapter3-1.mxd*'s data frame). Let's see this problem firsthand.

1. Use your **Pittsburgh** bookmark, and turn off the **Streets** and **Pool Tag Holders' Residences** map layers.

2. In the table of contents, right-click **Pools** and click **Properties**.
3. In the resulting Layer Properties window, click the **Source** tab, and note in the Data Source panel that Pools has geographic coordinates. *(The map document's data frame is in State Plane.)*
4. Click **Cancel**.
5. On the Standard toolbar, click the **ArcToolbox** icon 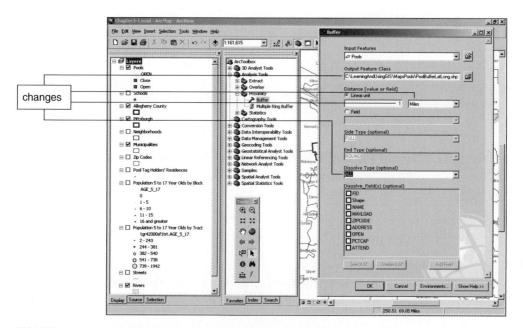.
6. In the resulting ArcToolbox panel, click expander boxes for **Analysis Tools** and **Proximity**, and double-click **Buffer**.
7. In the resulting Buffer window, make selection entries as shown in Figure 3-31. *(Having the Dissolve Type feature set to ALL causes overlapping buffers to be dissolved. If NONE were chosen for this parameter, every pool would have its own buffer and buffers of some adjacent pools would overlap.)*

FIGURE 3-31   ArcToolbox panel and buffer parameter settings

8. Click **OK** and click **Close**. See Figure 3-32. *(Here, you can see that the buffers are dissolved, forming amoeba-like structures, and the buffer shapes are not circular as desired. If you were to change the data frame's coordinate system to geographic, the buffers would be circular, but instead, you will project Pools to State Plane coordinates.)*
9. In the table of contents, right-click **PoolBufferLatLong** and click **Remove**.

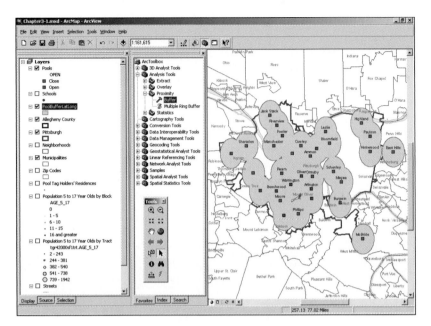

FIGURE 3-32   Pool buffers from geographic coordinates

Permanently Project Pools to Remedy Buffer Problem

To remedy the situation with pool buffer map layers, you need to project that layer to State Plane.

1. In the table of contents, right-click **Pools**, click **Data**, and click **Export Data**.
2. In the resulting Export Data window, click the **data frame** option button *(to use State Plane instead of geographic coordinates)*, click the **browse** button of the **Output shapefile or feature class** field, browse to **C:\LearningAndUsingGIS\MapsPools**, type **PoolsStatePlane** in the Name field, click **Save**, click **Yes**, click **OK**, and click **Yes**.
3. Right-click **PoolsStatePlane** and click **Properties**.
4. In the resulting Layer Properties window, click the **Symbology** tab, and click the **Import** button.
5. In the resulting Import Symbology window, click the **browse** button if necessary and browse to **C:\LearningAndUsingGIS\MapsPools**, click the **list arrow** in the **Layer** field, click **Pools**, click **OK**, click **OK**, and click **OK**.
6. Right-click the original **Pools** layer and click **Remove**.
7. Click the name label for **PoolsStatePlane**, wait a moment, click it again, and type a new name, **Pools**.

PRACTICE 3-11

Repeat Steps 4–7 of the Buffer Map Layers section to create PoolBufferStatePlane. Are its buffers circular? When finished, remove the new buffer layer from your map document.

Create Multiple Ring Buffer Map Layers

Often, as in the analysis of Pittsburgh's swimming pools, it is desirable to have several buffers for the same features. In the pools case, we want to see if the percentage of youths who have pool tags falls off with distance from open pools; therefore, you will create two buffers, one with a half-mile radius (2640 feet) and a second with a 1-mile radius (5280 feet). ArcGIS automates these steps with a tool that creates multiple-ring buffers. A nice feature is that the buffer polygons have rings for the 0.5- to 1-mile buffer, making analysis simple.

1. In the table of contents right-click **Pools**, click **Selection**, and click **Make This The Only Selectable Layer**.
2. On the main menu, click **Selection**, and then click **Select By Attributes**.
3. In the resulting Select By Attributes window, in the Layers field make sure that **Pools** is selected in the list of attributes, double-click **"OPEN"**, click the = button, type **1** after the = sign in the bottom panel, and click **OK**. *(That action selects all of the open pools.)*
4. On the Standard toolbar, click the **ArcToolbox** icon 📦.
5. In the resulting ArcToolbox panel, click **expander boxes** for **Analysis Tools** and **Proximity**, and double-click **Multiple Ring Buffer**.
6. In the Input Features field of the resulting Multiple Ring Buffer window, click the **list arrow** and click **Pools**, and click the **browse** button for the Output Feature class field.
7. In the resulting Output Feature class window, browse to **C:\LearningAndUsingGIS\FilesStudentWork**, type **OpenPoolBufferp5and1** in the Name field, and click **Save**.
8. Type **2640** in the Distances field, click the + button, type **5280** in the Distances field, and click the + button.

Getting Information from a GIS

9. Click the **list arrow** in the **Buffer Unit** field and click **Feet**. See Figure 3-33.

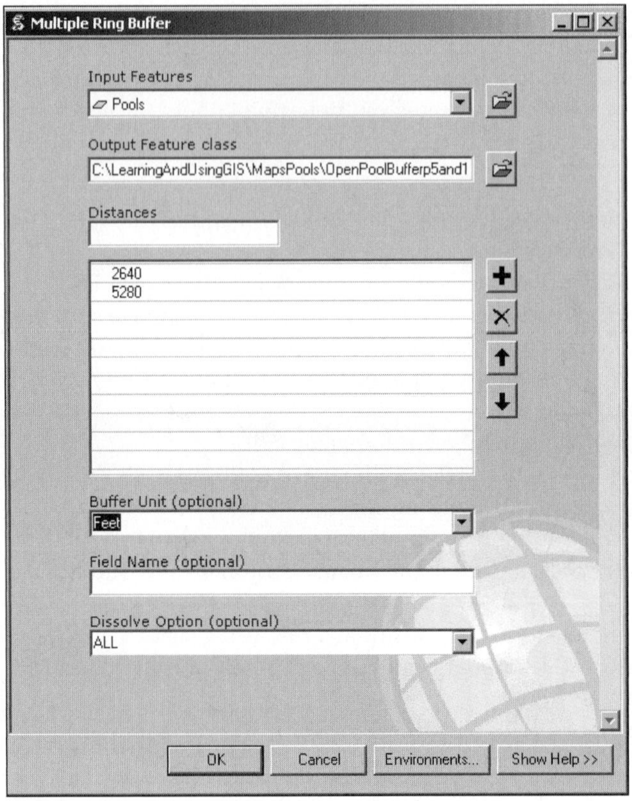

FIGURE 3-33 Multiple ring buffer parameters

10. Click **OK** and click **Close**. See Figure 3-34.

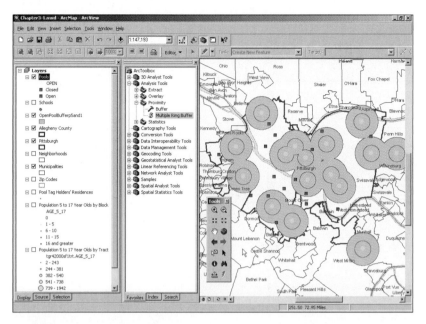

FIGURE 3-34   Multiple ring buffers

Conduct Buffer Analysis

Now you can use the two buffers—a 0.5-mile circular buffer and 0.5- to 1-mile ring—to select pool-tag-holders' residences and sum up their number in each buffer.

1. Set up the map: In the table of contents, drag **OpenPoolBufferp5and1** below Population 5 to 17 Year Olds by Block, turn on **Pool Tag Holders' Residences**, and close the ArcToolbox panel.
2. On the main menu, click **Selection**, and then click **Select By Attributes**.
3. In the resulting Select By Attributes window, click the **Clear** button, click the **list arrow** in the **Layer** field and click **OpenPoolBufferp5and1**. In the list of attributes panel, double-click **"distance"**, click the **=** button, click the **Get Unique Values** button, and double-click **2640** in the unique values list. See Figure 3-35. *(This selects the inner buffer of open pools.)*

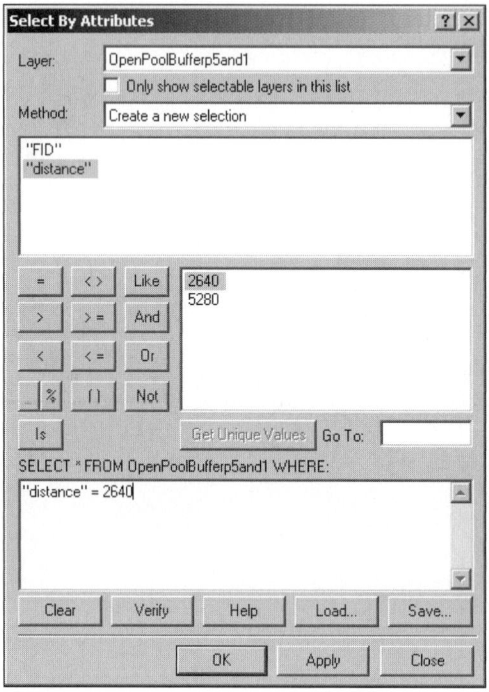

FIGURE 3-35 Buffer selection by attributes parameters

4. Click **OK**.
5. On the main menu, click **Selection**, and then click **Select By Location**.
6. In the resulting Select By Location window, turn on the **Pool Tag Holders' Residences** layer if it is not turned on, and make sure that all other select from layers are off.
7. In the features in this layer field, click the **list arrow** and click **OpenPoolBuffersp5and1**. See Figure 3-36.
8. Click **Apply** and click **Close**. See Figure 3-37.
9. Right-click **Pool Tag Holders' Residences**, and click **Open Attribute Table**.
10. In the resulting Pool Tag Holders' Residences attributes table, right-click the **NOPERSONS** column heading, and click **Statistics**. See Figure 3-38. *(You can see that there are 686 pool-tag-holder residences in that buffer with a total of 3813 pool tag holders.)*
11. Close the **Selection Statistics of pooltags** window, and close the **Attributes of Pool Tag Holders' Residences** window.

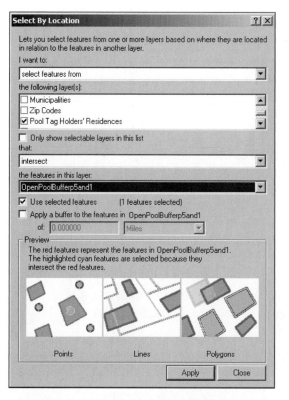

FIGURE 3-36 Pool Tag Holders' Residences selection parameters

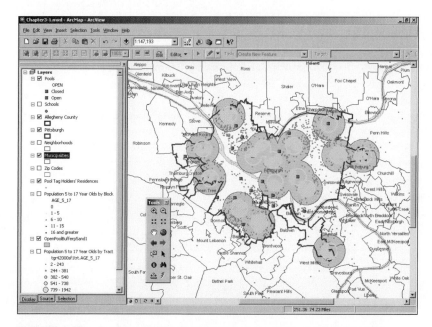

FIGURE 3-37 Pool Tag Holders' Residences selected in the 0.5-mile buffer

Getting Information from a GIS

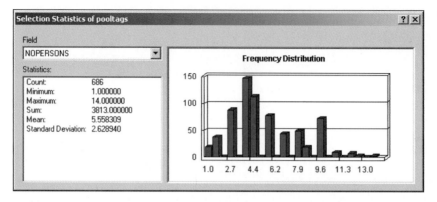

FIGURE 3-38 Statistics on pool tag holders in the 1-mile pool buffer

PRACTICE 3-12

Turn off Pool Tag Holder's Residences and turn on Population 5 to 17 Year Olds by Block. Repeat Steps 2–11 of the Buffer Analysis section except select the blockcentroids of Population 5 to 17 Year Olds by Block inside of the 0.5-mile buffer and sum up the number of 5- to 17-year-olds living in the buffer. What percentage of such youths have pool tags? You should find that there are 1930 blocks in the buffer with a 5- to 17-year-old population of 11,403. You found that the buffer has 686 pool tags. We provided an adjustment to scale such a sample to an estimated number of youths with pool tags: Multiply by 21 to get the total population of pool tags and then multiply by 0.47 to get the number of youths aged 5 to 17 with pool tags. Thus, $100 \times 21 \times 0.47 \times 686/11,403 =$ 59.4 percent of youths living within one-half mile of pools have pool tags. What do you suppose the percentage is for youths in the 0.5- to 1-mile buffer? Problem 4 of this chapter has you find the answer. When finished, save your project and exit ArcMap.

Chapter 3 Summary

A vector map can have one of many file formats. Four from ESRI include the shapefile, personal geodatabase, coverage, and E00 export format. Vector-based map layers have graphic features consisting of points, lines, and polygons. Attached to each graphic feature is a data record with attributes describing the graphic feature. Attributes can be of many data types (such as integer, decimal, text, date, and Boolean). The records of a map layer make up its feature attribute table. A data dictionary provides essential documentation for feature attribute tables. It lists all attributes, data types, and definitions.

Raster maps, by contrast, are images stored using digital-image formats—often as TIFF files—that consist of vast arrays of pixels. Each pixel is a tiny square that has a single color. Raster maps have an accompanying world file that provides data on how to display the image in projected coordinates. The world file includes the x- and y-coordinates of the upper-left corner of the image in map coordinates and the width of pixels in map distance.

GIS queries include attribute queries that are commonly used in databases, as well as spatial queries based on graphic features and their map coordinates. Spatial queries are unique to GIS.

Attribute queries applied to a GIS select records from the data stored in attribute tables. In turn, the corresponding graphic features in the map layer are selected automatically. ArcGIS usually uses a special selection color and icon to make these selections visible.

A simple attribute query has the form (<attribute name> <logical operator> <value>). Any attribute name of an attribute table can be used. Logical operators are the familiar ones from algebra (=, <, >, <=, >=), not equals (<>), and `like`. The `like` operator allows flexible queries of text values, such as all pool names starting with letters *Br*.

In ArcGIS, shapefile attribute names must appear in double quotes. Text values and dates must be placed in single quotes, but numeric values appear without special characters. Examples are (`"NAME"` = `'Riverview'`), (`"DateConstructed"` < `'1/1/1990'`), and (`"MAXLOAD"` >= `200`).

Compound queries combine two or more simple queries with AND or OR logical connectors. All simple conditions connected by AND must simultaneously be true for a record to be selected. By contrast, OR selects a record if any or all conditions are true.

Direct spatial queries depend on you being able to see what you want to select on a displayed map layer. You can use an ArcGIS tool to select any visible graphic features, highlighting them with the selection color. Such a spatial selection automatically selects corresponding records in the map layer's attribute table. With records selected spatially, you can analyze them in ArcGIS or export them and analyze them in another software package.

You can use ArcGIS to retrieve features within a polygon. An indirect but powerful means of making spatial queries is to build and use buffers. Point buffers are circular with a user-supplied radius. Line buffers of a single line look like a worm, and polygon buffers extend polygons outward and round off corners. You can use a buffer to select features from another map layer. For example, you can select the points representing pool-tag-holders' residences within a 1-mile radius of a pool.

Key Terms

Bit   The smallest computer storage unit. A bit, short for binary digit, has one of two values—on or off.

Boolean   A data type that has two possible values—true or false.

Byte   A storage unit on a computer, usually made up of 8 bits. Characters on a keyboard (and other special or foreign characters) are encoded as unique 8-bit patterns.

Color depth   Also known as *bit depth*; the number of colors an image file can display or store.

Compound query criterion   Two or more simple query criteria connected with the AND or OR logical connectives.

Coverage   An outdated GIS map file format designed by ESRI. A coverage has many files stored in a folder given the name of the coverage. Several of the files store intermediate results needed to speed up processing of advanced GIS procedures.

Data dictionary   Documentation for a database that includes (at a minimum) the names of data tables and their attributes' names, definitions, and data types.

Date   A data type for attribute storage of calendar dates.

Decimal   A data type for storing numbers that have fractional parts.

Digitize   The process of tracing an image or other graphic manuscript for the purpose of producing a vector-based drawing or map layer.

E00 export format   A map file format from ESRI used to store and transmit a map coverage as a single file.

Event theme   A data table that includes x- and y- map coordinates of point features.

False colors   Colors in the visible spectrum used to represent satellite images of reflected electromagnetic energy from Earth that is out of the color spectrum.

File compression   A technology for reducing the size of large files to facilitate storage or network transmission.

GIF (Graphic Interchange Format)   A digital image file format best suited for schematic drawings and other images without many color variations.

Integer   An attribute data type for storing numbers that do not have decimal parts.

JPEG (Joint Photographic Experts Group)   A digital image file format widely used for photographs. This format uses an adjustable amount of file compression to reduce file sizes, trading off image quality.

Logical connectives   The operators AND or OR, which are used to connect simple query criteria to produce a compound query criterion.

Personal geodatabase   A modern approach to storing both vector- and raster-based map layers in the Microsoft Access relational database package. The resulting layers are called feature classes and many or all layers of a GIS can be stored in a single Access file.

Proximity analysis   A study that identifies and analyzes entities of a selected type that are within a specified distance of other selected objects. An example is tabulating the number of 5- to 17-year-old youths within a 1-mile radius of open swimming pools.

Query   A process of selecting data records or graphic features that meet selection criteria.

Relational database   A collection of related rectangular data tables and accompanying programs or functions for input, processing, retrieval, and display of data.

Shapefile   A simple map format developed by ESRI. It is much simpler than the older coverage format but depends more on computing power to carry out advanced GIS processing.

Simple query criterion   A logical condition for selecting records from a data table of the form (<attribute name><logical operator><value>).

Spatial query   A means of selecting graphic features based on location in map coordinates or distance.

Text   An attribute data format for text strings.

TIFF (Tagged Image File Format)   A digital image file format widely used in publishing and other applications that require high-quality images.

Wildcard   A special character use to represent 0, 1, or more characters in queries using the `like` logical operator.

Short-Answer Questions

1. What is file compression, and why is it valuable for raster format maps?

2. The following four values have text data types: 3.141592, 300, argyle, and argument. Place these values in ascending order.

3. Sometimes a city is represented on a map as a point, and at other times as a polygon. What purposes and scales dictate such choices?

4. In advanced GISs, a street centerline map can be used to route vehicles across a street network. The routes attempt to minimize travel time. What do you think are some of the properties street maps need for such an application?

5. What are the important uses of raster maps? What are their limitations?

6. Would you ever expect to see a raster map, made from an aerial photograph, that is in geographic coordinates? Why or why not?

7. Give examples of state names that the following simple queries would select: (STATE like 'N*'), (STATE like '*a'), and (STATE like '*e*').

8. Suppose that there are 52 records describing the 52 playing cards in a deck. Attributes include Suit (clubs, spades, diamonds, or hearts), Color (red or black), and Name (such as 7, ace, or king). All attributes are text data type. What cards are retrieved with the following query criteria? ("Suit" = 'diamonds') AND ("Name" >= '3') AND ("Name" <='7'). ("Name" >= 'queen') AND (("Suit" <= 'diamonds') OR("Color" = 'red')).

9. Suppose that you have a boundary map that has the 87 neighborhoods of Pittsburgh. The Pool Tag Holders' Residences map layer does not include an attribute for neighborhood. Explain how you could select all the pool tag holders who live in the neighborhood of Shadyside using a GIS.

10. Suppose that you have selected all of the block centroids in the Shadyside neighborhood of Pittsburgh. Explain how to get the population of 5- to 17-year-old youths in Shadyside.

Exercises

1. **Swimming Pools in the Vicinity of Public High Schools.** In this exercise, you will use Select By Attributes or Select By Location in ArcMap.

   a. Open C:\LearningAndUsingGIS\Chapter3-1.mxd in ArcMap and save it as **C:\LearningAndUsingGIS\FilesStudentWork\Exercise3-1<YourName>.mxd**, where you substitute your name or other identifier for <YourName>. Remove layers until just the following remain and are turned on: Pools, Schools, AlleghenyCounty, Pittsburgh, Municipalities, Streets, and Rivers.

   b. Open a Microsoft Word document and save it as **C:\LearningAndUsingGIS\FilesStudentWork\Exercise3-1<YourName>.doc**.

   c. Out of all schools, select only public high schools that have the value "City of Pittsburg" (with no *h* at the end of Pittsburgh) for DISTRICT. Use your cursor to highlight your finished query criterion (in the Select By Attributes bottom panel), press Ctrl+C to copy the criterion, and paste it into your Word document. Label the query criterion in your document as Criterion to Select Public High Schools. Execute your query. How many public high schools are there in Pittsburgh? Click File and click Export Map to save a *.jpg* image of your resulting map. Include the image in your Word document. Do not clear your selection, but leave the public high schools selected.

   d. Select all pools within 0.2 miles of a public high school. (*Hint*: Use Select By Location with the **are within distance of** option.) How many pools are selected? List them in your Word document in alphabetical order.

   e. Save your Word and map documents.

2. **Intended Use Rate Estimates and Predictions for Pools.** We define the intended use rate for a buffer area to be the number of pool tag holders within the buffer area divided by the population of 5- to 17-year-olds living within the same buffer area.

   a. Open C:\LearningAndUsingGIS\Chapter3-1.mxd in ArcMap, and save it as **C:\LearningAndUsingGIS\FilesStudentWork\Exercise3-2<YourName>.mxd**, where you substitute your name for <YourName>. Remove layers until you just have the following layers remaining and turned on: Pools, AlleghenyCounty, Pittsburgh, Municipalities, Pool Tag Holders' Residences, Population 5 to 17 Year Olds by Block, and Rivers.

   b. Use **Select By Location** to estimate the individual use rates for a 1-mile buffer of Homewood, Jack Stack, and Magee Pools. Count pool tag holders and sum youths. You have to make two adjustments to the count of the tag holders per buffer. Make the adjustments to the counts of pool tag holders discussed in this chapter for scaling up from the random sample to the full population and for eliminating persons outside the 5- to 17-year-old interval (namely, multiply by 21 x 0.47 = 9.87).

   c. Using Excel, make a table including all of your estimates and use rates, and save it as **C:\LearningAndUsingGIS\FilesStudentWork\Exercise3-2<YourName>.xls**. Use four rows (with a header row at the top for column names and one row for each of the three pools). Include four columns (the first with pool name, two rows for the quantities tabulated from buffers, and the third for the finished use-rate ratio).

d. If Ream Pool were to be opened, predict the number of 5- to 17-year-olds who would sign up to get pool tags within 1 mile of the pool. Apply the average use rate from your three estimates in the previous step to make this prediction. Write down your steps and estimates for each step in your Excel spreadsheet.

e. Save your spreadsheet and map document.

3. **Estimate of McBride Pool Use by Residents of Munhall and West Mifflin.** The director of Pittsburgh's Citiparks Department asked us to estimate how many residents of West Mifflin and Munhall signed up to use McBride Pool. He was going to a meeting to persuade officials in those communities to contribute financially to McBride's operating costs. He reasoned that if many West Mifflin and Munhall residents used the pool, his case would be strengthened.

a. Open C:\LearningAndUsingGIS\Chapter3-1.mxd in ArcMap, and save it as **C:\LearningAndUsingGIS\FilesStudentWork\Exercise3-3<YourName>.mxd**, where you substitute your name or other identifier for <YourName>. Remove layers until you just have the following layers remaining and turned on: Pools, AlleghenyCounty, Pittsburgh, Municipalities, Pool Tag Holders' Residences, and Rivers.

b. Create a Word document called **C:\LearningAndUsingGIS\FilesStudentWork\ Exercise3-3<YourName>.doc**, where you substitute your name or other identifier for <YourName>.

c. Select features by location to determine the number of residents of West Mifflin and then Munhall who have pool tags for using Pittsburgh pools. Determine how many residents from each municipality intended to use McBride Pool or did not choose a pool for intended use. Assume those who did not select a pool for intended use would use McBride. Make the adjustment to the counts of pool tag holders discussed in this chapter for scaling up from the random sample to the full population of any age (multiply by 21). Write out all of your steps and calculations in your Word document. Copy the selection criterion for the attribute queries in your document.

d. For those residents who did not record a pool that they intended to use, include an estimate of how many likely used McBride. For example, if 90 percent of the persons who recorded a pool for intended use chose McBride, assume that 90 percent of those who did not record an intended pool also intended to use McBride. Write all steps and calculations in your Word document.

e. Click File and click Export Map to get a good map showing locations of sampled pool-tag-holders' residences in West Mifflin and Munhall and make it part of your document.

f. Save your Word and map documents.

4. **Reduction of Use Rate with Distance from a Pool.** We define the intended use rate of a swimming pool for a buffer area to be the number of pool tag holders within the buffer area divided by the population of 5- to 17-year-olds living within the same buffer area. Use rate should decline with distance from a pool.

a. Open C:\LearningAndUsingGIS\Chapter3-1.mxd in ArcMap, and save it as **C:\LearningAndUsingGIS\FilesStudentWork\Exercise3-4<YourName>.mxd**, where you substitute your name or other identifier for <YourName>. Remove layers until you just have the following layers remaining and turned on: AlleghenyCounty, Pittsburgh, Municipalities, Pool Tag Holders' Residences, and Rivers. Add and symbolize *poolsstateplane.shp* from C:\LearningAndUsingGIS\MapsPools. This version of pools is needed so that pool buffers will be circular, based on rectangular coordinates. The latitude/longitude coordinates of the original pool layer produces elliptical buffers, which are incorrect.

b. Create an Excel document called **C:\LearningAndUsingGIS\FilesStudentWork\ Exercise3-4<YourName>.xls**, where you substitute your name or other identifier for <YourName>.

c. Use a Multi Ring Buffer with 0.5-, 1-, and 2-mile radii for all open pools. Make the buffer unit be miles, and use the ALL value for dissolve option. Save your buffer map layer as **C:\LearningAndUsingGIS\FilesStudentWork\PoolBuffersExercise3-4.shp**. Make the adjustments to the counts of pool tag holders discussed in this chapter for scaling up from the random sample to the full population and for eliminating persons outside the 5- to 17-year-old interval (multiply the sampled number of pool tags by 9.87). Estimate the use rate for each of the three resultant buffers. Count pool tag holders and sum youths aged 5 to 17.

d. Click File and click Export Map to get a map of your buffers and pool-tag-holders' residences and make it part of your Excel document.

e. Save your Excel and Map documents.

References

ESRI Support Center, "FAQ: What Is the Format of the World File Used for Georeferencing Images?": Internet URL: http://support.esri.com/index.cfm?fa=knowledgebase.techArticles. articleShow&d=17489 (accessed February 25, 2005)

Koren, N. "Making Fine Prints in Your Digital Darkroom: Pixels, Images, and Files": Internet URL: http://www.normankoren.com/pixels_images.html (accessed February 25, 2005)

Wall, Roland. "Remote Sensing: The View From Above," The Academy of Natural Sciences: Internet URL: http://www.acnatsci.org/education/kye/te/kye52001.html (accessed February 27, 2005)

U.S. Census Bureau. TIGER Line/Files Technical Documentation: Internet URL: http://www. census.gov/geo/www/tiger/tigerua/ua2ktgr.pdf (accessed March 3, 2005)

CHAPTER **4**

DESIGNING MAPS

LEARNING OBJECTIVES

In this chapter, you will:

- Learn the principle of graphic hierarchy
- Determine how to use color
- Learn about map symbolization
- Learn to design maps for different audiences
- Symbolize maps using ArcGIS

Maybe orange with yellow polka dots...

INTRODUCTION

Thus far, you have been using ArcGIS map documents that we built for you. Now it is time for you to learn

how to design and build your own map documents.

When you design maps, you have a number of graphic elements at your disposal. **Graphic elements**

include the shapes, sizes, and colors of point markers; colors, widths, and styles of lines; and color fills and

patterns of polygons. Anybody can use a software package such as ArcGIS and easily choose colors and other graphic elements for maps. What will set you apart from the crowd are the graphic-design principles that you learn in this chapter, which will enable you to create professional-looking, effective maps.

Graphic hierarchy, an essential design principle, dictates that the most important aspects of a map composition (or any graphic arrangement) should be readily discernable. Color plays a central role in graphic hierarchy as well as in other aspects of graphic design, so we provide guidelines for using color. Another principle is to minimize ink: Make every pixel add value to the purpose of the graphic design, or leave pixels the equivalent of blanks—white, like paper, wherever possible.

There are two major audiences for maps: analysts and the general public. An analyst needs many graphic details to aid in the discovery of spatial patterns. Analysts will work hard, sorting through details, to find clues to the underlying behaviors of spatial phenomena. The general public is just the opposite: It needs to get your message clearly and without working to obtain it. Obviously, these two groups need different kinds of maps.

ArcGIS allows you to put graphic design principles to work. You can choose the color, size, widths, and shapes of graphic features based on the values of their attributes, using either unique values of codes or ranges of numeric variables. You also can label graphic features using attributes, such as names—and choose placement, fonts, and special effects. Finally, you can create a map layout with title, legend, scale, and other elements to produce maps that can be printed or inserted into other documents. All your selections are saved in the ArcGIS map document file.

MAP DESIGN

Cartography, the art of designing maps, is one of the oldest forms of graphic design. By **graphic design** we mean the choice of symbols, colors, text, patterns, and arrangements of graphic elements in visual displays whose primary function is to convey information (beauty is an important but secondary consideration). Mapmakers must represent a great quantity of data on relatively small sheets of paper, and over time this has led to the establishment of many principles, concepts, standards, and skills. Even if you do not consider yourself an artistic person, the knowledge that you will gain in this chapter will make you a successful map designer. The same ideas easily apply to other graphic applications, such as designing Web pages.

Graphic Hierarchy

As previously stated, one of the most useful graphic design principles is graphic hierarchy, the use of color and edge effects to draw attention to parts of a graphic display (MacEachren, 1994). For example, in the left panel of Figure 4-1, it is not clear what you should be studying—the lines, squares, or circles, whereas in the right panel, there is no doubt: The red circles almost jump off the page, while all else fades to context and background. The right panel uses graphic hierarchy.

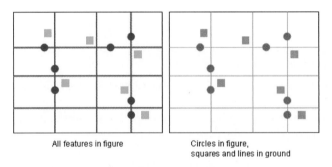

All features in figure   Circles in figure,
                                squares and lines in ground

FIGURE 4-1   Demonstration of graphic hierarchy

Here are guidelines for using graphic hierarchy:

- Assign bright colors, such as red, orange, yellow, green, or blue, to the most important graphic elements. Such graphic elements are called **figure**. These are the red circles in the right panel of Figure 4-1, which could mark the locations of some sort of incidents in a neighborhood, such as vandalism of parked cars.
- Assign drab colors to the graphic elements that provide orientation or context, especially shades of gray. The less important, the lighter the shade of gray you should use. Such graphic elements are called **ground**. These are the gray elements in the right panel of Figure 4-1, and they might represent streets and houses.
- Place a strong boundary, such as a black line, around polygons that are important to increase figure.
- Use a coarse, heavy crosshatch or pattern to make some polygons important, placing them in figure.

Minimizing Ink

A second important graphic principle, credited to Edward Tufte (2001), is simply this: *Minimize ink!* Make every pixel of a graphic design have a purpose. For example, as a guideline for map layouts in this chapter, we suggest not including a north arrow. Everyone already knows that the top of a map points north, so why waste ink on a north arrow? A north arrow is what Tufte calls **chart junk**, graphics with no payoff that clutter up a design.

Part of the minimize-ink principle is to minimize use of color. Use color only for truly important elements, as suggested by the graphic hierarchy principle. Really good designs, whether they are maps, Web pages, or PowerPoint slides, need a lot of white area and ground materials, and just a few valuable graphics and text in figure. For example, do not use color for areas such as states, counties, or zip codes unless you are color-coding them to represent a variable, such as population. Otherwise, leave them transparent with no color fill.

Color

Color is one of the most effective graphic elements for communication of spatial information, but it is easy to overuse. There is quite a bit to learn about color. First, you should learn these terms (Graphic Communication Program, 2005):

- **Hue** is the basic color. For example, green is the hue in both light green and dark green.
- **Color value** is the amount of white or black in the color. In relation to white paper or a white computer screen, white has low value and black has high value.
- **Monochromatic color scale** is a series of colors of the same hue with color value from low to high; for example, the value ranges from white to black on a monochromatic gray scale, from light to dark green in a green monochromatic scale, and so on.
- **Saturation** refers to a color scale that ranges from a pure hue to gray or black. The closer to black, the more saturated the color.

Map designers use monochromatic scales or saturated colors to represent the magnitude of numeric attributes, such as youth population, in color-coded polygon layers known as **choropleth maps**. Color value represents order in categories, ranging from low to high, and a key in a legend interprets the colors and magnitude ranges of the ordered categories. A **color ramp** is a particular arrangement of colors for this purpose. For example, see the map layout in Figure 4-2. Increasing value in gray scale of the color ramp corresponds to increasing intervals for the population of youths (age 5 to 17) per zip code area.

Figure 4-2 also has size-graduated point markers—an alternative to choropleth maps—for the population of Pittsburgh pool tag holders by zip code. The larger the circles, the higher the population. For many purposes, such point markers are easier to interpret visually than choropleth maps.

Some guidelines for using color scale on maps are as follows:

- Use monochromatic color scales to color-code most choropleth maps. An exception is where there is a natural middle-point of a scale, such as 0 for some quantities (profits and losses, increases and decreases). In such a case, use a

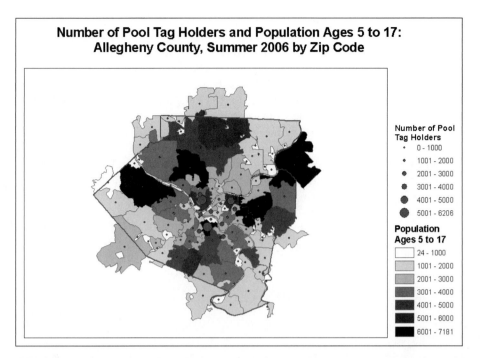

FIGURE 4-2   Choropleth map with size-graduated point markers

dichromatic color scale—two monochromatic scales joined together with a low color value in the center, with color value increasing toward both ends. For example, a dichromatic color scale might have blues on one end, reds on the other end, and white in the center. White in the center assumes that such areas should be denoted as ground—often the centers of scales are the least important for purposes at hand. It is helpful to the reader if you can keep the negative and positive numeric scales symmetric (that is, the same except for sign as the number decreases or increases). See Figure 4-3.

- The darker the color in a monochromatic scale, the more important the graphic feature. In Figure 4-2, the darker shades of gray are assigned to high intervals for youth population because high values are important for meeting demand for swimming pools.

- Use more light shades of a hue than dark shades in monochromatic scales. The human eye can better differentiate among light shades than dark shades.

- Do not use all of the colors of the **color spectrum**, as seen from a prism or in a rainbow, for color coding. Yellow, in the center of the scale, has the lowest color value, which is confusing because color value starts at a high value for red, decreases in moving to the right until attaining a minimum at yellow, and then increases through to the end at violet. Thus, the sequence of colors and color values in the spectrum cannot signify steadily increasing or decreasing quantities. See Figure 4-4. Instead of the entire color spectrum, use either half of the spectrum, the hot color (red) or cool color (blue) side.

- If you have relatively few points in a point layer, or if a user will normally be zoomed in to view parts of your map, use size (that is, size-graduated point markers) instead of color value to symbolize a numeric attribute. See Figure 4-2. The relatively small area of a point marker does not give color much room to send its message.

- If you need to compare two variables for the same set of polygons, a good option is to symbolize one variable—the less important one—as a choropleth map and the other as graduated point markers located at **centroids** of the polygons. The centroid of a polygon is its center point, on which it would balance if cut out of cardboard, for example. This was the design used in Figure 4-2.

- If you have a massive number of polygons to symbolize, it is much better to symbolize polygon centroid points—with a small, constant size and shape point marker and a color ramp—than to use choropleth maps. For example, we used the 24,283 blockcentroids in Allegheny County with a small, square point marker and a gray color ramp for the youth population in Chapter 2.

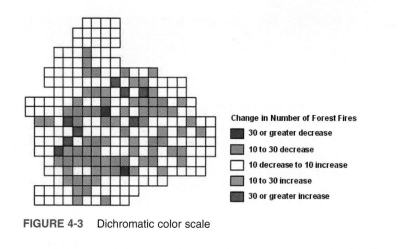

Change in Number of Forest Fires

- 30 or greater decrease
- 10 to 30 decrease
- 10 decrease to 10 increase
- 10 to 30 increase
- 30 or greater increase

FIGURE 4-3   Dichromatic color scale

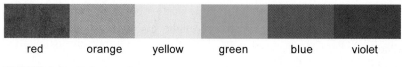

red   orange   yellow   green   blue   violet

FIGURE 4-4   Color spectrum

With the exception of choropleth maps, maps mostly use color to distinguish different kinds of graphic features from one another and to build graphic hierarchy. You already know to use bright colors for figure and dull, drab colors for ground. The **color wheel** is a device that provides further guidance in choosing colors, especially for differentiating features. It arranges colors in their order along the electromagnetic spectrum, but joins the two extremes, red and violet, on a circle. See Figure 4-5. Brewer (2005) is the ultimate book on choosing colors and designing maps. See Cindy Brewer's Web site, Color Brewer at *www.personal.psu.edu/cab38/ColorBrewer/ColorBrewer_intro.html*.

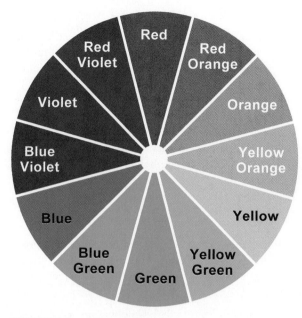

FIGURE 4-5 Color wheel

Guidelines for using the color wheel include the following:

- Use opposite colors—those directly across from one another—on the color wheel to differentiate graphic features. Opposites, such as yellow and violet or red and green, are known as **complementary colors**. When placed next to each other, complementary colors make each other look brighter, and produce a dramatic contrast.
- To differentiate graphic features, use three or four colors equally spaced around the wheel, such as red, blue, and yellow or red, blue violet, green, and yellow-orange. Use such choices for vector-based features (points, lines, and polygons) that have unique code values for classification and display. An example is point markers representing different types of recreation facilities with code values for swimming pool, tennis court, basketball court, and so on.
- Use adjacent colors for harmony, such as blue, blue green, and green or red, red-orange, and orange. These are known as **analogous colors**. They are less important in analytical mapping than complementary colors because we usually need to strongly differentiate features. Reference mapping makes more use of analogous colors.

Keep in mind that colors can have meaning through common experience, conventions, or cultural uses. Sometimes, you can put such knowledge to work on a map, tying symbols to well-known meanings. For example, we used blue for open swimming pools because water is blue. We used red for closed swimming pools because red signifies stop or danger. Color Wheel Pro (2005) has a fascinating list of colors and common uses and meanings.

Numeric Intervals

You often need to show variation in a numeric quantity, such as population, when designing an analytical map. To do so, you must break the numeric scale up into **numeric intervals**, which are nonoverlapping and exhaustive intervals covering the range of values for an attribute. Maps have many details, so keep the number of intervals as small as possible to help simplify the user's ability to absorb information. Research has shown that most people can hold seven items (plus or minus two) simultaneously in short-term memory. With maps, we reduce that a bit, to five sets of intervals (plus or minus two).

The number of pool-tag-holders residences per zip code area in Pittsburgh ranges from 0 to 6206. In this chapter's tutorial, you will use ArcGIS to symbolize this attribute using equal intervals: 0 to 1000, 1000 to 2000, 2000 to 3000, 3000 to 4000, 4000 to 5000, 5000 to 6000, and 6000 and greater (up to 6206). **Break values** are the higher values of intervals that break the total attribute range; namely, 1000, 2000, 3000, 4000, 5000, 6000, and 6206 for the preceding intervals.

Finally, you can select break values in several ways. Always use a mathematical progression or formula instead of picking arbitrary break values. You are less likely to be accused of manipulating a display to influence viewers' interpretation if break values have a logical progression. Some options follow.

- **Equal intervals**: As you can guess, equal intervals have constant widths; for example, 0 to 100, 100 to 200, 200 to 300, 300 and greater. Use equal width intervals in multiples of 2, 5, or 10. Equal intervals are easy to interpret.
- **Increasing interval widths**: Many populations in nature have **long-tailed distributions**, meaning that the data distributions are skewed and deviate from a bell-shaped curve by having one end elongated. The widths between intervals are increased to accommodate the elongated range of data. For example, many gymnasts have low-level skills, but a few have truly incredible skills. In such cases, it is necessary to stretch out the intervals for high numbers. One approach is to keep doubling the interval of each category; for example, intervals 0–5, 5–15, 15–35, and 35–75 have interval widths of 5, 10, 20, and 40. ArcGIS has a manual option for setting break values that allows any progression, including this one.
- **Exponential scale**: This is a popular method of increasing intervals. For example, use break values that are powers such as 2^n or 3^n, but generally you should start out with zero as an additional class if that value appears in your data. For example, 2^n for n = 0, 1, 2, 3, 4, ... yields the sequence 1, 2, 4, 8, 16, ... to which it is often relevant to add a separate class for 0. Hence, corresponding classes or intervals are: 0, 1–2, 3–4, 5–8, 9–16, and so forth for integer-value quantities. Corresponding break values are 0, 2, 4, 8, and 16.
- **Quantiles**: This refers to separating a distribution into equal sizes of attribute records per interval. For example, **quartiles**—a special case of the more general quantile with four categories—use break values that identify the 25 percent lowest values, the next 25 percent of values up to the **median** or middle point, the next 25 percent up from the median, and the top 25 percent. If there are five intervals, each has 20 percent of the distribution and so forth with other numbers of break values. Analysts use quantiles because they

provide information about the shape of the distribution. For example, if the top quartile has a relatively long interval width, the distribution is long-tailed. If the interval widths are all about the same size, the distribution is fairly uniform.

Point and Line Symbols

Points and lines are mathematical objects with no area or width. However, on a map or a graph, we use point markers with area and lines with width to make graphic elements visible. Location is the one aspect of point markers that we cannot vary as map designers. The other aspects are shape, size, color, and boundary. Here are some guidelines for varying these graphic elements for point markers:

- Use simple shapes. The simpler the shape, the easier it is to see spatial patterns. We suggest that the order of preference be circles, squares, triangles, stars, and then other solid shapes.
- Use point markers that have boundary lines and solid-color fill for important points. A boundary makes point markers more prominent (figure) and also allows use of some color fills that otherwise do not display well, such as yellow and light cyan.
- If you are using the size of point markers to symbolize a quantity, you have to exaggerate the differences in areas. Make the differences in sizes as large as possible. The human eye does not discriminate proportional changes in areas very well. Also, include a key in the map legend to convey magnitude.

Lines are easier to symbolize than points. Besides line features themselves, the boundaries of polygons are lines. Here are a few guidelines:

- For analytical maps, most lines are ground and should be black or shades of gray.
- Consider using dark gray instead of black for boundaries of most polygons. Dark gray makes the polygons prominent enough, but not so prominent that they compete for attention with more-important graphic elements in figure.
- Consider using dashed lines to signify less-important line features and solid lines for the important ones.

Map Layouts

A **map layout** includes all of the elements of a stand-alone map that you might use in a Microsoft PowerPoint presentation, a Microsoft Word document, or a bulletin board–sized paper map. Figure 4-2 is a map layout; it has a title, map, legend, and graphic scale. You will build this map layout later in this chapter. Here are the guidelines behind its design:

- Make the map the largest and most prominent element of the layout. Put a rectangular boundary around the map (called a **neat line** by cartographers) to help draw attention to it as the central element.
- Include a map title. The title needs to include information minimally answering the three questions *what, where, and when*. In Figure 4-2, the *what* is

"Number of Pool Tag Holders and Population Ages 5 to 17," the *where* is "Allegheny County," and the *when* is "Summer 2006." Center the title on the top of the map layout, and give it the largest font size on the map layout.

- Include a legend for symbols. Place it in the lower right of the layout. There is no need to label it *Legend*. Everyone will know what it is (this eliminates "chart junk").
- Include data sources. Maps that will be used by individuals not familiar with the mapped data need a note on the map layout stating data sources. Map users can then better judge the quality or nature of the data. However, maps for a client, such as Citiparks, might not need data sources listed because the intended map users already know that information. Thus, we did not include data sources in Figure 4-2. If, on the contrary, we determined that the map will be circulated widely, we would move the legend up an inch or so and add a note such as "Data Source: Pittsburgh Citiparks Department provided data on pools and pool-tag-holders residences."
- Ensure legibility. Make sure that the font sizes for labels on the map and legend are large enough to read.
- Include a graphic map scale. If your audience might not be familiar with the area shown, a graphic map scale is a valuable addition. Otherwise, you can omit a scale.
- Do not include a north arrow unless the top of your map is not north. Everyone knows that north is in the direction from the bottom to the top of a map. (Even cartographers in the Southern Hemisphere use north as the direction from the bottoms to the tops of their maps.)
- Occasionally include other components as needed. Sometimes, your map layout will need additional information, such as a data table listing, a frequency bar chart for the attribute of a choropleth map, or a photograph.

Map Audiences

Analytical maps have two primary audiences: analysts and the general public. The needs of these two audiences are different enough that mapmakers need to determine their audience before designing their maps. Analysts need maps with lots of details and layers so they can discover and analyze patterns. After an important pattern is discovered, the general public, or some part of it, needs a simple but dramatic map that strongly portrays the pattern.

Consider the difference between maps of crimes used by uniformed officers versus maps of crimes provided on Web sites for the public. One of the authors built a crime mapping system for the Pittsburgh Bureau of Police. At roll call and before going out on patrol, uniformed officers study maps of their patrol areas with crimes plotted over the last four weeks. Originally, there were seven crime types displayed on the same map—each with its own distinctive point marker—which made the maps quite cluttered from our perspective. Nevertheless, police officers wanted *more* crime types displayed. They wanted to study the entire crime picture—every crime point and type had meaning for them. By contrast, maps of crimes intended for the public, such as can be seen at the New Orleans Police Department's Web site *(www.cityofno.com/portal.aspx?portal=50)*, display only one crime type at a time.

Guidelines for analyst and general public audiences include the following:

- Use mostly simple shapes for point markers, but consider using mimetic point markers for general public maps. **Mimetic symbols** bear a resemblance to what they represent; for example, a mimetic railroad line on a map has cross lines for railroad ties, and the point marker for a state capital might look like a building with a flag on top.
- Use many break values for analytical choropleth maps, but use relatively few for general public maps.
- Use quantile numeric scales for analytical maps, but use equal interval scales for general public maps. Sometimes, you have to use an increasing interval scale for general public maps because of long-tailed distributions.
- Use a bright color for the monochromatic scale on a general public map.
- Build a stand-alone map layout for a general public map that includes map title, graphic scale, legend, and map.

ARCGIS FOR MAP DESIGN

In this tutorial, you will build a map document from scratch similar to those you have been using in previous chapters. In the process, you will use almost every kind of map design functionality that ArcMap has to offer.

Create a New Map Document

Before adding map layers to a new map document, it is a good idea to choose and set the data frame's coordinate system. You will use the State Plane projection system for *Chapter4-1.mxd*.

1. On your PC's desktop, click **Start**, click **All Programs**, click **ArcGIS**, and click **ArcMap**.
2. In the ArcMap window, with the **A new empty map** option button clicked, click **OK**.
3. In the table of contents, right-click **Layers**, and then click **Properties**.
4. In the resulting Data Frame Properties window, click the **General** tab, and change the name from Layers to **Pittsburgh Pools**.
5. Click the **Coordinate System** tab; click expander boxes for **Predefined**, **Projected Coordinate Systems, State Plane**, and **NAD 1983 (Feet)**; click **NAD 1983 StatePlane Pennsylvania South FIPS 3702 (Feet)**; and click **OK**. *(Although there is no evident change, you have just set the coordinate system to State Plane and feet for southern Pennsylvania. As you learned in Chapter 2, now ArcMap will project map layers added to the data frame on the fly to State Plane coordinates, if the map layers are in latitude and longitude coordinates or are in other coordinates but have spatial reference data.)*
6. Click the **Add Data** button ⬇; browse to your **C:\LearningAndUsingGIS\ MapsPools** folder; hold the **Ctrl** key down; click **blockcentroids.shp, pittsburgh.shp, pools.shp, railroads.shp, rivers.shp**, and **zipcodes.shp**; click **Add**; and click **OK to all**. See Figure 4-6. *(ArcMap adds all chosen layers to the*

map document with default symbols and random colors. Your colors will be different than those in Figure 4-6.)

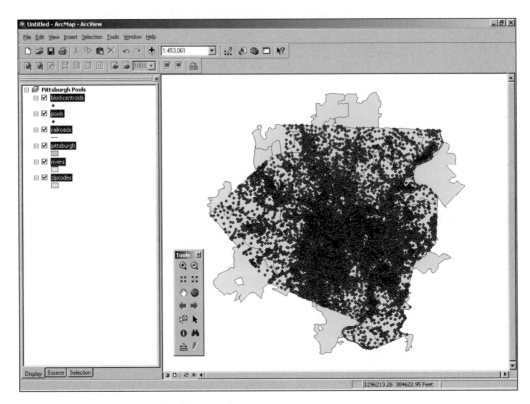

FIGURE 4-6   Initial layers added to map document

7. Click **File** and click **Save**.
8. In the resulting Save As window, browse to the **C:\LearningAndUsingGIS** folder, type **Chapter 4-1.mxd** in the File name field, and click **Save**.

PRACTICE 4-1

Add the following map layers from C:\LearningAndUsingGIS\MapsAlleghenyCounty\ that we downloaded from the Internet (you will learn how to download such files in Chapter 5): *tgr42003ccd00.shp* (municipalities), *tgr42003cty00.shp* (Allegheny County boundary), and *tgr42003lkA.shp* (streets). See Figure 4-7. The end result is a jumble of symbols.

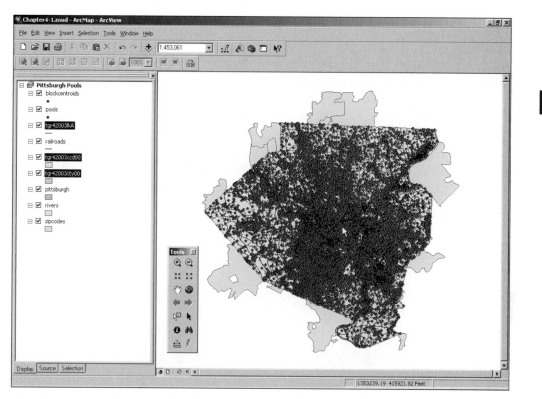

FIGURE 4-7   More layers added to map document

Apply Line Symbols and Properties

Mostly, we use line features for reference and context in analytical maps. Thus, such features generally should have background colors. If, however, you are working on transportation problems or other areas that focus on line features, you should use figure colors for lines.

1. Turn off all layers except **tgr42003lkA**.
2. On the Standard toolbar, type **1:24,000** in the scale field, and press the **Enter** key. (*The map zooms in to central Pittsburgh at the common scale of 1:24,000. In the following steps, you will set labels to turn on at this scale or larger.*)
3. Right-click **tgr42003lkA**, and then click **Properties**.
4. In the resulting properties window, click the **General** tab, and replace the Layer name tgr42003lkA with **Streets**.
5. Click the **Symbology** tab and click the large **Symbol** button.
6. In the resulting Symbol Selector window, click the **Color list** button in the Options panel, click the **Gray 50%** color chip (*1st column, 6th row*), and click **OK**.
7. Click the **Fields** tab and click off the following fields: **FID, Shape, TLID, FNODE, TNODE,** and **LENGTH**. (*After this step, the turned off fields will not*

display when using the Identify tool or when viewing this layer's attribute table.)

8. Click the **Labels** tab, click the **Label features in this layer** check box, click the **Color list** button in the Text Symbol panel, click the **Gray 50%** color chip, and click the **Scale Range** button.

9. In the resulting Scale Range window, click the **Don't show labels when zoomed** option button, type **24000** in the Out beyond field, click **OK**, click **Apply**, and click **OK**. See Figure 4-8.

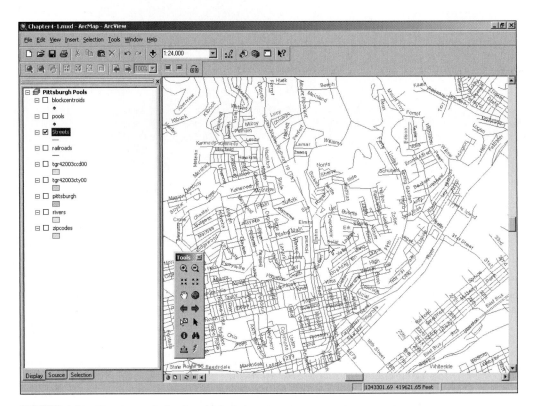

FIGURE 4-8   Streets symbolized and labeled

Turn on and symbolize and set properties for railroads: Capitalize the *R* in railroads, turn off all fields except FENAME and CFCC, use the railroads line symbol and Nubuck Tan color (third column, ninth row), label railroads with Nubuck Tan font color, and use the same label scale range as Streets. *Note: CFCC is a code used by the Census Bureau to classify line features, including streets and railroads. You can do an Internet search on the term to find a table of code values and descriptions.*

Apply Point Symbols and Properties

Symbolizing points is similar to symbolizing lines. Here, though, you will start using some more advanced ArcMap properties.

1. Turn on **pools**, right-click **pools**, and click **Zoom to Layer**.
2. Right-click **pools** and click **Properties**.
3. Set properties as follows: Capitalize **pools**, use a **Square 2** point marker symbol of size **8** and **Cretean blue** color *(10th column, third row)*, and turn off the **FID** and **Shape** fields. *(Leave the Properties window open. Next, you will build a definition query to display only open pools.)*
4. In the Properties window, click the **Definition Query** tab, click the **Query Builder** button, double-click "**OPEN**", click the = button, click the **Get Unique Values** button, double-click the resulting **1**, click **OK**, and then click **Apply**. *(Now, the map displays only the 16 open pools. If you were to open the Pools attribute table, you would see that now it too has only the open pools.)*
5. In the Properties window, click the **Labels** tab, click the **Label features in this layer** check box, click the **Color list** button in the Text Symbol panel, click the **Ultra Blue** color chip *(10th column, fifth row)*, and then click the **Placement Properties** button.
6. In the resulting Placement Properties window, click the **Change Location** button, scroll as necessary in the Initial point placement window, click **Top Only, Prefer Center**, click **OK**, click **OK** again, and then click **Apply**. *(Although the pools are labeled, the labels get lost in the Streets layer. To remedy this problem, you will add a white halo mask around the pool labels to make them stand out.)*
7. In the Text Symbol panel of the Labels tab, click the **Symbol** button; in the resulting Symbol Selector window, click the **Properties** button; then, in the resulting Editor window, click the **Mask** tab, click the **Halo** option button, type **1.5** for the size, click **OK**, click **OK** again, click **Apply**, and click **OK**. See Figure 4-9. *(That makes it a lot easier to see the pool labels. Note: There is an option to change the halo color.)*

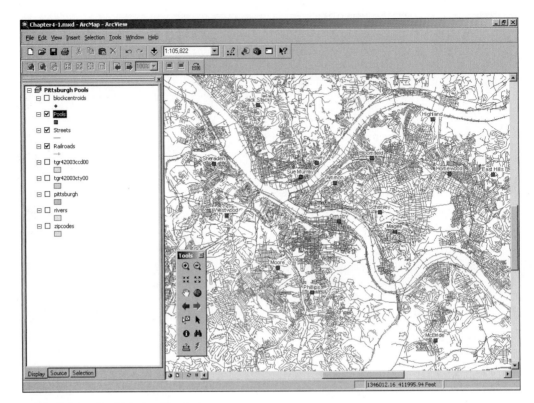

FIGURE 4-9   Pool labels with a halo

PRACTICE 4-3

Add schools from your C:\LearningAndUsingGIS\MapsPools\ folder to your map document. Use a pale green, size 7 Circle, 2 point marker. The pale green and smaller size will place schools more in the background, so as to not detract from Pools. Do not label the schools. See Figure 4-10.

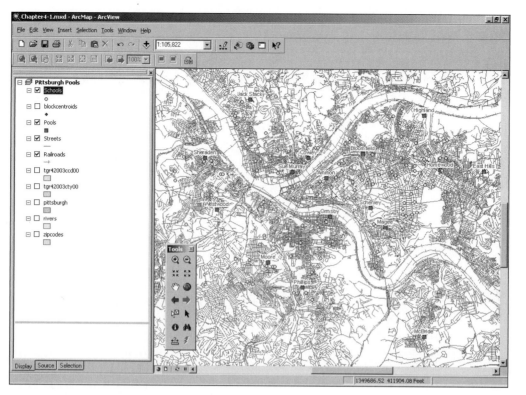

FIGURE 4-10   Schools symbolized

Create Map Hyperlinks

As in Web site graphics, you can add hyperlinks to map features. Next, you will add a photo of Cowley Pool through a map hyperlink. When you click Cowley Pool on the map, its picture will pop up.

1.   On the Tools toolbar, click the **Identify** tool 🛈.
2.   In the resulting Identify Results window, click the list arrow in the **Layers** field, click **Pools**, and click **Cowley Pool** on the map. See Figure 4-11. *(The right-click location is for Step 3, next.)*
3.   In the Identify Results window, right-click **Cowley** and click **Add Hyperlink**.
4.   In the resulting Add Hyperlink window, with the Link to a Document option button clicked, click the **browse** button under that option button, browse to your **C:\LearningAndUsingGIS\Data** folder, double-click **CowleyPool.jpg**, click **OK**, and close the **Identify Results** window.
5.   On the Tools toolbar, click the **Hyperlink** tool ⚡ *(the point marker for Cowley Pool gets a blue solid center indicating that it has a hyperlink),* hover your cursor over **Cowley Pool** until it turns dark in color and the path to the pool picture is displayed *(move your cursor around a bit if necessary),* and click **Cowley Pool.** *(If you have an application program on your computer associated with the .jpg extension, the application will open*

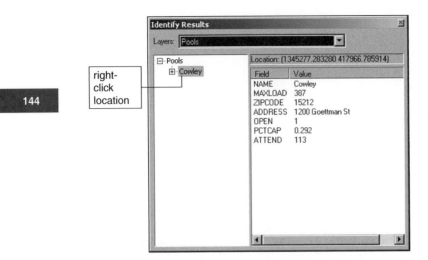

right-click location

FIGURE 4-11   Identify Results for Cowley Pool

with Cowley picture. If the image will not display and you have permissions to change settings on your computer, you can associate an application program with the .jpg extension. If necessary, switch to the Windows Classic desktop theme: Click Start, click Control Panel, double-click Display, click the Themes tab, click the list arrow in the Theme field, and then click Windows Classic. Click Start; click Control Panel; double-click Folder Options; click the File Types tab; scroll down in the extension panel to JPG; click the Change button; click Windows Picture and Fax Viewer (preferably), Paint, or some other image displaying application program; click OK; and then click Close. If you use Windows Picture and Fax Viewer, resize the image window approximately to that in Figure 4-12 and afterward the window will open to that size and position.)

6.   Close the **image** window.

PRACTICE 4-4

Add a hyperlink for Sheraden pool and C:\LearningAndUsingGIS\Data\
SheradenPool.jpg.

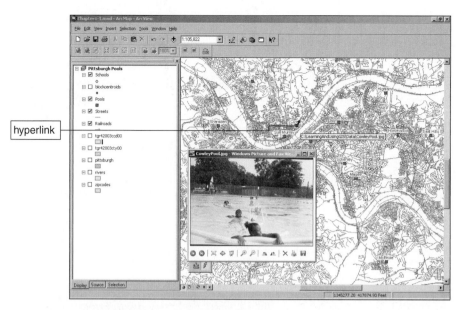

hyperlink

FIGURE 4-12   Hyperlinked image for Cowley Pool

Use Unique Symbols

If an attribute has a fixed set of values for classification, you can use those values to symbolize features. For example, you will identify open and closed schools with different symbols. Also, in the practice exercise for the following steps, you will use symbols to identify schools by type: Public, Catholic, and Private.

1. Right-click **Pools** and click **Properties**.
2. In the resulting Properties window, click the **Definition Query** tab, select **"OPEN" = 1** with your mouse (if not already selected), press the **Delete** key, and click **Apply**. *(All 32 pools are back on the map now, as well as in the Pools attribute table.)*
3. Click the **Symbology** tab, and in the Show panel, click **Categories**. *(ArcMap automatically selects the Unique values option under Categories.)*
4. Click the list arrow in the **Value Field**, click **OPEN**, click the **Add All Values** button, and click off the **<all other values>** check box. See Figure 4-13.
5. Double-click the symbol for the 0 value. See Figure 4-13.
6. In the resulting Symbol Selector window, make the following selections: **Square 2** point marker, **Mars Red** color *(second column, third row)*, and size **8**; and click **OK**.
7. Double-click the symbol for the **1** value and make the following selections: **Square 2** point marker, **Cretean Blue** color *(10th column, third row)*, and size **8**; and click **OK**. See Figure 4-14.
8. Click the **0** Label value (see Figure 4-14), and type **Closed**.
9. Click the **1** Label value (see Figure 4-14), and type **Open**.

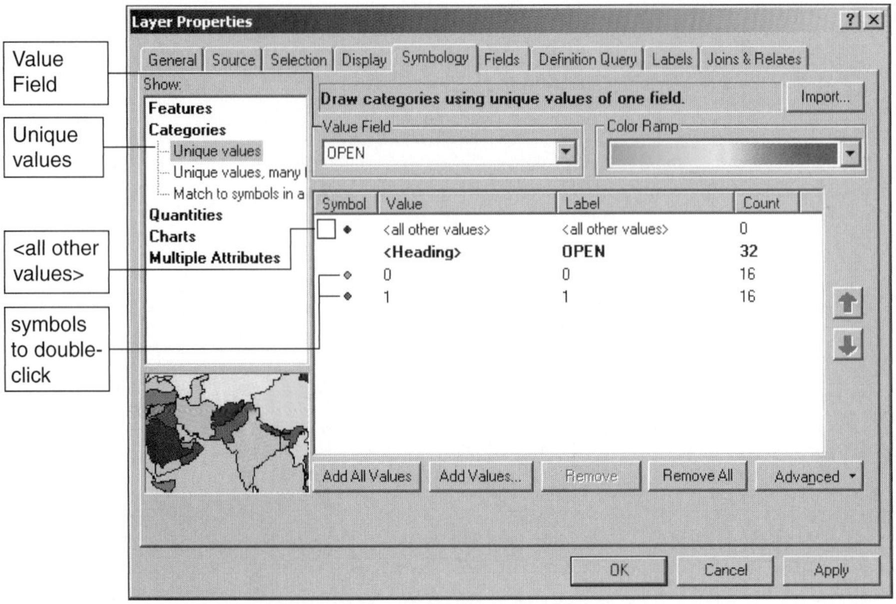

FIGURE 4-13 Symbology settings for Pools

10. Click **Apply** and click **OK**. See Figure 4-15. (*That nicely distinguishes open and closed pools.*)

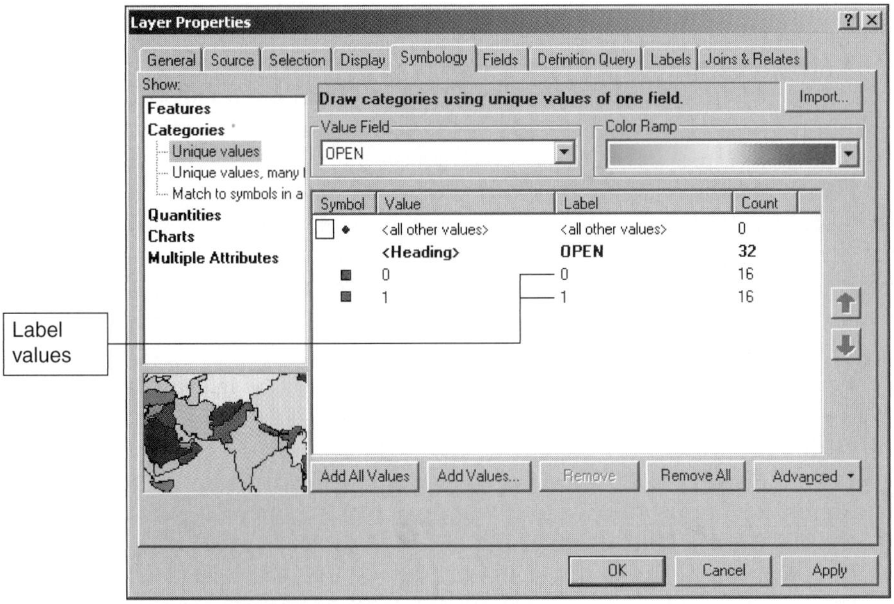

FIGURE 4-14 More symbology settings for Pools

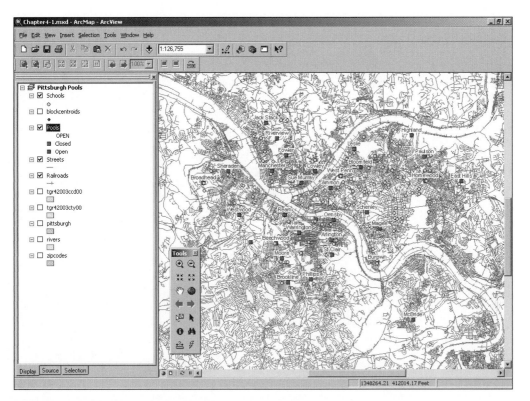

FIGURE 4-15   Pools with unique symbols

PRACTICE 4-5

Symbolize Schools with unique values, based on the DISTRICT attribute. Change labels so that City of Pittsburg [*sic*] becomes Public, Pittsburgh Dioces [*sic*] becomes Catholic, and Private School becomes Private. Use a size 7 Circle, 2 point marker, and pick three complementary colors from the second row of the color chip array. Turn off Pools for now. See Figure 4-16.

Designing Maps

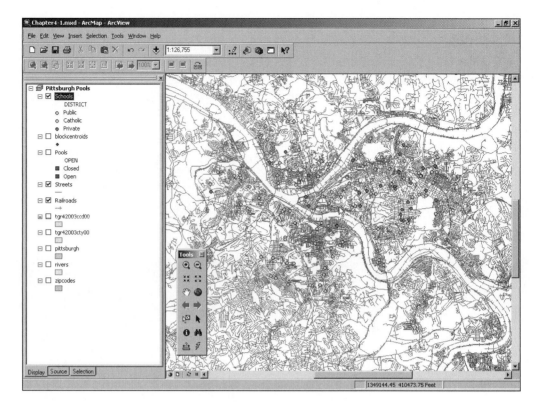

FIGURE 4-16 Schools with unique symbols

Create Labels Based on Class

If you have symbolized a map layer using classes—such as open and closed pools—you can label features in each class differently. Let's do that for pools.

1. Right-click **Pools** and click **Properties**.
2. In the Properties window, click the **Labels** tab, if not already selected.
3. Click the **Method** field list arrow, and click **Define classes of features and label each class differently**.
4. Click the **Get Symbol Classes** button. (*This step imports the open and closed classes from the map.*)
5. With the Closed class selected in the Class field, click the **Color fill** button, and click the **Tuscan Red** paint chip (*second column, fifth row*).
6. Click the **Class** field list arrow, and click **Open**. (*See that the font color for this class has the blue color that you selected earlier. This still works for this class.*)
7. Click **Apply** and click **OK**. See Figure 4-17.

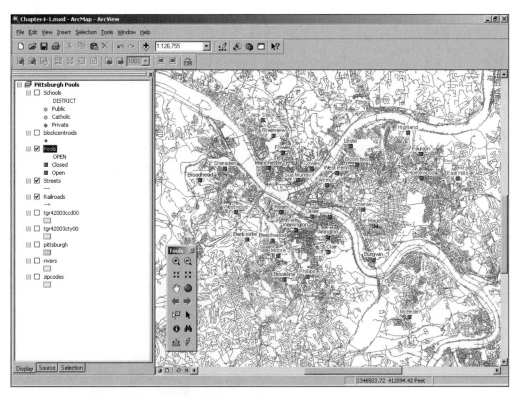

FIGURE 4-17 Pools with labeling by classes

Use Size-Graduated Point Markers

If an attribute is numeric, you can use it to change the size of point markers of the same shape. For example, you will use the MAXLOAD attribute for Pools to create a symbol to distinguish the capacity of pools. The trick here is to add a second copy of the Pools map and make its symbols larger than those of the current pool layer. Then, you can display both point markers for pools at the same time, with the benefit of having two attributes visible.

1. Turn off **Schools** and turn on **Pools**.
2. In the table of contents, right-click **Pools**, click **Copy**, then on the main menu click **Edit** and click **Paste**.
3. In the table of contents, drag the new copy of the **Pools** layer below the existing one.
4. Right-click the new copy of **Pools** and click **Properties**, then click the **General** tab, and change the name to **Pool Capacity (Persons)**.
5. In the Properties window, click the **Symbology** tab, click **Quantities** in the Show panel, and click **Graduated symbols** in the resulting Quantities options.
6. Click the **Field Values** field list arrow, and click **MAXLOAD**. (*ArcMap automatically chooses a numeric scale with five categories using a clustering method called Natural Breaks (Jenks)*).

7. Click the **Classify** button, then in the Classification window, click the **Method** field list arrow, click **Quantile**, and click **OK**.

8. In the Layer Properties window, change the symbol sizes "from **4** to **18**" to "from **10** to **22**". (*The other Pools layer has size 8 point markers. We want the new Pools layer to have larger point markers, so that each pool's capacity will be visible—with both Pool layers on.*)

9. Click the **Template** button, click the **Color list** button, click **Olivenite Green** (*fifth column, fifth row*) as the color, and then click **OK**.

10. Click the **Display** tab, type **50** in the Transparent field, click **Apply**, and then click **OK**. See Figure 4-18. (*The end result is very effective. You can now see the large versus small pools. Because you used transparent point markers, you can still see streets under the new point markers. Notice that many of the closed pools have small capacity, especially on the south side of Pittsburgh. This is something that you might expect, suggesting efficiency as a consideration in pool closings.*)

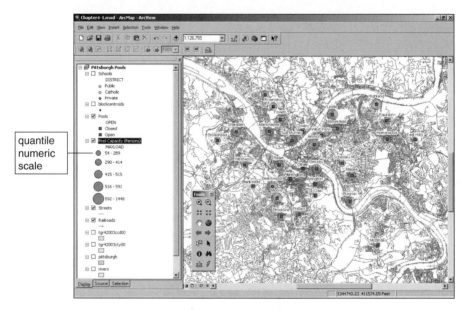

quantile numeric scale

FIGURE 4-18   Pools with size-graduated point markers

Build a Custom Numeric Scale

The quantile numeric scale for Pool Capacity is informative if you study it carefully. You will make it a bit easier to read by using a modified uniform scale, starting at 300 and with an interval width of 100.

1. Right-click **Pool Capacity** and click **Properties**.

2. In the Layer Properties window, click the **Symbology** tab and click the **Classify** button.

3. In the Classification window, click the **591** value in the Break Values panel,

type **600**, and press the **Enter** key. (*Generally, it is a good idea to work backward, from high to low values, when modifying break values because a new value that you enter might not exceed the next highest value. If you start on the low end and work up, you will likely violate this rule.*)

4. Do the same for **515**, replacing it with **500**; for **414**, replace it with **400**; and for **289**, replace it with **300**. See Figure 4-19.

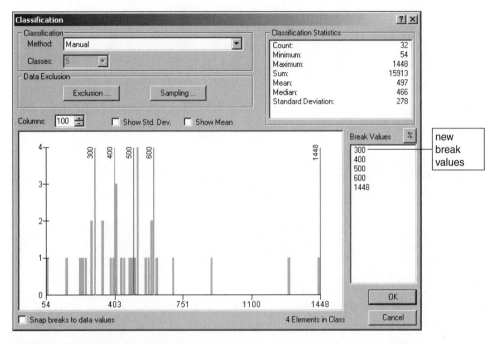

FIGURE 4-19 Entering break values

5. Click **OK**, click **Apply**, and then click **OK**. See Figure 4-20.

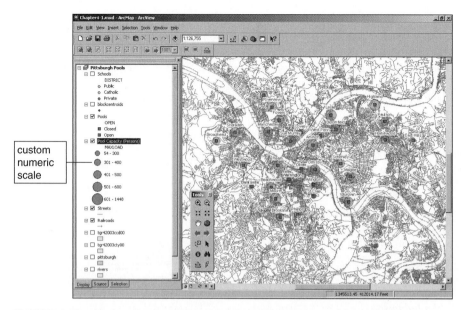

custom
numeric
scale

FIGURE 4-20   Pools with size-graduated point markers and custom numeric scale

PRACTICE 4-6

In this exercise, you will symbolize polygon boundaries that are only for spatial context. Instructions follow:

- *pittsburgh*: Capitalize its name, and make its boundary black with width 1.5.
- *rivers*: Capitalize its name, and give it a light blue color fill.
- *tgr42003cty00*: Change its name to *County*, and make its boundary black with width 1.5.
- *tgr42003ccd00*: Change its name to *Municipalities*, make its boundary a medium gray, and label it with a size 7, medium gray font.

Turn these layers on.

Create a Choropleth Map

In the next set of tasks, you symbolize polygons to convey numeric information. In particular, the Zip Codes map layer has two interesting attributes: POP5TO17, which is the population age 5 to 17 years, and NUMTAGS, which is the number of pool tag holders. You will plot the age distribution in Allegheny County as a choropleth map and then plot the distribution of pool tag holders using size-graduated point markers. ArcMap creates the polygon centroids on the fly for the point markers.

1. Turn off **Pools**, **Pool Capacity**, **Railroads**, and **Municipalities**, and turn on **zipcodes**.
2. Right-click **zipcodes** and click **Properties**.

3. In the Properties window, click the **General** tab, and change the name of the layer to **Zip Codes**.
4. Click the **Symbology** tab, and click **Quantities** in the Show panel. (*ArcMap automatically selects Graduated colors as the Quantities option, which is what you need.*)
5. Click the **Fields Value** field list arrow, and click **POP5TO17**.

6. Click the **Classify** button, then in the Classification window, click the **Classification method** field list arrow, click **Quantile**, and type **7** in the Classes field. (*Seven is about the maximum number of classes to use for most maps. After studying the break values, it looks like equal intervals of width 1000 would work well.*)
7. In the Break Values panel, replace the following values as instructed: **4549** with **6000**, **2956** with **5000**, **2154** with **4000**, **1474** with **3000**, **815** with **2000**, and **150** with **1000**.
8. Click **OK**.
9. If not yet selected, use the **gray color ramp**, with light grays on the left, and click **OK**. See Figure 4-21, where we have turned off Streets and clicked the Full Extent button. (*We chose the gray color ramp because we want to put population in the background. Next, you will put pool tag holder population by zip code more in figure because it is the subject of interest. Note: You can see that zip codes are "crazy quilt" patterns, spilling over the county's boundary and having unusual shapes. Quite a few zip codes in Pittsburgh have low youth populations.*)

PRACTICE 4-7

Turn off the current Zip Codes layer. Use the Add Data button on the Standard toolbar to add another copy of the Zip Codes layer to your map document. Design a numeric scale for POP5TO17 that has a scale that doubles with each larger class; for example, 500, 1000, 2000, 4000, and 7181. When finished, move your new Zip Codes layer to the bottom of the table of contents and turn it off. Turn on your original Zip Codes layer.

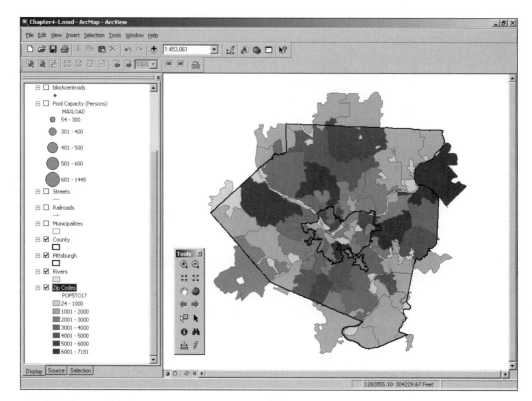

FIGURE 4-21 Choropleth map for zip codes

Use Size-Graduated Point Markers for Polygon Centroids

Just as you were able to display two variables for pools on the same map—whether a pool is open and pool capacity—you can display two variables for the same polygons: one using a choropleth map and the other using size-graduated point markers for polygon centroids.

1. In the table of contents, right-click **Zip Codes**, click **Copy**, then on the main menu click **Edit** and click **Paste**, and then drag the new copy of the **Zip Codes** layer just above the existing one.

2. Right-click the new copy of **Zip Codes** and click **Properties**, then click the **General** tab, and change the name to **Pool Tag Holder Population**.

3. Click the **Symbology** tab, click **Graduated symbols** in the Show panel, click the **Fields Value** field list arrow, click **NUMTAGS**, and then click the **Classify** button.

4. In the Classification window, click the **Classification method** field list arrow, and click **Equal Interval**. (*It is tricky to design a numeric scale for this attribute because most zip codes outside of Pittsburgh have very low values or zero. We really need a good scale for inside of Pittsburgh, where the high and interesting values lie. Let's use break values of 1000 through 5000 in intervals of 1000, but let's also have a separate class for the value "0".*)

5. In the Break Values panel for 5319 type **5000**, for 4433 type **4000**, for 3546 type **3000**, for 2660 type **2000**, for 1773 type **1000**, for 887 type **0**, and click **OK**.

6. Click the **Background** button; then, in the Symbol Selector window, click the **hollow fill** icon, and click **OK**.

7. Click the **Template** button; then, in the Symbol Selector window, click the **Color list** button, click the **Cretean Blue** chip *(10th column, third row)*, and click **OK**.

8. Change the Symbol Size *from* value to **2** and leave the *to* value at 18. (*Next, you will suppress the 0 class so that it does not get a visible point marker.*)

9. Double-click the symbol in the first row, for **0**; then, in the Symbol Selector window, click the **Color list** button, and click **No Color**.

10. Click the **Properties** button, click the **Color list** button, click **No Color**, click **OK**, and then click **OK** again.

11. Click the Label **0** in the first row, press the **Delete** key, click **Apply**, and click **OK**. See Figure 4-22. (*That eliminates the zero polygons from getting a point marker. Try right-clicking Pittsburgh and zooming to that layer to better study patterns. It appears that where there are more youths, there are more pool tag holders and vice versa. This indicates that the open pools generally meet needs. More details are needed on the performance of open pools, but this is a good result so far.*)

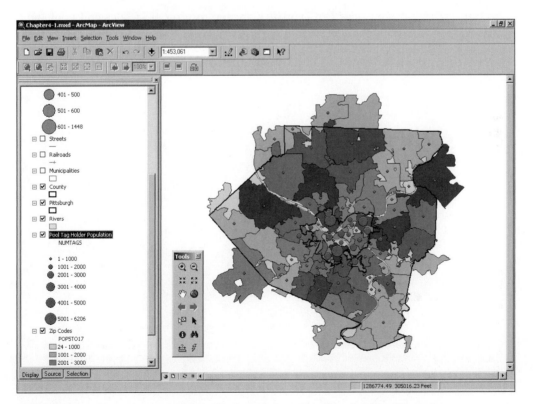

FIGURE 4-22   Zip codes symbolized with choropleth map and graduated point markers

Designing Maps

Create a Dot Density Map for Polygons

A third way to symbolize polygons is a dot density map. ArcMap places dots randomly within each polygon in proportion to the attribute being plotted. You can control the number of units each dot represents; for example, 5 persons per dot for a population attribute.

156

1. On the Tools toolbar, click the **Full Extent** button ⬤.
2. In the table of contents, turn off **Zip Codes** and **Pool Tag Holder Population**.
3. Right-click **Zip Codes**, click **Copy**, then on the main menu click **Edit** and click **Paste**, and then drag the new copy of the **Zip Codes** layer to the bottom of the table of contents.
4. Turn on the new copy of **Zip Codes**, right-click it, and click **Properties**.
5. Click the **General** tab, and change the Name to **Zip Codes Dot Density Map**.
6. Click the **Symbology** tab, and click **Dot Density** under Quantities in the Show panel.
7. In the Field Selection panel, click **POP5TO17** and click the **>** button.
8. Double-click the resulting small, green, **circular symbol**, then click the **Color list** button, click **Mars Red** *(second column, third row)*, and click **OK**.
9. In the Value Field, type **50** and click **OK**. See Figure 4-23. *(Thus, each dot represents 50 youths. Compare the resulting map to the choropleth map for the same attribute by clicking each one on and off. The dot density map has the advantage of conveying information about area density—how spread out a population is.)*
10. Turn off **Zip Codes Dot Density** map, and turn on **Zip Codes** and **Pool Tag Holder Population**.

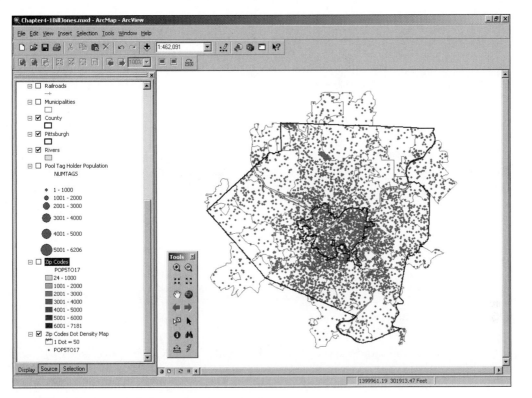

FIGURE 4-23 Zip codes symbolized with a dot density map

ARCGIS FOR MAP LAYOUTS

One use of a GIS is interactive, on your computer. You can make changes to your map, make queries as in Chapter 3, and so forth. Another use is to produce maps as outputs for display, reports, and presentations. In this section, you will learn how to use ArcMap's sophisticated but easy tools to produce map layouts for this latter purpose.

Set Up a Map Layout

Let's start by making a simple layout for your current map document that has zip code information. If you want to use your map in a PowerPoint presentation, a standard 8.5 x 11-inch paper size and landscape orientation is a good choice for your layout: Your map will fill an entire slide. This size also works well in Word documents, using about a half page when resized in the Word document.

1. On the Tools toolbar, click the **Full Extent** button .
2. On the main menu, click **View** and click **Layout View**. See Figure 4-24.
3. Right-click anywhere in the **white area** of the main window panel (*but not in the map frame, see Figure 4-24*), and click **Page and Print Setup**.
4. In the Page and Print Setup window, click the **Name** field list arrow, and click a printer that you can use with your computer.

Designing Maps

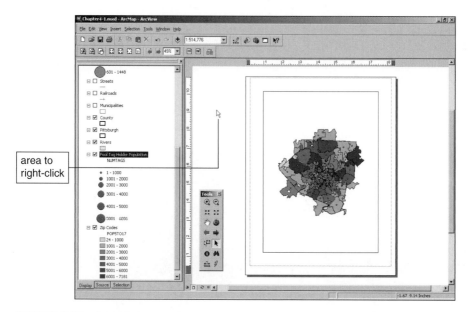

area to right-click

FIGURE 4-24   Layout view

5. Click the **Landscape** option button, and click **OK**. (*The page is set up as needed, but now the map frame needs to be resized.*)
6. Click the map to activate its frame, and then drag the **top middle grab handle** down to bring the frame inside the map layout. See Figure 4-25. (*Don't worry about the exact size and placement of the map because you will change these settings in the following steps. Next, you will set up some guide lines for aligning objects—such as the map, title, legend, and so on. Objects, such as the map and legend, will snap to the guides, making alignment easy.*)
7. Click the **horizontal ruler** (*see Figure 4-25*) at the **0.5"**, **1.0"**, **10"**, and **10.5"** points to create four vertical guide lines. See Figure 4-26. (*If you need to delete a guide, right-click the line's arrowhead on the ruler, and click Clear Guide.*)
8. Click the vertical ruler at the **0.5"**, **1.0"**, **7.5"**, and **8"** points to create four horizontal guides.

horizontal ruler

grab handle to drag

vertical ruler

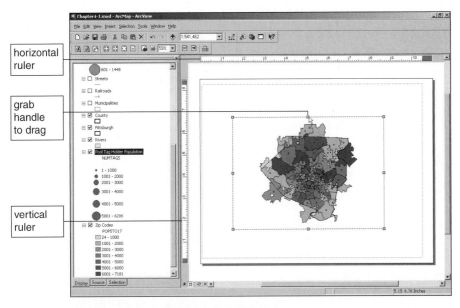

FIGURE 4-25 Layout with landscape page setup

guides

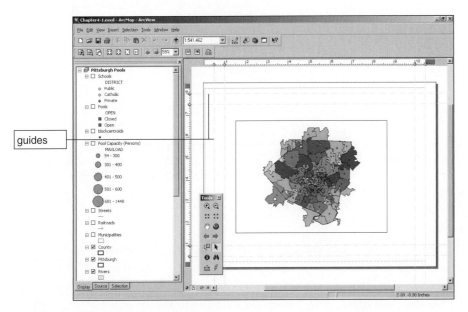

FIGURE 4-26 Layout guides

Adjust Map Position and Create a Title

ArcMap does most of the work in creating map elements for you. You just need to choose a few options and then insert and position the results on your map layout. Let's get started by resizing and positioning the map and inserting a map title.

1. Right-click the **map**, click **Properties**, and click the **Size and Position** tab.
2. Click the **Preserve Aspect Ratio** button *(to keep map proportions correct)*, type **8** for the width, click **OK**, and then click **OK** again.
3. Drag the map up to snap its upper-left corner to the intersection of 0.5" vertical and 7.5" horizontal guides.
4. On the main menu, click **Insert** and click **Title**.
5. Drag the title object so that it is centered in the layout and snaps on the top to the 8" horizontal guide.
6. Double-click the **title object**; then, in the Properties window, delete the text **Chapter4-1**, type **Youth Population and Pool Users in Allegheny County**, click the **Change Symbol** button, click the **bold** button, click **OK**, and then click **OK** again. See Figure 4-27.

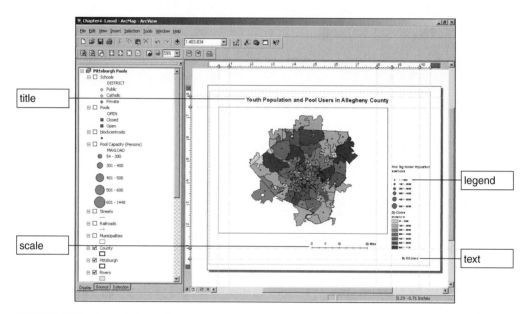

FIGURE 4-27 Layout elements

Create a Map Legend

Although it's possible to customize the map legend, you will use most of the default settings in the Map Legend Wizard.

1. Create a vertical guide at **8.7"**.
2. On the main menu, click **Insert** and click **Legend**.
3. In the Legend Wizard window and its Legend Items panel, click **County**, click the second button from the bottom with the single **<** sign, and do the same for **Pittsburgh** and **Rivers**. *(There is no need to have a legend for the county outline, nor for Pittsburgh and Rivers.)*
4. Click **Next** and delete the **Legend** title, click **Next** three times, and click **Finish**.

5. Drag the resulting legend so that its lower-right corner is at the intersection of the **1**" horizontal and **10.5**" vertical guides.
6. Use the top-left grab handle of the legend object to resize it so that its left side snaps to the **8.7**" guide. See Figure 4-27.

Create a Map Graphic Scale

Next, you will insert a graphic scale.

1. Create a vertical guide at **8**".
2. On the main menu, click **Insert** and click **Scale Bar**.
3. In the Scale Bar Selector window, click **Scale Line 2**.
4. Click the **Properties** button.
5. In the **Scale Bar** window, click the **Division Units** field list arrow, click **Miles**, click **OK**, and then click **OK** again.
6. Drag the resulting scale so that it is on the **1**" horizontal guide and has its right side on the **8**" vertical guide. See Figure 4-27.

PRACTICE 4-8

Use Insert and Text to create a text box to include your name as map author. See Figure 4-27, where we used the fictitious name, Bill Jones, for this purpose.

Export the Map Layout

Let's put the map layout to use. You will export a JPG image of the layout and then insert it into PowerPoint and Word documents.

1. Click **File** and click **Save**.
2. Click **File** and click **Export Map**.
3. In the resulting Export Map window, browse to your **C:\LearningAndUsingGIS\ FilesStudentWork** folder, change the filename to **ZipCodeMap.jpg**, and click **Save**.
4. Save your map document, and close ArcMap.

Use a Map Layout in PowerPoint

Next, you will import your map layout image into PowerPoint.

1. Open **PowerPoint**.
2. On the main menu, click **Format**, click **Slide Layout**, scroll down in the **Slide Layout** panel, and then click the **Blank** layout icon.
3. On the main menu, click **Insert**, click **Picture**, and click **From File**.
4. In the Insert Picture window, browse to your **C:\LearningAndUsingGIS\ FilesStudentWork** folder, and double-click **ZipCodeMap.jpg**.
5. On the main menu, click **View**, click **Zoom**, click the **33%** option button, click **OK**, resize the image so that it just fills the slide, and go through the zoom sequence again but use the **Fit** option button.

6. Save your PowerPoint presentation as **ZipCodeMap.ppt** in your **C:\LearningAndUsingGIS\FilesStudentWork** folder. See Figure 4-28. *(You now have a very professional looking map in a slide presentation.)*

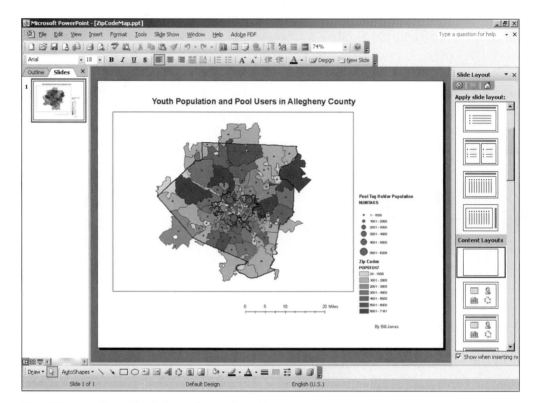

FIGURE 4-28 PowerPoint slide with map layout image

7. Close PowerPoint.

Use a Map Layout in Word

You'll do the same as in the preceding exercise, but now in Word.

1. Open **Word**.
2. Click **View** and click **Print Layout**.
3. Hold your **Enter** key down to open a page or two of lines and then go back to the top of your document. *(It is always a good idea to have many lines open when inserting images in Word.)*
4. Type the following text at the top: **Below is a map of Allegheny County showing youth population and number of Pittsburgh pool tag holders by zip code for a recent summer.**
5. On the main menu, click **View**, click **Toolbars**, and click **Drawing**.

6. On the Drawing toolbar (*bottom of document window*), click the **Text Box** tool 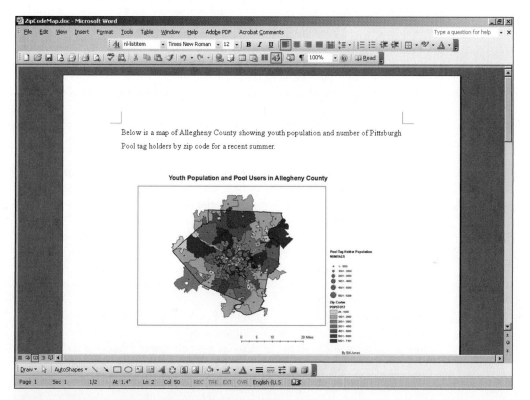, and drag a rectangle about half the page in size, within margins and below your text.

7. With the cursor inside the text box, on the main menu click **Insert**, **Picture**, **From File**, browse to your **C:\LearningAndUsingGIS\FilesStudentWork** folder, and double-click **ZipCodeMap.jpg**.

8. With your cursor still in the text box, on the Drawing toolbar click the **Line Color** tool, and click **No Line**. (*Now you have a very professional map in a Word document.*)

9. Save your Word document as **ZipCodeMap.doc** in your **C:\LearningAndUsingGIS\FilesStudentWork** folder. See Figure 4-29.

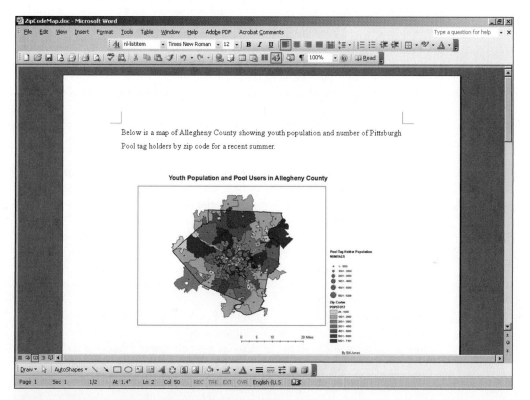

FIGURE 4-29   Word document with map layout image

PRACTICE 4-9

In ArcMap, zoom in to Pittsburgh, export a map called *PittsburghZipCodeMap.jpg* to your C:\LearningAndUsingGIS\FilesStudentWork\ folder, write some new text in *ZipCodeMap.doc* about the next map being a zoomed-in version of the previous map, create a second text box, and insert the new map image. Save and close Word.

Create a Second Data Frame

Thus far in this book, the ArcGIS map documents have had only a single map frame. It's possible, though, to have two or more map frames. Then, your map layouts can have more than one map. For example, sometimes you might want to show two or more maps because you want the reader to be able to compare several variables for the same features (for example, zip codes). *Note: In this case, it is important to keep map sizes identical.* There are other reasons to display two or more maps; for example, to create an overview map for your layout for the case when the main map is zoomed in. (Although ArcMap has a built-in overview map for Data view, it does not for Layout view, so you have to build your own.) Next, you will create an overview map for the layout.

1. Open **ArcMap** and open **C:\LearningAndUsingGIS\Chapter4-2.mxd**.
2. On the Tools toolbar, click the **Find** tool ⵌ, then in the Find window, type **Manchester** in the Find field, click the **In** field list arrow, click **Pools**, and click the **Find** button.
3. In the resulting values panel, right-click **Manchester**, click **Zoom to feature(s)**, and close the **Find** window. (*This is the main map for the layout. Next, you will create a second frame with just the Municipalities layer to serve as the overview map.*)
4. On the main menu, click **Insert** and click **Data Frame**. (*ArcMap creates a new data frame and activates it. In Data view, only one data frame can be activated at a time.*)
5. In the table of contents, right-click **New Data Frame**, and click **Properties**.
6. In the resulting Properties window, click the **General** tab, and then change the name to **Overview Map**. (*You have to set the coordinate system for each data frame, so you'll do that next.*)
7. Click the **Coordinate System** tab; click expander boxes for **Predefined**, **Project Coordinate Systems**, **State Plane**, and **NAD1983 (Feet)**; double-click **NAD 1983 StatePlane Pennsylvania South FIPS 3702 (Feet)** and click **OK**.
8. In the Pittsburgh Pools data frame, right-click **Municipalities** and click **Copy**.
9. Click **Edit** and click **Paste**.
10. In the Overview Map data frame, right-click **Municipalities** and click **Label Features** to toggle labeling off. See Figure 4-30. (*The resulting map has only the one map for context in the small-size overview map that you will create.*)

PRACTICE 4-10

Go to Layout view and rearrange the two data frames and add map elements freehand, without guides (this is to save time, so don't be too concerned about placement). Right-click the overview map frame, click Properties, click the Frame tab, and choose No Color for the border. Click the zoomed-in data frame before creating the legend. See Figure 4-31. *Note: It's important to position and size the maps before creating the overview rectangle in the following steps. If you resize the main map after creating the rectangle, the map's extent changes and the rectangle is no longer correct.*

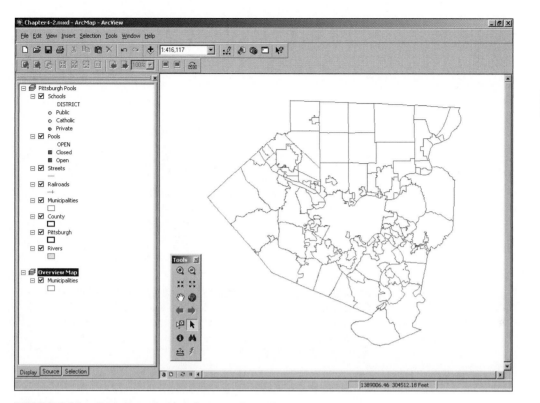

FIGURE 4-30   Overview map data frame and map layer

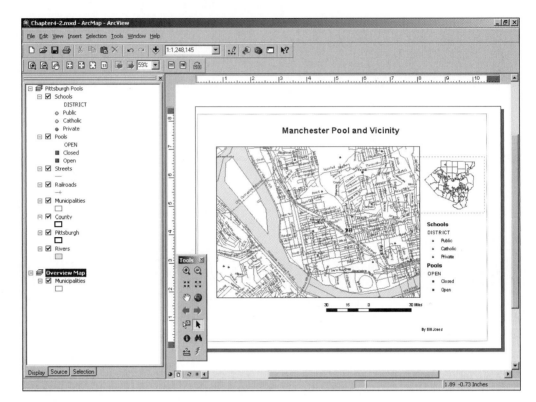

FIGURE 4-31   Map layout with overview map

Show Zoomed Map Position and Dimensions with a Rectangle

Your overview map needs to have a rectangle showing the extent of the main Pittsburgh Pools map. You will build a static rectangle—one that you would have to rebuild if you zoomed to another location on the map.

1. In the table of contents, right-click the **Pittsburgh Pools** data frame, and click **Activate**. (*Now the Pittsburgh Pools data frame is active, denoted by the Pittsburgh Pools name being in bold font. Next comes a trick to get the position and width of this data frame in projected units. You will draw a rectangle that covers the entire map and save its properties in a temporary file for copying and pasting. This saves you the work of copying by hand very long coordinate values and typing them.*)
2. On the main menu, click **View**, click **Toolbars**, and click **Draw**.
3. On the resulting Draw toolbar, click the **Rectangle** tool, drag a rectangle that exactly covers the map, right-click the **map**, click **Properties**, and then click the **Size and Position** tab. See Figure 4-32. (*Next, you will copy and paste these properties in Notepad, a simple text editor on your computer.*)
4. Select the value in the **X Position** field and press **Ctrl+C** to copy the value.

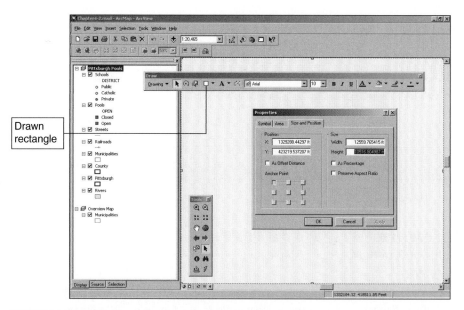

FIGURE 4-32   Pittsburgh Pools map covered by rectangle

5.   On your computer's desktop, click **Start**, point to **All Programs**, point to **Accessories**, click **Notepad** (*Notepad opens*), press **Ctrl+V** to paste the X Position value into Notepad, and then press **Enter** to go to a new line after the X value.

PRACTICE 4-11

Similarly, copy and paste the Y value, then the Width, and finally the Height in Notepad. See Figure 4-33. (Your rectangle's values will be different from those in Figure 4-33. You will have to restore Notepad by clicking its icon on your Windows Start toolbar or by using Alt+Tab to switch through your open applications until you come to Notepad.) When finished, close the Properties window, and delete the rectangle from the map.

FIGURE 4-33   Notepad with rectangle parameters

Create an Overview Map Extent Rectangle

Now, you will switch to the Overview Map data frame and create the desired rectangle for the zoomed-in map.

1. In the table of contents, right-click **Overview Map**, and click **Activate**.
2. On the Draw toolbar, click the **Rectangle** tool, draw any rectangle on the map, and close the Draw toolbar.
3. Right-click the resulting rectangle, and click **Properties**; then, in the resulting Properties window, click the **Symbol** tab.
4. Click the **Change Symbol** button; then, in the Symbol Selector window, scroll down, click the **10% Simple Hatch** icon, change the Fill color to **Mars Red** (*second column, third row*) and the Outline Color also to **Mars Red**, and then click **OK**.
5. In the Properties window, click the **Size and Position** tab.
6. Restore **Notepad**, select the first number (**1329288.44297** ft), press **Ctrl+C** to copy the number, select the value in the X field of the Properties window in ArcMap, and then press **Ctrl+V** keys to paste the value.

PRACTICE 4-12

Continue the process of copying values from Notepad to the Property window fields. See Figure 4-34. When finished, click Apply and click OK in the ArcMap Properties window. See Figure 4-35 for the resulting overview map with rectangle. Close Notepad. Save your map document, and close ArcMap.

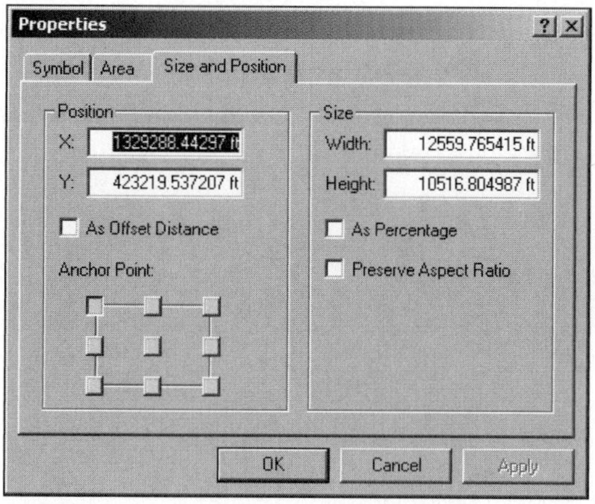

FIGURE 4-34   Overview map rectangle properties

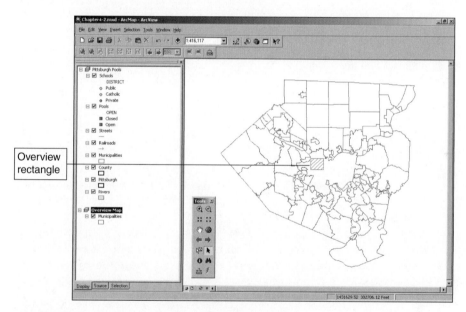

Overview
rectangle

FIGURE 4-35   Overview map with zoomed-in rectangle

Chapter 4 Summary

Graphic design is an art, but it is informed by principles, concepts, and knowledge—thus, everyone is capable of good graphic design, not just the artistically inclined.

Graphic hierarchy is a principle that dictates the use of figure and ground to direct the viewer's attention to important parts of a map, chart, or other graphic design. Many of the graphic features on a map provide context or reference material. Such features should be put into ground by the use of dull colors (mostly grays), weak or no boundaries, and thin or dashed lines. The subject of the map, the features that have important patterns, should be put into figure by the use of bright colors, wide, black edges, and other distinctive graphic elements.

As a graphic designer, be a minimalist: Make every pixel add meaning, or leave them white. Leave out chart junk, such as north arrows. Leave extra map layers out. Use color sparingly and for figure.

Hue, value, and saturation are terms associated with color. Blue is the hue in light blue and dark blue. Value signifies the amount of ink per square inch on an area, with a lot of white being low value, and a lot of black being high value. Saturation refers to a sequence of colors of the same hue that runs from the pure hue to gray or black.

Mapmakers often use monochromatic scales to represent increasing magnitudes on choropleth maps, running from low to high color value, or low to high saturation. Avoid using multiple hues for the same choropleth map. An exception is a dichromatic scale that combines two monochromatic scales; for example, blue for negative quantities and red for positive quantities to represent numeric attributes that have a natural center magnitude such as 0. Another exception is either half of the color spectrum (cool colors or hot colors) with yellow at one end, representing low value.

The color wheel is a device for picking good color combinations. Best for analytic maps are colors that provide the most differentiation—complementary colors (those that are opposite from each other or at equal intervals around the color wheel). Analogous colors are adjacent to each other on the color wheel and are used to show association (in contrast to differentiation).

Many map attributes have numeric scales, such as population counts and capacities of facilities. To represent such attributes on a map, the mapmaker must classify these variables into intervals by choosing break values along their range. Each interval is assigned a color from a monochromatic scale that portrays order through color value. A key in the map legend must provide each interval's end values and identify its color for interpretation. Good scales for general audiences are equal intervals in multiples of 2, 5, or 10—or exponential scales for long-tailed distributions such as powers of 2 or 3. Quantile scales are for analysts so they can see the shape of distributions; for example, if they are long-tailed, bell-shaped, or uniform.

Points and lines are mathematical objects with no area or width; nevertheless, mapmakers must show points with shape and area and lines with width. It is best to use simple point marker shapes, such as circles and squares because it is difficult to differentiate complex shapes and discover patterns among them. In analytic maps, most line features are ground and, thus, should have relatively narrow widths and gray color.

Analytical maps have two major audiences: the analysts who study maps and the general public, who needs to get the message of a map. Analysts require maps with many layers and details. Use relatively few intervals (up to 7) for choropleth maps, many different kinds of point markers that have simple symbols, and so forth. Maps for analysts may be used only on a computer screen in a GIS package. After analysts find an important pattern and want to make the public aware of it, the designer needs to create a simple map that dramatically portrays the pattern. Include the minimum layers to provide context and the subject and make good use of graphic hierarchy. Consider several map outputs, including images for Web sites and paper maps using a map layout, including a title, legend, and map graphic scale.

ArcGIS has powerful functionality for symbolizing maps. More complex layers get their symbols from the values of feature attributes that have code values or numeric scales. Use unique colors for point features that have codes, like that for open and closed pools. Use a sequence of sizes for point features that have numeric values converted into intervals. It is easy to create monochromatic and dichromatic scales for choropleth maps. A key feature of ArcGIS is that it allows the map designer to manually create break values for numeric attributes, allowing the use of any set of break values.

Key Terms

Analogous colors   Adjacent colors on the color wheel, used to depict association or harmony.

Break values   Points chosen along the range of a quantitative attribute for creating nonoverlapping, exhaustive intervals. The intervals make the attribute discrete so it can be represented as a bar chart or as a choropleth map.

Cartography   The art of choosing map layers and graphic elements to yield a map composition that meets a specified purpose.

Centroid   The center point of a polygon. It is a unique point that is calculated as the center of mass for a sheet with the polygon's shape and location. For unusual shapes of polygons, such as U-shaped polygons, centroids might not lie within their polygons.

Chart junk   Graphic elements and symbols that do not add value to charts, maps, graphs, or other graphic designs. Chart junk wastes ink and clutters maps.

Choropleth maps   Polygon map layers that have fill using color value to signify magnitude of an attribute.

Color ramp   A particular sequence or continuum of colors designed to represent numeric quantities. Color ramps that are very useful for analytic mapping are monochromatic or dichromatic.

Color spectrum   The sequence of colors determined by the increasing frequency of the visible range of electromagnetic waves as seen as light from a prism or in a rainbow.

Color value   The amount of white or black in a color. In relation to white paper or a white computer screen, white has low value and black has high value.

Color wheel   The a color-choosing guide, shaped like a wheel, that arrays colors in order of the color spectrum. Violet, the shortest-wavelength color is adjacent to red, the longest-wavelength color.

Complementary colors   Opposite colors on the color wheel. They combine a warm and cool color that look good together and provide large visual differentiation.

Continuous variable   A numeric variable with fractional parts, computed as a ratio or measured continuously, such as distances.

Dichromatic color scale   Two monochromatic scales joined together with low color value in the center and color value increasing toward either end. Such a scale is used for attributes that have a natural center, such as the value 0 for measures of increases and decreases.

Discrete variable   A variable that may take values only from a small set, such as small, medium, and large. Generally such variables cover all possibilities and all possible occurrences have values.

Equal intervals   Intervals with equal widths such as 0–5, 5–10, 10–15, and so on.

Exponential scale   A numeric scale with break values that follow an exponential sequence, such as 2^n or 3^n, where n takes on values 1, 2, 3, and so on. Often, the value 0 is included if the corresponding attribute's data includes values of 0.

Figure   A graphic feature given a bright color, distinctive boundaries, or other graphic designs to draw attention to it. Graphic features in figure are the subject being investigated or are of other high importance.

Graphic design   Choice of graphic features and elements yielding a map or other graphic display that meets an intended purpose.

Graphic elements   The graphic variables used to impart meaning to graphic design, including shape, size, width, and color.

Graphic hierarchy   A design principle that dictates the use of color, strong edges, and other graphic elements to direct the viewer's attention to important parts of a map, chart, or other graphic.

Ground   A graphic feature given dull colors, dashed lines, or other graphic designs to place it in the background. Ground features provide context and supplemental information.

Hue   The essence or distinguishing feature of color, for example, the blue in light blue and dark blue.

Increasing interval widths   A sequence of intervals covering the range of a variable that accommodates long-tailed representations in bar charts and choropleth maps.

Long-tailed distributions   Samples or populations whose distribution deviates from the normal, bell-shaped curve by having one tail elongated. The performance of athletes and computer programmers are examples of such distributions, with long tails on the right side of the distribution, as are many entities in nature.

Map Layout   A compostion of map, legend, title, graphic scale, and other components that allows anyone viewing it to be able to use and interpret the map correctly.

Median   The middle member of a distribution, with 50 percent of the sample being smaller and the other 50 percent being larger in magnitude.

Mimetic symbols   Graphic symbols that resemble what they represent, such as a cross-hatched line for a railroad on a map.

Monochromatic color scale   A series of colors of the same hue with color value varied from low to high; for example, the value ranges from white to black on a monochromatic gray scale, from light to dark green in a green monochromatic scale, and so on.

Neat line   A rectangle drawn around the map in a map layout to make the map attractive and prominent.

Numeric intervals   Nonoverlapping and exhaustive intervals covering the range of data values for an attribute, such as those associated with bars on a bar chart.

Quantiles   Numeric intervals for the range of an attribute that have equal numbers of members in each interval. The intervals are constructed by sorting an attribute and choosing break values along the sorted list of values that result in an equal number of data points in each interval.

Quartiles   Quantiles that have four intervals, each with 25 percent of an attribute's data values.

Saturation   A color scale that ranges from a pure hue to gray or black; for example, the closer to black, the more saturated the color.

Short-Answer Questions

1. Suppose that the following elements are individual map layers in an ArcGIS map document: streets, buildings, parks, motor vehicle accident points, stop signs, and stoplights. Suppose that you need a map for analysts. Describe which symbols you would use with each layer (shape, size, width, and color). Give a rationale for each choice that you make.

2. What is the best design for point marker classification using a numeric scale when there are relatively few points: (a) monochromatic color scale, (b) shapes ranging from circles through stars, (c) sequence of sizes, or (d) circles with increasingly thick black boundaries? Answer the same question for the case of a very large number of point markers (for example, 20,000). Provide a rationale for your choice.

3. Suppose that you have a point layer for sources of particulate air pollution in a city and that particulate emission rates range from 0.1 to 135.0 tons of particulates per day, but with most values in the range of 0.1 to 10 tons per day. Describe a graphic design and numeric scale to portray this map layer for use in a brochure for the Group Against Smog and Pollution. Provide rationales for your choices.

4. Suppose that you have county-level data on the population of white-tailed deer and deer hunting licenses in a state and a county polygon layer for the state. How would you portray these areas on a map and why?

5. Suppose that you have crime data points for a neighborhood classified by crime type, including larcenies, burglaries, motor vehicle thefts, and robberies. How would you symbolize these points?

6. Suppose that you have a polygon map layer for land use in an urban area that includes these nonoverlapping categories: industrial, commercial, residential, and nonprofit. How would you symbolize the polygons? Explain your choices.

7. Use the color wheel to produce four sets of three colors each for use in differentiating map features. Describe the four sets, indicate the one that you like the best, and tell why.

8. Suppose that you have used ArcGIS's quantile option for an attribute that has integer values and ranges from 0 to 72, and it produced break values 22, 25, 43, and 72. Describe the distribution of the attribute.

9. Map documents in Chapter 2 used blockcentroids instead of block polygons to represent the population of 5- to 17-year-old youths. What are the advantages of this choice?

10. Suppose that you have a layout with two choropleth maps for U.S. counties, one with population of Asians and the other with population of Hispanics. What are some ways to make the two maps on one layout easy to read and compare?

Exercises

1. **Map of the United States.** In this exercise, you will design a map of the lower 48 states with two data frames and a layout displaying the corresponding two maps.

a. Start ArcGIS and add the following layers from **C:\LearningAndUsingGIS\MapsUSA**: *counties.shp*, *states.shp*, and *water.shp*.

b. Save your map document file as **C:\LearningAndUsingGIS\FilesStudentWork\ Exercise4-1<YourName>.mxd**, where you substitute your name or other identifier for <YourName>.

c. Use the North_America_Albers_Equal_Area_Conic projection.

d. Symbolize *states.shp* with a hollow color fill and *water.shp* with a light blue color fill. Label states with state name, using a size 6 font and 1.5 halo mask. Copy your first data frame and paste to create a second.

e. In the first data frame, symbolize counties using CROP_ACR97 (acres in crops, 1997). Choose or design a numeric scale of your choice.

f. In the second data frame, symbolize counties using Med_AGE (median age). Again choose or design a numeric scale of your choice.

g. Design a layout with both maps, legends for both maps (just for counties), a title, graphic scale in miles, and a text box for your name. Use guides for placement. Export the map as C:\LearningAndUsingGIS\FilesStudentWork\Exercise4-1.jpg.

h. Create a Word document saved as **C:\LearningAndUsingGIS\FilesStudentWork\ Exercise4-1<YourName>.doc**. Include a title and your name. Then include the map image (*Exercise4-1.jpg*) with a paragraph that has bullets with some observations on patterns in both maps.

2. **Map with Two Point Markers Per Point.** In this exercise, you will display two copies of the Pool layer using size-graduated point markers for each. One will display average daily percent of capacity used (PCTCAP) and the other maximum capacity (MAXLOAD). The resulting map will show which pools have large capacities and which pools use a lot of their capacity.

a. Start a new map document and save it as **C:\LearningAndUsingGIS\FilesStudentWork\ Exercise4-2<YourName>.mxd**, where you substitute your name or other identifier for <YourName>. Set your map to use relative paths. Use the State Plane projection as done in the tutorials.

b. Add the following layers to your map document from C:\LearningAndUsingGIS\MapsPools\: *neighborhoods.shp*, *pittsburgh.shp*, and two copies of *pools.shp*. Limit pools to those that are open.

c. Design break values for each attribute using equal intervals with five classes per variable.

d. Make one variable's point markers range in size up to a maximum of 12 and the other to have a minimum of 12.

e. Symbolize other layers using good map design practices. Do not label neighborhoods, but label pools.

f. Build a map layout with title, map, legend, graphics scale (in miles), and a text box with your name. Export the map as a JPG image file, and insert it into a PowerPoint presentation that you save as **C:\LearningAndUsingGIS\FilesStudentWork\ Exercise4-2<YourName>.ppt**. Include a title slide with a title and your name. Make the second slide show your JPG map. Make the third slide by observations on patterns seen on the map.

3. **Three Ways to Symbolize Census Tracts.** The number of vacant houses in an area can be used as a measure of poverty. In this exercise, you will compare three versions of a map showing the number of vacant houses per census tract in Allegheny County. One version is a choropleth map of census tract polygons. A second version uses size-graduated point markers for tract polygon centroids. A third version uses a dot density map. You'll place each version of the map in a different data frame and compare all three in a single map layout.

a. Start ArcGIS and open a new empty map. Save this map document as **C:\LearningAndUsingGIS\FilesStudentWork\Exercise4-3<YourName>.mxd**, where you substitute your name or other identifier for <YourName>. Set map properties to store relative paths.

b. Add the following map layers and data table from C:\LearningAndUsingGIS\MapsAlleghenyCounty\: *tgr42003trt00.shp*, *tgr42003ccd00.shp* (municipalities), *tgr42003wat.shp* (water features), and *tgr42000sf1trt.dbf* (selected tract-level SF1 census attributes).

c. Set the data frame coordinate system to State Plane, 1983 (feet), Pennsylvania South. Symbolize municipalities with a hollow file and size 1 outline. Symbolize water features with a light blue color fill. Change the names of map layers in the table of contents to Municipalities, Tracts, and Water Features.

d. Next, you will follow directions to join *tgr42000sf1trt.dbf* to the attribute table of Tracts: (1) Right-click Tracts, click Joins and Relates, and click Join; (2) In the resulting Join window, make the following selections: Join attributes from a table, STFID, tgr42000sf1trt, and STFID, and click OK. You just added (joined) the census data to the map layer, making its attributes available for use.

e. Right-click the data frame in the table of contents, click Copy, and click Edit on the main menu, and click Paste to create a second data frame with all map layers of Census Tracts. Click Edit and click Paste again to create a third data frame. Name the three data frames, from top to bottom in the table of contents, Choropleth Map, Size-Graduated Point Markers Map, and Dot Density Map. Zoom each map to Pittsburgh by selecting Pittsburgh in the attributes of Municipalities map layer, right-clicking Municipalities, clicking Selection, and clicking Zoom to selected features.

f. Symbolize the tract maps for each data frame, using the attribute Vacant, according to the data frame name. Use break values of 50, 100, 200, and 585 for the choropleth maps and use a 1 dot = 5 households for the dot density map. Use a gray color ramp for the choropleth map and black for the point markers and dots.

g. Create a portrait map layout with all three data frames. Make each data frame be 3 inches wide by 2.5 inches high. Use guides to align and position map elements. Include a legend for each map. Include titles.

4. **Map of the World.** In this exercise, you will build a layout for a zoomed-in country of the world with an overview map to show its relative location on the world.

a. Start ArcGIS and add all three layers from C:\LearningAndUsingGIS\MapsWorld\.

b. Save your map document file as **C:\LearningAndUsingGIS\FilesStudentWork\Exercise4-4<YourName>.mxd**, where you substitute your name or other identifier for <YourName>.

c. Use the Robinson projection.

d. For the main map, use *cities.shp* and *countries.shp*. Zoom in to a country of your choice but about which you know little. Display cities with population 500,000 and greater. Symbolize these layers. Label countries with their names using a halo mask. Label cities with their names. If your country has an ocean coastline, use the data frame properties, Frame tab, to set the background color to a light blue. Then, the water will be blue.

e. For the overview map, use *countries.shp* and *latlong30.shp*. Use a hollow fill for *latlong30.shp*. Of course, do not label these layers. Create a rectangle, as in the tutorial of this chapter, for the extent of your zoomed-in country to display on the overview map.

f. For interactive use of your map, do an Internet search on two of the cities on your main map (use the name of your city and country and the word *picture*; for example, Delhi India picture) and copy an image for each (in your Web browser, right-click the image and click Save Picture As) in your C:\LearningAndUsingGIS\FilesStudentWork\ folder with the name of the city (for example, *Delhi.jpg*). Hyperlink the images to the cities.

g. Create a map layout. Be sure to size and position your map frames in the layout before creating the overview's rectangle for the main map. Click Insert and click Picture and insert your two images used for hyperlinks. Resize and reposition them so as not to interfere with the map of your country. Click View, click Toolbars, and click Draw to draw lines from your pictures to their cities.

h. Export your map layout and insert it into a Word document called **C:\LearningAndUsingGIS\FilesStudentWork\Exercise4-4<YourName>.doc**. Include a title, your name or other identifier, and a short paragraph describing the map.

References

Color Wheel Pro, "Color Meaning." Internet URL: http://www.color-wheel-pro.com/color-meaning.html (accessed March 2, 2005)

Brewer, C. A. *Designing Better Maps: A Guide for GIS Users*, ESRI Press, Redlands, CA, 2005.

Graphic Communications Program, NC State University College of Education "Color Principles—Hue, Saturation, and Value." Internet URL: http://www.ncsu.edu/scivis/lessons/colormodels/color_models2.html#saturation (accessed March 2, 2005)

MacEachren, A. M. *Some Truth with Maps: A Primer on Symbolization and Design*, Association of American Geographers, Washington D.C., 1994.

Tufte, E. R. *The Visual Display of Quantitative Information*, 2nd Ed., Graphics Press, Cheshire CT, 2001.

CHAPTER **5**

FINDING GIS RESOURCES

LEARNING OBJECTIVES

In this chapter, you will:

- Learn about free maps and data available from the U.S. Census Bureau and ESRI
- Download U.S. Census maps and data tables
- Download TIGER/Line maps and data tables
- Process downloaded layers in ArcGIS

Arthur and his crew looking for more pieces to build the world's first floating map...

INTRODUCTION

In previous chapters, you learned how to navigate, query, design, and build GIS map documents by using

map layers we provided for the Swimming Pool Case Study. In this chapter, you will learn how to download

base map layers for locations in the United States. There are two major sources of free map layers and

spatial data: the U.S. Census Bureau and ESRI Web sites. Both Web sites provide TIGER/Line maps for

the entire United States. We used these Web sites to obtain the blocks, municipalities, zip codes, streets,

and river maps for the Swimming Pool Case Study (maps you will continue to use in Chapters 6–9). In

Chapter 9, you will finish this case study in a project assignment, but you will also start working on projects in your own community using base maps from these Web sites.

Many more resources are available for map layers, and this chapter provides guidance on searching for specialized maps and data. Many states, counties, and cities have their own GIS departments that create map layers and make them available on the Internet. You will find that many map layers and data are free; others can be obtained for a small fee (typically just to cover duplication and handling costs), but some are quite expensive.

In addition to map layers, both the Census Bureau and ESRI Web sites provide data tables of **spatially referenced data**—data that is categorized by unique spatial identifiers. The identifiers—state names, county FIPS codes, five-digit zip codes, census tract numbers, and so forth—enable you to join the data to corresponding map layers. Joining data tables to maps is an example of some of the immediate steps that you will commonly perform after downloading data resources. In this chapter, you will learn how to repair spatial identifier values in a table so that they match the data format of the same identifier in another table, enabling table joins, and you will learn how to clean up other data problems, such as deleting extraneous data rows.

Also, you will learn how to create new variables in attribute tables from existing ones. Often, you will want to map a variable that is the sum or ratio of existing attributes; for example, the population in an age range that includes attributes for smaller ranges created by the Census Bureau.

One final task is to learn how to import shapefiles into a personal geodatabase, which is a modern relational database format for map layers. Many organizations prefer a database format for map layers rather than the individual files of shapefiles. You will gain a small introduction to geodatabases.

FREE RESOURCES ON THE INTERNET

There are more than 30 million GIS Web sites on the Internet at this writing—a year ago—it was *only* 10 million! Fortunately, many analytical U.S. mapping tasks require only the Census Bureau and ESRI Web sites. Although this chapter covers common formats including shapefiles, ArcInfo interchange (E00) files, ArcInfo coverages, and XY maps that have coordinates for points, you can import many more formats using ArcGIS.

U.S. Census Bureau Map Layers and Data

The U.S. Census Bureau began building a map infrastructure in the late 1970s and early 1980s. Its mapping needs were twofold: (1) to assign census employees to areas of responsibility, covering the entire country and its possessions, and (2) to report and display census tabulations by area. Officials determined that the smallest area needed for these purposes is a city block or its equivalent and, thus, set about compiling all line features that could be used to create a block map layer for the entire country. There was a preference for visible features—streets, streams, shorelines, and so forth—but officials also used invisible features when necessary—county lines, city limits, and so forth—to build block layers. In the end, the Census Bureau met its needs and, as a by-product, provided the major vector-based map infrastructure for the United States.

Any map features smaller than blocks—such as deeded land parcels, building outlines, street curbs, and parking lots—are the responsibility of local governments. There is no central repository for local-government map layers; to obtain such maps, you must search individual city and county Web sites. A small but increasing number of them provide GIS map layers.

TIGER/Line Files

As you learned in Chapter 1, TIGER/Line (Topologically Integrated Geographic Encoding and Referencing) files are the Census Bureau's product for digital mapping of the United States. The TIGER maps are available for the entire United States and its possessions, and the maps include geographic features such as roads and streets, railroads, rivers, lakes, political boundaries, and census statistical boundaries. Census statistical boundaries include the following:

- *Census tracts*: These are areas of population ranging from roughly 2500 to 8000. Census tracts are neighborhoods: Generally, they are homogeneous in terms of population, social-economic status, and living conditions. There were more than 60,000 census tracts in the 2000 Census.
- *Census block groups*: These are subdivisions of census tracts with an average population of around 1000.
- *Census blocks*: These are subdivisions of block groups, the smallest geographic areas for which the Census Bureau collects and tabulates census data.

TIGER/Line files can be downloaded for free in shapefile format from the U.S. Census Web site, from ESRI's site, and from many other sites. You can find definitions of all Census and TIGER/Line files at *www.census.gov/geo/www/tiger* and *www.census.gov/geo/www/garm.html*.

U.S. Census Bureau Data Files

The Census Bureau's boundary map layers do not contain demographic data. There are far too many census variables to be included with map layers—the maps files would be enormous, larger than permitted by PC file formats and databases, and too slow to process. Thus, it is the user's responsibility to choose one or more of the large number of census data tables available and then join them to a map's feature attribute table. Two major collections of data tables are the following:

- ***Census Summary File 1 (SF1)***: This collection has data tables on population, age, sex, race, Hispanic/Latino origin, household relationship, ownership of residences, and so forth for the entire population of people and housing units. This data is available for states, municipalities, zip codes, census tracts, census block groups, census blocks, and other types of areas.
- ***Census Summary File 3 (SF3)***: This collection has data tables for detailed population and housing characteristics—such as place of birth, educational attainment, employment status, income, value of housing unit, and the year in which a structure was built—collected from a 1-in-6 random sample and then weighted to represent the total population. This data is not available at the census block level, but only for census block groups and larger areas.

U.S. Census Bureau Data Web Site

The American Fact Finder Web site of the U.S. Census Bureau, *http://factfinder.census.gov*, has documentation for all census data sets and downloadable map layers in shapefile format. Census data is available in tabular format. This chapter's tutorial provides sufficient instructions to enable you to obtain maps and data that you need from the Census Bureau.

ESRI WEB Sites

As mentioned in previous chapters, ESRI, the maker of ArcGIS, is the world leader in GIS software. ESRI's data Web site, *www.esri.com/data*, is one of the first places that many people visit when looking for map layers. It provides links to download data, to order data on CDs, or to locate GIS data providers for a variety of industries. Examples of data you can download for free, or for a small fee, include the following:

- *ESRI World Basemap Data (free)*: These maps provide GIS layers from countries around the world in shapefile format.
- *Census 2000 TIGER/Line Data (free)*: These maps provide Census 2000 TIGER/Line maps in shapefile format by county.
- *U.S. Geological Survey (USGS) National Elevation Dataset (NED) Shaded Relief Imagery Data (free)*: These maps provide the highest-resolution elevation data available across the United States, in raster format.
- *GDT Dynamap/2000 U.S. Street Data (small fee for individual zip code layers)*: These map layers are the highest-quality street map layers in terms of appearance, completeness, and accuracy. These maps include more than 14 million U.S. street segments and include postal boundaries, landmarks, water features, and other features.

- *Titan Sure!MAPS RASTER Data (small fee for single map)*: These color raster maps are for selected areas. They include the USGS topographic maps at 1:24,000; 1:100,000; and 1:250,000 scales. Each map contains topographic contours, land-use features, political boundaries, streets, buildings, landmarks, and other cultural information.

ESRI's Geography Network site, *www.geographynetwork.com*, offers links to online dynamic maps and downloadable data. It provides a mechanism for GIS users to access GIS data and services worldwide. It is possible to search not only by location but also by industry-specific categories, such as agriculture and farming, biology and ecology, business and economy, and human health and disease. For example, you could search for the map layers for agriculture and farming near Cape Town, South Africa. ESRI also sponsors *www.gis.com*, with links to more free U.S. map data and free map and census data for Canada.

Additional GIS Data Web Sites

Numerous Web sites provide free map layers for download. Try doing some Web searches, such as for "GIS data download." Try adding the name of a state or city to the search criteria. Brown University has some good links at *www.brown.edu/Research/gis/webData. html* for international, national, state, and local GIS data sources. For example, almost any listing of GIS resources by state includes the Pennsylvania Spatial Data Access (PASDA), which is hosted and maintained by the Pennsylvania State University and is Pennsylvania's official geospatial data clearinghouse. The data on PASDA is provided by federal, state, local, and regional government agencies, nonprofit organizations, and academic institutions throughout the region. We obtained the Swimming Pool Case Study's raster maps from PASDA.

Data Table Formats

Data does not always come in exactly the right form or format for direct use in ArcGIS. Data might not be in table format, might not have the right file format, might not have identifiers in the right form or data format, and might not have attributes combined as needed.

A data table needs to have its first row be attribute names, and the names need to follow a naming convention. The usual naming convention specifies that the first letter be a letter and remaining characters be any letters, digits, or the underscore character. The dBase file format places a maximum length on attribute names of 10 characters, but newer formats do not have a limit that you will likely exceed. In addition, you should attempt to make attribute names self-documenting labels that you and others can recognize. Some good examples are Pop5To17, Area, and Capacity.

All additional rows of a data table, from row 2 through the last row, need to contain attribute values. None of the rows can be sums, averages, or other statistics. Census SF1 or SF3 tables that you download from the Census Bureau Web site use cryptic attribute names in the first row (like P030001), an extra second row with descriptive phrases defining attributes, and have all remaining rows as data records. Before using such data in ArcGIS, it is desirable to rename attributes, and it is necessary to delete the second row.

ArcGIS currently can import data tables easily in three file formats: a dBase table, text with comma- or tab-separated values, and a Microsoft Access table. In the future, ArcGIS will also be able to import Microsoft Excel tables directly.

Although not a requirement for using tables in ArcGIS, design principles dictate that each data table have a **primary key**. This is an attribute (or two or more attributes combined into a single composite attribute) that has two properties: Each value in the attribute column is unique—there are no duplicates of the same value in different rows—and there are no **null values**—these are missing values or data cells that were never assigned values. Sometimes, there are two or more alternate columns that have the properties needed to be a primary key. Then one such column is designated as the primary key, and the other qualifying columns are called **candidate keys**. This is a term from the database field where there are often alternative attributes that could serve as a primary key; for example, Social Security number or driver's license number.

Another data design principle is to not store redundant information in base tables made available for applications. For example, a table supplied by a Web site might have attributes for population in categories 0–5, 6–10, 11–20, 21–40, 41–60, and 61 and higher. The same table would not also include population data for ages 0–20 and 20–60 because you can calculate those attributes from the supplied attributes. It is perfectly acceptable, however, for you to create such attributes.

Table Joins

A **table join**—putting two tables together to make one table—is a common task. Our data joining needs for downloaded census data are simple. We need to join two tables one-to-one by row. This means that for every row of data in one table, we expect to find one and only one matching row in the other table. To join two such tables, you simply need to identify or create matching primary keys in both.

The primary key attributes do not need to have the same names in the tables to be joined, but they must have the same values and data types. For example, if one table stores primary key values, such as 15213, as a number and the other table stores them as text, you have to convert the data type of one of the attributes so that data types match. In ArcMap, you simply create a new attribute of the desired data type and use an expression to copy and convert the original values into it.

Sometimes, you have to combine two or more columns to create a primary key to match that in another table. For example, downloaded SF1 data for census tracts has tract numbers such as 42003480102. The *42* is the FIPS code for Pennsylvania, the *003* is the FIPS code for Allegheny County, and *480102* is tract 4801.02 in Allegheny County, Pennsylvania. The same data in the tract polygon map layer downloaded from the Census Bureau is in three numeric attributes: State with value *42*, County with value *003*, and Tract with value *4801.02*. You need to create a new attribute to combine separate attributes as follows: `Tract2=1,000,000,000*State + 1,000,000*County + 100*Tract`. In other cases, you will have to **concatenate** text attributes, using the "&" operator, to combine separate text values into a composite attribute. For example, if State and County were stored as text attributes, then `County2 = State & County` would yield 42003 for the preceding example.

U.S. CENSUS BUREAU WEB SITE

Next, you will follow steps for downloading census map files and spatially referenced data tables. *Note: If you are unsuccessful in downloading any files in this chapter, you will be able to get copies from the C:\LearningAndUsingGIS\MapsDownloaded\ BackupMapsDownloaded\ folder on your hard drive, which we downloaded.*

Download Map Boundary Files

The following steps show you how to access the U.S. Census Bureau Web site and download a shapefile with five-digit zip code area polygons for the entire state of Pennsylvania.

1. Open your Web browser and navigate to **http://www.census.gov**.
2. In the Geography section of the U.S. Census Bureau home page, click the **TIGER** link. See Figure 5-1.

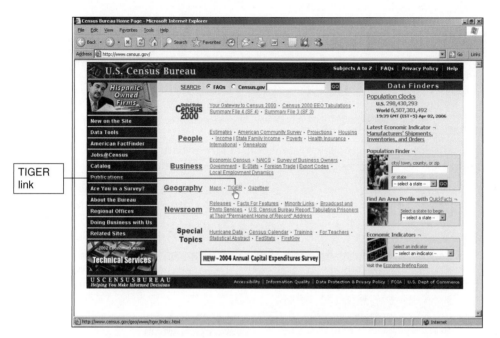

TIGER link

FIGURE 5-1   U.S. Census Bureau home page

3. On the left side of the TIGER page, click the **Cartographic Boundary Files** link.
4. On the Cartographic Boundary Files page, click the **Download Boundary Files** link.
5. Scroll down and click the **2000** link for 5-Digit ZIP Code Tabulation Areas (ZCTAs).
6. At the top of the resulting page, click the **ArcView Shapefile (.shp)** link, and then click the **zt42_d00_shp.zip** link for Pennsylvania.
7. Save the **zt42_d00_shp.zip** file in your C:\LearningAndUsingGIS\MapsDownloaded\ folder. *(This step might vary in detail, depending on which browser you are using and how you have it configured.)*
8. Click **Start**, click **My Computer**, browse to **C:\LearningAndUsingGIS\MapsDownloaded**, right-click **zt42_d00_shp.zip**, click **Extract All**, and extract to **C:\LearningAndUsingGIS\MapsDownloaded**.

(This step extracts the zt42_d00.dbf, zt42_d00.shp, and zt42_d00.shx files to your folder. Together, these three files make up the zt42_d00 shapefile.)

9. Delete **zt42_d00_shp.zip** and close the **My Computer** window.

184

PRACTICE 5-1

From the Census Web site's Cartographic Boundary section, download Pennsylvania's 2000 Census tracts, but this time use the ARC/INFO Export (*.e00*) file format. The file to download is *tr42_d00_e00.zip*. Download and extract *tr42_d00_e00.zip* to the C:\LearningAndUsingGIS\MapsDownloaded\ folder. Delete *tr42_d00_e00.zip,* and when you are finished, close your browser. You'll import the *tr42_d00.e00* file as an ArcInfo coverage and then convert it to a shapefile later in this chapter.

Download Summary File Tables

Next, you will download zip code–level census data for the entire United States that includes SF1 and SF3 variables. (Unfortunately, there is no option to download only Pennsylvania data.)

1. Start your Web browser and then navigate to **http://factfinder.census.gov/**. See Figure 5-2.

FIGURE 5-2 U.S. Census Bureau's FactFinder home page

2. Click the **Download Center** button, and then on the resulting page click the **Census 2000 Summary File 3 (SF 3) - Sample Data** link.
3. On the resulting page, click the **All 5 Digit ZIP Code Tabulation Areas (860)** link, and then click the **SELECTED DETAILED TABLES** option button and then click **GO**. *(The downloaded tables will be a text file in comma-separated format.)*
4. With the show all tables tab clicked on the resulting page, scroll down in the top panel, click the row for table **P30 Means of Transportation to Work for Workers 16+ Years**, and click the **Add** button.
5. In the same panel, scroll down to and click **P82 Per Capita Income in 1999 (Dollars)**, and click the **Add** button. See Figure 5-3. *(Two tables is enough for now. Take the time to scroll around in this list of tables, however, to get an idea of the kinds of data available.)*

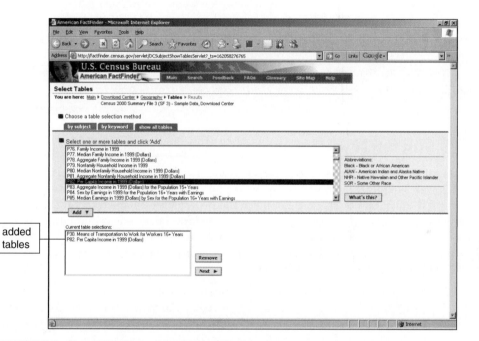

FIGURE 5-3 Two SF3 tables added for download

6. Click the **Next** button, and then on the resulting page click the **Start Download** button.
7. Save the resulting **dc_dec_2000_sf3_u.zip** file in your C:\LearningAndUsingGIS\ MapsDownloaded\ folder.
8. Click **Start**, click **My Computer**, browse to **C:\LearningAndUsingGIS\ MapsDownloaded**, right-click **dc_dec_2000_sf3_u.zip**, click **Extract All**, and extract to **C:\LearningAndUsingGIS\MapsDownloaded**. *(The extracted files are as follows: dc_dec_2000_sf3_u_data1.txt, dc_dec_2000_sf3_u_geo.txt, and readme_dec_2000_sf3.txt.)*

9. Using My Computer, delete **dc_dec_2000_sf3_u.zip** and two of the files you extracted: dc_dec_2000_sf3_u_geo.txt and readme_dec_2000_sf3.txt. *(The dc_dec_2000_sf3_u_data1.txt file is the only one that you need.)*

10. Using My Computer, rename dc_dec_2000_sf3_u_data1.txt to be **ZipCodeSF3Data.txt**, and then close the **My Computer** window. *(It is a good idea to rename this file so that you can recognize it later. Also, the Census Bureau gives all downloaded data of a certain geography, such as zip codes, the same name. So, renaming files will help you avoid deleting previously downloaded files and mixing files up.)*

PRACTICE 5-2

Use the same Web site to download census data for SF1. Start with the Census 2000 Summary File 1 (SF 1) 100-Percent Data link and then the All Census Tracts in a County (140) link. Next, select Pennsylvania from the drop-down menu, then the Web site will add a second drop-down menu for the county; select Allegheny. Download data for selected table H3 Occupancy by Status (Housing Units). After you extract files, delete the *.zip* file, the file ending with *geo.txt*, and the file starting with *readme*. Then rename the remaining new file *dc_dec_2000_sf1_u_data1.txt* to be *SF1Tracts.txt*.

ESRI WEBSITE

Next, you will visit ESRI's Web site to download additional Census Bureau TIGER maps and data. This Web site has some unique map layers; for example, it provides census blocks even though the Census Bureau does not make them available as map layers. It also has frequently used SF1 Census variables already downloaded from the Census Bureau's Web site and ready for use. Next, you will use the ESRI Web site to download shapefiles for Allegheny County, Pennsylvania, for its county boundary, census blocks, and streets. In addition, you will download SF1 data for blocks.

1. Start your Web browser and then navigate to **www.esri.com**.
2. At ESRI's home page, click the **Products** tab, and then in the resulting drop-down menu click **ESRI Data**. See Figure 5-4. *(The map or display on your Web page will differ from Figure 5-4 because ESRI changes the page periodically.)*
3. On the resulting page at the bottom of the left panel, click the **Geographic Data Portals** link; then, on the resulting page, click the **Census 2000 TIGER/Line Data** line, and click the **Preview and Download** link.
4. On the resulting page's map, click **Pennsylvania**. See Figure 5-5.

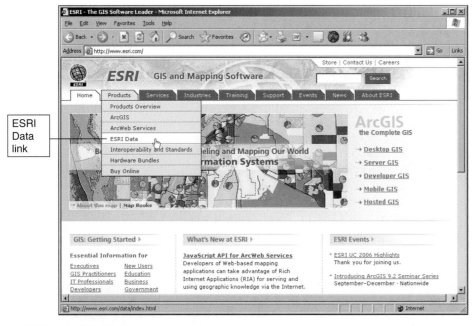

ESRI Data link

FIGURE 5-4 ESRI home page

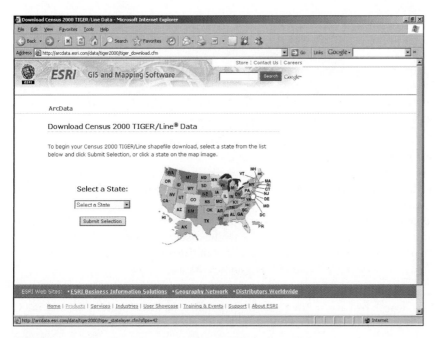

FIGURE 5-5 Download Census 2000 TIGER/Line Data Web page

Finding GIS Resources

5. On the resulting page, click the list arrow for **county**, scroll down, click **Allegheny**, and click the **Submit Selection** button directly under Allegheny. *(That results in a Web page with all of the TIGER map layers and Census Bureau data sets available for counties on this Web site.)*

6. Click check boxes on for **Census Blocks 2000**, **County 2000**, **Line Features-Roads**, and **Census Block Demographics (SF1)**, then scroll to the bottom of the page and click the **Proceed to Download** button, and, finally, on the resulting page, click the **Download File** button.

7. Save the resulting zip file in your C:\LearningAndUsingGIS\MapsDownloaded\ folder. *(The name of the file varies with each download; for example, one was called at_tigeresri8983115937.zip.)*

8. Click **Start**, click **My Computer**, browse to **C:\LearningAndUsingGIS\ MapsDownloaded**, right-click the **.zip** file just downloaded, click **Extract All**, and extract to **C:\LearningAndUsingGIS\MapsDownloaded**. *(After unzipping the downloaded file, you will find the result to be four more zipped files. So, there is a second round of unzipping needed next.)*

9. Use My Computer to extract files from the four resulting zipped files: **blk0042003.zip, cty0042003.zip, lkA42003.zip, and sf1blk42000.zip**. *(That creates three shapefiles—tgr1203blk00.shp, tgr12103cty00.shp, and tgr12103lkA.shp—and the very large data file tgr12000sf1blk.dbf.)*

10. Use **My Computer** to delete all *.zip* files. *(We suggest that you double-click the readme.html file to read some general documentation on the files you just downloaded.)*

PRACTICE 5-3

Download the water polygons shapefile for Allegheny County using the ESRI Web site. When finished, you should have *tgr12103wat.shp* in your C:\LearningAndUsingGIS\MapsDownloaded\ folder.

DOWNLOAD POINT DATA

Several Web sites have data on point locations. One is *www.hometownlocator.com*, which already has latitude and longitude coordinates included with the data. You will use this site to download data on Allegheny County's hospitals. Other sources, such as yellow pages listings on the Internet, provide business names and addresses by category of business, but do not provide coordinates. You will learn how to place address data as points on a street map in Chapter 7.

1. Start your Web browser and then navigate to **www.hometownlocator.com**.

2. In the Search by City or Town and State panel, type **Pittsburgh** in the city field, select **Pennsylvania** from the state field, and click **City Search**. See Figure 5-6.

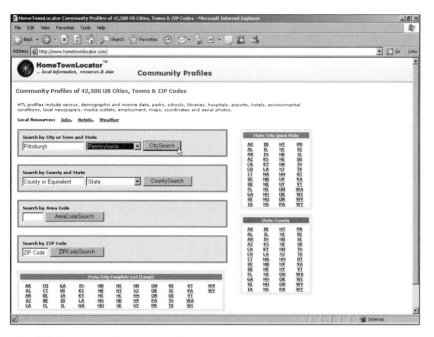

FIGURE 5-6   HomeTownLocator home page

3. On the resulting page, click the **Pittsburgh** link, on the next page click the **Health & Medical** link, and, finally, on the next page click the **Pittsburgh, Pennsylvania Hospitals (Local/Regional/State)** link. See Figure 5-7. *(That produces a list of 26 hospitals with name, latitude, and longitude coordinates. The coordinates are not precise because they only have two decimal points; nevertheless, the resulting point map is useful for general analysis.)*

4. Click, hold, and drag your mouse from the **Name** cell down and to the right through the **Maps** cell for Woodville State Hospital in the last row. *(That action selects all of the data.)*

5. On your browser's main menu, click **Edit**, click **Copy**, and close your browser.

6. Start **Microsoft Excel** and then on Excel's main menu, click **Edit** and click **Paste**.

7. Click **File** and click **Save As**, and then in the Save As window, browse to your **C:\LearningAndUsingGIS\MapsDownloaded** folder, change the Save as type to **DBF 4 (dBASEIV) (*.dbf)**, type **PghHospitals** in the File name field, click **Save**, click **OK**, and click **Yes**.

8. Hold the **Shift** key down, click the column selectors for columns **C** and **D**, and click **Format Cells**.

9. In the resulting Format Cells window, click the **Number** tab, if necessary click **Number** in the Category field, change Decimal Places to **2**, and click **OK**.

10. Click **File**, click **Save**, click **Yes**, and close **Excel** without saving. *(You've already saved the file.)*

Altogether, you should have all of the files shown in Figure 5-8. If not, copy any missing files from C:\LearningAndUsingGIS\MapsDownloaded\MapsDownloadedBackup\.

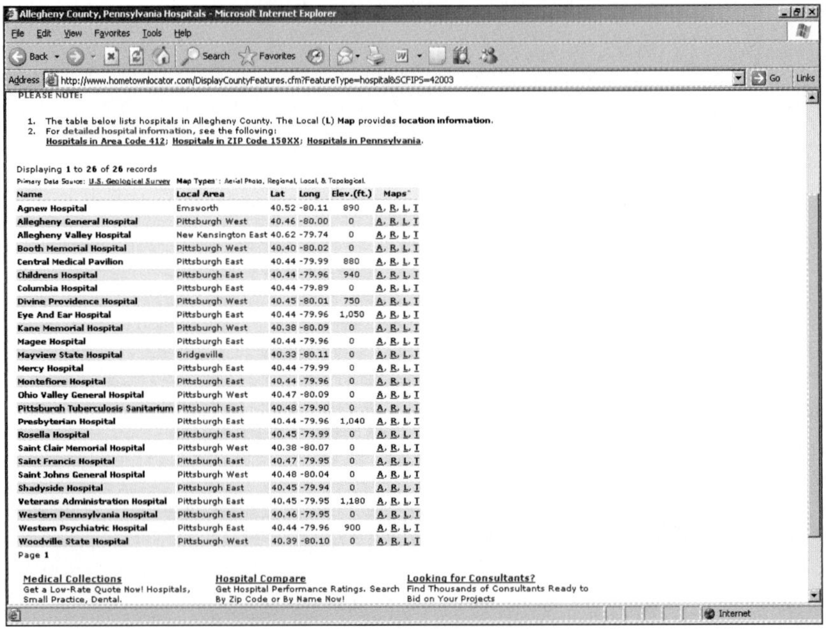

FIGURE 5-7   Listing of Pittsburgh hospitals

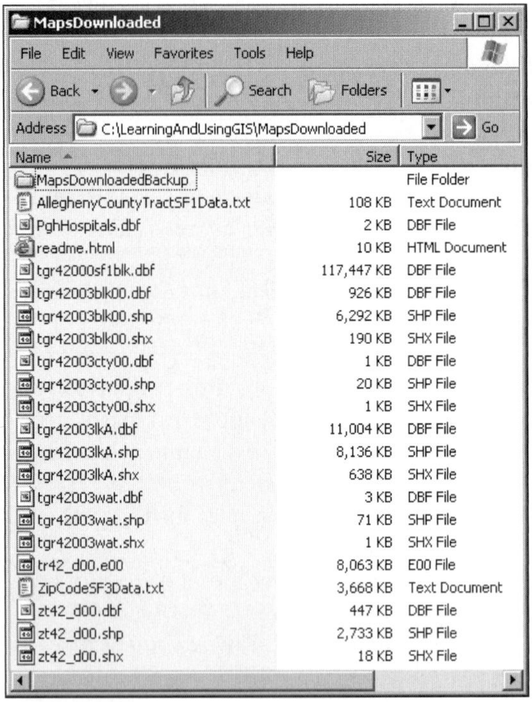

The browser window titled "Allegheny County, Pennsylvania Hospitals - Microsoft Internet Explorer" contains the following content:

PLEASE NOTE!

1. The table below lists hospitals in Allegheny County. The Local (L) Map provides location information.
2. For detailed hospital information, see the following:
   Hospitals in Area Code 412; Hospitals in ZIP Code 150XX; Hospitals in Pennsylvania.

Displaying 1 to 26 of 26 records
Primary Data Source: U.S. Geological Survey   Map Types : Aerial Photo, Regional, Local, & Topological.

Name	Local Area	Lat	Long	Elev.(ft.)	Maps*
Agnew Hospital	Emsworth	40.52	-80.11	890	A, R, L, T
Allegheny General Hospital	Pittsburgh West	40.46	-80.00	0	A, R, L, T
Allegheny Valley Hospital	New Kensington East	40.62	-79.74	0	A, R, L, T
Booth Memorial Hospital	Pittsburgh West	40.40	-80.02	0	A, R, L, T
Central Medical Pavilion	Pittsburgh East	40.44	-79.99	880	A, R, L, T
Childrens Hospital	Pittsburgh East	40.44	-79.96	940	A, R, L, T
Columbia Hospital	Pittsburgh East	40.44	-79.89	0	A, R, L, T
Divine Providence Hospital	Pittsburgh West	40.45	-80.01	750	A, R, L, T
Eye And Ear Hospital	Pittsburgh East	40.44	-79.96	1,050	A, R, L, T
Kane Memorial Hospital	Pittsburgh West	40.38	-80.09	0	A, R, L, T
Magee Hospital	Pittsburgh East	40.44	-79.96	0	A, R, L, T
Mayview State Hospital	Bridgeville	40.33	-80.11	0	A, R, L, T
Mercy Hospital	Pittsburgh East	40.44	-79.99	0	A, R, L, T
Montefiore Hospital	Pittsburgh East	40.44	-79.96	0	A, R, L, T
Ohio Valley General Hospital	Pittsburgh West	40.47	-80.09	0	A, R, L, T
Pittsburgh Tuberculosis Sanitarium	Pittsburgh East	40.48	-79.90	0	A, R, L, T
Presbyterian Hospital	Pittsburgh East	40.44	-79.96	1,040	A, R, L, T
Rosella Hospital	Pittsburgh East	40.45	-79.99	0	A, R, L, T
Saint Clair Memorial Hospital	Pittsburgh West	40.38	-80.07	0	A, R, L, T
Saint Francis Hospital	Pittsburgh East	40.47	-79.95	0	A, R, L, T
Saint Johns General Hospital	Pittsburgh West	40.48	-80.04	0	A, R, L, T
Shadyside Hospital	Pittsburgh East	40.45	-79.94	0	A, R, L, T
Veterans Administration Hospital	Pittsburgh East	40.45	-79.95	1,180	A, R, L, T
Western Pennsylvania Hospital	Pittsburgh East	40.46	-79.95	0	A, R, L, T
Western Psychiatric Hospital	Pittsburgh East	40.44	-79.96	900	A, R, L, T
Woodville State Hospital	Pittsburgh West	40.39	-80.10	0	A, R, L, T

Page 1

Medical Collections
Get a Low-Rate Quote Now! Hospitals, Small Practice, Dental.

Hospital Compare
Get Hospital Performance Ratings. Search By Zip Code or By Name Now!

Looking for Consultants?
Find Thousands of Consultants Ready to Bid on Your Projects

FIGURE 5-8   Downloaded files

The window titled "MapsDownloaded" shows Address C:\LearningAndUsingGIS\MapsDownloaded and contains:

Name	Size	Type
MapsDownloadedBackup		File Folder
AlleghenyCountyTractSF1Data.txt	108 KB	Text Document
PghHospitals.dbf	2 KB	DBF File
readme.html	10 KB	HTML Document
tgr2000sf1blk.dbf	117,447 KB	DBF File
tgr42003blk00.dbf	926 KB	DBF File
tgr42003blk00.shp	6,292 KB	SHP File
tgr42003blk00.shx	190 KB	SHX File
tgr42003cty00.dbf	1 KB	DBF File
tgr42003cty00.shp	20 KB	SHP File
tgr42003cty00.shx	1 KB	SHX File
tgr42003lkA.dbf	11,004 KB	DBF File
tgr42003lkA.shp	8,136 KB	SHP File
tgr42003lkA.shx	638 KB	SHX File
tgr42003wat.dbf	3 KB	DBF File
tgr42003wat.shp	71 KB	SHP File
tgr42003wat.shx	1 KB	SHX File
tr42_d00.e00	8,063 KB	E00 File
ZipCodeSF3Data.txt	3,668 KB	Text Document
zt42_d00.dbf	447 KB	DBF File
zt42_d00.shp	2,733 KB	SHP File
zt42_d00.shx	18 KB	SHX File

DOWNLOAD A RASTER MAP

Many state and municipal Web sites have raster maps for download: aerial photographs, mainly digital ortho quadrangles (DOQs) and scanned topographic maps (DRGs). Each Web site has a means of identifying the area of interest to you and then provides download capabilities. Here, you will download a DOQ for Pittsburgh from the Pennsylvania Data Access (PASDA). *Note: The file to be downloaded in this section is 45 MB in size, so you might only want to get to the point of downloading and stop, to save disk space on your computer. Alternatively, you can download the file, use it, and then delete it. The C:\LearningAndUsingGIS\MapsDownloaded\MapsDownloadedBackup\ folder does not have a copy of the raster map, to save on disk storage.*

1. Start your Web browser and then navigate to **www.pasda.psu.edu/**.
2. Click the **Access Data** link, and on the resulting page, click the **Data Access Wizard** link.
3. On the resulting Find Data page, type **DOQ** in the Search by Keyword(s) field and click **Submit**.
4. On the resulting Search Results page, click the **Digital Orthophoto Quarter Quadrangle images for Pennsylvania** link, and at the bottom of the resulting page click the **Data Applications & Viewers** link.
5. In the resulting Imagery Viewer & Download Tool page, click click the list arrow in the ZOOM TO A COUNTY field and click **Allegheny**.
6. Click the **Quarter-Quadrangles (DOWWs, Color Infrared)** option under the DISPLAY IMAGE TILES panel and click the **IDENTIFY & DOWNLOAD IMAGERY** button.

7. In the center of the resulting map, click the **small white square with the number 65.** *(This action provides information on the quadrangle of interest.)* See Figure 5-9.

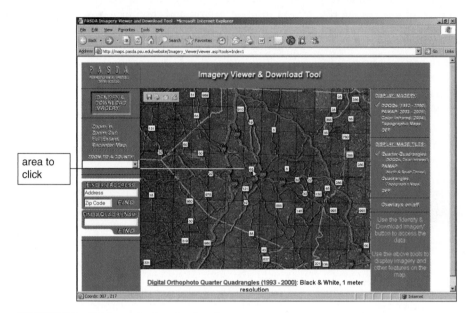

FIGURE 5-9 Grid area to download raster map

8. On the resulting page, in the NAPP II DOQQ: 4/7/1993 row and the under the FTP column, click the **TIFF** link.
9. Save and unzip the resulting files to your C:\LearningAndUsingGIS\ MapsDownloaded\ folder. *(Key resulting files are* pittsburgh_west_pa_ne.tif, *which stores the raster map, and* pittsburgh_west_pa_ne.tfw, *which is the map's world file.)*

PROCESS DOWNLOADED FILES

The next series of steps has you carry out preliminary work to process downloaded files in ArcCatalog.

Import an E00 File and ArcInfo Coverage

Your first task is to import the E00 interchange file that you downloaded from the Census Bureau Web site and transform it into an ArcInfo Coverage.

1. On your PC's desktop, click **Start**, click **All Programs**, click **ArcGIS**, and click **ArcCatalog**.
2. In the file tree in the left panel of ArcCatalog, click expander boxes for **LearningAndUsingGIS** and then for **MapsDownloaded**. See Figure 5-10.

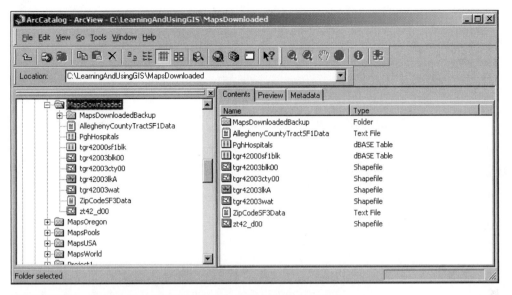

FIGURE 5-10 ArcCatalog with MapsDownloaded folder expanded

3. On the ArcCatalog main menu, click **View**, click **Toolbars**, and click **ArcView 8x Tools**. (*This toolbar provides access to some tools from an earlier version of ArcGIS.*)

4. In the ArcView 8x Tools window, click the **list arrow** to the right of Conversion Tools, and click **Import from Interchange File**.

5. In the ArcView Import from interchange File window, click the **browse** button for the Input file, browse to your **C:\LearningAndUsingGIS\MapsDownloaded** folder, and double-click **tr42_d00.e00**.

6. Click the **browse** button for the Output dataset field, browse to your **C:\LearningAndUsingGIS\MapsDownloaded** folder, type **tracts** in the Name field, leave **Coverages** as the Save as type, click **Save**, and click **OK**. (*That results in the tracts coverage in your file tree under MapsDownloaded.*)

7. Close the **ArcView 8x Tools** window.

Convert an ArcInfo Coverage to a Shapefile

An ArcInfo coverage's attribute table is in a proprietary format that you cannot edit. Later in this chapter, however, that's exactly what you will need to do before joining downloaded SF1 Census data to it for mapping. You will have to create a new attribute for the tract number that matches the tract number in the SF1 data. So next, you will convert the coverage to a shapefile, which is editable in ArcMap and elsewhere.

1. On your PC's desktop, click **Start**, click **All Programs**, click **ArcGIS**, click **ArcMap**, and click **OK** in the ArcMap window to yield a new, empty map.

2. Click the **Add Data** button ⬇, browse to your **C:\LearningAndUsingGIS\ MapsDownloaded** folder, click the **tracts** coverage, and click **Add**.

3. In the table of contents, right-click **tracts polygon**, click **Data**, and click **Export Data**.
4. In the Export Data window, click the **browse** button, browse to your **C:\LearningAndUsingGIS\MapsDownloaded** window, type **tracts** in the Name field, click **Save**, click **OK**, and click **Yes**.
5. Right-click **tracts polygon** and click **Remove**.
6. Click **File**, click **Save**, then in the Save As window browse to your **C:\LearningAndUsingGIS** window, type **Chapter5-1** in the File name field, and click **Save**.

Use ArcCatalog File Utilities

Shapefiles, as you know, are made of three or more individual files, each in the same folder and having the same filename, but with different file extensions. ArcCatalog makes it easy to work with a shapefile; for example, by representing it with one icon that you can rename instead of renaming its individual files.

1. Right-click the polygon shapefile, **tgr42003blk00**, click **Rename**, type **blocks**, and click anywhere in the **white area** of ArcCatalog.
2. Right-click the table, **tgr42000sf1blk**, click **Rename**, type **blockssf1**, and click anywhere in the **white area** of ArcCatalog.
3. Right-click the interchange file, **zt42d00**, click **Delete**, and click **Yes**. *(You do not need that file anymore because you just converted it to the ArcInfo coverage, tracts.)*

PRACTICE 5-4

Rename additional shapefiles as follows:
- tgr42003cty00 to county
- tgr42003lkA to streets
- tgr42003wat to water
- zt42_d00 to zipcodes

After finishing, your file tree should look similar to the one shown in Figure 5-11. Close ArcCatalog when you are finished.

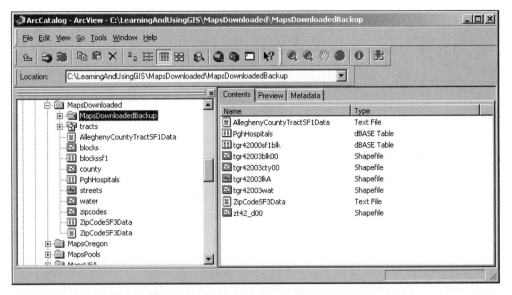

FIGURE 5-11 MapsDownloaded folder with renamed shapefiles and table

Prepare a Census Data Table

As discussed earlier in this chapter, data tables that you download from the Census Bureau are not in data table format, as needed by ArcGIS: There is an extra row of labels explaining the cryptic attribute names. Your next task is to rename attributes with self-documenting labels, create a data dictionary, delete the second row of descriptions, and save the results. You will do this work in Excel.

1. Start **Excel** on your computer.

2. On the main menu, click **File**, click **Open**, browse to
   C:\LearningAndUsingGIS\MapsDownloaded**, click the list arrow for **Files of type, click **All Files(*.*)**, and double-click **ZipCodeSF3Data.txt**.

3. In the Text Import Wizard window, Step 1, click the **Delimited** option button and click **Next**; then in the Step 2 window, click the **Comma** check box, uncheck the **Tab** check box, and click **Next**; and, finally, in the Step 3 window, click the column heading of the **second column** *(for GEO_ID2)*, click the **Text** option button *(so that leading zeros are not lost for the five-digit zip codes)*, and click **Finish**. See Figure 5-12.

4. Click the row selector for **row 2** *(see Figure 5-12)*; then on the main menu, click **Format**, click **Cells**, click the **Alignment** tab, click the list arrow under **Vertical**, scroll up, and, click **Top**; and, finally, click the **Wrap text** check box, and click**OK**. *(This action exposes all of the text in the second row.)*

5. Change the value in cell B1 from GEO_ID2 to **ZIPCODE**, and change cell **E1** from P030001 to **W** *(which stands for number of workers 16 years and over)*.

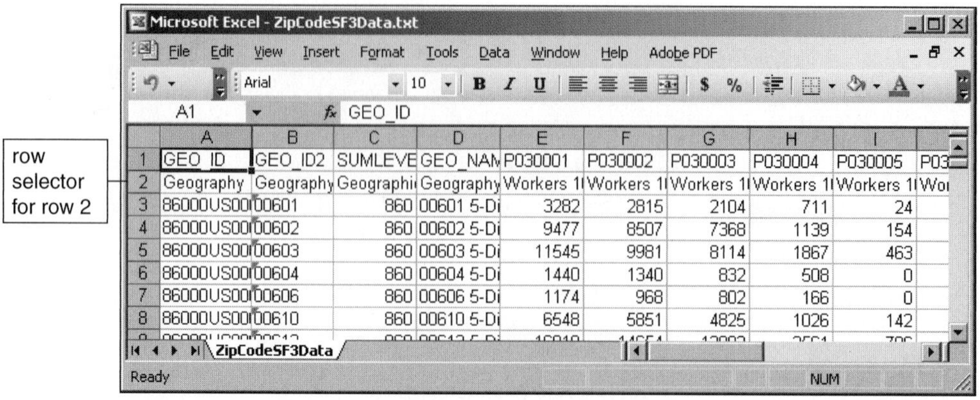

FIGURE 5-12   Excel with ZipCodeSF3Data.txt imported

PRACTICE 5-5

Rename additional cells in row 1, starting with F1 as follows: WCar, WCarAlone, WCar-Pool, WPublic, WBus, WTrolley, WSubway, WRailroad, WFerry, WTaxi, WMotorcycle, WBike, WWalk, WOther, WHome, and PCIncome.

Clean Up a Census Data Dictionary in Microsoft Excel

Although the extra row of attribute descriptions of the downloaded SF3 data cannot be kept in the data table for use in ArcMap, you can save it—along with attribute names—in a second worksheet as a data dictionary. You will do that, as well as save the data table in the dBase format, which is importable into ArcGIS, in the following steps.

1. Click the column selector for column **A**, then on the main menu, click **Edit** and click **Delete**.
2. Repeat Step 1 for the columns now in columns **B** and **C** (*SUMLEVEL and GEO_NAME*).
3. On the main menu, click **Insert** and click **Worksheet**.
4. Double-click the tab labeled **Sheet1**, and type **Data Dictionary**.
5. Click the **ZipCodeSF3Data** tab, then click the row selector for row **1**, hold your mouse key down, and slide down to also select row **2**.
6. Click **Edit**, click **Copy**, and click the **Data Dictionary** tab; then click cell **A1**, click **Edit**, and click **Paste Special**; and, finally, in the Paste Special window, click the **Transpose** check box, and click **OK**.
7. Change column widths and row heights as desired. See Figure 5-13.
8. Click the **ZipCodeSF3Data** tab, click the row selector for row **2**, click **Edit**, and click **Delete**. See Figure 5-14.

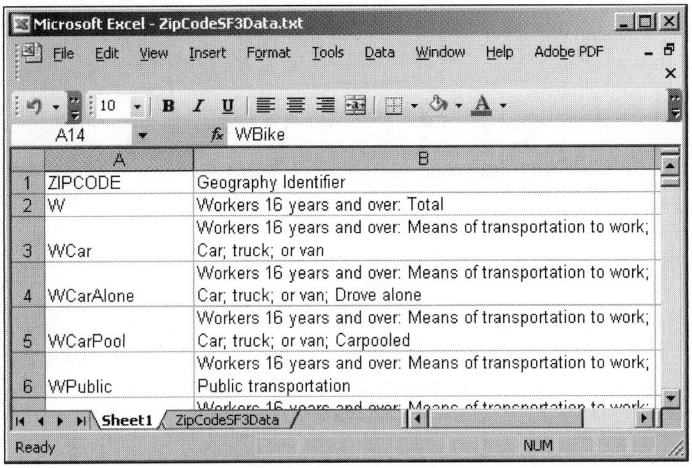

FIGURE 5-13 Data dictionary for zip code data

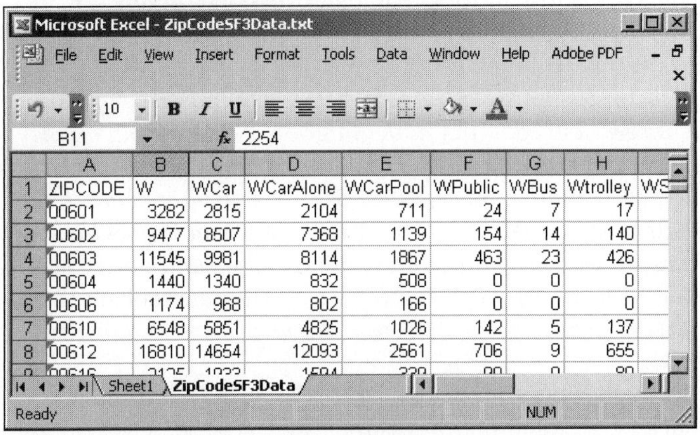

FIGURE 5-14 Prepared zip code data

9. Click **File** and click **Save As**; then, in the resulting Save As window, click the list arrow in the **Save as type** field, click **Microsoft Office Excel WorkBook (*.xls)**, and click **Save**. *(That saves both the data dictionary and the zip code data worksheets in an Excel workbook. ArcMap needs data tables in text or dBase IV format for import, so you'll save the data table alone in dBase format.)*

10. Click **File** and click **Save As**; then, in the resulting Save As window, click the list arrow in the **Save as type** field, click **DBF 4(dBASEIV)(*.dbf)**, click **Save**, click **OK**, and click **Yes**; and, finally, close **Excel** without saving. *(You've already saved the file.)*

Open *SF1Tracts.txt* in Excel. Rename the census data columns using HousingTotal for H003001, HousingOccupied for H003002, and HousingVacant for H003003. When you are finished, delete row 2 (do not save a data dictionary in this case), select all cells in the data region of the table, and save the resulting file as *SF1Tracts.dbf*.

Prepare a Census Tract Primary Key in ArcMap

The downloaded SF1 data in *AlleghenyCountyTractSF1Data.txt* has its census tract identifier in a single attribute (for example, 42003412001), whereas the census tract coverage that you imported and converted to a shapefile has the same identifier broken into three separate attributes (for example, 42, 003, and 412001). To enable joining the SF1 Data to the tract map for display, you will have to combine the coverage's separate pieces into a single, matching identifier. You need to use Excel for this task.

1. Start **Excel**, click **File**, click **Open**, browse to your **C:\LearningAndUsingGIS\MapsDownloaded** folder, and open **tracts.dbf**.
2. Adjust column widths by dragging the borders of column headings so that you can see the contents of all attributes.
3. Click the column selector for **TRACTS_** to select that column, and click **Insert Columns**. *(Always insert new columns in the interior of an existing dBase table, and never at its right end. If you do the latter, the results are not saved.)*
4. Click cell **C1** of the new column, and type **TractID**. *(Next, you will combine the three attributes that make up the full tract ID: State, County, and Name. These attributes are numeric, so you will combine the parts by multiplying by large numbers consisting of a 1 and the needed number of 0s to make the result have the right form. Be sure to get the number of zeros correct: 9, then 6, and then 2.)*
5. Click cell **C2**, type **=1000000000***, click cell **F2**, type **+1000000***, click cell **G2**, type **+100***, click cell **I2**, and then press the **Enter** key. See Figure 5-15. *(You might have to widen column C to see the results. Those actions build a cell formula for C2 that yields the desired tract number. Start over if the result does not look right. Cell C2 should have the value 42049011701. 00000000000.)*
6. Click the column selector for column **C**, click **Format**, click **Cells**; then, in the resulting Format Cells window, click the **Number** tab, change the Decimal places to **0**, and click **OK**.

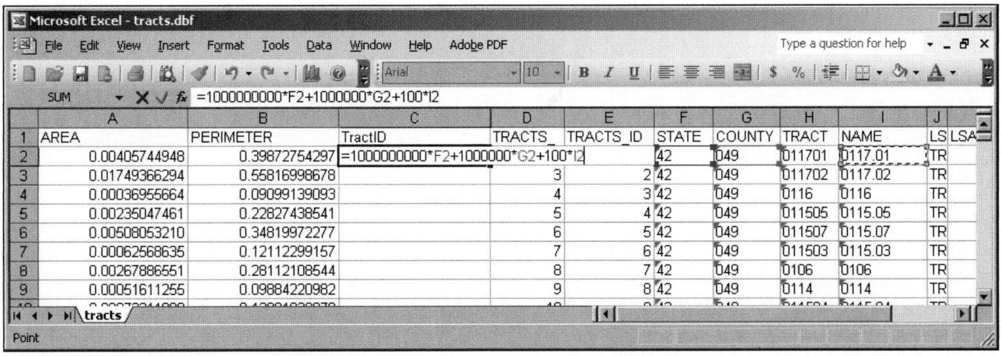

FIGURE 5-15 Cell formula for constructing the full census tract ID

7. Click **File**, click **Save**, and click **Yes**.
8. Close **Excel** without saving.

Create a New Attribute In ArcMap

As a demonstration of how you can create new attributes using ArcMap, you will create the attribute PVacantH = 100*HOUSINGVA/HOUSINGTO, the percentage of housing that is vacant. *Note: ArcMap truncates attribute names that you create to 10 characters because of the dBase format.*

1. On your PC computer's desktop, click **Start**, click **All Programs**, click **ArcGIS**, and click **ArcMap**.
2. In the ArcMap window, click the **An existing map** option button, double-click the **Browse for Maps** link, browse to your **C:\LearningAndUsingGIS** folder, and double-click **Chapter5-1.mxd**.
3. Click the **Add Data** button ✛, browse to your **C:\LearningAndUsingGIS\MapsPools\MapsDownloaded** folder, click **SF1Tracts.dbf**, click **Add**, and click **OK**.
4. Right-click **SF1Tracts** and click **Open**.
5. On the bottom right of the Attributes of tracts window, click the **Options** button and click **Add Field**.
6. In the resulting Add Field window, type **PVacantH**, change the type to **Float**, and click **OK**. See Figure 5-16.
7. Scroll to the right in the Attributes of tracts window, right-click the column heading for **PVacantH**, click **Calculate Values**, and click **Yes**.
8. In the Fields panel of the resulting Field Calculator window, click in the panel below **PVavcantH = **, type **100***, in the Fields panel double-click **HOUSINGVAC**, click the **division** button (with the "/" symbol), and double-click **HOUSINGTOT**. See Figure 5-17.

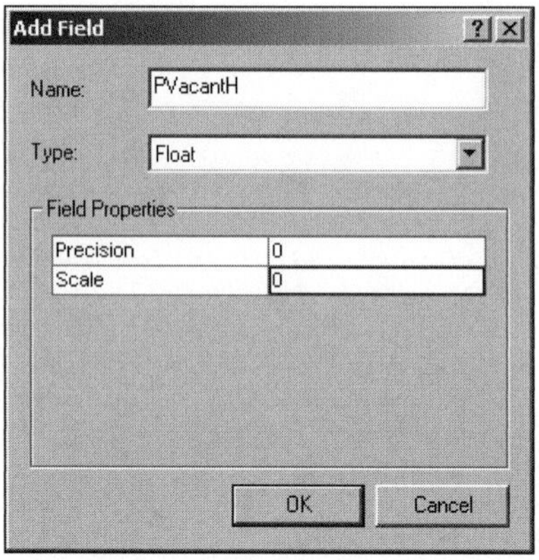

FIGURE 5-16 Parameters for creating a new attribute

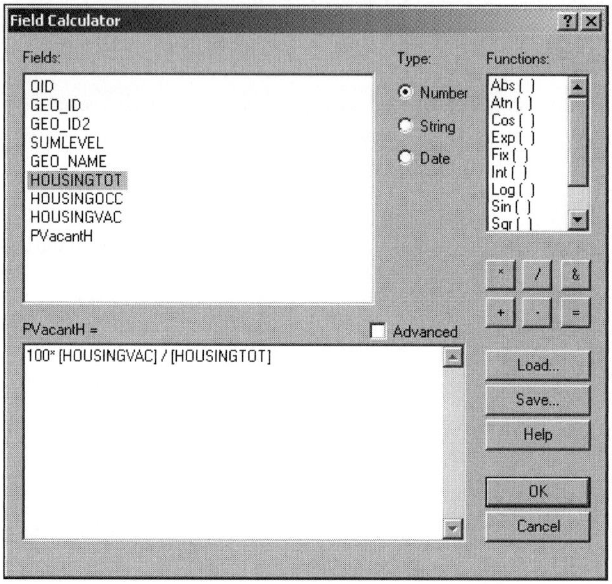

FIGURE 5-17 Formula for calculating a new attribute

9. Click **OK**. See Figure 5-18.
10. Close the table.

Join a Data Table to a Map Layer

Finally, you are ready to join census data to polygon maps. You will join the *SF1Tracts.dbf* table to the tracts polygon map. Now, *tracts.dbf* of the tracts shapefile has the numeric-value attribute, TractID, and the data table *SF1tracts.dbf* has the numeric-value attribute, GEO_ID2—both with matching tract IDs for Allegheny County.

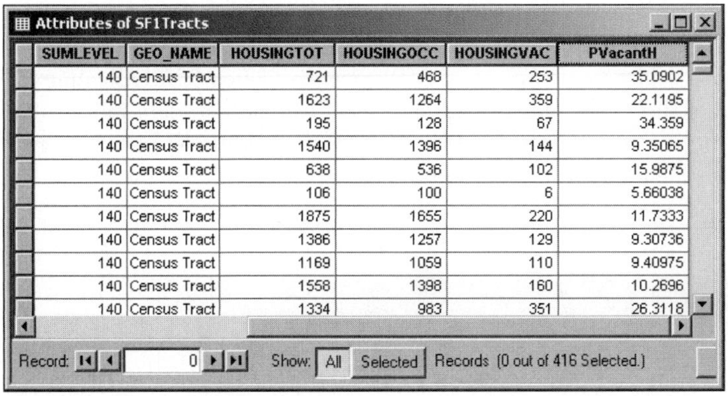

Attributes of SF1Tracts

SUMLEVEL	GEO_NAME	HOUSINGTOT	HOUSINGOCC	HOUSINGVAC	PVacantH
140	Census Tract	721	468	253	35.0902
140	Census Tract	1623	1264	359	22.1195
140	Census Tract	195	128	67	34.359
140	Census Tract	1540	1396	144	9.35065
140	Census Tract	638	536	102	15.9875
140	Census Tract	106	100	6	5.66038
140	Census Tract	1875	1655	220	11.7333
140	Census Tract	1386	1257	129	9.30736
140	Census Tract	1169	1059	110	9.40975
140	Census Tract	1558	1398	160	10.2696
140	Census Tract	1334	983	351	26.3118

Record: 0 Show: All Selected Records (0 out of 416 Selected.)

FIGURE 5-18 New attribute, PVacantH

1. Right-click **tracts**, click **Joins and Relates**, and click **Join**.
2. In the resulting Join Data window, make the selections shown in Figure 5-19.

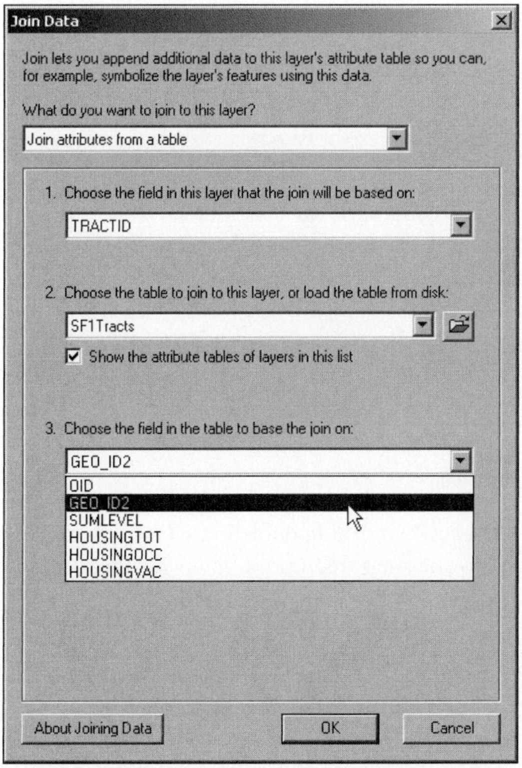

FIGURE 5-19 Selections for joining SF1Tracts to the tracts map layer

3. Click **OK** and click **Yes**.

4. Right-click **tracts** and click **Open Attribute Table**.
5. Scroll to the right, right-click **tracts.COUNTY**, and click **Sort Ascending**.
6. Scroll down until you come to tracts.COUNTY with values **003** (Allegheny County), then scroll to the right to see values for your joined data table, such as for SF1Tracts.HOUSINGTOT. See Figure 5-20. *(Notice that in the joined table attribute names have the name of the table from which they come as a prefix.)*

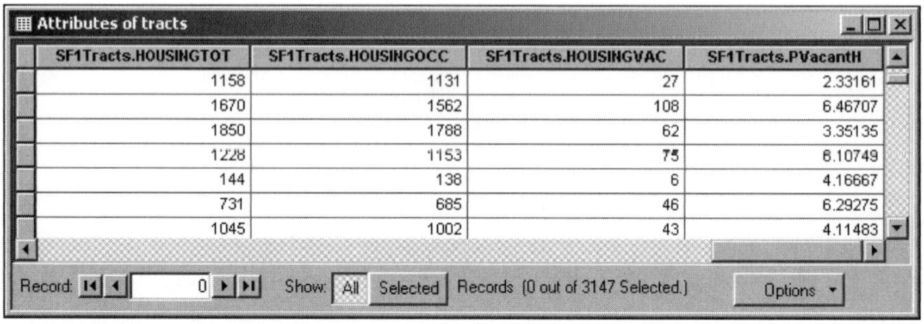

SF1Tracts.HOUSINGTOT	SF1Tracts.HOUSINGOCC	SF1Tracts.HOUSINGVAC	SF1Tracts.PVacantH
1158	1131	27	2.33161
1670	1562	108	6.46707
1850	1788	62	3.35135
1228	1153	75	6.10749
144	138	6	4.16667
731	685	46	6.29275
1045	1002	43	4.11483

Record: 0   Show: All Selected   Records (0 out of 3147 Selected.)   Options ▾

FIGURE 5-20   SF1Tracts table joined with the tracts map layer

7. Close the **Attributes of tracts** window.

PRACTICE 5-7

Add *zipcodes.shp* and *ZipCodeSF3Data.dbf* to *Chapter2-1.mdx* from the C:\LearningAndUsingGIS\MapsDownloaded\ folder and join *ZipCodeSF3Data.dbf* to *zipcodes.shp*. Open attribute tables for each table to find the names of matching attributes with text-value, five-digit zip code values. Text values are left-justified in their columns. Note that *ZipCodeSF3Data.dbf* has data for the entire United States, but only records matching zip codes in Pennsylvania are included in the join.

Add an XY Map to a Map Document

You downloaded hospital data, including latitude and longitude coordinates for Allegheny County hospitals. Next, you will add that data to the map document as an XY map, and then convert it to a shapefile.

1. On the main menu, click **Tools** and click **Add XY Data**.
2. In the resulting Add XY Data window, click the **browse** button at the top of the window, browse to **C:\LearningAndUsingGIS\MapsDownloaded**, click **PghHopsitals.dbf**, click **Add**, and click **OK**.
3. Right-click **PghHospitals Events** and click **Zoom to Layer**. See Figure 5-21. *(You can see that the coordinates for hospitals are not very precise because of the way that the points align either in the vertical or horizontal dimensions. It is more convenient to have a shapefile for hospitals instead of an XY data map. So next, you will convert the XY map to a shapefile.)*

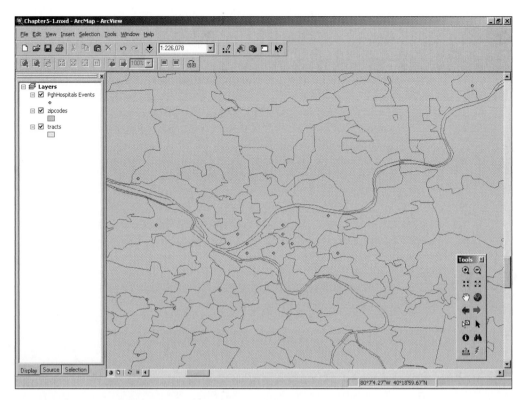

FIGURE 5-21 Map document with hospitals' XY data added

4. Right-click **PghHospitals Events**, click **Data**, and click **Export Data**.
5. In the resulting Export Data window, browse to
   C:\LearningAndUsingGIS\MapsDownloaded, change the Output shapefile
   name from *Export_Output.shp* to **Hospitals**, click **Save**, click **OK**, and
   click **Yes**.
6. Right-click **PghHospitals Events** and click **Remove**.
7. Save your map document and exit ArcMap.

PERSONAL GEODATABASES

Shapefiles are convenient because the format is so widely used. However, modern organizations prefer a database approach to working with map layers to match general practices in working with data. The file-based approach of shapefiles is a bit old-fashioned. Here,
therefore, you will get a brief exposure to importing map layers into a single personal geodatabase, to be named *Chapter5.mdb*. A map layer in a personal geodatabase is called
a **feature class**.

Create a Personal Geodatabase

The work to be done starts with ArcCatalog, to create a personal geodatabase and import map layers.

1. On your PC's desktop, click **Start**, click **All Programs**, click **ArcGIS**, and click **ArcCatalog**.
2. In the file and folder tree panel, right-click **MapsDownloaded**, click **New**, and click **Personal Geodatabase**. *(That action creates a new Microsoft Access file called* Personal Geodatabase.mdb.*)*
3. Right-click **Personal Geodatabase**, click **Rename**, type **Chapter5**, and click anywhere in the white space of the file and folder panel.
4. Right-click **Chapter5**, click **Import**, and click **Feature Class (single)**.
5. In the Feature Class To Feature Class window, click the **browse** button for Input Features, browse to **C:\LearningAndUsingGIS\MapsDownloaded**, click **Hospitals.shp**, type **Hospitals** in the Output Feature Class Name field, click **Add**, click **OK**, click **Close**, and then in the file and folders panel of ArcCatalog, click the expander box for **Chapter 5**. *(Now you have a feature class called hospitals, imported from* hospitals.shp. *You will be able to map the feature class just as you would a shapefile.)*

PRACTICE 5-8

Import *tracts.shp* and *water.shp* from C:\LearningAndUsingGIS\MapsDownloaded\ into *Chapter5.mdb* as feature classes Tracts and Water, respectively. See Figure 5-22. When you are finished, close ArcCatalog.

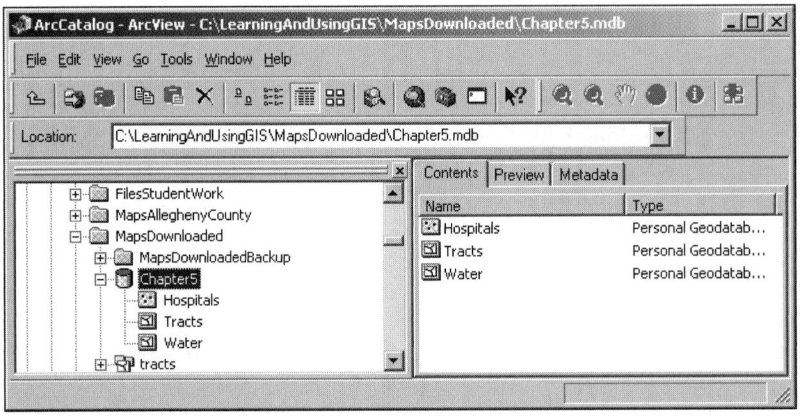

FIGURE 5-22 Chapter5.mdb with three feature classes imported

Create a Map Display from a Personal Geodatabase

To wrap up this chapter's tutorial, you will add map layers from your personal geodatabase to a map document. Also, just so that you can see the raster map you downloaded from the PASDA Web site, you also will add it to your map document.

1. On your PC computer's desktop, click **Start**, click **All Programs**, click **ArcGIS**, and click **ArcMap**.*(Currently, the data frame of your map document is not projected, and all added map layers are in latitude and longitude coordinates. You could add and display a raster map, but shapes would be distorted. So before adding the raster map, you will project the data frame to State Plane.)*

2. In the ArcMap window, click the **A new empty map** option button, and click **OK**.

3. In the table of contents, right-click **Layers**, click **Properties**, and then in the resulting Data Frame Properties window, click the **Coordinate System** tab.

4. In the Select a coordinate system panel, click expander boxes for **Predefined**, **Projected Coordinate Systems**, **State Plane**, and **NAD 1983 (Feet)**, and then click **NAD 1983 StatePlane Pennsylvania South FIPS 3702 (Feet)**, and click **OK**.

5. Click the **Add Data** button ✚, browse to your **C:\LearningAndUsingGIS\ MapsPools\MapsDownloaded** folder, double-click **Chapter5.mdb**, and double-click **Hospitals**. *(That action adds the Hospitals feature class to your map. You will see that working with a feature class is the same as working with a shapefile, for the most part. The feature class has properties, an attribute table, and other characteristics that are the same as those of shapefiles.)*

6. Similarly, add the **Tracts** and **Water** feature classes to your map document and symbolize all layers *(give Tracts a hollow fill)*. *(You might not have a raster map if you chose not to download it to save on disk storage space. If that is the case, just skip Steps 7 and 8 and examine Figure 5-22.)*

7. Click the **Add Data** button ✚, browse to your **C:\LearningAndUsingGIS\ MapsPools\MapsDownloaded** folder, click **pittsburgh_west_pa_ne.tif**, and click **Add**.

8. Zoom in to the **island area** of the rivers for a closer look. See Figure 5-23.
9. Save your map document as **Chapter5.2.mxd** in C:\LearningAndUsingGIS, and close ArcMap.

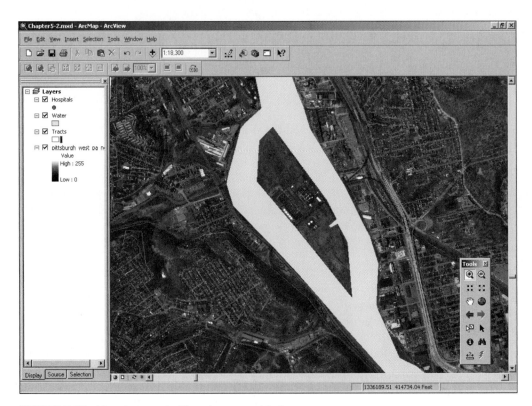

FIGURE 5-23   Map document with raster map added

Chapter 5 Summary

We obtained most of the base-map layers for the Swimming Pool Case Study—the blocks, municipalities, zip codes, streets, and rivers—for free on the Internet. You can get these and additional map layers and data for GIS projects for your own or other communities. We created a few of the map layers from scratch using methods that you will learn in Chapters 6 and 7. In all such cases, some of the downloaded maps were needed for processing.

The U.S. Census Bureau is a good source of map layers and data that you can add to a GIS project. These resources are free for all states and counties. GIS resources provided include TIGER/Line map layers—which show streets, rivers, states, counties, municipalities, census tracts, and so forth—and summary file tables, which contain census data tabulations that can be joined to corresponding map boundary layers. Two important summary files are Census Summary File 1, which has census data on basic population and housing characteristics from the complete census, and Census Summary File 3, which has a random sample of the population and housing with detailed characteristics, including place of birth, educational attainment, employment status, income, value of housing unit, and so forth. Census Bureau staff scaled sampled data tabulations up to full population levels. You can download these map layers and data tables from *www.census.gov* or *www.esri.com/data*.

The ESRI Web site has several additional map resources, from maps for countries around the world to the province/state level and from shaded relief maps for elevation to topographic raster maps. In addition, ESRI sponsors the *www.geographynetwork.com* Web site that has unique search capabilities by industry type and location for many vendors of map layers and their products. Another Web site sponsored in part by ESRI is *www.gis.com*, which also has links to map sources.

Many states have GIS clearinghouses on the Internet, such as the Pennsylvania site, PASDA, to provide map layers and data. You can find several Web pages with links to GISs for all states and many cities; for example, a good one is provided by Brown University (*www.brown.edu/Research/gis/webData.html*). Local governments are sources for map layers for features smaller than city blocks, such as building outlines, curbs, parking lots, and deeded properties. An increasing number of local governments are making their specialized GIS layers available for public use.

Data tables that you download for use in a GIS are not always in a format ready for use. Even the summary file tables from the Census Bureau need some preprocessing and cleanup. Microsoft Excel is a convenient tool for some of this work, which includes renaming attributes, deleting extraneous columns and rows, building composite primary keys, changing the data types of attributes, and creating new variables from existing ones such as ratios and sums.

With data tables ready for use and imported into a map document in ArcMap, you next need to join them to map layers, using table joins. Both the data table and the map layer's attribute table need to have the same primary key values for this task to be successful. ArcMap has very powerful and convenient functionality for joining tables.

Staff in organizations today are accustomed to working with databases, so a GIS with shapefiles seems a bit old-fashioned. ArcMap comes with the capacity to build a personal geodatabase, using Microsoft Access, to provide a database approach to GIS. The resultant map layers, called feature classes, function in many ways like shapefiles, except that they are stored in a single database file.

Key Terms

Candidate key A column in a data table that has unique values and no missing or null values. If there are two or more such columns, only one is designated as the primary key.

Census blocks The smallest statistical tabulation area used by the U.S. Census Bureau for reporting census variables. In urban areas, census blocks are also city blocks. Their boundaries are made up mostly of streets, but they also include rivers, lakes, county lines, and many other line features.

Census block groups Collections of census blocks yielding approximately 1000 population. This is the smallest tabulation available for SF3 data.

Census Summary File 1 (SF1) A collection of data tables from the complete census of persons and households. Included are population, age, sex, race, Hispanic/Latino origin, household relationship, ownership of residences, and so forth.

Census Summary File 3 (SF3) A collection of data tables from the 1-in-6 random sample of the population. Included are variables such as place of birth, educational attainment, employment status, income, value of a housing unit, and construction year for structures.

Census tracts Collections of census block groups yielding approximately 4000 population each. Census tracts are the primary statistical tabulation area for the census.

Concatenate A process of combining text values to create a new composite value using the "&" operator. For example, `"Bill" & " " & "Jones"` yields `"Bill Jones"`.

Feature class A map layer stored in a personal geodatabase. It is possible to import shapefiles and maps in other file formats into a personal geodatabase as feature classes. The feature classes behave, for the most part, like shapefiles when symbolizing maps and carrying out other common GIS steps.

Null value A cell in a data table that does not have a value. Often, a special, nonprinting symbol is used to denote such a cell.

Primary key A column in a data table that has unique and nonnull values and that has been designated to be the primary identifier of rows.

Spatially referenced data Data tables that include unique identifiers for geographic area, such as state names, county FIPS codes, five-digit zip codes, or census tract numbers. Such tables can be joined to feature attribute tables of corresponding map layers.

Table join A process that combines two tables, row by row, to create a new table. Often, rows are matched using a primary key.

Short-Answer Questions

1. Suppose that you have a map layer of U.S. Census Bureau tract boundaries for a county that has urban, suburban, and rural areas. How would you expect the size of census tracts, in acres, to vary across those three kinds of areas? Why?

2. Describe the relationship between Census Bureau tracts, block groups, and blocks. What are advantages of such a design for reporting the census?

3. Explain the differences between the Census Summary File 1 and Census Summary File 3 data collections. What do you think the Census Bureau's motivation was for designing these two data collections?

4. Why are Census Bureau boundary files supplied without census data already attached to them? Describe the computer skills that you need to use SF1 and SF3 data in a GIS.

5. Why doesn't the Census Bureau build map layers of deeded land parcels?

6. What major Web site do you visit to learn about map layers depicting human health in Africa?

7. What data do you download to identify the poverty-stricken areas of a state?

8. If you were the city official in charge of GIS and needed a street layer for use in dispatching emergency vehicles (police, fire, and ambulances), which map layer would you obtain? Why?

9. Why did the Census Bureau base its map layers on line features?

10. Suppose that a data table that you download won't join to its corresponding map layer, downloaded from a different Web site. What are potential causes of the problem, and how do you remedy them?

Exercises

1. **Download GIS Layers from Sarasota County, Florida.** An example of a local government providing map layers on the Internet is Sarasota County, Florida.

   a. Create the subfolder **C:\LearningAndUsingGIS\FilesStudentWork\Exercise5-1**.

   b. Open your Web browser and then open Sarasota County's Web site, *http://gis.co.sarasota.fl.us*. Scroll to the Maps and Data section.

   c. Click GIS DATA and download the following layers: Coast Line, County Line, Major Roads, Parks Polygons, and School Points.

   d. Create a map document called **Exercise5-1.mxd** and save it in the C:\LearningAndUsingGIS\FilesStudentWork\ folder (and not in the C:\LearningAndUsingGIS\FilesStudentWork\Exercise5-1\ subfolder).

   e. Add your map layers to the map document. Symbolize map layers using good map design principles. Zoom in to the northwest area of the county, which has the high density of schools. Create a layout in your map document with title, map, legend, and scale in miles.

   f. Create a Microsoft PowerPoint document called **Exercise5-1<YourName>.ppt** saved in the C:\LearningAndUsingGIS\FilesStudentWork\ folder, where you substitute your name or other identifier for <YourName>. Include a title slide for your PowerPoint document (such as Map of Sarasota, Florida) and your name or other identifier. Next create a bulleted slide listing the input data source and layers. Export your map layout as a *.jpg* image, and place it in the third slide.

2. **Create and Input an XY Map for Places of Interest in Your County.** In this exercise, you will download map layers for your county including a street map, find several points of interest using the street map, record the points' coordinates and other attributes in a dBase table, and plot them as an XY map.

   a. Create the subfolder **C:\LearningAndUsingGIS\FilesStudentWork\Exercise5-2**.

   b. Start your Web browser and download the following map layers from the ESRI TIGER Web site for your county into C:\LearningAndUsingGIS\FilesStudentWork\Exercise5-2\: 2000 county subdivisions, roads, and water polygons.

c. Create a map document called **Exercise5-2.mxd** and save it in the C:\LearningAndUsingGIS\FilesStudentWork\ folder (and not in the C:\LearningAndUsingGIS\FilesStudentWork\Exercise5-2\ subfolder).

d. Use a search engine on the Internet to find a State Plane zone map so that you can look up the State Plane zone for your county, and project the map document's data frame to that State Plane zone in feet.

e. Add your downloaded map layers to the map document. Symbolize map layers, using good design principles.

f. Compile a list of six places of interest to you in your county for which you can obtain street addresses or otherwise find locations on the map. For example, use a Web site such as *www.yellow.com*. Open Excel and type the following column headings in row 1: Name, Address, Zipcode, X, and Y. Type names and addresses for the six places of interest in the table. In ArcMap, use the attribute table of roads (sort by the name of streets), select the street segment record that has the desired street number in its range, and zoom to selected features to find the street segments of interest. Hover your cursor over the approximate location of a place of interest and record corresponding coordinates in the X and Y cells of the place of interest's row. When you are finished, save the spreadsheet as a DBF 4 (dBASE IV) (*.dbf*) file called **Interests.dbf** in your C:\LearningAndUsingGIS\FilesStudentWork\Exercise5-2\ folder.

g. Add **Interests.dbf** to your map document as an XY map, and label the points with its Name attribute. Create a layout in your map document with title, map, legend, and scale.

h. Create a Microsoft Word document called **Exercise5-2<YourName>.doc** and save it in the C:\LearningAndUsingGIS\FilesStudentWork\ folder, where you substitute your name or other identifier for <YourName>. Include a title for your Word document (such as My Places of Interest Map), your name or other identifier, and a paragraph listing the input data sources and where you obtained them. Copy and paste your table, *Interests.dbf*, in your Word document. Lastly, export your layout as a *.jpg* image, and place it in your Word document.

3. **Download Map Layers for Oregon's Urban Growth Areas.** Oregon's 241 cities are surrounded by urban growth areas delimited by urban growth boundaries (UGBs). A UGB shows where a city expects growth; land outside the UGB will remain rural. In this exercise, you will download Census Bureau boundary maps necessary to build a map document showing where Oregon's urban growth boundaries are compared with existing urban and rural areas.

a. Create the subfolder **C:\LearningAndUsingGIS\FilesStudentWork\Exercise5-3**.

b. Open a Web browser and go to the *www.census.gov*, TIGER link in the Geography section, Cartographic Boundary Files link, Oregon Urban Growth Areas link, and so forth. Download the following boundary map layers for Oregon into the Exercise5-3 folder: 2000 Oregon Urban Growth Areas and 2000 county subdivisions. Be sure to scroll down and get shapefiles.

c. Open the American Fact Finder Web site in your browser and use the following links and selections: Download Center, Census 2000 Summary File 1 (SF 1) 100-Percent Data, State Level, All County Subdivisions in a State, Oregon, Selected Tables, P2 (Urban and Rural, Total Population).

d. Extract the shapefiles and data table from the downloaded files to C:\LearningAndUsingGIS\FilesStudentWork\Exercise5-3\.

e. In your data table, use Excel to create a new attribute called PUrban = 100*P002002/P002001, delete the second row of the table, and save the results as **UrbanPop.dbf** in C:\LearningAndUsingGIS\FilesStudentWork\Exercise5-3\. *Hint: Create PUrban in the middle of the table and not the extreme right—the .dbf format does not allow you to add new columns at the extreme right.* In your municipalities shapefile, combine STATE (41), COUNTY (for example, 001), and COUSUBFP (for example, 90204) to yield a double field called GEO_ID2 (for example, 4100190204).

f. Create a map document called **Exercise5-3.mxd**, and save it in C:\LearningAndUsingGIS\FilesStudentWork\ folder (and not in the C:\LearningAndUsingGIS\FilesStudentWork\Exercise5-3\ subfolder).

g. Use a search engine on the Internet to find a UTM zone map so that you can look up a UTM zone for Oregon (use the one that includes the coast), and project the map document's data frame to that UTM zone.

h. Add the downloaded data layers to your map document. Join *UrbanPop.dbf* to the municipalities attribute table and create a choropleth map for PUrban. Symbolize layers using good map design principles. Create a layout in your map document with title, map, legend, and scale. *Hint 1: To use color fill for both the choropleth map and the urban growth areas, open the property sheet for growth areas, click the Display tab, and set transparency to 50 percent. Hint 2: You can modify the legend of your layout by right-clicking it, clicking Convert to Graphics, right-clicking it again, and clicking Ungroup. Then, you can change the text in text boxes, delete undesirable text boxes, and so forth.*

i. Create a PowerPoint document called **Exercise5-3<YourName>.ppt** saved in the C:\LearningAndUsingGIS\FilesStudentWork\ folder, where you substitute your name or other identifier for <YourName>. Include a title slide for your PowerPoint document (such as Map of Oregon Urban Growth Boundaries) and your name or other identifier. Next create a bulleted slide listing the input data source and shapefiles. Export your map layout, zoomed to the full extent as a *.jpg* image and place it in the third slide. For the fourth slide, zoom to Portland and click the fixed zoom out button once, turn on labeling for municipalities, and export the layout again. Finally, in the fourth slide, describe one or more patterns in the census attribute spatial distribution of your maps.

4. **Download Map Layers and Data Tables for Your County.** In this exercise, you will download TIGER maps and a demographic data table from the ESRI and Census Bureau Web sites to build a map of a county of your choice.

a. Create the subfolder **C:\LearningAndUsingGIS\FilesStudentWork\Exercise5-4\.**

b. Open your Web browser, download shapefiles from the ESRI TIGER Web site and Census data from the Census Web site into C:\LearningAndUsingGIS\FilesStudentWork\Exercise5-4\ as follows: 2000 census tracts, county boundary, 2000 county census divisions (municipalities), and a single SF3 data table of your choice for 2000 census tracts.

c. Create a map document called **Exercise5-4.mxd**, and save it in the C:\LearningAndUsingGIS\FilesStudentWork\ folder (and not in the C:\LearningAndUsingGIS\FilesStudentWork\Exercise5-4\ subfolder).

d. Use a search engine on the Internet to find a State Plane zone map so that you can look up the zone for your county, and project the map document's data frame to that State Plane zone in feet.

e. Add your map layers to the map document. Do data preparation as necessary for joining your census tract data table to the tract map. In this case, add your downloaded census data map to your map document, open it, add a new text field called STFID, and calculate it to equal GEO_ID2. This transforms the numeric GEO_ID2 attribute to be the text STFID attribute, matching the STFID in your census map layer.

f. Make the join and create a choropleth map for a census attribute in your tract data table. Symbolize other map layers, using good design principles. Label municipalities. Create a layout in your map document with title, map, legend, and scale. See Hint 2 of Exercise 5-3.

g. Create a Word document called **Exercise5-4<YourName>.doc** saved in the C:\LearningAndUsingGIS\FilesStudentWork\ folder, where you substitute your name or other identifier for <YourName>. Include a title for your Word document (such as Map of My County), your name or other identifier, a paragraph listing the input data sources and where you obtained them, and the projection used for your layout. Export your layout as a *.jpg* image, and place it in your Word document. Describe one or more patterns of the census attribute spatial distribution of your choropleth map.

References

Department of Land Conservation and Development (DLCD), Oregon Urban Growth Boundary, Internet URL: http://*darkwing.uoregon.edu/~pppm/landuse/UGB.html*, accessed March 23, 2005.

ESRI Downloadable Data, Internet URL: www.esri.com/data/download/index.html, accessed March 5, 2005.

ESRI Geography Network, Internet URL: www.geographynetwork.com, accessed March 7, 2005.

U.S. Census Bureau Tiger Overview, Internet URL: www.census.gov/geo/www/tiger/overview.html, accessed March 11, 2005.

U.S. Census Bureau Cartographic Boundary Files, Internet URL: www.census.gov/geo/www/cob/index.html, accessed March 12, 2005.

USGS National Elevation Dataset, Internet URL: http://gisdata.usgs.net/ned, accessed March 23, 2005.

BUILDING A GIS STUDY AREA

LEARNING OBJECTIVES

In this chapter, you will:

- Understand variations in study areas
- Identify various approaches for extracting portions of maps
- Learn about administrative areas
- Learn about appending maps
- Extract and clip portions of maps using ArcGIS
- Dissolve and append map layers using ArcGIS
- Run a script to build a centroid map using ArcGIS
- Write a macro using ArcGIS ModelBuilder

Jimmy extracts himself from an area of the pool

INTRODUCTION

In Chapter 5, you learned that there is a multitude of map layers available for you to download from the Internet—all paid for by tax dollars and part of our country's digital infrastructure. These map layers generally come in certain area units, such as country, state, county, and grid areas (for raster maps). What if, however, you want to build a GIS for an area different from any available? For example, the Swimming Pool Case Study concerns the City of Pittsburgh, which is a subset of Allegheny County but is not available as a separate set of map layers. What if you want your maps to only have the Pittsburgh area? In that case, you must extract a subset of features from available county or state maps for your **study area** of Pittsburgh. In other cases, your study area must be built from a combination of several downloaded maps to build a larger area. For example, to create a GIS to study water quality in the Santee River Basin in South Carolina, you would need to **append** map layers for five counties—Berkeley, Clarendon, Charleston, Georgetown, and Williamsburg.

Several GIS tools are available for extracting portions of map layers to create new map layers. You will learn how to select features by attribute, for which you use an attribute query to select features; by shape, for which you use some spatial features to select others; and by means of **clipping**, in which you use a fixed area as a "cookie cutter" to chop out features.

To go from small to larger areas, you have two options. The first is to use the **dissolve** function. Dissolving is a good means of building administrative areas—such as police patrol areas, school districts, and so on—from census blocks, block groups, or tracts. The second option is to append one or more adjoining map layers to make a larger area.

When building study areas, it is sometimes necessary to use special programs, or scripts, that do not appear on any of the ArcGIS menus or toolbars, but nevertheless are available. You will learn how to run a script in the ArcGIS Field Calculator for creating a centroid point layer from a polygon layer. In addition, sometimes it is necessary to reuse a series of interactive steps in ArcGIS, over and over. For automating such work, ArcGIS has a **macro** builder, called ModelBuilder, that you will use to combine two or more steps into a single macro.

STUDY AREAS

The construction of a GIS starts with a problem definition that stems from the mission of an organization, the purpose of a project, or the problem to be solved. For example, if you work for a city's parks and recreation department, your GIS probably needs to have the city's boundary as its study area. If you have a project for the Group Against Water Pollution in the Santee River Basin, you need to use the multiple-county region in South Carolina in which the river flows as the study area. If you want to analyze traffic and pedestrian accidents around a college campus, you probably need to limit your GIS to a buffered area of the campus boundary. The geographic area for a problem definition is its study area.

When you build a study area, your starting point is base maps available on CD or downloaded from the Internet. These are polygon, line, point, and raster maps provided mainly by government agencies. In addition, vendors provide enhanced government maps and specialized map layers. Base maps are the inputs to **geoprocessing** functions—computer programs available as tools in ArcToolbox—that can extract features or combine features in building a study region.

FEATURE EXTRACTION

Selecting a subset of existing features—points, lines, or polygons—from an existing map layer is straightforward. You can click features' records in the map layer's attribute table or execute an attribute query. Also, you can use the Select Features tool on the Standard toolbar to select features from a map, by direct inspection. You can also save selected features as a new shapefile as part of your study area.

The first map layer to save for a study area is its boundary, which is generally a single polygon. This is simple if the boundary already exists as a single polygon in a base map, such as for a city. Figure 6-1 shows the TIGER base map of municipalities in Allegheny County with Pittsburgh selected for the study area boundary. Pittsburgh has the interesting case of Mount Oliver, a municipality entirely within Pittsburgh. The Pittsburgh boundary thus has Mount Oliver as a "hole" or island as part of its polygon.

Later in this chapter, you will learn how to make a boundary map for a study area that consists of two or more polygons from a single map layer, such as several census tracts. With the study area boundary saved as a new map layer, you can use it to select or clip out other features, such a streets, for the study area GIS.

When adding more layers to a study area, such as Pittsburgh, you must determine how to handle the case of features that cross the study area's boundary. Two good examples are

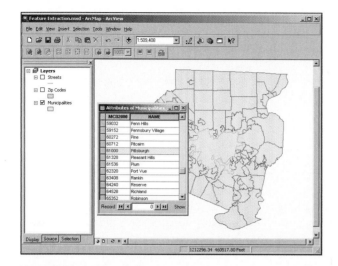

FIGURE 6-1 Pittsburgh's boundary polygon selected for use as a study area boundary

zip code polygons and streets lines. See the zip codes in Figure 6-2. The left panel shows all the zip codes that are inside Pittsburgh or cross its boundary. The right panel has zip codes clipped to Pittsburgh's boundary.

If you can guarantee that all data that you would display using zip code boundaries, such as counts of pool tag holders, are for points only inside of Pittsburgh, you could use the clipped zip codes. Clipping, however, is not correct for pool-tag-holders' residence zip codes. Pool tag holders can live outside of Pittsburgh, so you need to use the other version of the study-area zip codes, shown in the left panel of Figure 6-2.

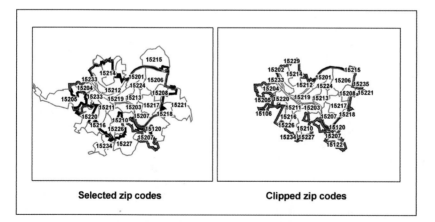

FIGURE 6-2 Selected zip code polygons that cross Pittsburgh's boundary, and zip code polygons clipped to Pittsburgh's boundary

Whether to select or clip streets is a bit more complicated. Each block-long TIGER street segment has street numbers only for its beginning and end—apparently that is all the information the Census Bureau needs when using street maps to conduct the census. Figure 6-3 illustrates a street segment. When you use ArcGIS's geocoding or address-matching capability in Chapter 7 to place points on the street network from street address data, the algorithm will linearly interpolate the point location along the street segment, given the street numbers at each end of the street. For example, ArcGIS would place the address, 450 Eureka St, approximately halfway between the end points of the street segment, which ranges between 400 and 498 on the even side of the street. This nature of TIGER streets and address matching have the following consequence: You should not clip (shorten) street segments that cross your study area's boundary, but select and retain original street segments. If you clip a street segment, the resultant line feature, of course, will be shorter, but will retain its original attribute record and street numbers. Thus, interpolation and placement will be incorrect.

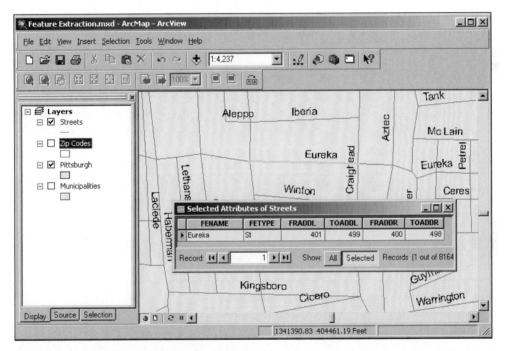

FIGURE 6-3 TIGER street segment and record

A good approach to building a study area that doesn't cut street segments into pieces is to aggregate blocks or other census areas as the basis of the study area—because those areas are mostly made up of whole street segments. The dissolve tool in the next section enables you to carry out that task.

Dissolving Polygons

The dissolve function combines adjacent polygons to create new, larger polygons. For example, Pittsburgh neighborhoods each consist of one or more census tracts. To create neighborhood polygons from tract polygons, you need to create a dissolve attribute in tracts that contains the name of each tract's neighborhood ID or name. ArcGIS's dissolve tool uses that information to remove tract interior lines within each neighborhood, forming the neighborhood polygons. The dissolve function can also aggregate (for example, sum) census data from the input tracts up to the neighborhood level. Having population and other data available for dissolved polygons is valuable for analysis and decision making.

Let's apply this tool to the simpler task of creating the single polygon of a study area from several adjoining census tracts. To apply the dissolve tool, all you need is an attribute that has the same value for all tracts in the study area because the dissolve tool uses unique values in the dissolve attribute to identify polygons that are to be combined. If all of the values are the same in the attributes column, then only one, large polygon results. FIPSSTO, the FIPS code of the county, is just such an existing TIGER map attribute for tracts. Figure 6-4 shows the starting four census tracts of the Hill District study area of Pittsburgh, their attribute table with the FIPSSTO attribute serving as the dissolve field, and the resulting output of the dissolved, study-area polygon.

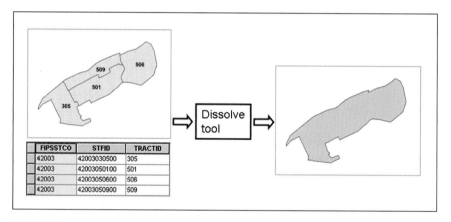

FIGURE 6-4 Dissolving tracts to form a study-area boundary

Dissolving polygons to form fewer larger polygons follows the same process, except that each output polygon's ID or name must be repeated in the dissolve column of the input polygons forming a larger one. It is easy to enter values into a dissolve column of an attribute table: You only need to select all input polygons of an output dissolved polygon using the map and then to enter the common ID or name in the corresponding selected rows for the dissolve column.

Cities and other organizations commonly build administrative areas from census polygons including blocks, block groups, or tracts. This practice makes census data readily available for analysis at the dissolved level. For example, as part of the dissolve process, ArcGIS aggregates input attributes up to the dissolved-polygon level. For example, if you are dissolving tracts to make neighborhoods, you can get the population by age and gender for neighborhoods as a by-product of dissolving. Such demographic data and other attributes can be critically important for policy and management decision-making purposes. For example, in the emergency medical services (EMS) case later in this chapter, public safety officials might want to analyze the number of EMS calls per 1000 population in each EMS zone dissolved from census polygons.

When selecting input polygons for building administrative areas you should consider the kind of census data available versus size of polygons. Using blocks as the input enables you to create just about any shape of administrative area because blocks are so small. The limitation of blocks, however, is that only SF1 census data is available for them, from the full census. To provide SF3 detailed data on income, educational attainment, and so on, you must use block groups or tracts as the inputs, which, of course, are larger in size than blocks and therefore less flexible.

Appending Map Layers

Suppose that you have downloaded map layers for three counties for your study area. To build study-area map layers, you need to append the input map layers. The append process normally takes adjacent map layers as inputs, each with the same feature type (point, line, polygon, or raster), and the same attribute **table schema**. A table's schema consists of the names and data types of its attributes. So in this case, each input layer must have the same attributes, which is no problem when combining multiple map layers downloaded from the same source.

Scripts

Visual Basic for Applications (VBA) is a trimmed-down version of Microsoft's Visual Basic computer language. It was designed for writing **scripts**—small programs—that provide custom functionality for use in application packages, including Microsoft Office (Word, Excel, and so on) and ESRI's ArcGIS. We do not expect you to write scripts, but you can use some scripts available from ArcGIS Desktop Help for GIS tasks not available in any of ArcGIS's menus or toolbars. A script that you will use takes polygons as the input, calculates the coordinates of the polygons' centroids, and writes them in the polygon attribute table. From there, in a few steps you can create a new point layer of centroids that can be very useful for analysis or map display.

To introduce you to Visual Basic scripts, let's take a look at a script that calculates the x-coordinate of a centroid, obtained from the ArcGIS Desktop Help topic "centroid":

```
Dim dblX As Double
Dim pArea As IArea
Set pArea = [Shape]
dblX = pArea.Centroid.X
```

The two `Dim` statements create ("dimension") new variables in the computer's memory. `dblX` is a double precision number, with 15 digits of precision, for storing the x-coordinate of a centroid. The second `Dim` statement creates an instance of a predefined object of type `IArea`, a polygon in this case. The third line sets `pArea` to be a specific polygon, one of the polygons of the map layer being processed. The fourth line executes a method or program associated with the `pArea` object called `Centroid`, which in this case is for the x dimension. The script for calculating the y-coordinate of centroids is identical to the one above after substituting y for x.

A characteristic of VBA, being a scripting language, is that its programming code cannot be executed as a stand-alone program but must be embedded in an application program such as ArcMap. ArcMap places the script in a loop that processes all polygons of the map layer and writes results to the x-coordinate attribute of the attribute table.

Other scripts readily available for use calculate the area, perimeter, and lengths of features in their permanently projected coordinates. In addition, you can find user-supplied scripts on the ESRI Web site, *http://support.esri.com/index.cfm*. Create an account, log in, click the Downloads tab, click the ArcScripts tab, and search for Visual Basic language scripts for ArcGIS – ArcView. A well-documented script with example data is the spider diagram. A **spider diagram** connects central points, such as a person's residence, with lines to related points, such as all restaurants visited in a year. It thus depicts spatial relationships between different kinds of entities. See Figure 6-5 for a sample spider map.

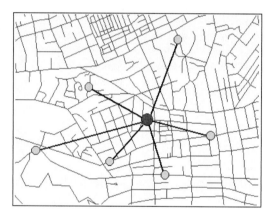

FIGURE 6-5 Spider map

ModelBuilder

One thing that we have always loved about ESRI is how it keeps its software on the frontier of computing. A great example of this is its ModelBuilder, which has a graphical user interface for building macros. You have used some of the many geoprocessing tools available in ArcToolbox, each of which has a form that accepts inputs and parameters for producing outputs, such as the input map layers to append or dissolve. Using ModelBuilder, you can string together two or more such tools by dragging and dropping icons to produce a macro, which is a script that runs the tools in the sequence of the diagram that you build. The end result provides a reusable sequence of steps that can be modified by changing the inputs to tools. You run a model in a single action and it carries out the string of detailed steps with tools. You will use ModelBuilder in the tutorial of this chapter to join tables and then clip an associated map layer.

USING ARCGIS FOR BUILDING STUDY AREAS

To get started, you will start ArcMap and open the *Chapter6-1.mxd* map document. This document contains map layers for Allegheny County, Pennsylvania, that you will use to build a study area for Pittsburgh.

Chapter6-1.mxd Map Document

1. On your computer's desktop, click **Start**, click **All Programs**, click **ArcGIS**, and click **ArcMap**.
2. In the ArcMap window, click the **An existing map** option button, and double-click **Browse for maps** in the panel below the option button.
3. In the Open window, browse to your **LearningAndUsingGIS** folder and double-click **Chapter6-1.mxd**. See Figure 6-6. *(The* Chapter6-1.mxd *map document window opens in ArcMap showing the Allegheny County municipalities layer turned on. Other map layers in the map document include Census Tracts, Census Block Groups, Census Blocks, Rivers, Streets, and Roailroads.)*

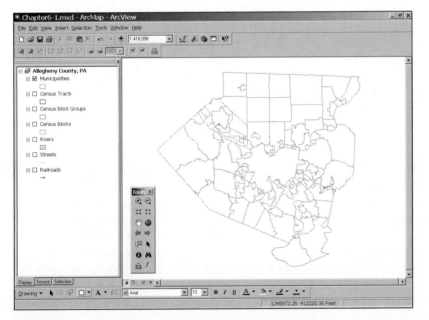

FIGURE 6-6   Chapter6-1.mxd map document

Feature Extraction By Attribute

Two common methods for extracting GIS features are selecting by attribute and selecting by location. First you will use attributes to create the study area of Pittsburgh, then you will use location selection to extract census layers for Pittsburgh from larger Allegheny County map layers.

1. On the main menu, click **Selection**, click **Select by Attributes**, and then in the resulting Select By Attributes window, make sure that **Municipalities** is selected as the Layer and **Create a new selection** is selected as the Method.
2. In the large panel listing attributes of the Pools attribute table, double-click "**NAME**", click the **=** button, click the **Get Unique Values** button, double-click '**Pittsburgh**' and click **OK**. See Figure 6-7. *(The result is that only the City of Pittsburgh municipality is selected.)*

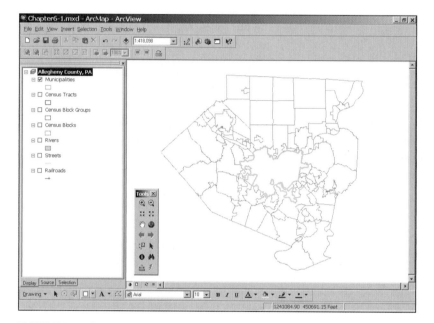

FIGURE 6-7 Query with unique value for NAME entered

3. In the table of contents, right-click the **Municipalities** map layer, click **Data**, and click **Export Data**. Then, in the resulting Export Data window, click the **Output** shapefile box, type **C:\LearningAndUsingGIS\FilesStudentWork\ Pittsburgh.shp**, click **OK**, and click **Yes** to add the exported data to the map as a layer.
4. In the table of contents, turn off the Municipalities map layer.
5. In the table of contents, right-click **Pittsburgh**, click **Properties**, click the **Symbology** tab, and click the button in the Symbol section. Then, in the resulting Symbol Selector window, click the **Hollow** color swatch in the left panel, double-click the **Outline Width** box, type **1.15**, click **OK**, and click **OK** again.
6. In the table of contents, right-click **Pittsburgh** and click **Zoom to Layer**. See Figure 6-8. *(This is the new study area—an outline of the City of Pittsburgh.)*

7. In the table of contents, click the **Census Tracts** map layer on.

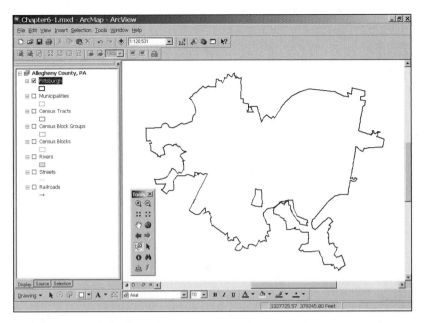

FIGURE 6-8   New study area—City of Pittsburgh

Feature Extraction By Location

Now that you have created Pittsburgh's outline as a separate map layer, you can use it to select other features from Allegheny County maps that are in Pittsburgh.

1. On the main menu, click **Selection** and click **Select by Location**. In the resulting Select by Location window, make sure that **select features from** is selected in the **I want to** field. In the following layer(s) field, click the **Census Tracts** check box, make sure that **have their center in** is selected, click the **list arrow** in the last field, click **Pittsburgh**, click **Apply**, and click **Close**. See Figure 6-9.

2. In the table of contents, right-click the **Census Tracts** map layer, click **Data**, and click **Export Data**. In the resulting Export Data window, click the **Output** shapefile box, type **C:\LearningAndUsingGIS\FilesStudentWork\ PghCensusTracts.shp**, click **OK**, and click **Yes** to add the exported data to the map as a layer.

3. In the table of contents, turn off the **Census Tracts** map layer.

4. In the table of contents, click and drag the **PghCensusTracts** map layer below the Pittsburgh map layer and symbolize as a hollow fill with a medium red outline. See Figure 6-10.

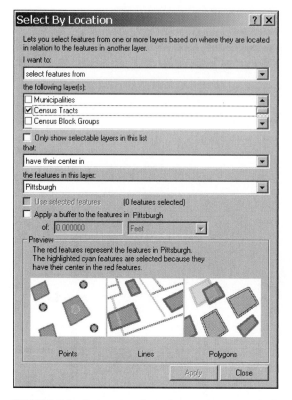

FIGURE 6-9   Parameters for select census tracts by location

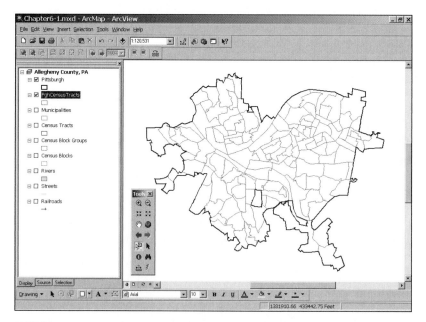

FIGURE 6-10   Census tracts for City of Pittsburgh study area

PRACTICE 6-1

Use Select By Location to select census block groups whose centers are completely within the Pittsburgh map layer and create a new shapefile of just these block groups. Add the new shapefile to your map document just below PghCensusTracts, and symbolize with a hollow fill and a light red outline. See Figure 6-11.

Geoprocessing Clip Tool

Using the Geoprocessing Clip tool, you can use the Pittsburgh shapefile as a cookie cutter to clip features such as river polygons that overlap the city boundary.

    1.   In the table of contents, click the **Rivers** map layer on. See Figure 6-11. *(Notice that the Rivers polygon layer extends well beyond the Pittsburgh layer. Clipping will cut Rivers to the exact boundary of the City of Pittsburgh.)*

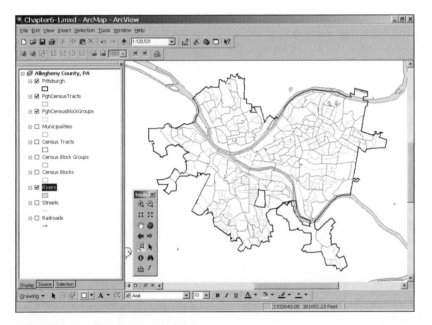

FIGURE 6-11   Rivers layer turned on

    2.   On the Standard toolbar, click the **ArcToolbox** tool.
    3.   In the ArcToolbox window, click expander boxes for **Analysis Tools** and **Extract**, and double-click **Clip**.
    4.   In the Input Features field of the resulting Clip window, make sure that **Rivers** is selected. In the Clip Features field, make sure that **Pittsburgh** is selected, and in the Output Features field, type **C:\LearningAndUsingGIS\FilesStudentWork\ PghRivers.shp**. See Figure 6-12.
    5.   Click **OK** and click **Close**.

Building a GIS Study Area

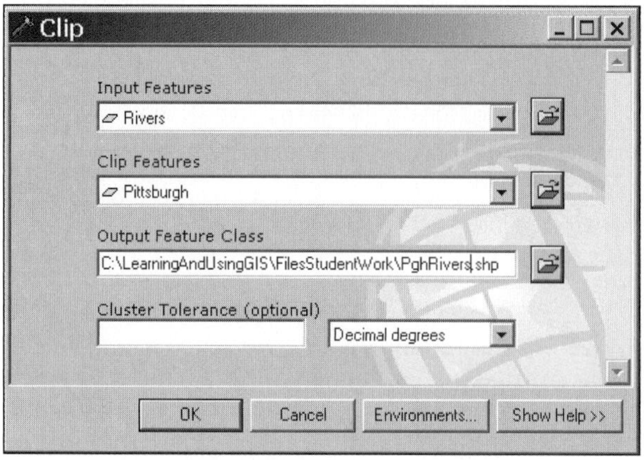

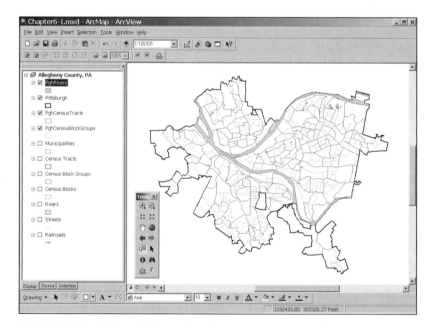

FIGURE 6-12 Clip settings for Pittsburgh rivers

6. In the table of contents, click the **Rivers** map layer to turn it off.
7. Close the ArcToolbox window.
8. Symbolize the **PghRivers** layer with a light blue fill color. See Figure 6-13.

FIGURE 6-13 Pittsburgh rivers clipped

9. On the main menu, click **File**, and click **Save**.

Create a Dissolve Attribute

You are about to use the Geoprocessing Dissolve tool to create a new shapefile by dissolving polygons within a given map layer that have a common, dissolve attribute value. In particular, you will dissolve neighborhood boundaries to create emergency medical services
(EMS) zones. The mechanism for this work depends on giving each neighborhood to be
dissolved for a specific EMS zone the same value for the dissolve attribute. In this section, you will use a version of the neighborhoods shapefile that has five attributes:
POP2000 (total population), AGE_5_17 (population ages 5 to 17), FHH_CHILD (number
of female-headed households with children), HOUSEHOLDS (number of households), and
EMSZONES2 (the finished dissolve column). *Note: We included EMSZONES2, the
finished dissolve attribute, to save you some time later. For now, suppose that it does not
exist and start to build it from scratch with a new attribute that you will create called
EMSZONE.*

1. On the main menu, click **File** and click **Open**.
2. In the Open window, browse to your **LearningAndUsingGIS** folder and double-
   click **Chapter6-2.mxd**. See Figure 6-14. *(The* Chapter6-2.mxd *map
   document window opens in ArcMap showing the Pittsburgh neighborhoods
   layer turned on. You will use this map layer to create new emergency
   medical services [EMS] zones.)*
3. In the table of contents, right-click the **projectedneighborhoods** map layer,
   click **Data**, and click **Export Data**. In the Export Data window click the **Output**
   shapefile box, type **C:\LearningAndUsingGIS\FilesStudentWork\
   PittsburghNeighborhoods.shp**, click **OK**, and click **Yes**. *(This adds a copy of
   the neighborhoods layer that you will use to add a field for dissolving
   neighborhoods to EMS zones.)*
4. In the table of contents, click the **projectedneighborhoods** map layer off.
5. In the table of contents, right-click the **PittsburghNeighborhoods** map layer,
   and click **Open Attribute Table**.
6. In the Attributes of PittsburghNeighborhoods table, click the **Options** button,
   and click **Add Field**.
7. In the resulting Add Field window, type **EMSZONE** as the field Name, click
   Short Integer as the field Type. See Figure 6-15.
8. Click **OK**.

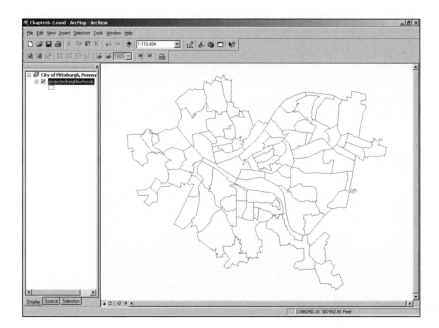

FIGURE 6-14 Chapter6-2.mxd map document with Pittsburgh neighborhoods layer

FIGURE 6-15 New EMSZONE field parameters

Calculate Dissolve Attribute Values

In practice, you would have a list of neighborhoods or a paper map of neighborhoods with notes and colored areas to designate which neighborhoods make up EMS zones. We provide the list as you proceed through the tutorial.

1. In the Attributes of PittsburghNeighborhoods table, hold down the Ctrl key and click row selectors to select the following neighborhoods: **East Hills, Homewood North, Homewood South, Homewood West, Larimer, Lincoln-Lemington-Belma, Point Breeze, Point Breeze North, Regent Square, Shadyside**, and **Squirrel Hill North**. *(These are neighborhoods that make up EMS Zone 1.)*

2. Click the **Selected** button at the bottom of the Attributes of PittsburghNeighborhoods table. See Figure 6-16. *(Note that only the selected neighborhoods are displayed. When you calculate new values for this table, only selected rows are affected.)*

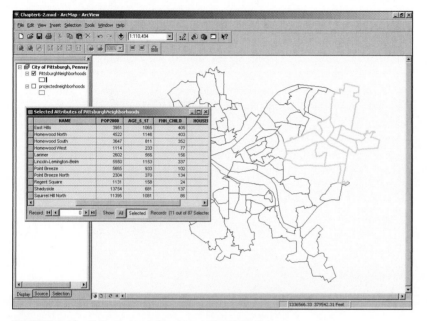

FIGURE 6-16 Selected neighborhoods for EMS Zone 1

3. In the Attributes of PittsburghNeighborhoods table, scroll to the right if necessary, right-click the **EMSZONE** column selector, click **Calculate Values**, and click **Yes**.

4. In the resulting Field Calculator window, click in the window below EMSZONE= and type **1**. See Figure 6-17.

5. Click **OK**. *(This places a value of 1 in the record for each of the selected neighborhoods. You will later dissolve the boundaries of these neighborhoods to make up EMS Zone 1.)*

6. In the Attributes of PittsburghNeighborhoods table, click the **All** button, click the **Options** button, and click **Clear Selection**.

PRACTICE 6-3

Repeat the steps from the previous section for one or more of the following EMS zones. When you feel comfortable with the process, you can stop. In the next section, you will use the finished EMSZONE2 to dissolve the EMS zones. When done, close the Attributes of PittsburghNeighborhoods table.

- *EMS Zone 2*: Beltzhoover, Bon Air, Brookline, Carrick, Knoxville, Mt. Oliver, Overbrook, St. Clair
- *EMS Zone 3*: Allentown, Banksville, Beechview, Chartiers City, Crafton Heights, Duquesne Heights, East Carnegie, Elliott, Fairywood, Mount Washington, Oakwood, Ridgemont, Sheraden, South Shore, West End, Westwood, Windgap
- *EMS Zone 4*: Allegheny Center, Allegheny West, Brighton Heights, California-Kirkbride, Central Northside, East Allegheny, Fineview, Manchester, Marshall-Shadeland, North Shore, Northview Heights, Perry North, Perry South, Spring Hill-City View, Summer Hill, Troy Hill
- *EMS Zone 5*: Bedford Dwellings, Bluff, Central Oakland, Crawford-Roberts, Middle Hill, North Oakland, Polish Hill, South Oakland, Strip District, Terrace Village, Upper Hill, West Oakland
- *EMS Zone 6*: Bloomfield, Central Lawrenceville, East Liberty, Friendship, Garfield, Highland Park, Lower Lawrenceville, Morningside, Stanton Heights, Upper Lawrenceville
- *EMS Zone 7*: Glen Hazel, Greenfield, Hays, Hazelwood, Lincoln Place, New Homestead, Squirrel Hill South, Swisshelm Park
- *EMS Zone 8*: Arlington, Arlington Heights, Southside Flats, Southside Slopes
- *EMS Zone 9*: Central business district

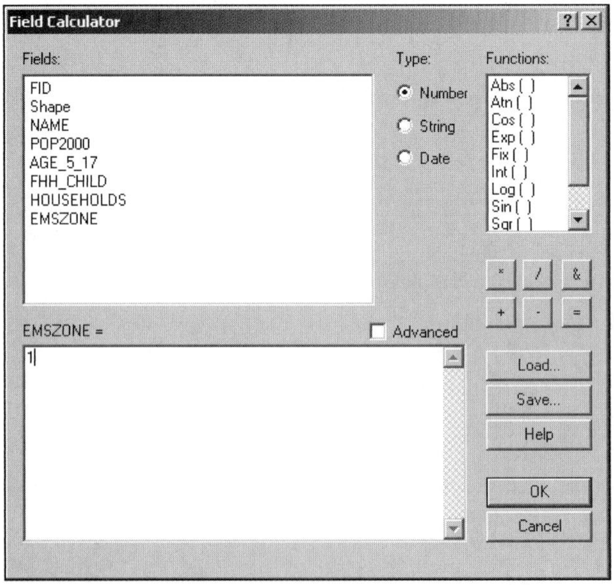

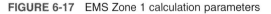

FIGURE 6-17   EMS Zone 1 calculation parameters

Dissolve Geoprocessing Tool

With the dissolve function, you can easily create EMS zones using the finished EMSZone2 dissolve field. Neighborhoods with the same EMSZone2 number will have their borders dissolved to create an EMS zone polygon.

1. On the main menu, click **Selection** and click **Clear Selected Features**. *(This selection might be grayed out if there aren't any features selected.)*
2. On the Standard toolbar, click the **ArcToolbox** tool 🔲.
3. In the ArcToolbox window, click expander boxes for **Data Management Tools** and **Generalization** *(not General)*, and double-click **Dissolve**.
4. In the resulting Dissolve window, in the Input Features field click the list arrow and click **PittsburghNeighborhoods**. In the Output Features field, type **C:\LearningAndUsingGIS\FilesStudentWork\PittsburghEMSZones.shp**, and in the Dissolve Field window click the box beside **EMSZone2** *(do not click OK yet)*. *(Next, you will designate which attributes to aggregate from the neighborhood up to the EMS zone level.)*

Aggregation of Attributes for Dissolved Polygons

The Dissolve tool has the capacity to aggregate attributes up to the dissolved polygon level from the input polygons' attribute table.

1. Click the list arrow in the **Statistics Field(s)** field, click **POP2000**, click in the resultant Statistic Type cell of the **POP2000** row, and click **SUM**.
2. Repeat Step 1 to add **AGE_5_17**, **FHH_CHILD**, and **HOUSEHOLDS**—all summed. See Figure 6-18. *(Note that we have aggregated only raw count attributes. Attributes that are ratios or percentages cannot be aggregated directly. Instead, you must aggregate the components of ratios or percentages—their numerators and denominators—and then compute them at the aggregate level.)*
3. Click **OK**, click **Close**, and close **ArcToolbox**.
4. In the table of contents, right-click the **PittsburghEMSZones** map layer, and click **Label Features**. See Figure 6-19. *(You successfully dissolved Pittsburgh neighborhoods to create emergency medical services zones.)*
5. In the table of contents, right-click **PittsburghEMSZones**, click **Open Attribute Table**, and examine the aggregated census attributes. See Figure 6-20.

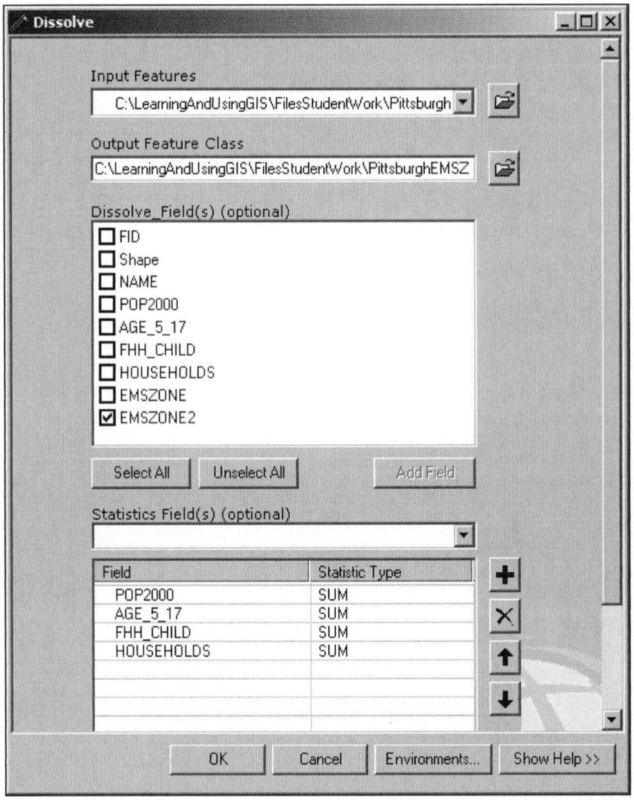

FIGURE 6-18   Dissolve parameters

6.   Right-click the column heading for **SUM_POP200** and click **Statistics**. *(You will see that the sum of this column is 334,563, which is the population of Pittsburgh. So the aggregation worked correctly.)*

7.   Close the statistics and attributes windows. On the main menu click **File** and click **Save**.

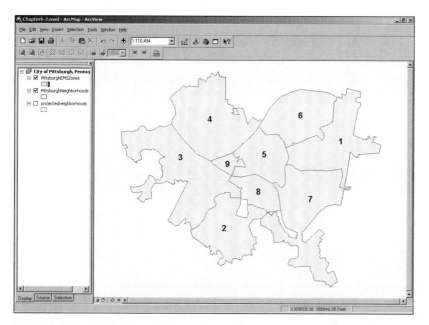

FIGURE 6-19 EMS zones labeled

FID	Shape*	EMSZONE2	SUM_POP200	SUM_AGE_5_	SUM_FHH_CH	SUM_HOUSEH
0	Polygon	1	55635	8197	2213	24139
1	Polygon	2	39185	6811	1401	16169
2	Polygon	3	51602	7784	1787	22465
3	Polygon	4	48151	8681	2687	19774
4	Polygon	5	37946	3541	1543	14885
5	Polygon	6	48931	7538	2192	23048
6	Polygon	7	34921	4950	790	15680
7	Polygon	8	12970	1347	308	6315
8	Polygon	9	5222	52	6	1264

Record: 1 Show: All Selected Records (0 out of 9 Selected.) Options ▾

FIGURE 6-20 Attributes of EMS zones

Append Geoprocessing Tool

Sometimes you need to combine multiple shapefiles to create one shapefile. In this example, suppose that two individuals worked on preparing maps for residences of pool tag holders, each for half of the city, and as a result there are two separate shapefiles, **PghPoolTags1** and **PghPoolTags2**. Your task is to append one of the shapefiles to the other, yielding a single, combined shapefile for mapping all residences.

1. On the main menu, click **File** and click **Open**.
2. In the Open window, browse to your **LearningAndUsingGIS** folder and double-click **Chapter6-3.mxd**. See Figure 6-21. *(The* Chapter6-3.mxd *map document window opens in ArcMap showing Pittsburgh Neighborhoods, Pooltags1, and Pooltags2 layers turned on.)*

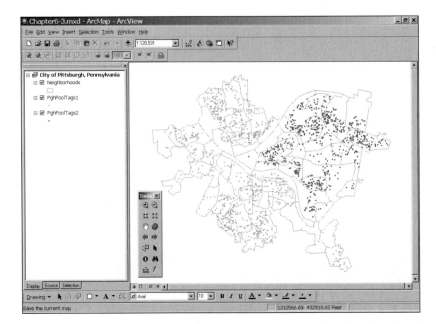

FIGURE 6-21 Chapter6-3.mxd map document with neighborhoods and pool tag layers

3. On the Standard toolbar, click the **ArcToolbox** tool.

4. In the ArcToolbox window, click expander boxes for **Data Management Tools** and **General**, and double-click **Append**.

5. In the resulting Dissolve window, make sure that **PghPoolTags1** is selected in the Input Features field, and make sure that **PghPoolTags2** is selected from the drop-down menu in the Output Features field. See Figure 6-22.

6. Click **OK** and click **Close**.

7. Close the **ArcToolbox** window.

8. In the table of contents, click the **PghPoolTags1** map layer off. See Figure 6-23. *(You can now see that the Pooltags2 layer contains points from both shapefiles.)*

9. In the table of contents, right-click the **PghPoolTags2** map layer, click **Data**, and click **Export Data**. In the Export Data window click the **Output** shapefile box, type **C:\LearningAndUsingGIS\FilesStudentWork\PghPools.shp**, click **OK**, and click **Yes** to add the exported data to the map as a layer.

10. On the main menu, click **File** and click **Save**.

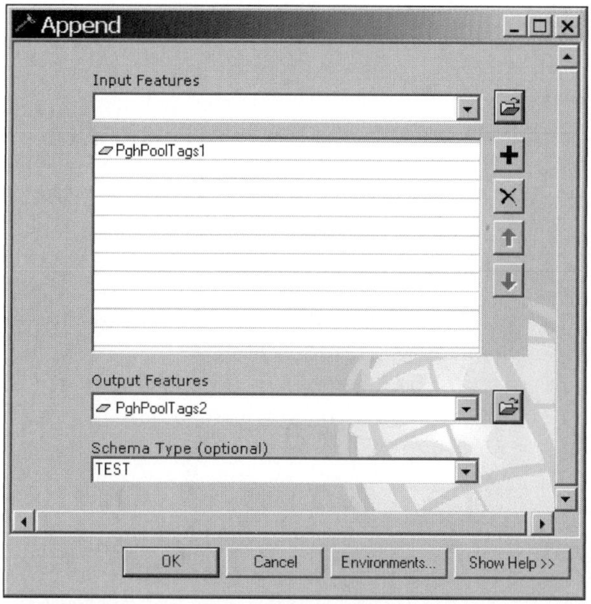

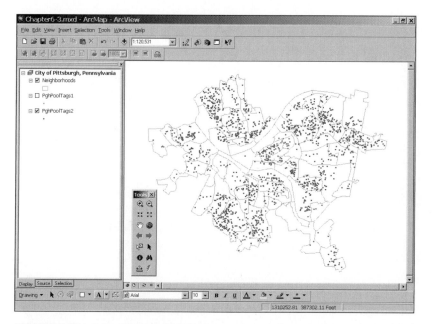

FIGURE 6-22 Append parameters

FIGURE 6-23 Appended pool tag layer

ADVANCED GEOPROCESSING TOOLS

ArcView's advanced geoprocessing functions are powerful tools that allow you to use VBA scripts to manipulate GIS data sets. Next, you will use such a script to create point centroids for census block groups.

Chapter6-4.mxd Map Document

1. On your computer's desktop, click **Start**, click **All Programs**, click **ArcGIS**, and click **ArcMap**.
2. In the ArcMap window, click the **An existing map** option button, and double-click **Browse for maps** in the panel below the option button.
3. In the Open window, browse to your **LearningAndUsingGIS** folder and double-click **Chapter6-4.mxd**. See Figure 6-24. *(The* Chapter6-4.mxd *map document window opens in ArcMap showing Allegheny County Census Block Groups layer turned on.)*

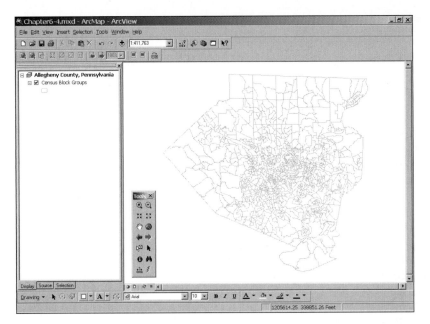

FIGURE 6-24 Chapter6-4.mxd map document with Census Block Groups layer on

Centroid Fields

Before you can create point centroids, you need to create X and Y fields in the appropriate attribute table to store the centroid locations for the polygons.

1. In the table of contents, right-click the **Census Block Groups** layer, and click **Open Attribute Table**.
2. In the resulting Attributes of Census Block Groups window, click **Options** and click **Add Field**.

3. In the resulting Add Field window, type **X** as the field Name, click **Double** as the field Type, and click **OK**. See Figure 6-25.

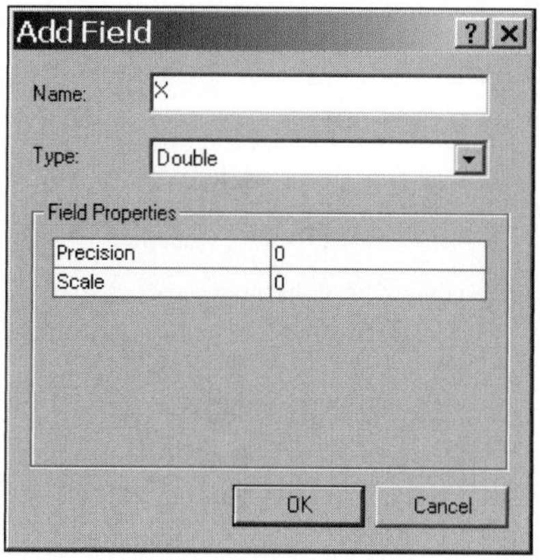

FIGURE 6-25 X field parameters

4. In the Attributes of Census Block Groups window, right-click the **X** field, click **Calculate Values**, and click **Yes**.
5. In the resulting Field Calculator window, click the **Advanced** check box.
6. In the first text box (Pre-Logic VBA Script Code), type the following:
   Dim dblX As Double
   Dim pArea As IArea
   Set pArea = [Shape]
   dblX = pArea.Centroid.X
   (You can find this code, and code for other advanced tasks, by using ArcGIS Help. For example, on the main menu click Help, click ArcGIS Desktop Help, type centroid in the Keyword to Find field, click Calculating for polygons under the resulting centroid listing, and click the link Adding the x,y coordinates of the centroid of a polygon layer to a new field. As an alternative to typing the preceding code, you could copy and paste the code from Help.)
7. In the second text box (X=), type **dblX**. See Figure 6-26.
8. Click **OK**. See Figure 6-27. *(The X field should be populated with the X centroid values.)*

PRACTICE 6-4

Create a new Y field with the same parameters as shown in Step 6 to calculate the Y centroid value, but replace the X parameter with Y. See Help to copy and paste code for the Y centroid.

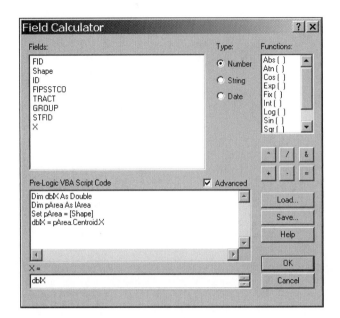

FIGURE 6-26 VBA script for X field centroid

	FID	Shape	ID	FIPSSTCO	TRACT	GROUP	STFID	X	
	0	Polygon	1	42003	010300	1	420030103001	-79.983147	
	1	Polygon	2	42003	010300	2	420030103002	-79.990130	
	2	Polygon	3	42003	020100	1	420030201001	-80.003750	
	3	Polygon	4	42003	020100	2	420030201002	-80.001895	
	4	Polygon	5	42003	020100	3	420030201003	-79.995889	
	5	Polygon	6	42003	020100	4	420030201004	-79.968840	

Record: 0   Show: All Selected   Records (0 out of 1107 Selected.)   Options ▾

FIGURE 6-27 X field values

Centroid Shapefile

Now that you have X and Y values for the centroid of your polygons, you can create a point file for the polygon centroids.

1. In the Attributes of Block Groups window, click **Options** and click **Export**.
2. In the resulting Export Data window, click the Output shapefile box, type **C:\LearningAndUsingGIS\FilesStudentWork\BlockGroupCentroidTable.shp**, click **OK**, and click **Yes** to add the exported data to the map as a table.
3. Close the **Attributes of Block Groups** table.
4. In the table of contents, click the **Source** tab.
5. In the table of contents, right-click the **Block Group Centroid** layer, and click **Display XY Data**.
6. In the resulting Display XY Data window, be sure **X** is selected as the X field and **Y** is selected as the Y field, and click **OK**. See Figure 6-28. (*This adds the*

*centroids as points on the map. Although the points are displayed, they still
need to be exported as a point shapefile.)*

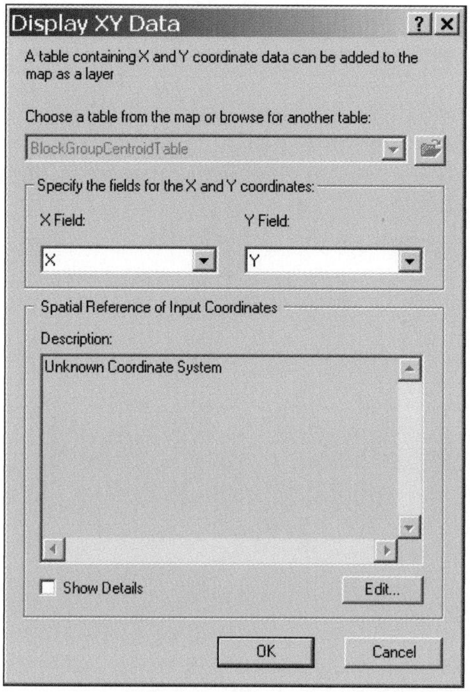

FIGURE 6-28 Display XY Data window parameters

7. In the table of contents, right-click the **BlockGroupCentroidTableEvents** layer,
    click **Data**, click **Export**, click **OK**, and click **Yes**.
8. In the table of contents, right-click the **BlockGroupCentroidTableEvents** layer,
    and click **Remove**.
9. Save your map document.

PRACTICE 6-5

Finish your map by removing the CensusBlockGroupCentroidTableEvents layer, and
symbolize the CensusBlockGroupCentroids as Square2 size 4.

Area Field Script

Another useful Visual Basic for Applications script adds an area field to a polygon shapefile.
Here you will create an area field for the City of Pittsburgh neighborhoods. The version of
the neighborhoods that you will use has coordinates permanently projected to State
Plane in feet. *Note: The area script that you will use calculates area in the stored
coordinate units in the map layer, regardless of the projection used in the map*

document's data frame. Do not make the mistake of calculating area for map layers that have latitude/longitude coordinates stored: The area script only works for rectangular coordinates such as in State Plane or UTM projections.

1. On your computer's desktop, click **Start**, click **All Programs**, click **ArcGIS**, and click **ArcMap**.
2. In the ArcMap window, click the **An existing map** option button, and double-click **Browse for maps** in the panel below the option button.
3. In the Open window, browse to your **LearningAndUsingGIS** folder, and double-click **Chapter6-5.mxd**. *(The* Chapter6-5.mxd *map document opens with the* projectedneighborhoods *layer added.)*
4. In the table of contents, right-click the **projectedneighborhoods** layer, and click **Open Attribute Table**.
5. In the Attributes of projectedneighborhoods window, click **Options**, and click **Add Field**.
6. In the Add Field window, type **AREA** as the field Name, click **Double** as the field Type, and click **OK**.
7. In the Attributes of projectedneighborhoods window, right-click the **AREA** field, click **Calculate Values**, and click **Yes**.
8. In the Field Calculator window, click the **Advanced** check box.
9. In the Pre-Logic VBA Script Code text box, type the following:
   Dim dblArea as double
   Dim pArea as IArea
   Set pArea = [shape]
   dblArea = pArea.area
10. In the second text box (AREA=), type **dblArea**. See Figure 6-29.

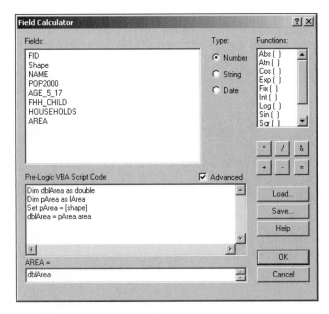

FIGURE 6-29 AREA field VBA parameters

11. Click **OK**. See Figure 6-30. *(The AREA field is populated with area values.)*

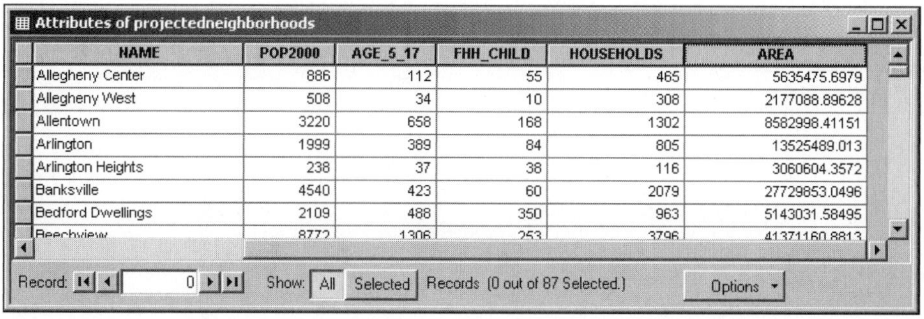

NAME	POP2000	AGE_5_17	FHH_CHILD	HOUSEHOLDS	AREA
Allegheny Center	886	112	55	465	5635475.6979
Allegheny West	508	34	10	308	2177088.89628
Allentown	3220	658	168	1302	8582998.41151
Arlington	1999	389	84	805	13525489.013
Arlington Heights	238	37	38	116	3060604.3572
Banksville	4540	423	60	2079	27729853.0496
Bedford Dwellings	2109	488	350	963	5143031.58495
Beechview	8772	1306	253	3796	41371160.8813

Record: [◄] [◄] 0 [►] [►|] Show: All | Selected Records (0 out of 87 Selected.) Options ▼

FIGURE 6-30 AREA field

PRACTICE 6-6

Add the EMSZones shapefile that you created to the map document, and calculate the area field for its polygons. When you are finished, save your map document.

MODEL BUILDER

The previous examples showed the power of ArcView's geoprocessing tools. Sometimes, you will need to carry out a sequence of geoprocessing steps. If those steps need to be reused periodically, it is possible to use ArcGIS's ModelBuilder to write a macro that will run all the steps in a single command. With ModelBuilder, you simply drag and drop geoprocessing functions into the ModelBuilder window to write the macro. ModelBuilder writes VBA code for you, based on your interactions.

Chapter6-6.mxd Map Document

1. On your computer's desktop, click **Start**, click **All Programs**, click **ArcGIS**, and click **ArcMap**.
2. In the ArcMap window, click the **An existing map** option button, and double-click **Browse for maps** in the panel below the option button.
3. In the Open window, browse to your **LearningAndUsingGIS** folder, double-click **Chapter6-6.mxd**, and click the **Source** tab at the bottom of the table of contents. See Figure 6-31. *(The Chapter6-6.mxd map document window opens in ArcMap showing Allegheny County census block group layer, Allegheny County census block group SF1 data table, and City of Pittsburgh outline turned on.)*

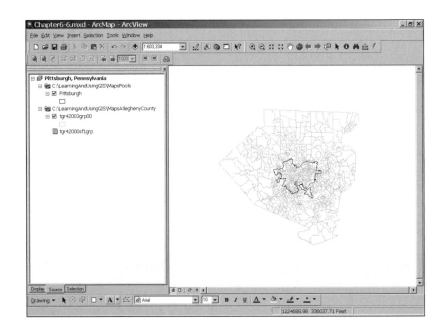

FIGURE 6-31 Chapter6-6.mxd map document with census block groups and Pittsburgh outline

4. In the table of contents, right-click the **tgr42003grp00** layer, and click **Open Attribute Table**.

5. Browse the fields and records for this table to become familiar with it.

PRACTICE 6-7

Open the tgr42000sf1grp table and browse its fields and records.

Model Builder to Join and Clip

In the following section you will build a macro to join the Allegheny County census block group table to the attribute table for census block group polygons and then clip the polygons to the outline for the City of Pittsburgh.

1. On the Standard toolbar, click the **ArcToolbox** tool.

2. In the ArcToolbox window, right-click **ArcToolbox** from the top of the window, click **New Toolbox**, and type **Join Clip Tool** as the new toolbox name.

3. In the ArcToolbox window, right-click **Join Clip Tool**, click **New**, and click **Model**.

4. Drag the **Model window** to the lower-right corner of the screen. See Figure 6-32. *(You are now ready to drag and drop objects to define the model.)*

5. In the table of contents, drag **tgr42003grp00** into the Model window.

6. In the ArcToolbox window, click expander boxes for **Data Management Tools** and **Join** and drag **Add Join** to the Model window. See Figure 6-33.

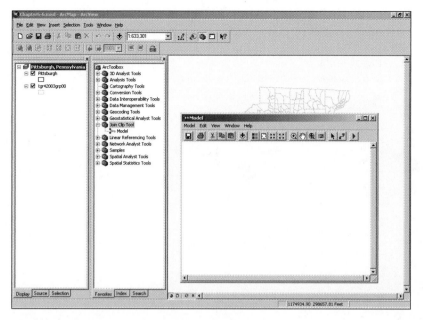

FIGURE 6-32   Empty model builder window

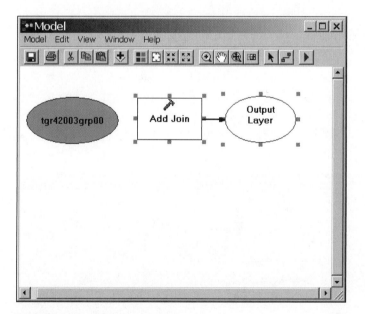

FIGURE 6-33   Beginning model

7. In the Model window, click the **Add Connection** tool ![icon], then drag a line from **tgr42003grp00** to the **Add Join** box.

8. In the Model window, click the **Select** tool ⬉ , double-click the **Add Join** box, and then in the resulting Add Join window, select **STFID** as the Input Join Field, select **tgr42000sf1grp** as the Join Table, and select **STFID** as the Output Join Field. See Figure 6-34.

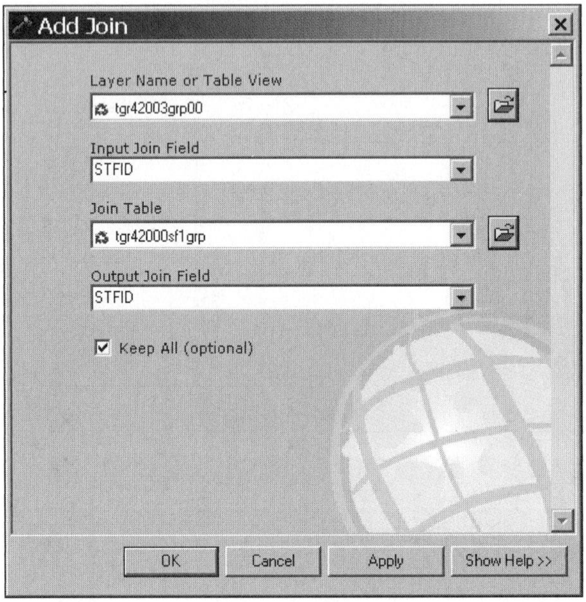

FIGURE 6-34   Add Join parameters

9. Click **Apply**, click **OK**, and rearrange elements in the model as shown in Figure 6-35. *(You can see in the model window that the census block group attribute tables are joined, and the result is an output shapefile called tgr42003grp00 (2).)*

PRACTICE 6-8

Drag the Pittsburgh shapefile and Clip Analysis tool (from ArcToolbox under Analysis Tools and Extract) into your model. Use the Add Connection tool to connect the Pittsburgh shapefile and the output shapefile from the final step to the clip tool. This will result in a new output shapefile. Change its name to C:\LearningAndUsingGIS\ FilesStudentWork\PittsburgCensusBlkGroupsJoined.shp. See Figure 6-36 for the finished model.

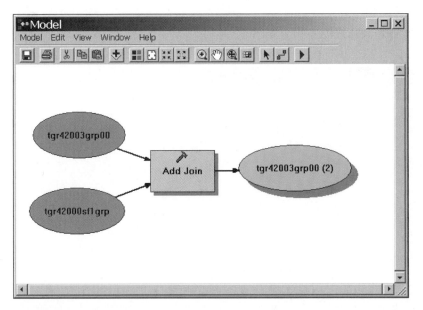

FIGURE 6-35   Join model

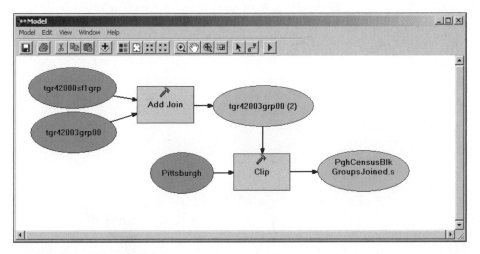

FIGURE 6-36   Finished model

Model Run

Now that your model is defined, you can run the model, and the result will be a shapefile
with census block group tables joined and clipped within the City of Pittsburgh outline.

1. In the model window, click the **Run** tool ▶.
2. Click **Close**.
3. Add the newly created shapefile, called **PghCensusBlkGroupsJoined.shp**, to
   your project.

4. In the table of contents, right-click the **PghCensusBlkGroupsJoined** layer, and click **Zoom to Layer**. See Figure 6-37.

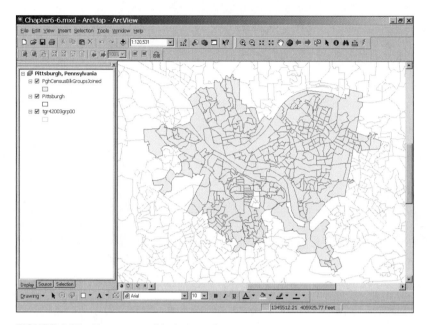

FIGURE 6-37   New census block group layer

5. In the table of contents, right-click the **PghCensusBlkGroupsJoined** layer, click **Open Attribute Table**, and note the new fields in the census block group table.
6. Save **Chapter6-6.mxd** and close.

Chapter 6 Summary

Each GIS has specific needs in regard to the geographic areas it represents. Governments and vendors provide base maps for areas such as countries, states, counties, and grids. Often, you will have a study area that is either a subset of available base maps or one that requires you to combine adjoining base maps. In either case, GIS has several geoprocessing tools to help you produce study-area map layers.

To extract features from base maps, you have three alternatives. If there are attributes of the base map that identify the area you need, you can execute an attribute query to select the desired features and then convert them into a new shapefile. If you can visually identify the features that you need on the map, you can select them directly and save them as a new shapefile. Lastly, if you have created a boundary map for your study area, you can use it to either select or clip features, resulting in new shapefiles.

To create larger areas from smaller ones, you use the dissolve tool in ArcToolbox. If you select all of the blocks for your study area, you can save them as a new shapefile and then dissolve them to a single, outline polygon. There are many advantages to using blocks or other census areas such as building blocks, including the availability of census data for applications of your study area. If there are subsets of your study area made up of several blocks each that are areas of interest for analysis, you can create polygons for them using the dissolve tool.

To combine adjoining map layers you can use the append tool. The input map layers need to be of the same feature type (point, line, polygon, or raster) and have the same table schema.

You can obtain geoprocessing tools in addition to the ones available in ArcGIS's standard user interface by using scripts. Macros string two or more tools together to automate processing. ArcGIS has a very modern drag-and-drop interface, ModelBuilder, for building macros without any knowledge of computer programming.

Key Terms

Append   A geoprocessing tool that combines two or more map layers for adjacent areas, such as neighboring counties, to make a new map layer.

Clipping   A process using a geoprocessing tool for extracting features from a map layer based on a "cookie cutter" or clip polygon. The extracted features are those that lie within or on the boundary of the clip polygon.

Dissolve   A geoprocessing tool for creating polygons out of smaller polygons. The input set of polygons must have an attribute, a dissolve column, that repeats a unique value for each set of two or more polygons that are to be dissolved. Dissolving removes interior lines of each set, leaving only a bounding polygon.

Geoprocessing   The use of specialized programs or functions in a GIS for processing map layers that produce analytic results, modify or transform map layers, or produce new map layers from existing ones.

Macro   A computer program created by a user that executes one or more functions generally found in an interactive software package's menus or toolbars. Macros are generally not written by users, but instead are created by means of computer interactions that the software uses to write the macro program.

Script   A short computer program written in a scripting language, such as Visual Basic for Applications, that performs a single function. An example is the script available from ArcGIS Help for creating and populating the area attribute of polygons in a polygon map layer.

Spider diagram   A graphic display used to show the relationship between two kinds of points on a map. For example, such maps are used to study the hunting grounds of animals of prey by connecting the den or home location of a hunting animal with straight lines to points where it has made kills. Generally, the result for each animal of prey has the appearance of a simplified spider's web.

Study area   The geographic area, generally defined by a polygon, for use in a GIS that meets the needs of a defined problem or organization. For example, for a city's streets maintenance department, it would be the city's boundary.

Table schema   The layout for a data table, consisting of attribute names and data types.

Visual Basic for Applications (VBA)   A scripting language provided by Microsoft for use in extending or customizing application programs, such as Word and Excel. It is a subset of the larger Visual Basic computer language.

Short-Answer Questions

1. Suppose that you are designing a GIS for some problem in your community or your region of the country. State a problem definition or issue to study. Briefly describe the study area including its outer boundary and important map layers.

2. A shopping mall owner is considering adding a large new entertainment complex to the mall. She is concerned about traffic patterns and parking lot capacity at the mall. What areas do you think the study area should include? What map layers would be important to include? How would you build the outline polygon of the study area? What if it were possible to conduct a survey of moviegoers to get their demographics and area of residence?

3. The fire chief in your town wants to draw new fire demand zones on the map for each fire station. If there is a fire within a fire station's zone, it is designated as the first responder and must send equipment and personnel to the fire. The chief and his staff have a lot of expertise about firefighting and would like to simply draw lines on the map. What do you recommend they do to design fire demand zones? Why?

4. Your study area is a city, and you have a polygon for it in a map layer. Explain how to use a county map for census tracts to make trash collection zones from the tracts, assuming that they are the building blocks.

5. What would you do if you had two map layers to append, both with points? One map layer's attribute table has the attributes Name (text) and DateBuilt (date) and the other's attribute table has Facility (text), ConstructionDate (date), and Comment (text). Both layers are for locations of medical clinic buildings, and each is for a unique list of nonoverlapping clinics. How do you prepare for appending the two layers?

6. Suppose you have a map document with a raster image from a high-quality aerial photograph and a street centerline map that aligns perfectly with the image. If an address-matching algorithm places a point for a residence at 450 Bayview Drive, would you expect to see the point in front of a rooftop?

7. Suppose that you have a study area that was originally drawn freehand on a map and then turned into a polygon in a map layer, using the drawing as a guideline. If you needed to include street centerlines for the study area only, what approach would you take to extracting them?

8. What is the purpose of a `Dim` statement in a VBA script?

9. What would be an application of a spider diagram, that you can envision, in your community?

10. By tradition, the first program that a beginning programming student writes is called Hello World. All it does is to write the message "Hello World" on your computer screen. If you knew the programming statements to do that, could you run VBA script for it on your computer? Why or why not?

Exercises

1. **Study Area for a Pittsburgh Neighborhood.** This exercise uses the Select by Location and geoprocessing Clip tools to create a study area for a Pittsburgh neighborhood, the South Side Flats.

   a. Create a new folder called **C:\LearningAndUsingGIS\FilesStudentWork\Exercise6-1**.

   b. Create a new map document called **C:\LearningAndUsingGIS\FilesStudentWork\Exercise6-1<YourName>.mxd**, where you substitute your name or other identifier for <YourName>. Set the coordinate system for the layer to be State Plane, Pennsylvania South zone, and name the data frame **South Side Flats**.

   c. From C:\LearningAndUsingGIS\MapPools\ add the *neighborhoods.shp* and *pittsburgh_east_pa_sw.tif* map layers, and from C:\LearningAndUsingGIS\MapsAlleghenyCounty\, add *tgr42003lkA.shp* (streets) and *tgr42003trt00.shp* (census tracts) to your map document.

   d. In the neighborhoods map layer, select the South Side Flats neighborhood, create a new shapefile called **C:\LearningAndUsingGIS\FilesStudentWork\SouthSideFlats.shp** of just this neighborhood, and add it to your map document. Remove the original neighborhoods map layer from your map document.

   e. Extract the following layers for the South Side Flats as new layers stored in C:\LearningAndUsingGIS\FilesStudentWork\: **SouthSideTracts** from *tgr42003trt00.shp* and **SouthSideStreets** from *tgr42003lkA.shp*. Add these layers to your map document, and remove the corresponding original layers.

   f. Clip the aerial photo to the South Side Flats neighborhood. Click **View**, click **Data Frame Properties**, click the **Data Frame** tab, click **Enable** under Clip to Shape, click the **Specify Shape** button, click **South Side Flats** as the Outline of Features layer, click **OK**, and click **OK** again.

   g. Symbolize SouthSideTracts to have a hollow fill with size 2 red outline and SouthSideStreets to have a tan size 2 line.

   h. Save the map document.

2. **Appended Neighborhoods.** Sometimes you have separate shapefiles that you need to merge, or append, into one shapefile. For example, the South Side of Pittsburgh is divided into two neighborhoods, South Side Flats and South Side Slopes. In this exercise, you will combine shapefiles for the boundaries and streets of these two neighborhoods into one larger neighborhood, called South Side.

   a. Create a new map document called **C:\LearningAndUsingGIS\FilesStudentWork\ Exercise6-2<YourName>.mxd**, where you substitute your name or other identifier for <YourName>. Set the coordinate system for the layer to be State Plane, Pennsylvania South zone, and name the data frame **South Side**.

   b. Add all four layers for both the South Side neighborhoods found in C:\LearningAndUsingGIS\MapsPools\: *SouthSideFlats.shp*, *SouthSideSlopes.shp*, *SouthSideFlatsStreets.shp*, and *SouthSideSlopesStreets.shp*.

   c. Using the ArcToolbox Append tool, append *SouthSideFlats.shp* to *SouthSideSlopes.shp*, and append *SouthSideFlatsStreets.shp* to *SouthSideSlopesStreets.shp*.

   d. Save **C:\LearningAndUsingGIS\FilesStudentWork\Exercise6-2<YourName>.mxd** and close.

   e. Create a new folder called **C:\LearningAndUsingGIS\FilesStudentWork\ Exercise6-2**.

   f. Open ArcCatalog. Copy *SouthSideSlopes.shp* and *SouthSideSlopesStreets.shp* from C:\LearningAndUsingGIS\MapsPools\ to C:\LearningAndUsingGIS\FilesStudentWork\ Exercise6-2\. In C:\LearningAndUsingGIS\FilesStudentWork\Exercise6-2\, rename *SouthSideSlopes.shp* to **SouthSide.shp** and *SouthSideSlopesStreets.shp* to **SouthSideStreets.shp**, and close ArcCatalog.

   g. Reopen *Exercise6-2<YourName>.mxd*. Remove all map layers, and add *SouthSide.shp* and *SouthSideStreets.shp* from C:\LearningAndUsingGIS\FilesStudentWork\ Exercise6-2\. Symbolize these map layers, and save your map document.

3. **Census Tract Centroids.** Polygon centroids have many uses as separate map layers. In Chapter 3, for example, you used blockcentroids selected by buffers to estimate buffer demographics from census data. In this exercise you will create census tract centroids for Allegheny County and then create a map for that area comparing overall population and population between ages 5 and 17.

   a. Create a new folder called **C:\LearningAndUsingGIS\FilesStudentWork\ Exercise6-3**.

   b. Create a new map document called **C:\LearningAndUsingGIS\FilesStudentWork\ Exercise6-3<YourName>.mxd**, where you substitute your name or other identifier for <YourName>. Set the coordinate system for the layer to be State Plane, Pennsylvania South zone, and name the data frame **Allegheny County**.

   c. Add the table *tgr42000sf1trt.dbf* and the map layer *tgr42003trt00.shp* from C:\LearningAndUsingGIS\MapsAlleghenyCounty\ to your map document.

   d. In the Attributes of the *tgr42003trt00.shp* table, create fields for the X and Y centroids.

   e. Join *tgr42000sf1trt.dbf* to *tgr42003trt00.shp*.

f. Export the *tgr42003trt00.shp* attribute table as *TractsXY.dbf*, add it to your map as an XY event file, and export the new event points as **C:\LearningAndUsingGIS\FilesStudentWork\TractCentroids.shp**.

g. Create a choropleth map showing the total population, a point map showing the population, and a point map using graduated point markers for youths between 5 and 17 years of age. Use quantiles for both maps. Save your map document.

4. **Model for Extracting Neighborhood Data.** Extracting data for a study area is an excellent candidate for a ModelBuilder application. In this exercise, you will create a model that extracts GIS layers for a selected Pittsburgh neighborhood. To extract data for other neighborhoods, you would simply need to plug in a different neighborhood name or layer to clip.

a. Create a new folder called **C:\LearningAndUsingGIS\FilesStudentWork\Exercise6-4**.

b. Create a new map document called **C:\LearningAndUsingGIS\FilesStudentWork\Exercise6-4<YourName>.mxd**, where you substitute your name or other identifier for <YourName>. Set the coordinate system for the layer to be State Plane, Pennsylvania South zone, and name the data frame **Allegheny County**.

c. From C:\LearningAndUsingGIS\MapsAlleghenyCounty add *tgr42003lkA.shp* (streets), and from C:\LearningAndUsingGIS\MapsPools\ add *neighborhoods.shp* and *schools.shp* to your map document.

d. In the ArcToolbox, create a new toolbox called **Neighborhood Extraction**, and add a new model to this toolbox.

e. Add the neighborhoods layer to the model, a script to select layer by attribute (found under ArcToolbox, Data Management Tools, Layers and Table Views), and connect the neighborhoods to the Select Layer By Attribute script. Double-click the script to set parameters, including a query to select the Allentown neighborhood.

f. Add the script to clip features (found under ArcToolBox, Analysis Tools, Extract) and add the streets layer to the model. Connect the streets layer to the clip script. Double-click the clip script and set parameters, including an output feature class of C:\LearningAndUsingGIS\FilesStudentWork\Exercise6-4\AllentownStreets.shp.

g. Run the entire model, and add the resultant *AllentownStreets.shp* to your map document.

h. Double-click the *tgr42003lka.shp* input layer to the clip script in the model, and select Schools. Double-click the *AllentownStreets.shp* output layer of the Clip script, and change its shapefile name to *AllentownSchools.shp*.

i. Rerun the entire model, add the new *AllentownSchools.shp* to your map document, turn off the non-Allentown layers (but do not remove these inputs to the model), symbolize layers, and save your map document. (*Note:* If you need to use your model again and it responds that the model has no parameters, close the model, right-click it in the ArcToolBox, and click Edit. Make any repairs necessary, and run it.)

CHAPTER **7**

GEOCODING YOUR DATA

LEARNING OBJECTIVES

In this chapter, you will:

- Transform street address data into point maps
- Learn about U.S. postal street address standards
- Use algorithms to geocode street address data
- Learn strategies for cleaning street address data
- Build address locators using ArcGIS
- Batch and interactively geocode data using ArcGIS
- Report geocoding performance using ArcGIS

Allison wonders how much longer she has to be the point marker at 33 Pool Lane

INTRODUCTION

Thus far in this book you have used base map layers provided by the U.S. government to build and analyze map documents. You learned how to use these base maps to construct new map layers by selecting subsets of map features, appending map layers, dissolving polygons, and creating centroid points for polygons. What if, however, you have your own data, not part of any base map, and you want to map it? If your data has street addresses and other location data such as zip codes, you can use a GIS process called **geocoding** (or address matching) to do just that.

Geocoding is a sophisticated GIS function that uses street centerline maps or other spatial references—such as zip code maps—as the basis for location. It places points on or near streets for which there is a good match between address attributes in your data and in the street map. To do this, it uses many of the same analytical skills that your postal carrier uses to get a piece of mail to you. If an address has a misspelling, is missing a street type, uses a strange abbreviation, and so forth, no problem! The mail still gets to you. Likewise, geocoding is able to use address data to find a point on the street map. As you can imagine, the computer program that does this work is quite sophisticated. Sometimes, though, like its human counterpart, it makes mistakes.

Before delving into the subject of geocoding, you should know that there are other ways to get original data onto a map. One is by means of global positioning system (GPS) data, captured with a GPS unit. So, for example, if you are studying a network of medical clinics in a developing nation that does not have a digital street map (or even streets in some cases), you might have to get latitude/longitude coordinates using a GPS unit while visiting the clinics. Then it is easy to add GPS data to a map as an XY data layer, as done in Chapter 5. You could also use **heads-up digitizing**, a process in which you create new points, lines, or polygons using base maps as guides. You will learn about this in Chapter 8.

ADDRESS STANDARDS

Postal Addressing Standards, Publication 28 of the U.S. Post Office (2000), is the ultimate source on mailing address formats and codes. It provides standard street address formats and abbreviations for the purpose of increasing efficiency and completeness of mail delivery. These same standards are the basis for geocoding too. Let's take a look at a typical address format and then some irregular ones.

The following street address meets all the requirements of the post office:

> 533 W Old Main ST Apt 3
> Mars, PA 16046-3121

The parts of this address are shown in Table 7-1.

TABLE 7-1   Parts of typical address 533 W Old Main ST Apt 3, Mars, PA 16046-3121

533	House number
W	Prefix directional (postfix directional would appear after ST)
Old Main	Street name
ST	Street suffix abbreviation (conforms to Appendix C, Street Abbreviations of *Postal Addressing Standards*)
Apt	Common unit designator abbreviation for apartment (conforms to table on page 6 of *Postal Addressing Standards*)
Mars	City
PA	State abbreviation (conforms to Appendix B, Two-Letter State and Possession Abbreviations of *Postal Addressing Standards*)

TABLE 7-1 Parts of typical address 533 W Old Main ST Apt 3, Mars, PA 16046-3121 (continued)

16046	Five-digit zip code (available in the City State File of the U.S. Postal Service)
3121	Zip+4 extension to zip codes providing block-level locations (available in the City State File of the U.S. Postal Service)

This might surprise you: ArcGIS needs the street address in a single field, rather than having all the parts of Table 7-1 in separate fields. Furthermore, TIGER street maps only have five-digit zip codes, so you must extract only the first five digits of the full zip code for geocoding. Table 7-2 gives an example table schema for address data. Only Address is needed if the study area is within a single city and you have extracted the street map for just the city. If the study area covers a multiple-city or state region, then either zip code or city, called the **zone** in this context, is also needed to distinguish locations that share the same street and number. Addresses can repeat in different municipalities; for example, several cities or towns could have the address 100 Main ST. TIGER maps do not have apartment number data, so that information is not used in geocoding and is best placed in a separate attribute.

TABLE 7-2 Example table schema for address data

Address	Apartment	City	State	Zip code
533 Old Main ST	3	Mars	PA	16046
4800 Forbes AV		Pittsburgh	PA	15213
1200 E Broad ST	25	Columbus	OH	43205
Smithfield ST & 7th AV		Pittsburgh	PA	15213

Geocoding can also handle street intersections, as shown in the final row of Table 7-2. You need to specify and use a special character, such as the & in the table, as the separator for the two streets of the intersection. It is also possible to geocode using highway mile markers and other kinds of location data.

MAPPING DATA WITH POLYGON IDENTIFIERS

If your data only has the identifier of a polygon—such as a zip code, city, or county—the best method for mapping your data is to create an aggregate table with a single record for each unique polygon and the count of records for each polygon. You can join such a table to the corresponding polygon layer and symbolize it with a choropleth map or size-graduated point markers.

PROBLEM ADDRESS DATA

There are addresses that organizations use that cannot be mapped directly without some data preparation. For example, post office box numbers, such as PO Box 781, will not geocode. In the worst case, sometimes data collection or entry personnel will leave address data blank for some records.

It is common for organizations to use **place-names**, such as JFK Airport, for an address. For such cases, ArcGIS allows you to use an **alias table** for geocoding that has attributes for the place-name alias and a legitimate street address for geocoding. Before geocoding, ArcGIS first makes a pass through your address data to see if there are any matches in the alias table. If so, it replaces the alias with the street address from the alias table. Then geocoding proceeds. An alias table is valuable for applications in which field personnel record event data (including addresses) on a regular basis, and feed them into a GIS. For example, police and firefighters write or input incident reports that get mapped. Repeated responses to the same location, for example a sports arena or airport, are more easily recorded using aliases rather than addresses.

Data cleaning is a preprocessing step in which you make adjustments or corrections to problem data. One example of data that can be cleaned is "block of" addresses such as "500 block of Main ST." Geocoding cannot directly process such data, but you can use Microsoft Excel to remove "block of" and add 50 to the house number to generate an approximate location. The end result of data cleaning is 550 Main ST, which will probably geocode. Another example is when street addresses are stored in separate attributes, such as house number, name, postfix directional, and so on. Then you have to concatenate values to produce a street address attribute.

Some parts of the United States have addresses that do not conform to the standard format as shown in Table 7-1, but have irregular address formats. These irregularities are documented in *Postal Addressing Standards* and include the following:

- *Hyphenated address ranges*: These are prevalent in New York City, Hawaii, and areas of southern California. An example address is 112-14 Johnson ST. Generally, you can determine an appropriate data cleaning step by examining a corresponding street centerline map's attribute data. For example, simply deleting the dashes in the house numbers of your input data often results in values that match those in the street map.
- *Grid style addresses*: These contain additional punctuation, such as periods (for example, 39.2 Marlin Ave). You can simply delete the periods in most cases. There are also grid style addresses in Salt Lake City that include double directionals (for example, in 842 E 1700 S, E is a predirectional, S is a postdirectional, and 1700 is located in the primary name field). Some commercial street centerline maps, such as GDT Dynamap/2000, handle such cases automatically.
- *Alphanumeric combinations of address ranges*: An example is N6E23001 Redmond RD and is found in Wisconsin and Northern Illinois. A solution that generally works is to delete all characters in the street number up through the last alpha character.

GEOCODING

Geocoding uses an **expert system** approach to matching your address data with attributes in street centerline maps. An expert system attempts to replicate the judgment of experts by using logic and rules. Geocoding uses a **geocoding engine**, which is a computer program that employs code tables to standardize address components for spelling and rules for identifying parts of addresses and errors in addresses. Here are the major steps in geocoding:

1. *Parse the address attribute*: This step uses rules that identify and standardize the parts of the street address. The process finds the house number, prefix and postfix directionals, street name, and street suffix and standardizes the spelling of the various parts that are codes (directionals and street suffix). The end result is a standardized house number and street name that matches the format of TIGER files.

2. *Match address attributes with street attributes*: The matching process has several steps and rules. To allow for misspellings of the street name, the geocoding engine transforms the street name into a **SOUNDEX key**, an index based on a limited alphabet that yields the same index values for names that sound alike. For example, Smith and Smythe have the same SOUNDEX key, S530 (see *www.sconsig.com/sastips/soundex-01.htm*). For a street segment to be considered a candidate match, the SOUNDEX keys of the input data street name and street centerline name must match. If there is a zone, such as zip code, it must match. The house number of the input address, depending on whether it is even or odd, must lie within the range of the corresponding even or odd side of the street segment.

3. *Compute a matching score*: Each address begins the process with a perfect score of 100. For each error in the match, such as a misspelled name or missing directional, points are deducted from the score.

4. *Select a match and determine a point*: The user determines a threshold below which matching scores are unacceptable. If there is more than one candidate street match for an address, the one that maximizes the matching score wins and is accepted as the location of the address. The geocoding engine then calculates a location for the address, using **linear interpolation** between the beginning and ending house numbers of the winning street segment.

Interpolation just uses ratios to determine location. For example, for the address of Beechwood Swimming Pool in Pittsburgh, 1249 Rockland Street, the resulting point is the fraction 49/(1299 – 1201) along the distance from the point locations of 1201 to 1299. See Figure 7-1, where we have selected and identified the street segment on which the pool is located.

ArcGIS provides two ways to geocode: (1) **batch geocoding**, in which it attempts to match all input addresses automatically, and (2) **interactive rematching**, for which there is a sophisticated user interface to repair problems and search for unmatched addresses. An expert on local streets or on the geocoding process can often find additional matches using interactive rematching. If an organization has good practices in entering address

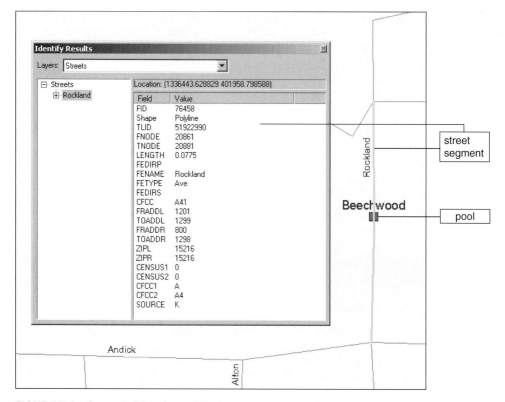

FIGURE 7-1   Geocoded Beechwood Pool at 1249 Rockland Street

data into their databases, such as always requiring a street address in a U.S. postal format, TIGER maps can batch match upward of 85 to 95 percent of addresses automatically without additional work. If an organization has poor practices, such as allowing any form of address to be entered, a matching rate of approximately 70 percent or worse is likely.

If you have a list of addresses that must be matched 100 percent and accurately, you can be successful with sufficient effort. After passing through batch matching and rematching steps, the next step is to find unmatched addresses using an online geocoding service, such as MapQuest or Google Maps. Such service providers have the best commercial street centerline maps, and using them you can often find your previously unmatched address. If you can find the location on one of these services, you can generally fix the problem. Often the problem is that TIGER maps are missing attribute values, such as house numbers, for the needed street segment. Other times the input street address data is simply incorrect.

What are the match rates and accuracy needs for geocoding? The answer depends on the nature of your problem area. If your job is to dispatch emergency services, such as ambulances, you need 100 percent matching and accuracy. As a backup, you can request a nearby street intersection as a second address. Obviously, the dispatching personnel need to have knowledge of the area and the best commercial street maps. Any errors need to be logged, reviewed, and then fixed with either a change in the street centerline map or data input practices. If, however, you need to determine residential patterns of customers for a facility, such as a retail store, you can accept 85 percent address matching rates and some inaccuracies. The patterns will still be valid for facility location planning and analysis.

REPORTING MATCHING RATES

You can gauge the success of geocoding using address match rates supplied by ArcGIS. First, however, you need to adjust reported match rates by determining the number of address records that are unmatchable—that have null address values, do not have street numbers and are not on the alias list of place-names, or do not have street numbers and do not have separators for intersections. Then subtract that number from the denominator of the ratio for calculating the match rate. The resulting match rate better estimates the capacity of geocoding and highlights problem cases that might have several remedies on the address data-entry side.

MAPPING ZIP CODE DATA

City of Pittsburgh officials created a data set for all pool tag holders in a recent summer season, including pool tag holder name, personal identifiers, and five-digit zip code, but no street address. Later, we obtained copies of paper records that included street addresses and input a small random sample of pool tag holders including street address, which we geocoded and used in earlier chapters. In the next section , you will map the original data with zip codes for 48,366 pool tag holders who had nonnull values for zip codes.

Prepare the Map Document for Geocoding to Zip Codes

1. On your PC computer's desktop, click **Start**, click **All Programs**, click **ArcGIS**, and click **ArcMap**.
2. In the ArcMap window, click the **An existing map** option button and double-click **Browse for maps** in the panel below the option button.
3. In the Open window, browse to your **LearningAndUsingGIS** folder and double-click **Chapter7-1.mxd**. See Figure 7-2. *(The* Chapter7-1.mxd *map document window opens in ArcMap showing the Allegheny County Zip Codes layer turned on. Next, you will add the table with zip code data to this map document.)*
4. On the Standard toolbar, click the **Add Data** tool ⬇.
5. Browse to **C:\LearningAndUsingGIS\Data** and double-click **TagsByZIP.dbf**. *(This action adds the zip code data table to your map document.)*
6. In the table of contents, right-click **TagsByZIP**, click **Open**, and observe the data in the table. See Figure 7-3. *(You can see that there are duplicates of zip codes in the table, as expected.)*

Count Records by Zip Code

The next step in the geocoding process is to create a new table with the number of records for each zip code.

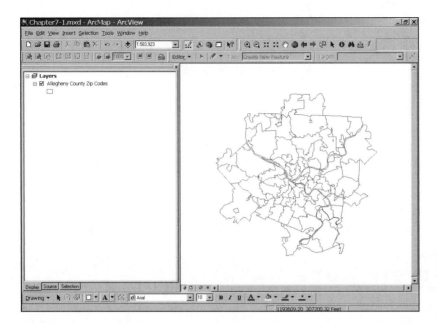

FIGURE 7-2 Chapter7-1.mxd map document

	OID	TAGNO	ZIPCODE
►	0	22253	15212
	1	35128	15213
	2	26262	15211
	3	26422	15203
	4	35776	15219
	5	38303	15214
	6	44229	15219

Attributes of TagsByZip

Record: 1   Show: All Selected   Records (0 out of 48366 Selected.)

FIGURE 7-3 Zip code address table

1. In the Attributes of TagsByZip window, right-click **ZIPCODE** and click **Summarize**.
2. In the resulting Summarize table, make sure that **ZIPCODE** is the selection for the field to summarize. In the Specify output table field, type **C:\LearningAndUsingGIS\FilesStudentWork\NumTags.dbf**, click **OK**, and in the Summarize Completed window click **Yes** to add the new table to the map document.
3. In the table of contents, right-click **NumTags** and click **Open**. See Figure 7-4. *(ArcGIS automatically adds the Count_ZIPCODE field to the new table with the count of records for each zip code. The resultant table only has 132 records, for each zip code that has one or more pool tag holders in residence.)*
4. Close the **Attributes of TagsbyZip** and **Attributes of NumTags** tables.

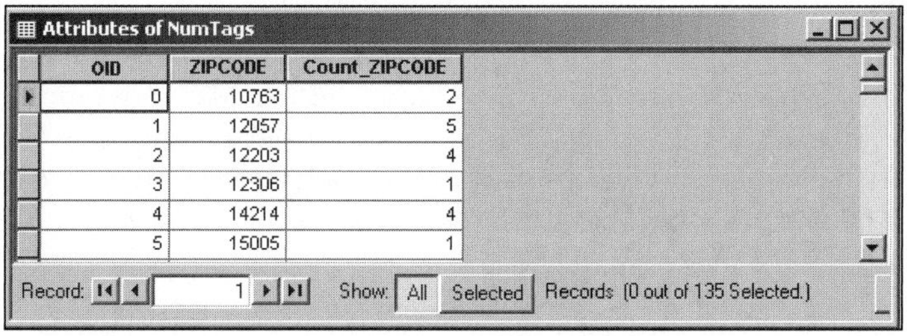

FIGURE 7-4   Records in the aggregate NumTags table

Join and Map the Zip Code Data

Finally, you can join the NumTags table to the Attributes of Allegheny County Zip Codes and then symbolize zip codes to show the distribution of pool tag holders in Allegheny County.

1. In the table of contents, right-click **Allegheny County Zip Codes**, click **Joins and Relates**, and click **Join**.
2. Make the selections shown in Figure 7-5.

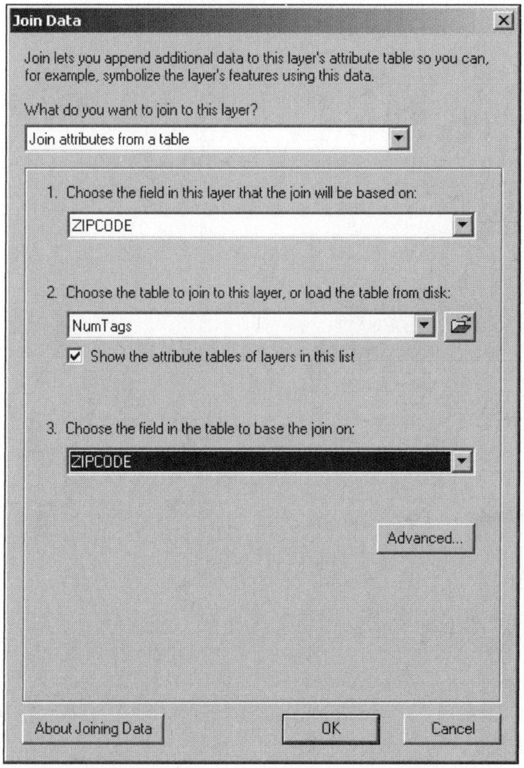

FIGURE 7-5   Join Data parameter selections

3. Click **OK** and click **Yes**.

4. Right-click **Allegheny County Zip Codes** and click **Open Attribute Table**. *(Some zip codes have null values for Count_ZIPCODE because those zip codes do not have any pool tag holders. You will need a second copy of Allegheny County Zip Codes to display all zip code boundaries after symbolizing one of the copies using Cnt_ZIPCOD because zip codes with null values for that attribute will not display.)*

5. Right-click **Allegheny County Zip Codes** and click **Copy**.

6. On the main menu, click **Edit** and click **Paste**.

7. Make sure that the Display tab is selected at the bottom of the table of contents, then Right-click the second copy from the top of **Allegheny County Zip Codes** and click **Properties**.

8. In the resulting Layer Properties window, click the **Symbology** tab, click **Quantities** in the left panel, click the list arrow in the **Value** field, click **NumTags.Count_ZIPCODE**, click **Classify**, click the list arrow for **Method**, click **Quantile**, click **OK**, select a **monochromatic color ramp** of your choice, and click **OK** again. See Figure 7-6.

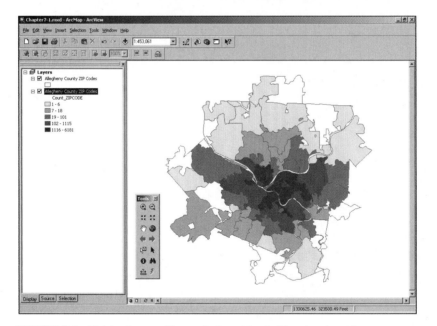

FIGURE 7-6   Finished map with count of pool tag holders by zip code

9. Save your map document and close ArcMap.

GEOCODING STREET ADDRESS DATA WITH A ZIP CODE ZONE

The best way to geocode address data from two or more municipalities is to have a street address attribute with a zip code zone. Zip codes are easy to enter accurately into data sets; other zone identifiers, such as municipality names, can have variations in spelling that generate matching errors. Let's get started with geocoding a zip code zone.

Prepare the Map Document for Geocoding to Streets with a Zip Code Zone

1. On your PC's desktop, click **Start**, click **All Programs**, click **ArcGIS**, and click **ArcMap**.
2. In the ArcMap window, click the **An existing map** option button and double-click **Browse for maps** in the panel below the option button.
3. In the Open window, browse to your **LearningAndUsingGIS** folder and double-click **Chapter7-2.mxd**. See Figure 7-7. *(The* Chapter7-2.mxd *map document window opens in ArcMap showing the Allegheny County Streets layer turned on.)*

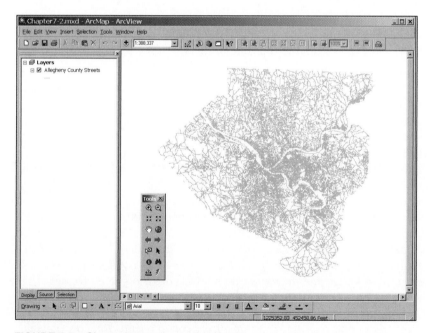

FIGURE 7-7   Chapter7-2.mxd map document

4. On the Standard toolbar, click the **Add Data** tool ⬇.
5. Browse to **C:\LearningAndUsingGIS\Data**, and double-click **emssites.dbf**.
   (This action adds a data table of EMS site addresses to your map document.)

6. In the table of contents, right-click **emssites.dbf**, click **Open**, and examine the data in the table. See Figure 7-8. *(You will see that each record has the name of the EMS site, a street address or intersection, and a zip code. Notice the variations in spelling and abbreviations of street types, such as* Avenue. Ave., *and* Av.*)*

OID	NAME	ADDRESS	ZIPCODE
0	MEDIC 4	200 Lafayette Street	15214
1	MEDIC 1,11	519 N Dallas Ave & Hamilton Ave	15208
2	MEDIC 3	320 S Main St.	15220
3	MEDIC 2	430 Matthews Avenue	15210
4	MEDIC 8	1720 Mary Street	15203
5	MEDIC 14	101 River Ave.	15212
6	MEDIC 9,15	2200 Liberty Av	15222

Record: 8 Show: All Selected Records (0 out of 13 Selected.)

FIGURE 7-8   EMS sites address table

7. Close the Attributes of emssites table.

Build the Street Address Locator

The next step in the geocoding process is to create an address locator for Allegheny County streets. In this case, the address locator is US Streets with Zone because you have street address and zip code, which is considered the zone in this example.

1. On the Standard toolbar, click the **ArcCatalog** tool.
2. In the Catalog Tree window, scroll to the bottom of the window, click the expander box for **Address Locators**, and double-click **Create New Address Locator**.
3. In the resulting Create New Address Locator window, scroll down, and click **US Streets with Zone (File)**. See Figure 7-9.
4. Click **OK**.
5. In the resulting New US Streets with Zone (File) Address Locator window, the Name field type **Allegheny County Streets**.
6. In the Reference data field of the Primary Table window, browse for or type **C:\LearningAndUsingGIS\MapsAlleghenyCounty\tgr42003lkA.shp** and click **Add**. *See Figure 7-10. (The street address fields should appear automatically. Check to be sure your settings are the same as Figure 7-10. The right panel has additional default settings for tuning parameters or options that you will simply accept. Notice that the minimum match score is 60, so addresses with a best matching score less than 60 are classified as unmatched. Also notice that & is a recognized connector for intersection streets, corresponding to intersections in* emssites.dbf. *The side offset is often useful. You can specify a distance from the street centerline for plotting geocoded points—on the correct odd or even side of the street—such as 20 feet.)*
7. Click **OK** and close **ArcCatalog**. *(ArcCatalog builds an index file, called* tgr42003lkA.shp.aig, *as an ingredient to geocoding.)*

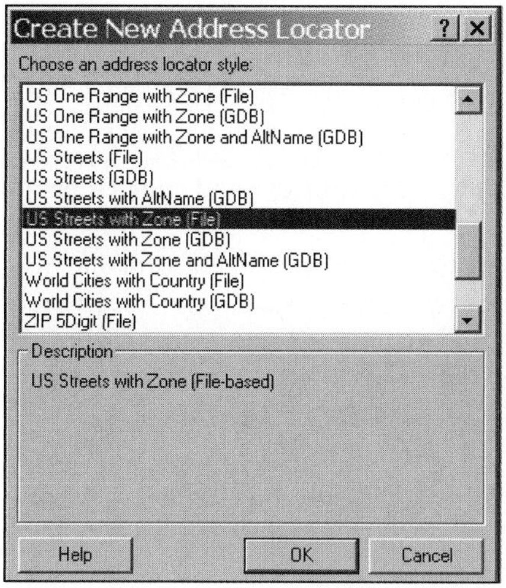

FIGURE 7-9 US Streets with Zone (File) address locator selection

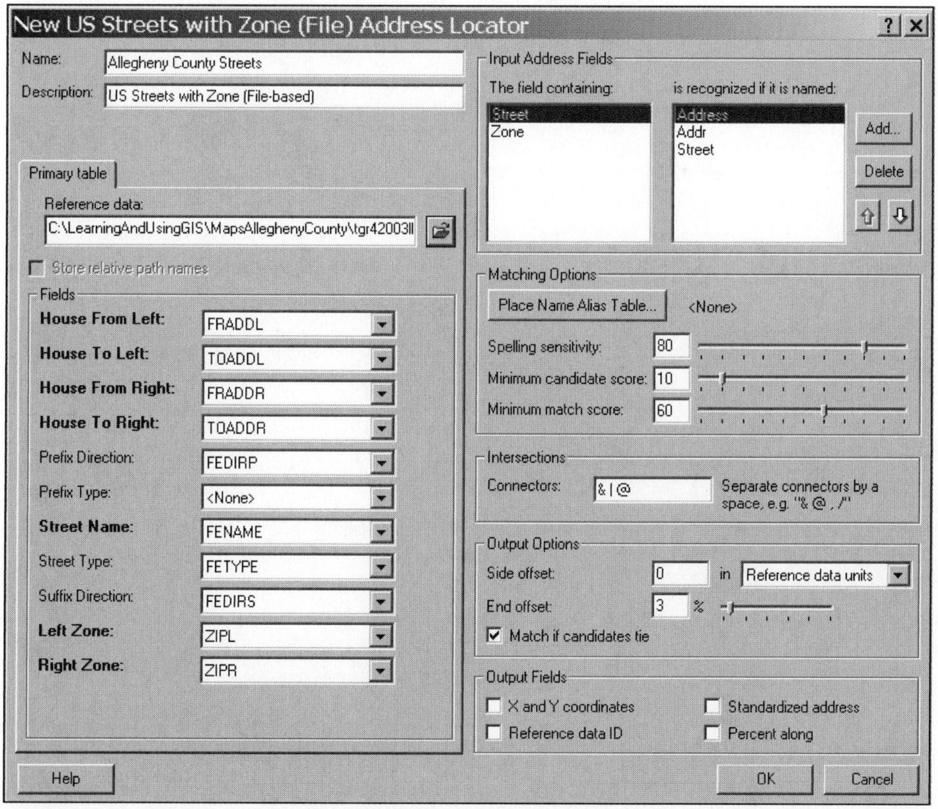

FIGURE 7-10 Allegheny County streets with zone address locator settings

Geocode Addresses with a Zip Code Zone

Now that you have an address locator for Allegheny County streets, you can geocode the original emssites table to the Allegheny County TIGER streets. This will yield a point shapefile of addresses on the streets.

1. In ArcMap, in the table of contents, right-click **emssites.dbf** and click **Geocode Addresses**.
2. In the resulting Choose an address locator to use window, click **Add**, click the **Look In** list arrow, click **Address Locators**, click **LoginName.Allegheny County Streets** (*where you replace LoginName with your login name*), click **Add**, and click **OK**. (*In the resulting Geocode Addresses window, notice that ArcMap automatically selected Address as the street address input and ZIPCODE as the zone.*)
3. In the resulting Geocode Addresses window, in the Output shapefile or feature class field, type **C:\LearningAndUsingGIS\FilesStudentWork\ EMSSites.shp**. See Figure 7-11.

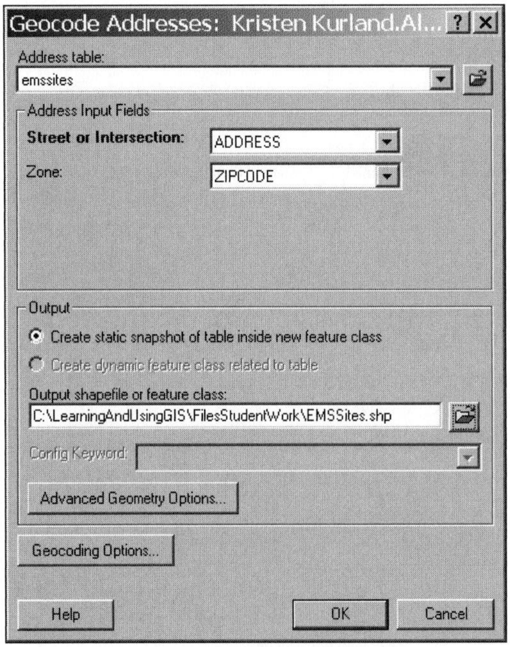

FIGURE 7-11 Geocode settings for streets

4. Click **OK**.
5. In the Review/Rematch Addresses window, you should have 9 (69%) matched with a score 80–100, 0 (0%) matched with a score less than 80, and 4 (31%) unmatched. See Figure 7-12.
6. Click **Done**. (*ArcMap adds the newly geocoded shapefile, EMSSites, to your map document.*)

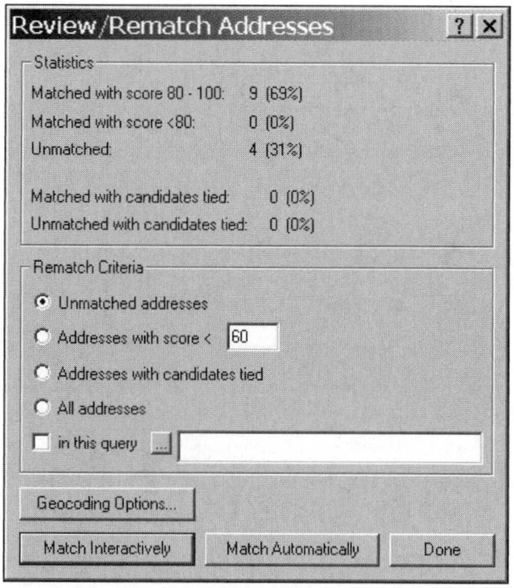

FIGURE 7-12 Address match statistics

PRACTICE 7-1

Open the attribute table for Geocoding Result: EMSSites and examine it. The Status column has values *M* for addresses geocoded successfully and *U* for those unmatched. The Side column indicates whether the address is on the right or left side of the street. Finally, ArcMap made copies of the STREET and ZIPCODE input attributes, calling them ARC_Street and ARC_Zone, that it used for geocoding. Close the table when you are finished.

Prepare a Log File of Unmatched Addresses

It is a good idea to keep a log file of the unmatched addresses that includes reasons why the addresses didn't geocode and any solutions or remedies. The log is useful for future work in cleaning addresses or repairing street maps. This can be a Microsoft Word document or Excel spreadsheet.

1. Start **Microsoft Word**.
2. Create a table that includes a column with the incorrect address and a column with the possible reason or solution for the incorrect address and remedy.
3. Copy and paste the four unmatched addresses in the attributes of Geocoding Result: EMSSites table to your new document. See Figure 7-13.
4. Save your Word document as **C:\LearningAndUsingGIS\FilesStudentWork\ AddressMatchingLog.doc**.

Incorrect address	Possible reason/solution
519 N DALLAS AVE & HAMILTON AVE	
4720 MOSSFIELD BLVD	
42000 WINTERBURN AVE	
2500 ALLIQUIPP ST	

FIGURE 7-13 Address matching log

Investigate Unmatched Addresses

Let's investigate the unmatched addresses. Generally, this requires experience with this task and knowledge of local streets, but we'll guide you through an exercise.

1. In the table of contents, right-click the **Allegheny County Streets** map layer and click **Open Attribute Table**.
2. In the resulting Attributes of Allegheny County Streets table, right-click **FENAME** and click **Sort Ascending**.
3. Scroll through the street names to see if you can find the street name ALLQUIPP. See Figure 7-14. *(You will notice that there are no streets named ALLIQUIP but there are streets named ALLEQUIPPA that includes the house number 2500. We recognized ALLQUIP as a potential typographical error because Allequippa is the name of a town near Pittsburgh.)*

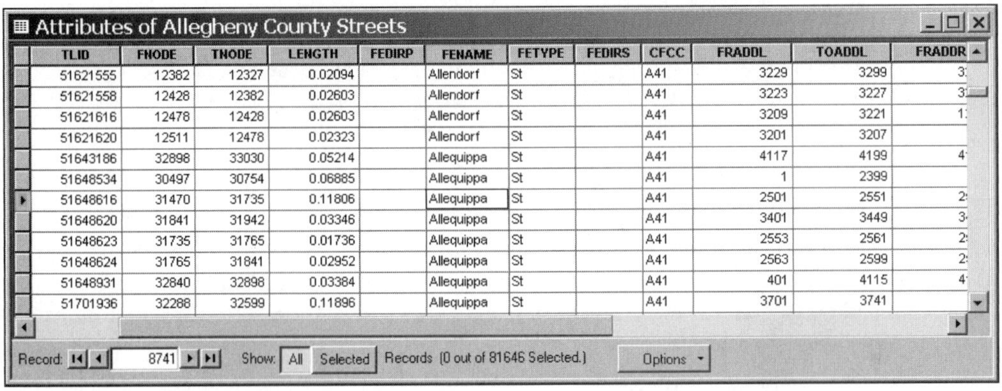

Attributes of Allegheny County Streets

TLID	FNODE	TNODE	LENGTH	FEDIRP	FENAME	FETYPE	FEDIRS	CFCC	FRADDL	TOADDL	FRADDR
51621555	12382	12327	0.02094		Allendorf	St		A41	3229	3299	3
51621558	12428	12382	0.02603		Allendorf	St		A41	3223	3227	3
51621616	12478	12428	0.02603		Allendorf	St		A41	3209	3221	1
51621620	12511	12478	0.02323		Allendorf	St		A41	3201	3207	
51643186	32898	33030	0.05214		Allequippa	St		A41	4117	4199	4
51648534	30497	30754	0.06885		Allequippa	St		A41	1	2399	
51648616	31470	31735	0.11806		Allequippa	St		A41	2501	2551	2
51648620	31841	31942	0.03346		Allequippa	St		A41	3401	3449	3
51648623	31735	31765	0.01736		Allequippa	St		A41	2553	2561	2
51648624	31765	31841	0.02952		Allequippa	St		A41	2563	2599	2
51648931	32840	32898	0.03384		Allequippa	St		A41	401	4115	4
51701936	32288	32599	0.11896		Allequippa	St		A41	3701	3741	

Record: 8741 Show: All Selected Records (0 out of 81646 Selected.) Options

FIGURE 7-14 Allequippa streets

4. In your Word document log file, in the row for 2500 ALLIQUIPP, make a note that the street name is misspelled. See Figure7-15.

Incorrect address	Possible reason/solution
519 N DALLAS AVE & HAMILTON AVE	
4720 MOSSFIELD BLVD	
42000 WINTERBURN AVE	
2500 ALLIQUIPP ST	Street name misspelled – should be ALLEQUIPPA

FIGURE 7-15 Allequippa address solution

PRACTICE 7-2

Search the streets attribute table for possible reasons that two other street addresses (4720 MOSSFIELD BLVD, 15232, and 42000 WINTERBURN AVE, 15207) didn't match and add notes to your log file. Be sure to check the zip codes for the streets. These are sometimes entered incorrectly. Close the Attributes of Allegheny County Streets table when finished.

Use Online Mapping to Troubleshoot Incorrect Addresses

Sometimes you can use online tools to determine address locations. Some of the common Web sites that are used for directions can help you find missing or incorrect addresses. Here you will use Google Maps to determine if North Dallas and Hamilton streets actually intersect for the unmatched street intersection.

1. Start a Web browser, such as Microsoft Internet Explorer.
2. Enter the URL **http://maps.google.com/**.
3. Type **N Dallas & Hamilton 15208** in the search field and click **Search**. (*The streets intersect.*)
4. Make a note in your log that the intersection exists.

PRACTICE 7-3

Use Google Maps to search for 4720 MOSSFIELD BLVD, 15232, and 42000 WINTER-BURN AVE, 15207. Try searching other Internet mapping sites such as *www.mapquest.com* and *http://maps.yahoo.com/*.

Rematch Addresses Interactively

You can now use the address matching log to try to rematch addresses.

1. In ArcMap on the main menu, click **Tools** and click **Geocoding**, click **Review/Rematch Addresses**, click **Geocoding Result: EMSSites**, and click **Yes**.
2. In the Review/Rematch Addresses window, click **Match Interactively**. (*The first unmatched address, 519 N Dallas and Hamilton, appears highlighted.*)

3. In the Street or Intersection field, delete the house number **519** and press **Enter**. See Figure 7-16. (*A candidate address with a perfect score of 100 percent appears.*)

candidate address

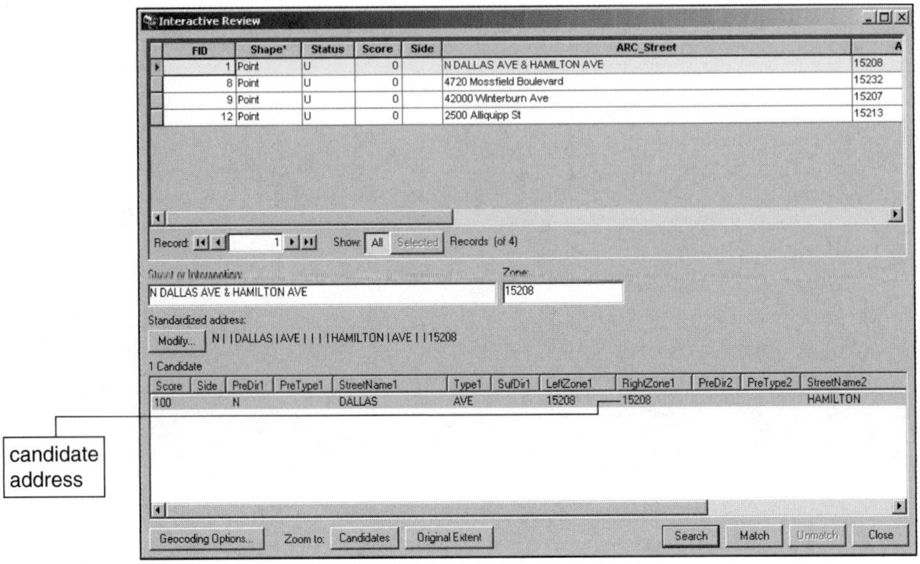

FIGURE 7-16   N DALLAS AVE & HAMILTON AVE candidate address

4. Click **Match**.
5. In the Interactive Review table, click the next unmatched address, **4720 MOSSFIELD BLVD**. (*This address has an incorrect street type and zip code. Instead of BOULEVARD the street type should be ST and instead of 15232, the zip code should be 15224.*)
6. In the Street or Intersection field, replace **BOULEVARD** with **ST** and in the ZONE field, enter **15224** and press **Enter**. See Figure 7-17. (A candidate address with a score of 100 percent appears.)
7. Click **Match**.

	FID	Shape*	Status	Score	Side	ARC_Street		ARC_Zone	
	1	Point	M	100		N DALLAS AVE & HAMILTON AVE		15208	M
▶	8	Point	U	0		4720 MOSSFIELD ST		15224	M
	9	Point	U	0		42000 Winterburn Ave		15207	M
	12	Point	U	0		2500 Aliquipp St		15213	M

Record: |◄ ◄ [2] ► ►| Show: All | Selected | Records (of 4)

Street or Intersection:
4720 MOSSFIELD ST

Zone:
15224

Standardized address:
[Modify...] 4720 | | | MOSSFIELD | ST | | 15224

2 Candidates

Score	Side	LeftFrom	LeftTo	RightFrom	RightTo	PreDir	PreType	StreetName	StreetType	SufDir	LeftZone	RightZone	
100	R	4701	4703	4700	4726			MOSSFIELD	ST		15224	15224	
51		4705	4829	4728	4844			MOSSFIELD	ST		15224	15224	

candidate address

[Geocoding Options...] Zoom to: [Candidates] [Original Extent]   [Search] [Match] [Unmatch] [Close]

FIGURE 7-17   4720 MOSSFIELD BLVD candidate address

PRACTICE 7-4

Rematch the remaining unmatched addresses by removing the extra zero in 42000 WIN-TERBURN AVE and correctly typing ALLEQUIPPA. Close the Interactive Review window when you are finished and click Done. You should have 100 percent of your addresses matched.

Produce the Final Map with EMS Sites

Now that your EMS sites are all matched, you can create a map showing the EMS sites near pools. This map is the basis for estimating the distance to the nearest EMS site for each pool—a performance measure that officials can use in determining which pools to keep open.

1. On the main menu, click the **Add Data** tool ✛, browse to **C:\LearningAnd UsingGIS\MapPools**, click **pools.shp**, press the **Ctrl** key, click **rivers.shp**, and click **Add**. *(If a warning message appears, dismiss it.)*

2. Symbolize **pools** with a **blue square 2**, size **10**, EMS Sites as a **bright red circle 2**, size **8**, rivers with a **light blue color fill**, and zoom into the map to see all of the pools and EMS sites close up. See Figure 7-18. *(You can see that some pools are quite far from the nearest EMS site. If you had time, you could add an attribute, EMSDist, to the attributes of pools table, use the Measure tool, and estimate travel distances.)*

3. When you are finished, save your map document and close ArcMap.

271

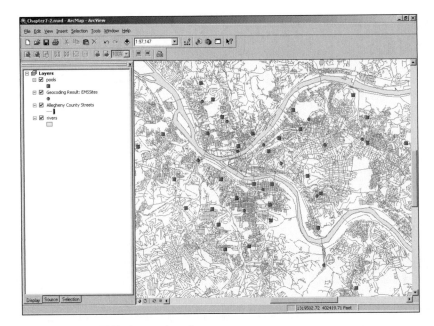

FIGURE 7-18 EMS sites and pools

GEOCODING STREET ADDRESS DATA WITH A MUNICIPALITY ZONE

Sometimes address data contains street address and municipality attributes, but no zip code attribute. TIGER streets include just streets and zip codes, so to geocode address data with municipality as the zone, you will have to add a municipality attribute to streets. You can easily do this with a spatial intersection. Then, you can build a new locator for streets, using municipality for the zone.

Prepare the Map Document for Geocoding to Streets with a Municipality Zone

1. On your PC's desktop, click **Start**, click **All Programs**, click **ArcGIS**, and click **ArcMap**.
2. In the ArcMap window, click the **An existing map** option button and double-click **Browse for maps** in the panel below the option button.
3. In the Open window, browse to your **LearningAndUsingGIS** folder and double-click **Chapter7-3.mxd**. See Figure 7-19. *(The Chapter7-3.mxd map document window opens in ArcMap showing the Allegheny County Streets and Municipalities layers turned on.)*
4. In the table of contents, right-click **Streets** and click **Open Attribute Table**. *(Notice that the municipality name is not included in this table.)*
5. Close the **Attributes of Streets** table.

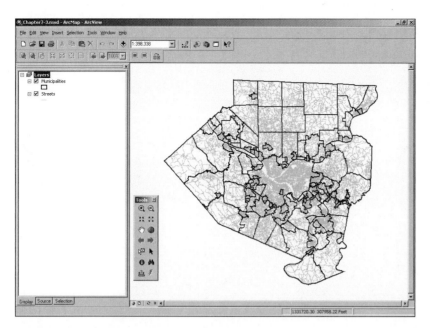

FIGURE 7-19   Chapter7-3.mxd map document

6. At the bottom of the table of contents, click the **Source** tab, right-click the **YMCA** table, and click **Open**. *(Notice that there are no zip codes in this table, but instead it has municipality names.)*
7. Close the **Attributes of YMCA** table.

Intersect Streets and Municipalities

Next you use ArcToolbox's Intersect function to create a new streets layer that includes the municipality name.

1. On the Standard toolbar, click the **ArcToolbox** tool .
2. In the ArcToolbox window, click expander boxes for **Analysis Tools** and **Overlay** and double-click **Intersect**.
3. In the Intersect window, click the list arrow in the **Input Feature** field, and click **Municipalities**.
4. Click the same list arrow and click **Streets**.
5. In the Output Features field type **C:\LearningAndUsingGIS\FilesStudentWork\ StreetsMCD.shp**. See Figure 7-20.
6. Click **OK** and click **Close**. *(This creates a new shapefile that combines streets and municipality names that ArcMap automatically adds to your map document. Note: MCD is the U.S. Census Bureau abbreviation for minor civil divisions, which is the same as municipalities.)*
7. Close **ArcToolbox**.
8. At the bottom of the table of contents, click the **Display** tab. In the table of contents turn the original **Streets** off, move the new **StreetsMCD** layer below the Municipalities layer, and symbolize it with a **gray** color.

Geocoding Your Data

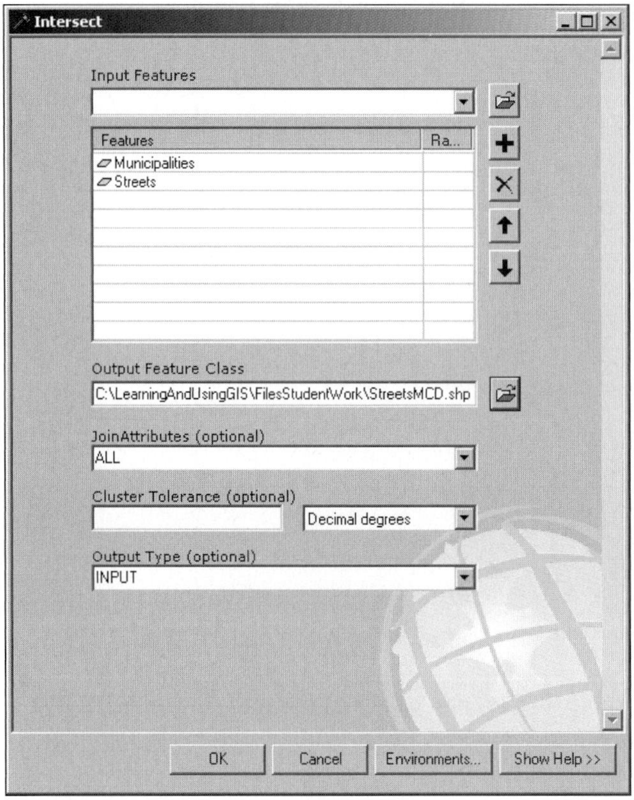

FIGURE 7-20 Settings for intersection

9. Right-click **StreetsMCD** and click **Open Attribute Table**. See Figure 7-21. *(See that municipality names are now in the street attribute table.)*

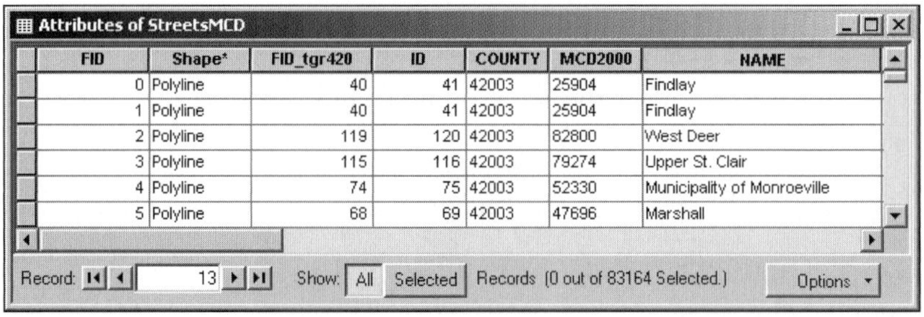
Attributes of StreetsMCD

FID	Shape*	FID_tgr420	ID	COUNTY	MCD2000	NAME
0	Polyline	40	41	42003	25904	Findlay
1	Polyline	40	41	42003	25904	Findlay
2	Polyline	119	120	42003	82800	West Deer
3	Polyline	115	116	42003	79274	Upper St. Clair
4	Polyline	74	75	42003	52330	Municipality of Monroeville
5	Polyline	68	69	42003	47696	Marshall

Record: 13 Show: All Selected Records (0 out of 83164 Selected.) Options

FIGURE 7-21 Streets with municipality names

10. Close **Attributes of StreetsMCD**.

Build an Address Locator for Streets with Municipality as Zone

The next step is to build a new address locator for Allegheny County Streets using the municipality name as the zone.

1. On the Standard toolbar, click the **ArcCatalog** tool [icon].
2. In the Catalog Tree window, scroll down, click the expander box for **Address Locators**, and double-click **Create New Address Locator**.
3. In the Create New Address Locator window, click **US Streets with Zone (File)**, and click **OK**.
4. In the Name field of the New US Streets with Zone (File) Address Locator window, type **Allegheny County Streets with MCD Name**.
5. In the Reference data field, browse to or type **C:\LearningAndUsingGIS\ FilesStudentWork\StreetsMCD.shp**.
6. In the Fields section, change both **Left Zone** and **Right Zone** to **NAME**.
7. In the Side offset field type **20**, change the corresponding units to **Feet**, and click the **Reference data ID** check box. See Figure 7-22.

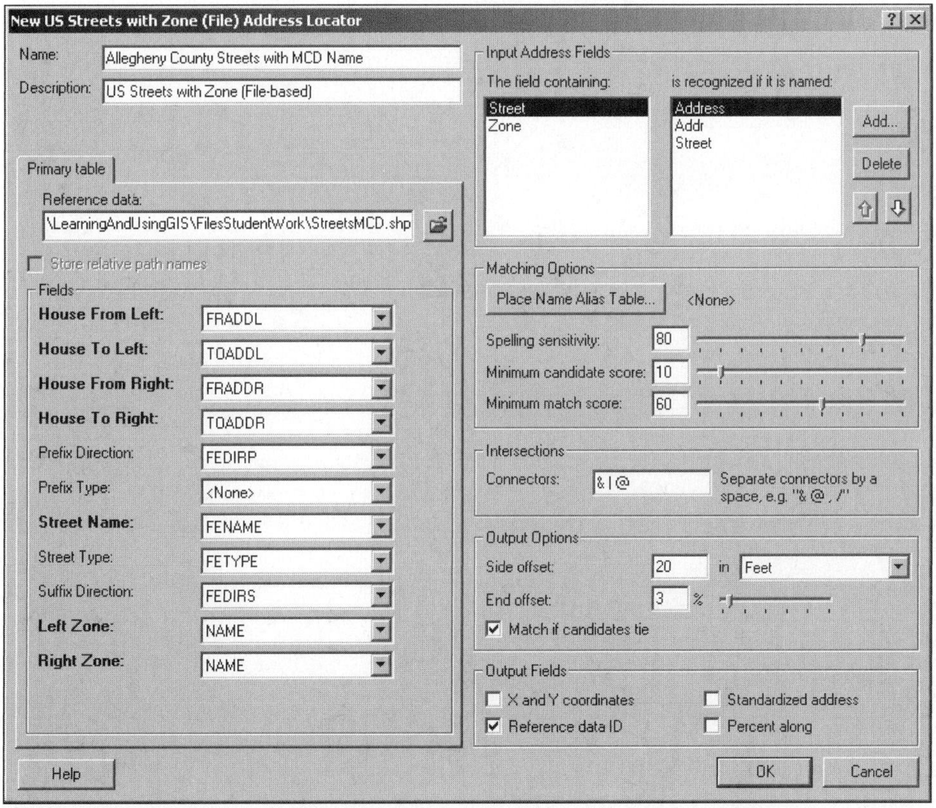

FIGURE 7-22 Allegheny County streets with MCD name address locator settings

8. Click **OK** and close **ArcCatalog**.

Geocode Street Address Data with Municipality as Zone

Now that you have a new address locator for Allegheny County Streets with the Municipality name, you can geocode the YMCA table using the StreetsMCD layer.

1. In the table of contents, click the **Source** tab, right-click **YMCA**, and click **Geocode Addresses**.
2. In the resulting Choose an address locator to use window, click **Add**, click the **Look in** list arrow, click **Address Locators**, click **LoginName.Allegheny County Streets with MCD Name** (*where you substitute your login name for Login-Name*), click **Add**, and click **OK**.
3. In the Address Input Fields section of the resulting Geocode Addresses window, click the **Zone** list arrow, and click **NAME**.
4. In the Output shapefile or feature class field, type **C:\LearningAndUsingGIS\ FilesStudentWork\YMCASites.shp** as the new point shapefile for YMCA sites. See Figure 7-23.

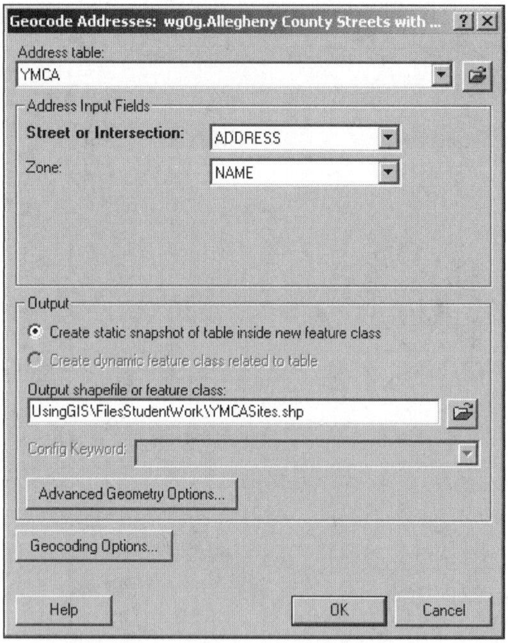

FIGURE 7-23   Settings for geocoding YMCA data

5. Click **OK**. (*In the resulting Review/Rematch Addresses window, you should have 26 (68%) matched with a score 80–100, 0 (0%) matched with a score less than 80, and 12 (32%) unmatched.*)

Click the Match Interactively button and try to match the YMCA locations in the municipality of Pittsburgh that did not match. The address 730 WILLIAM PITT UN is actually
4450 Bigelow Blvd (that was way off!). BLVD OF THE ALLIES should be BOULEVARD
OF THE ALLIES. For this address, you will have to click the Modify button under Standardized address, delete BLVD as a PreDir, type BOULEVARD as the start of the Street-
Name, and press Enter. When finished, close the following windows: Edit Standardization
window, Interactive Review window, and Review/Rematch Address.

Produce a Map with Geocoded YMCA Facilities and Pools

Because most YMCA locations have indoor pools, it would be interesting to see the locations of YMCAs and Pittsburgh pools.

1.   On the Standard toolbar, click the **Add Data** tool ⬇.
2.   Browse to **C:\LearningAndUsingGIS\MapPools**, and add **pools.shp**. (*If a
     warning message appears, dismiss it.*)
3.   Symbolize **pools** and **YMCASites** to your liking. See Figure 7-24.
4.   Save your map document.

Build the Alias Table

An alias table is not particularly valuable for geocoding YMCAs because geocoding YMCAs
is a one-time process. It would be valuable to include YMCA locations in an alias table for
EMS data entered by ambulance drivers because EMS data collection and geocoding is a
repeated process. As explained earlier in this chapter, an alias is useful for locations that
occur frequently and have familiar place-names. Nevertheless, we have you create an alias
table here for practice. If you were to open the YMCASites attribute table, you would find
two place-names: Memorial Field in Wilmerding, PA, and YMCA Plum in Plum, PA. Of
course, neither is matched. It is easy to find addresses for these YMCAs using Google Maps.
For Memorial Field, we took a nearby street address of 299 Western Ave, McKeesport,
which is on our street map. For YMCA Plum we took the nearest address on our street map,
103 Kane Rd, Plum.

1.   Start **Excel**, create the spreadsheet shown in Figure 7-25, and save it as
     C:\LearningAndUsingGIS\FilesStudentWork\YMCAAlias.dbf.

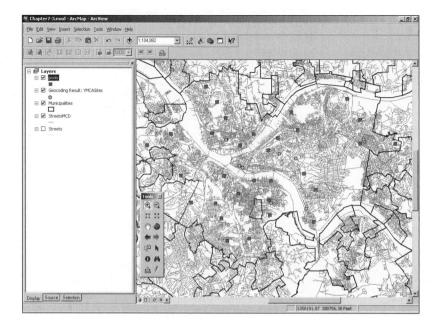

FIGURE 7-24 Pools and YMCA sites

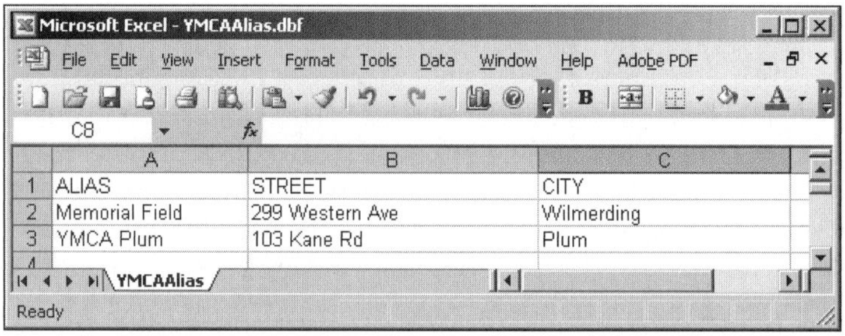

	A	B	C
1	ALIAS	STREET	CITY
2	Memorial Field	299 Western Ave	Wilmerding
3	YMCA Plum	103 Kane Rd	Plum

FIGURE 7-25 YMCA alias table

2. On the Standard toolbar, click the **Add Data** tool ✛.
3. Browse to **C:\LearningAndUsingGIS\FilesStudentWork**, and double-click **YMCAAlias.dbf**.

Modify the Street Address Locator for Alias Table

1. On the Standard toolbar, click the **ArcCatalog** tool 📖.
2. In the Catalog Tree window, scroll to the bottom of the window, click the expander box for **Address Locators**, and double-click **Allegheny County Streets with MCD Name**.

3. Click the **Place Name Alias Table** button. In the Alias Table window, browse to **C:\LearningAndUsingGIS\FilesStudentWork**, and double-click **YMCAAlias.dbf**.
4. Click the list arrow in the **Alias** field, click **Alias**, and click **OK**.
5. Close ArcCatalog.

Geocode Street Address Data with Municipality as Zone

1. In the table of contents, click the **Source** tab, right-click **YMCA.dbf**, and click **Geocode Addresses**.
2. In the Choose an address locator to use window, click **LoginName.Allegheny County Streets with MCD Name** *(where you substitute your login name for LoginName)*, and click **OK**.
3. In the Address Input Fields section of the resulting Geocode Addresses window, click the **Zone** list arrow, and click **NAME**.
4. In the Output shapefile or feature class field, type **C:\LearningAndUsingGIS\FilesStudentWork\YMCASitesWithAlias.shp** as the new point shapefile for YMCA Sites.
5. Click **OK**. *(In the resulting Review/Rematch Addresses window, you should have 28 (74%) matched with a score 80–100, 0 (0%) matched with a score less than 80, and 10 (32%) unmatched. There are two more matches for a total of 28 compared to your early batch geocode results without the alias table of 26. Of course, the two additional matches are from your alias table.)*
6. Save your map document and close ArcMap.

Chapter 7 Summary

Mailing addresses make possible mail delivery to residences, businesses, and other facilities on the street network. Likewise, mailing addresses in the form of tabular data can be used to place points on a GIS street map layer. Three components make mapping address data possible: (1) the table of address data that you obtain or supply, (2) a TIGER street map or other spatial reference data, and (3) a geocoding engine that matches address data attributes to those in the attribute table of the street map for placement of a point.

The address data needs to be in a standard format as provided by the U.S. post office. Components are a house number, prefix or postfix directional (N, E, S, or W) if part of the address, street name, street suffix (St, Ave, Blvd, and so on), common unit designator (such as Apt), city name, state abbreviation, and five-digit zip code. If your data and map are for a single city or smaller, you only need the street address (house number, prefix or postfix directional, street name, and street suffix). If your data and map are for a larger area than a city, you need to have either zip code or city name or ID for use as a geocoding zone to break ties for multiple occurrences of the same street address. For example, 100 5th Ave could be used in more than one city.

If your data only contains the ID or name of a polygon—such as a zip code or city name—you can associate data records with polygons and produce choropleth maps or size-graduated point marker maps displaying the number of records associated with each polygon.

Poor address data practices and certain practices in location references introduce some complications in geocoding. For example, many organizations use place-names for famous or well-known locations. Yankee Stadium, Dulles Airport, and Point State Park are examples. For such cases ArcGIS allows you to build an alias table listing the place-names and corresponding legitimate street addresses. Geocoding uses the table to replace place-names with the addresses as a first step. Then the address-matching process can proceed.

Data cleaning is a preliminary step that is sometimes necessary when placing address data into an acceptable format. Sometimes attributes need to be concatenated to form a street address field. Other times, it is necessary to delete characters, such as *block of* in *500 block of Main ST*. Also, some parts of the United States have irregular street address formats such as letters, periods, or dashes included in the house number. In most cases a simple adjustment, such as deleting the nonnumeric characters, solves the problem.

A geocoding engine is an expert system computer program that goes through steps similar to those of your postal carrier in delivering the mail. Spelling errors, variations in abbreviations, and other nonmatches with the official street address (the attributes in the street map) are all handled with much success, but sometimes result in errors. One error inherent in TIGER street maps are positional. TIGER street maps do not have precise locations for street placement and only have starting and ending house numbers on the left and right side of each block-long street segment. So, an address such as 125 Main ST results in an interpolated point, 25 percent of the distance between the end points of 101 and 199.

If you have high-quality address data, you can expect around 85 to 95 percent of addresses to geocode in a batch processing—a single step. With extra effort, reviewing one unmatched address at a time in ArcGIS's interactive rematching interface, you can make more matches, but this is time consuming. The match rate is a good performance measure for geocoding, but it does not identify major errors in location. Only an expert on local streets or experience in attempting to reach the geocoded point can identify such errors.

Key Terms

Alias table   A table of place-names and corresponding street addresses used during the geo-coding process. Before address matching, the geocoding engine searches for aliases from the alias table in the input address data table and replaces them with the corresponding street addresses.

Batch geocoding   An automated process that attempts to geocode all of the addresses in an input data table.

Data cleaning   A process for adjusting data for computer processing, for example to prepare addresses for geocoding. If an address contains *block of*, it is cleaned by deleting *block of* and adding 50 to the house number. For example, 300 block of Main ST becomes 350 Main ST.

Expert system   A set of rules and processes used by a computer to attempt to replicate the judg-ments of an expert. For example, a geocoding engine attempts to match imperfect address data to attributes in street centerline maps.

Geocoding   The process of transforming tabular address data into point locations on a map using sophisticated matching algorithms for street addresses or simple table joins for poly-gon locations such as zip codes or counties.

Geocoding engine   The complex set of software programs that carry out the geocoding process.

Heads-up digitizing   The use of existing map layers as guides on the computer screen for drawing new vector map layers. It is possible to digitize points, lines, or polygons.

Interactive rematching   An interactive interface used to process one unmatched street address at a time from batch geocoding in an attempt to repair the address or otherwise find a match-ing street segment and point.

Linear interpolation   As applied to placing points at house numbers on TIGER streets, the use of proportions for approximate location. For example, if a TIGER street segment has even street numbers 300 and 398 as its recorded starting and ending values, a house number of 320 is located the fraction 20/(398 − 300) of the distance from the 300 point location to the 398 location.

Place-names   The use of a familiar name rather than an address, for example JFK Airport.

SOUNDEX key   A code generated using a fixed set of rules and limited alphabet to represent words that sound alike. Each word that sounds alike has the same SOUNDEX key value. Thus, the SOUNDEX key can be used to match words that have minor variations in spellings.

Zone   A polygon ID or name used in geocoding to select the correct location among identical streets. For example, a state might have several streets in different municipalities with the address 123 Main St. In such a case, it is possible to select the correct location given a zip code or municipality as the tie breaker.

Short-Answer Questions

1. What are the advantage(s) of storing street address data in many attributes, one for each row in Table 7-1?

2. Suppose that a demolition crew has a GPS unit so that they can locate themselves accu-rately and you gave them the location of a property to demolish from geocoding with TIGER streets. Could this lead to any problems? Why?

3. What do you suppose would be the problem if delivery persons, who provide address data for locations they visit, include field notes in the address field; for example, "123 Main ST—vicious dog in rear"? How would you repair the data?

4. A street in Pittsburgh is named E North Avenue. Do you suppose that a geocoding engine could handle such an address?

5. Suppose that your data—all from the same state— includes a single spatial identifier, county name. How would you go about mapping such data?

6. Suppose that Carnegie Mellon University (CMU) is a place-name for 5000 Forbes Ave, 15213. How many records would you suggest adding for CMU in an alias table?

7. Read up on the SOUNDEX key at *www.sconsig.com/sastips/soundex-01.htm*. What are SOUNDEX key values for the following names: BEADLES, BEATLES, RENOLDS, RYNOLDS, STEWART, and STUART.

8. Suppose that you geocode addresses and then want to count them up by census block group, using spatial intersection of the two layers. Would you recommend using a side off-set in geocoding for this purpose? Explain.

9. If you needed to geocode a set of facilities with 100 percent accuracy, how would you go about collecting address data? What would you do for facilities that do not match with available data?

10. Suppose you have a large amount of address data that contain many place-names. How could you go about mining the data for place-names?

Exercises

1. **Geocode Hospitals to Pittsburgh Streets.** Sometimes it is necessary to geocode data 100 percent; for example, when mapping facilities such as hospitals. Nevertheless, not all records in a data table with addresses will match at first. You have to do additional research and draw on additional resources to match unmatched records. This exercise uses a Pittsburgh street layer and a data table to create a geocoded point shapefile of hospitals. To enable you to practice the mechanics of this process, we allow you to make "big" assumptions to geocode the hospitals 100 percent, including changing street numbers and zip codes.

   a. Open C:\LearningAndUsingGIS\Chapter7-2.mxd in ArcMap and save it as **C:\LearningAndUsingGIS\FilesStudentWork\Exercise7-1<YourName>.mxd**, where you substitute your name or other identifier for <YourName>. Add the data table, hospitals.dbf, from C:\LearningAndUsingGIS\Data\ and the shapefiles pools.shp, Pittsburgh.shp, and rivers.shp from C:\LearningAndUsingGIS\MapsPools\ to the map document. Symbolize your map.

   b. Create a US Streets with Zone (File) address locator called Hospital using default settings, C:\LearningAndUsingGIS\MapsAlleghenyCounty\tgr42003lkA.shp as the reference data, and zip code as the zone.

   c. Create a new folder called **C:\LearningAndUsingGIS\FilesStudentWork\ Exercise7-1**. Geocode the hospitals table to the Pittsburgh streets, creating a shapefile called **C:\LearningAndUsingGIS\FilesStudentWork\Exercise7-1\ PghHospitals.shp**.

d. Use the PghStreets attribute table to determine why the unmatched addresses did not match. Create a new Word document called **C:\LearningAndUsingGIS\ FilesStudentWork\Exercise7-1\Exercise7-1<YourName>.doc**, where you substitute your name or other identifier for <YourName>. Include a title and create a table that includes three columns, one for the incorrect address, one for the zip code, and one for the possible remedy. Include a header row with column names.

e. Use your Word document as a guide and ArcMap's Interactive Rematch tool to match 100 percent of the hospital addresses.

f. Symbolize hospitals using the More Symbols button in the Symbol Selector window, the Civic symbols, and the Hospital 1 symbol.

g. Create a map layout with title, map, and legend. Turn off streets. Export the layout as Exercise7-1.jpg to **C:\LearningAndUsingGIS\FilesStudentWork\Exercise7-1** and add it to your Word document. Comment on the distribution of pools and hospitals. Is it good that pools are nearby hospitals?

2. **Geocode Fast Food Places to Allegheny County Zip Codes.** Even though data might be available with street addresses in addition to zip codes, sometimes it's desirable to just produce maps with counts of records or statistics by zip code. Resulting maps display spatial patterns while protecting the privacy of persons residing at addresses—if the data is on individuals. In this exercise you geocode a table of fast food restaurants in Allegheny County, Pennsylvania using a zip code map. While there is no need to protect privacy in this case, you will nevertheless get experience with geocoding zip code data.

a. Create a new map document saved as **C:\LearningAndUsingGIS\FilesStudentWork\ Exercise7-2<YourName>.mxd**, where you substitute your name or other identifier for <YourName>. Change the coordinate system of the data frame in the project to the State Plane, 1984 NAD (Feet), Pennsylvania South projection. Add zipcodes.shp, pools. shp, and Pittsburgh.shp from C:\LearningAndUsingGIS\MapsPools\; tgr42003lkA.shp and tgr42003cty00.shp from C:\LearningAndUsingGIS\MapsAlleghenyCounty; and the comma separated text file, FastFood.csv, from C:\LearningAndUsingGIS\Data\.

b. Create a new folder called **C:\LearningAndUsingGIS\FilesStudentWork\ Exercise7-2**.

c. Summarize FastFood.csv by producing a new table, called **C:\LearningAndUsingGIS\ FilesStudentWork\Exercise7-2\FFoodZip.dbf**, in ArcMap that includes the count of fast food restaurants by zip code. *Hint: Check your work by counting records for a zip code in FastFood.csv and seeing that FFoodZip.dbf has the correct count for that zip code.*

d. Join FFoodZip.dbf to the zip code map.

e. Symbolize your map, using 5 classes with quantiles, to display the spatial distribution of fast food restaurants in Allegheny County and Pittsburgh. *Hint: Add a second copy of zipcodes.shp and symbolize it with hollow fill to fill out the map for zip codes that do not have restaurants.* Produce a map layout with map, title, and legend. Zoom in to Pittsburgh and export your map layout as **C:\LearningAndUsingGIS\FilesStudentWork\ Exercise7-2\Exercise7-2.jpg**.

f. Create a Word document called **C:\LearningAndUsingGIS\FilesStudentWork\ Exercise7-2\Exercise7-2<YourName>.doc.** Include a title, your map layout image, and a discussion of the distribution of pools versus fast food restaurants. Is it good or bad that fast food restaurants are in the vicinity of pools?

3. **Geocode Fast Food locations to Allegheny County Streets.** This exercise uses an Allegheny County street layer and a data table of fast food locations to create a geocoded shapefile of fast food sites.

a. Create a new map document saved as **C:\LearningAndUsingGIS\FilesStudentWork\ Exercise7-3<YourName>.mxd,** where you substitute your name or other identifier for <YourName>. Change the coordinate system of the data frame in the project to the State Plane, 1984 NAD (Feet), Pennsylvania South projection. Add zipcodes.shp, pools. shp, and Pittsburgh.shp from C:\LearningAndUsingGIS\MapsPools\; tgr42003lkA.shp and tgr42003cty00.shp from C:\LearningAndUsingGIS\MapsAlleghenyCounty; and the comma separated text file, FastFood.csv, from C:\LearningAndUsingGIS\Data\. *Hint: If you did problem 7-2, save Exercise7-2<YourName>.mxd as Exercise7-3 <YourName>.mxd and modify it as needed.*

b. Create a new folder called **C:\LearningAndUsingGIS\FilesStudentWork\ Exercise7-3\.**

c. Create a US Streets with Zone (File) address locator called FastFood using a 20 foot off-set and default settings for the other parameters, C:\LearningAndUsingGIS\ MapsAlleghenyCounty\tgr42003lkA.shp as the reference data, and zip code as the zone. Save your geocoded file called **C:\LearningAndUsingGIS\FilesStudentWork\ Exercise7-3\FastFoodRestaurants.shp.**

d. Notice that many addresses did not match. Find and document five address problems. Create a new Word document called **C:\LearningAndUsingGIS\FilesStudentWork\ Exercise7-1\Exercise7-3<YourName>.doc,** where you substitute your name or other identifier for <YourName>. Include a title and create a table that includes three columns, one for the incorrect address, one for the zip code, and one for the possible remedy. Include a header row with column names. Use Web sites such as Google Maps, Mapquest, Yahoo Maps, and the fast food restaurants (e.g. McDonalds, Wendy's, Burger King) to find correct addresses.

e. Use ArcMap's Interactive Rematch tool to match five more fast food addresses accurately.

f. Create a layout of your map with a title, map, and legend. Export the layout to **C:\LearningAndUsingGIS\FilesStudentWork\Exercise7-3** as Exercise7-3.jpg.

g. Create a new Word document called **C:\LearningAndUsingGIS\FilesStudentWork\ Exercise7-3\Exercise7-3<YourName>.doc,** where you substitute your name or other identifier for <YourName>. Include a title. Insert your map image, Exercise7-3.jpg and comment on the distribution of fast food restaurants compared to pools.

4. **Alias table for Hospitals.** Suppose that ambulance drivers file electronic reports for trips made taking patients to hospitals. Instead of recording the address of the hospital, they would like to have an alias for each hospital.

a. Create a new map document saved as **C:\LearningAndUsingGIS\FilesStudentWork\ Exercise7-4<YourName>.mxd**, where you substitute your name or other identifier for <YourName>. Change the coordinate system of the data frame in the project to the State Plane, 1984 NAD (Feet), Pennsylvania South projection. Add Pittsburgh.shp from C:\LearningAndUsingGIS\MapsPools\ and tgr42003lkA.shp and tgr42003cty00.shp from C:\LearningAndUsingGIS\MapsAlleghenyCounty; and the comma separated text file, FastFood.csv, from C:\LearningAndUsingGIS\Data\. *Hint: If you did problems 7-2 or 7-3, save Exercise7-2<YourName>.mxd or Exercise7-3<YourName>.mxd as Exercise7-4<YourName>.mxd and modify it as needed.*

b. Create a new folder called **C:\LearningAndUsingGIS\FilesStudentWork\ Exercise7-4**.

c. Open hospitals.dbf from C:\LearningAndUsingGIS\Data\ in Excel and add a column called ALIAS after NAME. Enter a short alias for each hospital and save the file to C:\LearningAndUsingGIS\FilesStudentWork\Exercise7-4\.

d. In Excel, create a spreadsheet with three columns as follows where you substitute the appropriate alias from your alias table if different from that listed:

TripID	Date	Address	ZipCode	Hospital
1001	12/1/2006	4010 Forbes Ave	15213	Allegheny
1002	12/1/2006	100 Grant St	15222	Childrens
1003	12/1/2006	310 5th Ave	15222	Providence

e. Create a US Streets with Zone (File) address locator called HospitalAlias using default settings and C:\LearningAndUsingGIS\MapsAlleghenyCounty\tgr42003lkA.shp as the reference data, and zip code as the zone. *Hint: You will have to add Hospital to the Input Address Fields and remove all other field names.*

f. Address match trips.dbf using Hospital as the address.

g. Create a new Word document called **C:\LearningAndUsingGIS\FilesStudentWork\ Exercise7-4\Exercise7-4<YourName>.doc**, where you substitute your name or other identifier for <YourName>. Include a title. Copy and paste your trips.dbf table into your Word document (open the dbf file in Excel, select desired cells, copy, and paste). Simply export your map as a jpg image from the data view of ArcMap as C:\LearningAndUsingGIS\FilesStudentWork\Exercise7-4\Exercise7-1.jpg and add it to your Word document.

References

Postal Addressing Standards, Publication 28 of the U.S. Post Office (2000). Internet URL: http://pe.usps.com/cpim/ftp/pubs/Pub417/pub417.pdf (accessed May 18, 2006)
SAS Consultant Special Interest Group, "What is SOUNDEX?" Internet URL: http://www.sconsig. com/sastips/soundex-01.htm (accessed May 18, 2006)

CHAPTER **8**

DIGITIZING MAP FEATURES

LEARNING OBJECTIVES

In this chapter, you will:

- Learn about control networks for spatial location referencing
- Learn about GPS and its role in providing known locations
- Learn how to digitize maps from hard copy and scanned manuscripts
- Edit point locations using a raster base map as reference
- Create new shapefiles
- Create new line features
- Edit polygon features

Eric and friends are vertices in a nice but temporary line at the pool's edge...

INTRODUCTION

Most applied GIS work uses map layers created by others. For example, you have downloaded and

directly used base maps. You have selected features from vector base maps to save as new map layers,

dissolved polygon base maps to create new polygon layers, and appended base maps to form new layers.

The closest you have come to creating original map layers was to geocode street addresses to place points on or near street centerline base maps. What if, however, you need a map layer that is not available or easily derived from a vector base map?

We take you one step further toward creating map layers in this chapter by showing you how to do heads-up digitizing. Recall that this is the process of creating or editing a vector map layer using existing map layers, including aerial photographs, as guides. You view the guide map layers on your computer's screen ("heads up"), use your cursor as a drawing tool, and click on the screen to create new points or vertices for lines and polygons. Likewise, you can move points or vertices of any existing shapefile or add new vertices and delete old ones as desired.

For example, in this chapter we have you edit existing vector map files for physical features—swimming pools and river shores—using an aerial photograph as the guide for more accurately repositioning previously digitized points. You move the pool point markers, and you add and move new vertices to the river's shores. We also have you create a portion of a bus route that serves a swimming pool, again using the aerial photo.

To further your general GIS education, we briefly discuss some additional digitizing topics. These include **raster-to-vector conversion software** for automating digitizing of electronically scanned paper maps, the **digitizing tablet** for digitizing paper maps, control networks of benchmark points for referencing survey methods to known locations vertically and horizontally, such as the **National Spatial Reference System (NSRS)**, and GPS methods for locating features. The NSRS is a dense network of benchmarks provided by the **National Geodetic Survey (NGS)**, the federal agency responsible for this system.

NATIONAL SPATIAL REFERENCE SYSTEM

No doubt, you have seen surveyors along or on roadways peering through their **transits** at a pole being held by an assistant. What are these people doing? They are taking measurements—angles and distances—from *known locations* on Earth to accurately locate points, paths of various kinds, and boundaries. What and where are these known locations, and who established them?

Let's start with who establishes the known points. Primarily it is a federal agency known as the National Geodetic Survey (NGS) in the United States. The NGS established and maintained a national network of control points (small brass disks with identifiers and marks) placed on permanent structures such as concrete posts. There is a network for elevation above mean sea level and another network for horizontal location. If you have any 7.5 minute USGS topographic maps, look for vertical control points (called benchmarks) labeled with *BM* and an elevation beside the point marked with an *X*. The precise locations of these points were determined using advanced survey methods.

By the early 1990s, however, GPS became the dominant means to establishing the locations of control points, both in the vertical and horizontal directions. Today there is a very precise network, known as the National Spatial Reference System, of GPS-located control points maintained by the NGS (Vorhauer, 2005). In addition, cities often maintain their own control points; for example, Pittsburgh was the first U.S. city to use GPS to establish control points for its GIS map layers. Figure 8-1 is a photo of one of Pittsburgh's monument markers, located on Panther Hollow Bridge at the boundary of Carnegie Mellon University and the University of Pittsburgh.

FIGURE 8-1 City of Pittsburgh control point benchmark

GPS

The U.S. Department of Defense built the global positioning system (GPS), consisting of a network of up to 24 satellites in Earth orbit, in the 1970s and opened it up for civilian use in the 1980s, free of charge. To use it, one must have a GPS receiver, which today can be hand-held and is often built in to new cell phones.

The basic way that GPS works is triangulation. A GPS receiver has stored in it data and programs that determine the precise location of each satellite at each instant. So, if a GPS receiver detects a signal from a satellite, it can identify the satellite and determine its location relative to Earth. The satellite measures and transmits its distance, but not direction, from the GPS unit. Thus a single satellite limits the location of the GPS unit to the surface of a sphere centered on the satellite with the measured radius. With signals from two satellites, the location of the GPS unit is limited to the intersection of two spheres, which is a circle. With three satellites, it is one of two points of which one easily can be eliminated. With four satellites the precision of location improves.

Uncorrected GPS signals have an error that averages around 70 meters, but with a second fixed receiver, called a **base station** that has a known position, it is possible to get the accuracy to within 1 to 5 meters. This process is known as **differential correction**, and the base station is often at a control point with location determined by survey methods. Finally, there are advanced error correction methods using a base station and roving station that can get the error down to centimeters. To learn more about GPS, see Trimble (2006) or Halsall (2000).

It is easy to input GPS data into a GIS and process it further to edit features graphically and add attributes. Of course, GPS is most valuable when there are no base maps sufficient to guide drawing new features. A good example is a project one of our students did, using our GPS unit, for a Girl Scout camp in West Virginia. He walked all the trails of the camp and used GPS to record corresponding line features. He then processed the GPS coordinates using differential correction and software that came with our GPS unit. Next, he edited the lines, added attribute data, and created a map document using base maps and his new trails line shapefile. Finally, he produced a beautiful map layout, plotted it in color using our 3-foot wide plotter, and mounted it for display at the campground headquarters.

DIGITIZING

One way to digitize a hard copy map is to use a digitizing tablet or board. These devices have a fine grid of wires or other conductive materials (horizontal and vertical) embedded beneath their surfaces and a pointing device, called a puck, that has crosshairs and can sense the nearest intersection of two wires when placed on the tablet. The digitizer tablet can then transform the wire intersection location into coordinates of the tablet's coordinate system. The grids of wires are quite fine, leading to errors as small as plus or minus 0.002 inches.

The steps for digitizing are roughly as follows. Suppose that you have a paper cadastral map showing boundaries of deeded land parcels that you want to digitize. Step 1 is to tape the map to the digitizer. Step 2 is map registration, which requires digitizing at least four known points (control points) on the map. The known points have projected map coordinates (UTM or State Plane), and digitizing produces digitizer-tablet coordinates. Step 3 is to estimate two conversion equations, one for the vertical and the other for the horizontal coordinates, to convert from digitizer coordinates to projected map coordinates. Step 4 is to digitize vector features.

It is possible to digitize manually, clicking each vertex of a line or polygon, or to use **stream digitizing** in which the user moves the puck over the line feature and software collects and stores vertices at a fixed rate. Often the vector line or polygon features resulting from stream digitizing must be **generalized**, using software that deletes vertices to reduce file sizes, while retaining the basic shape of features.

RASTER-TO-VECTOR CONVERSION

Satellite images and aerial photographs provide rich raster maps with much detail. One of the tasks of local governments and other organizations is to convert such raster maps to vector layers for physical features such as pavement edges, building outlines, parking lots, and so on. It is possible to digitize features directly from hard copies of images, but that process is very time consuming and tedious. Today, organizations use automated raster-to-vector conversion programs with scanned, electronic images as the input instead. For example, such a program can draw the outline of a building with a single click of the mouse or follow a line and digitize until the line intersects another line. Then, a single click on the correct path on the other side of the intersection starts the process going on its own again.

Many software options for vectorization of raster images are available. ESRI's product is called ArcScan (Arcscan, 2006). Wikipedia has a good article comparing many such packages, several of which are free (Comparison of Raster-to-Vector Conversion Software, 2006).

HEADS-UP DIGITIZING IN ARCGIS

Let's have you begin digitizing using ArcMap to edit graphic features and ArcCatalog to create new shapefiles. Your task will be to use your mouse and screen cursor as drawing and editing tools over the top of base maps. You will edit existing points by moving them, create a new point, create new lines and edit them, and add more details to polygons.

Edit Point Features

To get started, you will start ArcMap and open the *Chapter8-1.mxd* map document. This document contains vector map layers for Pittsburgh's pools and an aerial photo for a portion of the city. You will edit the pool locations using the photo as a guide.

Examine Point Location Errors

We created the Pools map layer for Pittsburgh swimming pools by geocoding their street addresses. Consequently, you would not expect the resulting point features to plot directly on the visible pools in the photo. Your task in the following steps is to move mapped points to lie over the actual pools.

1. On your PC's desktop, click **Start**, click **All Programs**, click **ArcGIS**, and click **ArcMap**.

2. In the ArcMap window, click the **An existing map** option button and double-click **Browse for maps** in the panel below the option button.
3. In the Open window, browse to your **LearningAndUsingGIS** folder, and double-click **Chapter8-1.mxd**. See Figure 8-2.

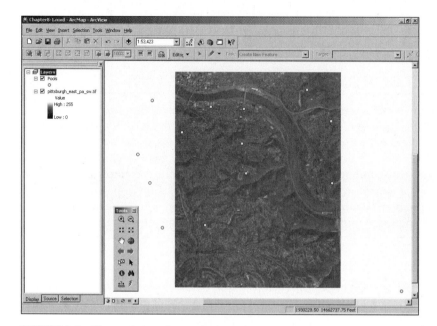

FIGURE 8-2   Chapter8-1.mxd map document

4. On the main menu, click **View**, click **Bookmarks**, and click **St. Clair**. See Figure 8-3. *(Note that the St. Clair Pool point feature, as suspected, is not over the actual pool.)*

St. Claire point feature

pool in aerial photo

FIGURE 8-3   St. Clair Pool point feature and actual pool in aerial photo

Move Point Features

Next you will edit pool point features and move them to the actual pools on the aerial photo.

1. On the main menu, click **Tools** and click **Editor Toolbar**.
2. Drag the **Editor** toolbar below the Standard toolbar and dock it there.
3. On the Editor toolbar, click **Editor**, click **Start Editing**, and then in the Starting to Edit window, verify that **C:\LearningAndUsingGIS\MapsPools** is selected, and click **Start Editing**.
4. On the Editor toolbar, click the **Edit** tool .
5. Click the **St. Clair Pool** point feature, drag the **point feature** to the pool in the aerial photo, and release.
6. Click **Editor**, click **Stop Editing**, and click **Yes** to save your edits. See Figure 8-4.

moved
point
feature

FIGURE 8-4 Moved St. Clair Pool point feature

Add a New Point Feature

Suppose that a wealthy person made a gift to the City of Pittsburgh. She provided funding to build a new swimming pool at McKinley Park in her childhood neighborhood. You'd like to add the new pool to your Pools map layer, directly digitizing the new point. This is a good skill to have as a supplement for geocoding. Sometimes you will know where a point should lie but simply won't be able to find a street address that geocodes. In such a case you can simply zoom in to the area of the point in ArcMap and click the map to create the point.

1. On the main menu, click **View**, click **Bookmarks**, and click **McKinley**. See Figure 8-5. *(We marked the approximate location for the new pool in Figure 8-5.)*
2. On the main menu, click **Tools** and click **Editor Toolbar**.
3. On the Editor toolbar, click **Editor**, click **Start Editing**, and then in the Starting to Edit window, verify that **C:\LearningAndUsingGIS\MapsPools** is selected, and click **Start Editing**.
4. On the Editor toolbar, click the **Task** list arrow, and click **Create New Feature**.

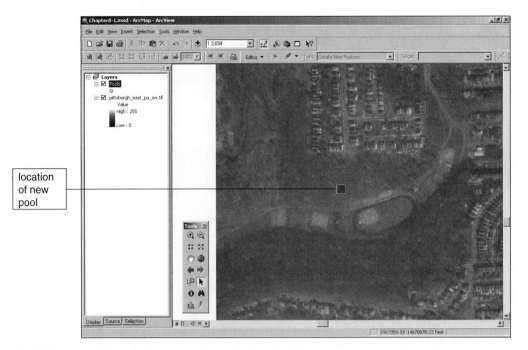

location of new pool

FIGURE 8-5 McKinley Park bookmark

(Pools will be the target for creating the new feature because it is the only vector feature in the map document. If there were two or more vector features, you'd have to select one.)

5.   Click the **Sketch** tool . *(The cursor turns into a cross hair.)*

6.   Click the map approximately at the point as indicated in Figure 8-5. *(That adds a new point to Pools. The point has the selection point marker because ArcMap automatically selects it after creating it.)*

7.   In the table of contents, right-click **Pools** and click **Open Attribute Table**.

8.   Enter values **McKinley**, **198 Amesbury St**, and **1**, as shown in Figure 8-6, and then close the Attributes of Pools window.

9.   On the Editor toolbar, click **Editor**, click **Stop Editing**, click **Yes** to save edits, and observe your new pool point feature.

10.   Save your map document and close ArcMap.

Attributes of Pools

FID	Shape*	NAME	MAXLOAD	ZIPCODE	ADDRESS	OPEN	PCTCAP	ATTEND
25	Point	Beechwood	596	15216	1249 Rockland St	0	0	0
26	Point	St Clair	230	15210	901 Cresswell St	0	0	0
27	Point	Moore	1282	15226	1801 Pioneer Ave	1	0.25	321
28	Point	Burgwin	522	15207	328 Mansion St	0	0	0
29	Point	Phillips	390	15210	203 Parkfield St	1	0.692	270
30	Point	Brookline	488	15226	1400 Oakridge St	0	0	0
31	Point	McBride	54	15207	1785 McBride Ave	1	1.574	85
33	Point	McKinley	0	0	198 Amesbury St	1	0	0

Record: 33 Show: All Selected Records (1 out of 33 Selected.) Options

FIGURE 8-6 Pools attribute table with new pool record

EDIT LINE FEATURES

In the following steps, you will create a new line feature and use it to digitize a portion of bus route 51G. You will use ArcCatalog to create a new shapefile, add it to ArcMap, and digitize its features.

Create a New Line Shapefile

1. On your PC's desktop, click **Start**, click **All Programs**, click **ArcGIS**, and click **ArcCatalog**.
2. In ArcCatalog's left-panel folder and file tree, click expander boxes for **C:** and **LearningAndUsingGIS**, and click the **FilesStudentWork** folder.
3. On the main menu, click **File**, click **New**, and click **Shapefile**.
4. In the Create New Shapefile window, type **BusRoute51G** as the new shapefile name, click the list arrow for **Feature Type**, and click **Polyline**.
5. Click **Edit**; in the Spatial Reference Properties window, click **Select**.
6. In the Browse for Coordinate System window, double-click **Projected Coordinate Systems**, double-click **State Plane**, double-click **NAD 1983 (feet)**, click **NAD 1983 StatePlane Pennsylvania South FIPS 3702 (Feet)**, click **Add**, click **Apply**, click **OK**, and click **OK** again. *(Now BusRoute51G is a line feature shapefile under the FilesStudentWork folder.)*
7. Close ArcCatalog.

Add the New Line Shapefile to ArcMap

Next you will add the bus route 51G shapefile to map document *Chapter8-2.mxd*.

1. On your PC's desktop, click **Start**, click **All Programs**, click **ArcGIS**, and click **ArcMap**.
2. In the ArcMap window, click the **An existing map** option button and double-click **Browse for maps** in the panel below the option button.
3. In the Open window, browse to your **LearningAndUsingGIS** folder, and double-click **Chapter8-2.mxd**. *(The* Chapter8-2.mxd *map document window opens in ArcMap showing the aerial photo of a section of Pittsburgh and the St. Claire pool. Figure 8-7 shows the map document with an addition for your*

instructions: It includes the end-product of digitizing work that you are about to do. You will digitize the yellow Bus Route 51G in segments identified by the red capital letters seen in the figure. This route serves the St. Clair swimming pool.) Note: Your map document does not have the red capital letters seen in Figure 8-7. We added them to help guide your upcoming digitizing steps.

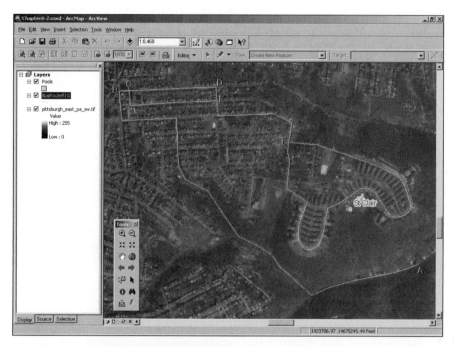

FIGURE 8-7 Chapter8-2.mxd map document

4. On the Standard toolbar, click the **Add Data** tool ⬦, browse to **C:\LearningAndUsingGIS\FilesStudentWork**, and double-click **BusRoute51G.shp**.

5. Symbolize **BusRoute 51G** to have a yellow line color. *(Of course, this is an empty shapefile now. You will add the first line to it in the next set of steps.)*

Digitize a Line Feature

You are now ready to initially digitize bus route 51G. You will first do this at a scale of the current view (spatial bookmark Bus Route 51G). Then, you will zoom in to more precisely edit the line feature to match the streets in the aerial photo. This is a good approach for digitizing: Rough in the line features, and then edit them zoomed in for precision.

1. On the Editor toolbar, click **Editor**, click **Start Editing**, and then in the Start Editing window, verify that **C:\LearningAndUsingGIS\FilesStudentWork** is selected, and click **OK**.

2. On the Editor toolbar, click the **Task** list arrow, click **Create New Feature**, and click the **Sketch** tool ✎. *(On the Editor toolbar, BusRoute51G is selected as the target for new features because it is the only vector shapefile in the map document.)*

3. Click points along the streets in the aerial photo to roughly digitize the line segment from points A to B in Figure 8-7, and double-click the **last point (B)** to end your line feature. See Figure 8-8. *(It is difficult to match Figure 8-7 perfectly, so just do as well as you can. If you make a major mistake, click your line with the Edit tool to select it, and press Delete. Then you can start over. Also, you can click the Undo button or the Edit tool, double-click your line, right-click a vertex, and click Delete to delete a vertex.)*

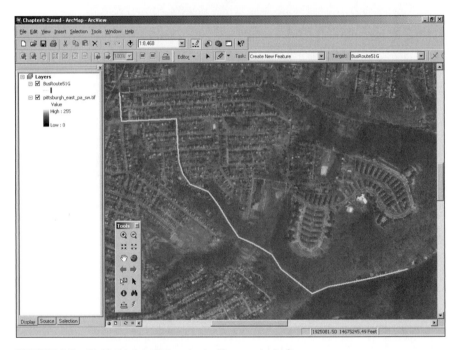

FIGURE 8-8 Digitized A-to-B segment of bus route 51G

PRACTICE 8-2

Digitize each remaining line segments (BDEF, CE, and FF). When you are finished, click Editor, click Stop Editing, and click Yes to save your edits.

Edit a Line Feature

After you digitize the initial bus route you can zoom in to the map to see more details and edit the initial lines. You will want to move vertices and add new vertices to get more precision in your digitized bus route.

1. On the main menu, click **View**, click **Bookmarks**, and click **St. Clair Village**.
2. On the Editor toolbar, click **Editor**, click **Start Editing**, and then in the Start Editing window, verify that **C:\LearningAndUsingGIS\FilesStudentWork** is selected, and click **Start Editing**.
3. On the Editor toolbar, click the **Edit tool** .
4. Double-click the **BusRoute51G** polyline feature so its vertex points appear.
5. Right-click a line feature of BusRoute51G where you want to insert a new vertex point, and click **Insert Vertex**.
6. Move the **vertex** to the center of the street in the aerial photo.

PRACTICE 8-3

Continue to add and/or move vertices of BusRoute51G for the St. Claire Village bookmark until you feel comfortable with this process. The end result does not need to be perfect. You can always use the Undo button to correct errors. See Figure 8-9. When you are finished, click Editor, click Stop Editing, and click Yes to save your edits. Save your map document.

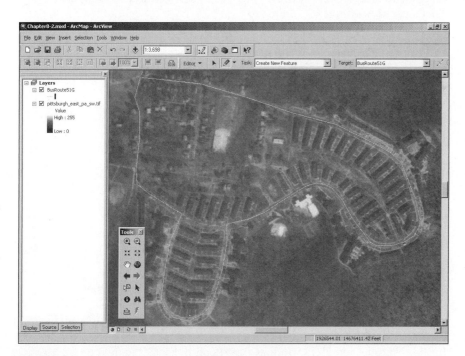

FIGURE 8-9   Edited bus route 51G in St. Claire Village

Add Attribute Data to the Line Shapefile

Suppose that your goal is to digitize all bus routes, and that after all routes are digitized as separate shapefiles, you plan to append them into a single shapefile. It is important to have an attribute that identifies each bus route to be used for labeling and other purposes. Now that you have successfully digitized Bus Route 51G, you can add data to its attribute table. The initial attribute table for the shapefile, created automatically during digitizing, contains three attributes: an internal sequence number for records, the Shape type (polyline), and an ID, which has value 0 for all records. You will create a new attribute, called Route, and enter values for it.

1. In the table of contents, right-click the **BusRoute51G** map layer, and click **Open Attribute Table**.
2. In the Attributes of BusRoute51G table, click the **Options** button, and click **Add Field**.
3. In the resulting Add Field window, type **ROUTE** as the field name, click **Text** as the field type, click **15** as the length, and click **OK**.
4. On the Editor toolbar, click **Editor**, click **Start Editing**, and then in the Start Editing window, verify that **C:\LearningAndUsingGIS\FilesStudentWork** is selected, and click **Start Editing**.
5. In the Attributes of BusRoute51G table, double-click the record for the first bus route segment in the cell **Route**, and type **51G** as the bus route.
6. Enter **51G** for the remaining records that make up the bus route. See Figure 8-10.
7. Click **Editor**, click **Stop Editing**, click **Yes** to save your edits, and close the Attributes of BusRoute51G window.

FID	Shape*	Id	Route
0	Polyline	0	51G
1	Polyline	0	51G
3	Polyline	0	51G
2	Polyline	0	51G

FIGURE 8-10   Bus route data in attribute table

Calculate Line Lengths

Some applications of GIS need to use lengths of features, such as when determining the length of a bus ride to a pool. You can get ArcMap to calculate and store lengths of line features, but it takes a VBA script to accomplish this.

1. In the table of contents, right-click **BusRoute51G**, and click **Open Attribute Table**.
2. In the Attributes of BusRoutes51G table, click the **Options** button, and click **Add Field**.
3. In the resulting Add Field window, type **Length_FT** as the field name, click **Double** as the field type, and click **OK**.

4. In the Attributes of BusRoutes51G table, right-click **Length_FT**, click **Calculate Values**, and click **Yes**.

5. In the resulting Field Calculator window, click the **Advanced** check box to select it.

6. In the Pre-Logic VBA Script Code panel, type the following *(or copy and paste the code from ArcGIS Desktop Help, Length, Calculating for Lines, Updating length for a shapefile)*:

```
Dim dblLength as double
Dim pCurve as ICurve
Set pCurve = [shape]
dblLength = pCurve.Length
```

7. In the Length_FT= field, type the following:

```
dblLength
```

See Figure 8-11.

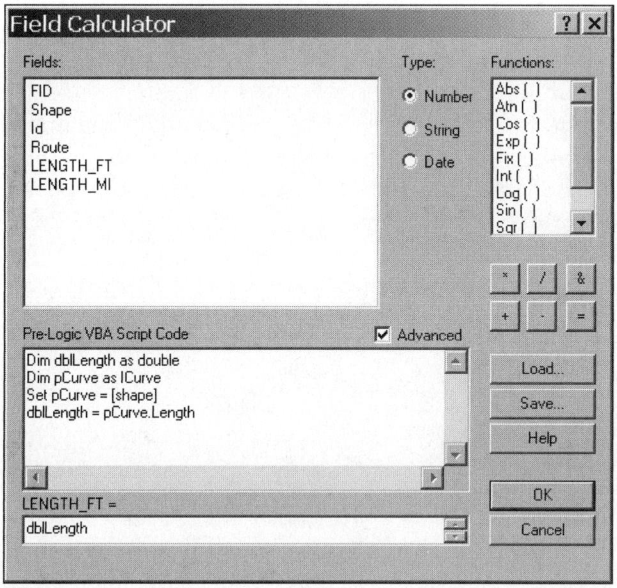

FIGURE 8-11 VBA script for length calculation

8. Click **OK** and close the **Attributes of BusRoute51G table**. *(The resulting length is in feet.)*

9. Save your **map document**, and close ArcMap.

EDIT POLYGON FEATURES

Polygon features are somewhat more complicated to edit than point or line features. They have three or more lines connected to form a closed area, so there are more elements to edit.

Examine Polygon Feature Location Precision

First, you will check the accuracy of the TIGER Rivers polygon layer of *Chapter8-3.mxd*. You will see that the Rivers layer is crude compared to the aerial photograph in the same map document. The Census Bureau created the Rivers map layer for small-scale thematic maps (zoomed far out), but your map document is zoomed far in. Next, you will edit the Rivers polygon feature to improve it for the current large-scale map document by adding more vertices and moving them so that it better matches the actual river shore in the aerial photo.

1. On your PC's desktop, click **Start**, click **All Programs**, click **ArcGIS**, and click **ArcMap**.
2. In the ArcMap window, click the **An existing map** option button and double-click **Browse for maps** in the panel below the option button.
3. In the Open window, browse to your **LearningAndUsingGIS** folder, and double-click **Chapter8-3.mxd**. See Figure 8-12. *(Notice the large discrepancies between the highly generalized Rivers polygon and river shore in the aerial photo.)*

digitized Rivers polygon

river shore

FIGURE 8-12 Rivers polygon compared to actual river shore

4. In the table of contents, right-click **Rivers**, click **Properties**, and click the **Display** tab. *(Note that we have set the transparency of the Rivers layer to 40 percent, which makes the aerial photo partially visible from below the Rivers map layer. This makes it easier for you to use the photo as a guideline in editing Rivers.)*
5. Close the **Layer Properties** window.

Move Polygon Features

When editing a polygon feature, you can either move the entire feature or edit individual vertices (points) to adjust just part of the polygon. You will begin by moving an entire polygon feature, but will not keep the edits.

1. On the Editor toolbar, click **Editor** and click **Start Editing**.
2. In the resulting Starting To Edit window, verify that **C:\LearningAndUsingGIS\MapPools** is the folder entered in which you want to edit, and click **Start Editing**.
3. On the Editor toolbar, click the **Edit** tool ▶.
4. Click and drag the **Rivers** polygon feature to any new location and release. *(This step is just for practice. You will not save edits, so Rivers will return to its original location.)*
5. Click anywhere outside the Rivers polygon feature.
6. On the Editor toolbar, click **Editor**, click **Stop Editing**, and click **No** to discard your edits. *(Rivers moves back to its original location.)*

Edit Polygon Vertices

Often, when editing polygon features, you need to move, add, or delete individual vertices. You will begin editing the Rivers shapefile by moving vertex points to better match the shore of the rivers to the aerial photo.

1. On the Editor toolbar, click **Editor** and click **Start Editing**.
2. In the resulting Start Editing window, verify that **C:\LearningAndUsingGIS\MapPools** is the folder entered in which you want to edit, and click **Start Editing**.
3. On the Editor toolbar, click the **Edit** tool ▶.
4. Double-click anywhere inside the **Rivers** polygon. See Figure 8-13. *(This action makes the polygon's vertices visible with square point markers.)*

vertex to
move

FIGURE 8-13   Rivers polygon vertices

5. Click the vertex noted in Figure 8-13 *(the vertex point marker changes to two thick, short orange lines to indicate that it is selected)*, drag the selected vertex down to the **river's shore** on the photo, release, and click anywhere outside the Rivers polygon feature to register your moved vertex. See Figure 8-14.

6. Double-click inside the **Rivers** polygon, click **another vertex**, and move it to the corresponding **river shore** in the photo. *(If you make an error, click the Undo button* ↰ *on the Standard toolbar.)*

PRACTICE 8-4

Move more vertices in the Rivers spatial bookmark area to the shore in the photo. Your moves do not have to be perfect. Also, if moves create new problems, such as lines of the polygon crossing the shore line, do not be concerned. In the next set of steps, you will create new vertices to correct such problems. When you are finished, on the Editor toolbar, click Editor, click Stop Editing, and click Yes to save your edits. See Figure 8-15.

moved
vertex

FIGURE 8-14 Result of moving a vertex

location
for new
vertex

FIGURE 8-15 Edited polygon feature

Digitizing Map Features

Create New Vertices

Additional vertex points are often needed to better edit polygons. The more vertex points, the smoother the polygons appear.

1. On the Editor toolbar, click **Editor** and click **Start Editing**.
2. In the resulting Start Editing window, verify that **C:\LearningAndUsingGIS\MapPools** is the folder entered in which you want to edit, and click **Start Editing**.
3. On the Editor toolbar, click the **Edit tool** .
4. Double-click inside the **Rivers** polygon feature to make vertex point markers appear.
5. Right-click the edge of the Rivers polygon at the location noted in Figure 8-14 for a new vertex, and in the resulting context menu, click **Insert Vertex**.
6. Double-click anywhere inside the Rivers polygon.
7. Click your new vertex , drag it to the **river's shore** on the photo and release, and click anywhere outside the Rivers polygon feature to register your moved vertex. See Figure 8-16.

FIGURE 8-16 New vertex moved

8. Click **Editor**, click **Stop Editing**, and click **Yes** to save your edits.

In the Rivers bookmark area, create a few additional new vertices and move them to improve the digitized polygon. When you are finished, click Editor, click Stop Editing, and click Yes to save your edits. See Figure 8-17.

FIGURE 8-17 Rivers polygon with new vertices moved to position

Cut Polygons

The Rivers polygon feature is made up of four polygons, one for each river in Allegheny County: the Allegheny, Ohio, Monongahela, and Youghiogheny Rivers. These polygons cross over bridges and other man-made features. For some purposes, it would be useful to break the four polygons down into smaller polygons that cover only the river areas between bridges. In the following steps, you will "cut" polygons that cross bridges on a portion of the Monongahela River.

1. On the main menu, click **View**, click **Bookmarks**, and click **River**.
2. On the Editor toolbar, click **Editor** and click **Start Editing**.
3. On the Editor toolbar, click the **Task** list arrow, and click the **Cut Polygon Features** item under Modify Tasks. (*You will create two break points, using the Editor's Sketch tool.*)
4. Click inside the **Rivers** polygon. (*This action selects the polygon, turning its outline the selection color.*)

5. On the Editor toolbar, click the **Sketch** tool ![Sketch tool icon].
6. Click outside the northern edge of the **Rivers** polygon to the right of the bridge shown in Figure 8-18. *(This creates the first cut point.)*
7. Double-click the opposite side of the **Rivers** polygon to the right of the bridge, as shown in Figure 8-18. See Figure 8-19.
8. Click outside the **Rivers** polygon, and on the Editor toolbar, click the **Edit** tool ![Edit tool icon].
9. Double-click one of the **newly cut polygons**, move vertex points so that the cut line is on the center of the bridge, and then do the same for the other polygon. See Figure 8-20. *(Try zooming in to the bridge to get more precision, and use the River spatial bookmark to zoom back out.)*

PRACTICE 8-6

Continue breaking polygons on opposite sides of the bridges and move vertex points in the Rivers bookmarked view so there is a break between the river polygons and bridges. Remember that you have to click in a polygon with the Edit tool to be able to cut it. When you are finished, on the Editor toolbar, click Editor, click Stop Editing, and click Yes to save your edits. Then save your map document, and close ArcMap.

first polygon cut point

second polygon cut point

FIGURE 8-18 First click for breaking polygons

FIGURE 8-19 Cut polygons

cut
polygons

FIGURE 8-20 Polygons cut and moved

cut and
moved
polygons

Chapter 8 Summary

ArcMap not only allows you to create and edit map attribute data, but you can also do the same for vector features including points, lines, and polygons. The reference system for creating vector features consists of control points with known locations, determined with surveying methods or GPS. In the United States, this system is known as the National Spatial Reference System, which is maintained by the National Geodetic Survey. The control points are on permanent structures, such as brass markers on concrete posts, with separate control points for horizontal and vertical positions.

GPS is becoming the predominant method of determining the location of control points. Even with a handheld GPS unit, it is possible to determine locations with an accuracy of a few meters. The U.S. Department of Defense built and maintains the constellation of 24 satellites that constitutes the global positioning system.

The process of creating vector features from a manuscript, such as a hard copy map, is called digitizing. Digitizing a paper map requires that you have a digitizing tablet or table—a special device with a flat surface and fine grid of wires embedded in it that can detect the location of a pointing device called the puck.

If the manuscript is a scanned map in electronic form, you can use specialized software to automate digitizing that is capable of drawing lines largely on its own. This is one form of heads-up digitizing. Another form of heads-up digitizing uses a raster map from an aerial photograph as a background to guide digitizing physical features that can be seen in the photograph. A common use for this capacity is for correcting location and shape of vector features for physical map layers, such as street centerlines or shores of bodies of water.

Key Terms

Base station A fixed GPS receiver that has known coordinates and records GPS signals that it receives on its location over time.

Differential correction The use of a base station to determine error correction of GPS signals by comparing the GPS-determined location with the actual location. The resulting correction can be used in an area up to a hundred miles from the base station or more, but the further from the base station the higher the error.

Digitizing tablet A drawing board with an embedded grid of wires and a pointing device for inputting vertices of vector features into a digital format from a hard copy manuscript.

Generalization A software function for line and polygon map features that reduces the number of vertices while retaining the shape of the feature. One application is to reduce the file size of stream-digitized features.

National Geodetic Survey (NGS) The federal agency responsible for establishing and maintaining the National Spatial Reference System.

National Spatial Reference System (NRSR) Networks of control points with known altitude above mean sea level and known horizontal coordinates. Surveyors measure angles and distances from control points to determine map coordinates for various vector features. GISs use the control points to reference digitized features to geographic coordinate systems.

Raster-to-vector conversion software A software package with many functions available for heads-up digitizing of scanned maps. One set of functions automates drawing of line and polygon features using software that automatically follows lines and saves vertices.

Stream digitizing   Software for automating digitizer tablet digitizing of line or polygon features. As the user moves the digitizer puck over line features, the software collects and inputs vertices from the puck's path.

Transit   A telescope mounted on a tripod used by surveyors to measure vertical and horizontal angles.

Short-Answer Questions

1. TIGER street centerlines are not accurate in their position and also do not have much detail in terms of shape. If you needed a more accurate street map for a neighborhood, how could you fix a TIGER map?

2. What are the differences between digitizing and heads-up digitizing?

3. Name some map layer types that can and cannot be digitized from an aerial photo map.

4. Why do you suppose that the vertical and horizontal networks of control points are different?

5. Suppose that you are a police officer in a rural jurisdiction and that crimes you investigate often occur off the road network. How could you get all crimes into a point map layer?

6. Suppose that you are digitizing a 7.5 minute, 1:24,000 USGS topographic map. If your digitizer has an expected error of plus or minus 0.002 inches, what is the corresponding error for geographic coordinates in feet?

7. If you remove a paper map manuscript from a digitizer tablet, but later decide that you need to add more features to a layer that you digitized, is it possible to relocate the manuscript so that you can continue digitizing? Explain.

8. If you were designing a software program to generalize line features, what might some strategies be for preserving shape?

9. Suppose that you have street address data for a set of your organization's facilities and you need to map 100 percent of them. If geocoding fails to achieve a 100-percent match rate, how could you go about adding the nonmatched addresses to your point shapefile?

10. Suppose that you have a polygon map layer but need a new map layer with a set of smaller coterminous polygons (that is, that partition and share boundaries with the original polygons). How could you go about this task?

Exercises

1. **Digitize Bus Stops.** In this exercise, you will create a new point shapefile and digitize a sample of bus stops for routes 51C and 51G.

    a. Open C:\LearningAndUsingGIS\Chapter8-2.mxd in ArcMap, and save it as **C:\LearningAndUsingGIS\FilesStudentWork\Exercise8-1<YourName>.mxd**, where you substitute your name or other identifier for <YourName>.

    b. Create a new folder, **C:\LearningAndUsingGIS\FilesStudentWork\Exercise8-1**.

    c. Create a new point shapefile called **C:\LearningAndUsingGIS\FilesStudentWork\ Exercise8-1\BusStops.shp**. In the Create New Shapefile window, click Edit, and in the Spatial Reference Properties window, click Select. In the Browse for Coordinate System window, double-click Projected Coordinate Systems, double-click State Plane, double-click NAD 1983 (feet), click NAD 1983 StatePlane Pennsylvania South FIPS 3702 (Feet), click Add, click Apply, click OK, and click OK again.

d. Digitize the sample of bus stops, as shown in Figure 8-21. Zoom so that you have the map extent, roughly, of the figure. Your map document does not have the 51C route nor all of 51G, so locate stops as best you can by studying features of the aerial photo.

FIGURE 8-21   Bus stops on routes 51C and 51G

e. In the attributes table of BusStops, number the ID column, add a field for the route number, and calculate the values *51C* and *51G* for appropriate rows. There are three stops for 51C along the central east-west route and two stops on the far north east-west route. The rest of the stops are for 51G. (*Hint:* After selecting bus stops for one route, click Options and click Switch Selection in the attribute table of BusStops to get the selection for the remaining route.)

f. Create a layout with title and legend. Export the layout as **C:\LearningAndUsingGIS\ FilesStudentWork\Exercise8-1\Exercise8-1.jpg**.

g. Create a Microsoft Word document, **C:\LearningAndUsingGIS\FilesStudentWork\ Exercise8-1\.Exercise8-1.doc**. Include a title and insert *Exercise8-1.jpg* into the document. Open C:\LearningAndUsingGIS\FilesStudentWork\Exercise8-1\BusStops.dbf in Microsoft Excel, select the cells of the table, click Copy, and paste it into your Word document.

2. **Digitize a New Bus Route.** In this exercise, you will digitize route 51C.

    a. Open C:\LearningAndUsingGIS\Chapter8-2.mxd in ArcMap, and save it as **C:\LearningAndUsingGIS\FilesStudentWork\Exercise8-2<YourName>.mxd**, where you substitute your name or other identifier for <YourName>. Remove bus route 51G from the table of contents.

    b. Create a new folder, **C:\LearningAndUsingGIS\FilesStudentWork\Exercise8-2**.

    c. Create a new polyline shapefile called **BusRoute51C.shp** in C:\LearningAndUsingGIS\ FilesStudentWork\Exercise8-2\. In the Create New Shapefile window, click Edit, and in the Spatial Reference Properties window, click Select. In the Browse for Coordinate System window, double-click Projected Coordinate Systems, double-click State Plane, double-click NAD 1983 (feet), click NAD 1983 StatePlane Pennsylvania South FIPS 3702 (Feet), click Add, click Apply, click OK, and click OK again.

    d. Digitize route 51C in *BusRoute51C.shp*. Use Figure 8-22 as a guide. Zoom out in your map document until you can see the area in Figure 8-22, and then zoom in to it. Digitize it roughly at first, and then zoom in to edit the route to digitize it more accurately. Just attempt to get your bus route to follow street centerlines, even if it does not match Figure 8-22 precisely.

FIGURE 8-22   Bus route 51C

    e. Add an attribute called Route to the attribute table of BusRoute51C with the text data field type and 15 length. Also add Length_ft with the double data field type in the attribute table, and calculate its line length in feet. (*Hint:* Use ArcMap's Help to copy and paste the script for calculating length.)

f. Save the edits to *BusRoute51C.shp*, and your map document.

g. Create a layout with title and legend. Export the layout as **C:\LearningAndUsingGIS\FilesStudentWork\Exercise8-2\Exercise8-2.jpg**.

h. Create a Word document, **C:\LearningAndUsingGIS\FilesStudentWork\Exercise8-2\.Exercise8-2.doc**. Include a title and insert *Exercise8-2.jpg* into the document. Open C:\LearningAndUsingGIS\FilesStudentWork\Exercise8-2\BusRoute51C.dbf in Excel, select the cells of the table, click Copy, and paste it into your Word document.

3. **Digitize Routes from Pools to EMS Sites**. A useful layer is routes from pools to the EMS sites. With it we can provide another performance measure for assessing pools: the distance to the nearest EMS site for a pool.

a. Create a new folder, **C:\LearningAndUsingGIS\FilesStudentWork\Exercise8-3**.

b. Create a new shapefile called **C:\LearningAndUsingGIS\FilesStudentWork\Exercise8-3<YourName>.mxd**, where you substitute your name or other identifier for <YourName>.

c. Change the coordinate system of the data frame in the project to the State Plane, 1984 NAD (Feet), Pennsylvania South projection. Add and symbolize the shapefiles C:\LearningAndUsingGIS\FilesStudentWork\EMSSites.shp, C:\LearningAndUsingGIS\MapsPools\pools.shp, C:\LearningAndUsingGIS\MapsPools\rivers.shp, and C:\LearningAndUsingGIS\MapsAlleghenyCounty\tgr42003lkA.shp.

d. Create a new polyline shapefile called **C:\LearningAndUsingGIS\FilesStudentWork\Exercise8-3\EMSRoutes.shp**. In the Create New Shapefile window, click Edit, and in the Spatial Reference Properties window click Select. In the Browse for Coordinate System window, double-click Projected Coordinate Systems, double-click State Plane, double-click NAD 1983 (feet), click NAD 1983 StatePlane Pennsylvania South FIPS 3702 (Feet), click Add, click Apply, click OK, and click OK again.

e. Zoom in to the area that has the pools north of the major rivers in Pittsburgh, Jack Stack, Riverview, and so forth. Using your judgment, along with the assumptions that there are no one-way streets and all turns are possible, assign each pool to the nearest medic site, either Medic 4, Medic 10, or Medic 14. Then digitize emergency EMS routes for each pool to its nearest medic site. (*Hint 1*: Zoom in for each route. *Hint 2*: Save edits for each route after creating it. Then you can quit editing and not save a route in progress that you do not like. *Hint 3*: For some of the shorter routes, try using the Snap tool. With your Sketch tool on, press the T key at any time to show the tolerance area for snapping to an existing feature. Click the starting point of a route, move your cursor to the nearest vertex on the street network, right-click the vertex within the tolerance area, click Snap to Feature, and click Edge. Alternatively, you can press shortcut keys Shift+F10, N, and E. Keep this process up as long as you want.)

f. Create an attribute called Name in *EMSRoutes.dbf*, and give each route the name of its pool. Calculate the length of each route in feet, and save it in an attribute called Length_ft.

g. Create a layout with title and legend. Export the layout as **C:\LearningAndUsingGIS\FilesStudentWork\Exercise8-3\Exercise8-3.jpg**.

h. Create a Word document **C:\LearningAndUsingGIS\FilesStudentWork\Exercise8-3\. Exercise8-3.doc**. Include a title and insert *Exercise8-3.jpg* into the document. Open C:\LearningAndUsingGIS\FilesStudentWork\Exercise8-3\EMSRoutes.dbf in Excel, select the cells of the table, click Copy, and paste it into your Word document.

4. **Digitize Parks.** Pools are not the only public places for physical activities in Pittsburgh. City parks are also an excellent resource for active living. In this exercise, you will digitize parks in the South Side neighborhoods of Pittsburgh using an aerial photo as a guide.

    a. Create a new folder, **C:\LearningAndUsingGIS\FilesStudentWork\Exercise8-4\.**

    b. Open C:\LearningAndUsingGIS\Chapter8-3.mxd in ArcMap, and save it as **C:\LearningAndUsingGIS\FilesStudentWork\Exercise8-4<YourName>.mxd**, where you substitute your name or other identifier for <YourName>. Remove Rivers from the table of contents.

    c. Add and symbolize *neighborhoods.shp* and *pools.shp* from C:\LearningAndUsingGIS\ MapsPools\ to your map document.

    d. Create a new polygon shapefile called **C:\LearningAndUsingGIS\FilesStudentWork\ Exercise8-4\Parks.shp**. In the Create New Shapefile window, click Edit, and in the Spatial Reference Properties window, click Select. In the Browse for Coordinate System window, double-click Projected Coordinate Systems, double-click State Plane, double-click NAD 1983 (feet), click NAD 1983 StatePlane Pennsylvania South FIPS 3702 (Feet), click Add, click Apply, click OK, and click OK again.

    e. Digitize the parks shown in Figure 8-23. Leave out some details, such as interior lines, and just digitize simple polygons. (*Hint*: Zoom in to each park area and save edits after digitizing each park.)

    f. In the attribute table of Parks, create a new text data type field called Name for the park name. Enter the name of each park. Also, add a double data type attribute, Area, and calculate the area for each park in square feet.

    g. Create a layout with title and legend. Export the layout as **C:\LearningAndUsingGIS\ FilesStudentWork\Exercise8-4\Exercise8-4.jpg**.

    h. Create a Word document, **C:\LearningAndUsingGIS\FilesStudentWork\Exercise8-4\. Exercise8-4.doc**. Include a title and insert *Exercise8-4.jpg* into the document. Open C:\LearningAndUsingGIS\FilesStudentWork\Exercise8-4\Pakrs.dbf in Excel, select the cells of the table, click Copy, and paste it into your Word document.

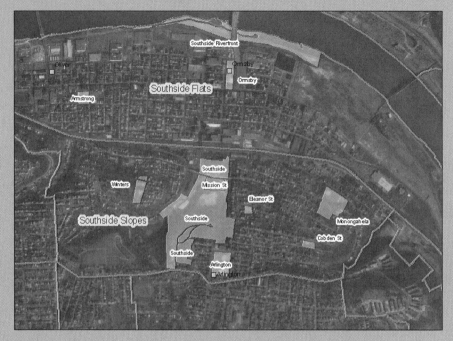

FIGURE 8-23   Southside parks

References

ArcScan flier, ESRI, Internet URL: http://www.esri.com/library/fliers/pdfs/arcscan-for-arcgis.pdf (accessed June 1, 2006)

Comparison of Raster-to-Vector Conversion Software, Wikipedia, the free encyclopedia, Internet URL: http://en.wikipedia.org/wiki/Comparison_of_raster_to_vector_conversion_software (accessed June 1, 2006)

Halsall, C. "Where Are You Exactly? A GPS Introduction," O'Reilly Wireless DevCenter. Internet URL: http://www.oreillynet.com/pub/a/wireless/2000/12/08/gps_intro.html (accessed June 1, 2006)

Trimble GPS Tutorial, Internet URL: http://www.oreillynet.com/pub/a/wireless/2000/12/08/gps_intro.html (accessed June 1, 2006)

Vorhauer, M. "National Spatial Reference System Readjustment Starting June 2005," GIS/LIS News, Internet URL: http://www.mngislis.org/newsletter/issue39/National%20Spatial%20Reference%20System%20Readjustment%20Starting%20June%202005.htm (accessed June 1, 2006)

CHAPTER **9**

WORKING ON GIS PROJECTS

LEARNING OBJECTIVES

In this chapter, you will:

- Learn project management methods for GIS
- Learn how to structure GIS projects
- Study two solved projects
- Use this chapter's solved projects as templates for your own projects

Now you are getting the idea!

INTRODUCTION

You have studied GIS facts, concepts, and principles; worked through tutorial steps; and completed

practice and end-of-chapter exercises. Your introduction to GIS is almost complete! The final step is to do

a GIS project independently or as a member of a small team. You will execute the phases of building an

analytical GIS, from initially defining the problem to finding, downloading, and processing map layers and

data; building map compositions and layouts; and reporting results.

To prepare you for independent project work, we begin by surveying the basics of project management in the context of GIS. You will learn about project life cycles and project components. After you've learned basic project structure and management, we will review two completed projects, which are written in first person, as if presented by a student in the style of a GIS professional for a target audience. The first project assesses the need for and utilization of public transportation in Phoenix, Arizona. The second project maps major air pollution point sources of toxic emissions in Minneapolis, Minnesota, and then makes a preliminary assessment of their potential impact on black and white populations. We give solutions and implications for further study for both projects.

The Exercises section presents four projects, or extended exercises. In Exercises 1 and 2, you carry out the public transportation and environmental pollution projects for counties or cities of your choice. You use the Phoenix and Minneapolis projects as templates for carrying out your projects. The third exercise challenges you to complete the Swimming Pool Case Study, given new data on actual pool visits by pool tag holders to two pools. Exercise 4 is an open-ended, independent project. You or your instructor identify a new project that needs a GIS solution.

PROJECT MANAGEMENT

Real-world projects are challenging! You must define the problem, decide which factors to ignore and which are important, deal with uncertainties (including whether the project outcome will be valuable), and so on. Fortunately, the field of project management brings structure to GIS project work. Entire textbooks and courses are devoted to studying project management, but the few concepts we introduce here will give you a good start on managing GIS projects. We define these concepts in terms of components of GIS projects.

Project Life Cycle

Projects have phases that can be organized in a **systems development life cycle**. The most widely used model is called the **waterfall model** because it assumes that a project flows from one phase to the next, like water going over a series of waterfalls. Ideally—like water, which does not reverse direction and flow upstream—project phases move forward sequentially. After a phase is completed, it is not revisited. However, in reality most projects cycle back to earlier phases, repeating parts of the earlier phases, with steps being reexamined and modified as one learns or as conditions change. Nevertheless, the waterfall model is useful.

The major phases of any project are as follows (Kendall and Kendall, 1995). Each project phase is described in terms of what you must do.

- *Problem identification phase*: State the problem, opportunity, issue, or objective; provide an approach for a solution; and define the **scope** of the project—that is, what it will and will not attempt to solve. It is important to restrict a project to only a few issues, and to state them clearly. Include background on the problem area and a few references for general information. Generally, it is also a good idea to provide a rationale for why the parts studied are important. The **deliverable**, or product of this phase, is a memorandum or short report that is a project proposal. A client (or your instructor) must comment on and approve the proposal, and you should expect some helpful suggestions.
- *Analysis phase*: Determine the specifics of a solution, collect data, and represent the solution on paper. You should identify data sources and collect the data, determine specific attributes (variables) that represent underlying performance or behavioral measures, and provide a verbal or schematic representation of the finished system that can be discussed and easily modified before proceeding to building the solution. Early in this phase, if the project is a team effort, you should produce a **work-breakdown structure**, which is simply a list of tasks, who will do them, and their due dates.
- *Design phase*: Process data and build the system or models that provide a solution. Both problem identification and analysis focus on thought processes and the feasibility of carrying out the project. Most of the computer and other hands-on work occurs in the design phase. The deliverable for this phase is a working system, ready for use.
- *Implementation phase*: Provide access to the solution as a computer system or reports. If others need to use the computer system, documentation is another deliverable.

GIS Project Components

Because we present simple projects for an introductory GIS experience, we use an abbreviated systems development life cycle in this chapter. We have combined and streamlined project phases into three components:

- *Project proposal*: This phase of the project's deliverable combines the phases for problem identification and analysis. The proposal states the problem or issue, limits the scope of the project to a geographic area and specific purposes, lists map layers and data to be downloaded or otherwise obtained, provides a computer folder and file structure for all project components, and if a team is involved, it provides a work-breakdown structure. The project proposal is a Microsoft Word document that can be evaluated and commented upon by a client or an instructor. Some of the text and other material of the proposal can be reused in the project's report.

- *Process log*: The deliverable for this project phase lists each major step you've taken to build the analytical GIS. We have a well-developed and structured approach for building a GIS, so you already know how to design and build much of the solution. Thus, you can just list major steps. Also, if you have an instructor, she might want you to elaborate in more detail. A detailed log is useful if you have to revise parts of the project, so you do not have to reinvent steps. Include the process log as an appendix in your report. A process log is especially valuable for student projects so instructors can assess and diagnose student work and provide feedback. Otherwise, many of the processing steps could remain hidden, and students would not get credit for their hard work. For GIS professionals, a process log is also valuable, but it might be maintained only as an internal team document and used as the basis for writing a report section on computer processing steps.

- *Report*: A report and the folders and files of your GIS are the major deliverables of the project. Map layouts, such as the ones built in Chapter 4, are key parts of the report, which can be a Word document, Microsoft PowerPoint presentation, or both. The report structure follows the lines of the systems development life cycle: problem identification, analysis, solution, and results. Also, include a paragraph on future work with notes on implications for additional study. There is always more that can be done on a project, and it is important to summarize your ideas about additional work that might be done if time and resources are available.

Next, let's look at two projects and their solutions. You should also review the Project1 and Project2 subfolders in the LearningAndUsingGIS folder. In addition to the input data files, finished map layers, and documents, you will also find ArcGIS document files that you can open and study on your computer.

PROJECT 1: PUBLIC TRANSPORTATION: SUPPLY AND DEMAND IMBALANCES

The material we present on this project is in the form of project deliverables—proposal, process log, and report—as if written by a student or GIS professional. The deliverables are "bare bones": We have not elaborated on points, and we kept text to a minimum. Our comments to you, which are not included in deliverables, are in square brackets.

Proposal

[You might find that preparing the proposal is the most difficult part of a GIS project. Finding a problem and structuring it into a feasible project is a challenge. The following components exemplify a good GIS project proposal.]

Background

An efficient and well-designed public transit system is a vital component of a thriving and growing community. Although it is not the only force that influences neighborhood life, public transit is a significant force because it can add social, economic, and environmental value to a community.

Public transit yields numerous benefits, three of which are (1) affordable mobility, (2) congestion management, and (3) economic growth. The Federal Transit Administration states that the fundamental reason for offering public transit is to provide low-cost mobility to those who cannot own or operate an automobile, such as the young, the aged, and the infirm (see *www.fta.dot.gov*). Public transportation provides a means for accessing employment, schools, medical services, shopping, entertainment, recreation, and other social opportunities. As such, effective public transportation helps promote equal opportunity across all income levels. See the Public Transportation Partnership for Tomorrow Web site at *www.publictransportation.org* for reports on the many benefits of public transportation.

The Problem and an Approach to a Solution

The problem to be addressed concerns public transportation in low-income areas of Phoenix, Arizona. I propose to compare maps displaying use of public transportation for traveling to work compared to the percent of female-headed households with children, all by 2000 census tracts. Gaps in transportation coverage, if they exist, should be evident as areas having high percentages of female-headed households with children but relatively low public transportation use.

Scope

Statistically, the census description "female-headed households with children" designates one of the poorest segments of the total population. Of course, not every such household is poor, but a great many are. Federal policies are forcing the employable-but-unemployed segments of this population off of welfare and into employment. Often, jobs are available but not in the distressed, low-rent areas in which many female-headed households with children are located. Public transportation is an important link, literally, between such households and jobs.

Data and Map Layer Sources

I need relatively few map layers: Minor Civil Divisions, Census Tracts, and Streets. They are for Maricopa County, Arizona, which includes the city of Phoenix.

I will download these map layers from the ESRI Tiger/Line 2000 Web site, *www.esri. com/data/download/census2000_tigerline/index.html*. This Web site also has tables of selected 2000 Census SF1 variables, including the number of Female-Headed Households with Children and the Total Number of Households.

Additional data will come from the 2000 Census; namely, the Summary File 3 (SF3) data found in table P30, Means of Transportation to Work for Workers 16+ Years. This data is available from *http://factfinder.census.gov/*. The main variables of interest are the total number of workers age 16 or older and the subset of them who take public transportation to work.

Note that there are additional SF3 tables that could be used to expand this study; for example, P32 (Travel Time to Work by Means of Transportation to Work for Workers 16+ Years Who Did Not Work at Home), P52 (Household Income in 1999), and P87 (Poverty Status in 1999 by Age).

Folder and File Structure

The proposed folder and file structure for the project is as follows where the Project1<MyName> folder is a subfolder of the LearningAndUsingGIS folder.

- *Project1<MyName>* : This will be the overall project folder. At this level, it will contain *PublicTransportationMaricopaCounty.mxd*, the final GIS map composition.
- *Project1<MyName>\DownloadedFiles* : This folder will contain original map and data files that have been downloaded. Some of the files expanded from zipped files will be moved to other folders.
- *Project1<MyName>\ProcessedFiles* : This folder will contain files that are intermediate steps along the way to producing finished map layers. Any explanations needed from these files will be in *ReadMe.doc* files. This folder will also contain any images exported from ArcMap (or elsewhere) before they are inserted into the final report.
- *Project1<MyName>\Maps* : This folder will have the finished map layers used in the GIS. They will have the original map layer names as downloaded. Again, *Readme.doc* files might be included for documentation.
- *Project1<MyName>\Documents* : This folder will contain the final report or PowerPoint presentation. It will also contain the proposal and process log documents.

Process Log

This section has the list of major steps that I took to complete my project. Further details are in steps identified by lowercase letter (a, b, c, and so forth).

Note: The numbered steps in the next section are necessary for the process log. We have also included detailed steps denoted a, b, c, and so forth. Normally, you would not include all detailed steps unless required by your instructor. Some detailed steps, however, are important documentation, and you should include them, such as the ones we have placed in italic. In general, use your judgment and document details that might be useful to you or your instructor to explain your work.

Download Files

1. Start a **Web browser**, open **http://factfinder.census.gov/**, and download **SF3 table P30** for year 2000 census tracts of Maricopa County, Arizona.
   a. Click the **Download Center** button.
   b. Click the **Census 2000 Summary File 3 (SF3) – Sample Data** link.
   c. Click the **All Census Tracts in a County (140)** link.
   d. Click **Arizona** under Select a State, and click **Maricopa County** under Select a County.
   e. Click the **Selected Detailed Tables** button.
   f. Click **Go**.
   g. Click **P30, Means of Transportation to Work for Workers 16+ Years**, click **Add**, click **Next**, and click **Start Download**.
   h. Save the compressed file, **dc_dec_2000_sf3_u.zip**, in the **C:\LearningAndUsingGIS\Project1\DownloadedFiles** folder, and extract **dc_dec_2000_sf3_u_data1.txt** to the same folder.
2. Open **http://www.esri.com/data/download/census2000_tigerline/index.html**, and download map layers for Maricopa County, Arizona, Census Tracts, SF1 data, Municipalities, and Streets.
   a. Click **Preview and Download**.
   b. Click **Arizona** and click **Submit Selection**.
   c. Click the list arrow for **Select a County**, click **Maricopa**, and click **Submit Selection**.
   d. Click **Census Tracts 2000**, click **County Census Divisions 2000 (Cities)**, click **Line Features - Roads**, and click **Census Tract Demographics (SF1)**.
   e. Click **Proceed to Download**.
   f. Click **Download File**.
   g. Click **Extract**, and save **at_tigeresri56276406.zip** to the **C:\LearningAndUsingGIS\Project1\DownloadedFiles** folder.
   h. Decompress **at_tigeresri56276406.zip** in the same folder to yield *trt0004013.zip, ccd0004013.zip, sf1trt04000.zip,* and *lkA04013.zip*.
   i. Decompress **trt0004013.zip, ccd0004013.zip, sf1trt04000.zip**, and **lkA04013.zip** to the **C:\LearningAndUsingGIS\Project1\Maps** folder to yield *tgr04013trt00.shp, tgr04013ccd00.shp, tgr04000sf1trt.dbf,* and *tgr04013lkA.shp*.
   j. Change the name of **tgr04000sf1trt.dbf** to **SF1.dbf**. (Otherwise, the long name interferes with reading attribute names in a drop-down list later when creating new attributes in ArcGIS.)

Prepare Files

1. Import **dc_dec_2000_sf3_u_data1.txt** into Microsoft Excel. The downloaded table is not in standard table format because it has two rows of column headings instead of a single column heading. One has code values, such as P030003, and the other has descriptive phrases. Thus the task is to create a row of self-descriptive attribute names and to delete the other two heading columns.

   a. Start Excel and open **C:\LearningAndUsingGIS\Project1\ DownloadedFiles\dt dc_dec_2000_sf3_u_data1.txt**.

   b. Use the **Text Import Wizard** to import comma-delimited text.

   c. Save the file as the *.dbf* file **C:\LearningAndUsingGIS\Project1\ ProcessedFiles\SF3.dbf**.

   d. Delete columns **SUMLEVEL, GEO_NAME, P030003, P030004, P030006** through **P030012**, and **P030015**.

   e. Click in **2nd row cells** and read the full contents above in Excel's cell contents box.

   f. Change top-row column names:
      i.   **P030001** to **Worker16P**
      ii. **P030002** to **Drive**
      iii. **P030005** to **PubTrans**
      iv. **P030013** to **Bike**
      v.   **P030014** to **Walk**
      vi. **P030016** to **WorkHome**

   g. Delete **row 2** (that has the descriptive labels for columns).

   h. Insert a new column to the right of GEO_ID2 called **STFID** (this is needed as the join column to match the STFID column in *tgr04013trt00.shp*).

   i. In the new column, in cell C2, type the cell formula **= 0 & B2** (concatenating a 0 to GEO_ID2) and press **Enter** (that creates a text value, 04013010100, which is what is desired).

   j. Copy the **C2** formula through the rest of the column, range **C3:C664**.

   k. Save the file and exit Excel.

Build the ArcMap Document

1. Start **ArcMap** and add **tgr04013trt00.shp, tgr04013lkA.shp**, and **tgr04013ccd00.shp**.

2. Add a second copy of **tgr04013trt00.shp**.

   a. Google **UTM Zone** to look up Arizona's UTM zone (which is 12N).

   b. Set the layer projection to be **UTM**, zone **12N**, and **NAD 1983**.

   c. Set Map Properties to use **relative paths** for files.

3. Symbolize layers and save the map document.

   a. Symbolize **tgr04013lkA.shp** with a gray color, and change its name to **Streets**.

   b. Symbolize **tgr04013ccd00.shp** with no color fill and an outline 3 pixels wide. Change its name to **Cities**.

   c. Turn labeling on for Cities.

    d.   Zoom in to Phoenix, and create a spatial bookmark called **Phoenix** for it.

    e.   Save the map document as **C:\LearningAndUsingGISPristine\Project1\project1.mxd**.

Join SF3 and SF1 Tables to Tract Maps

1. Add tables **C:\LearningAndUsingGISPristine\Project1\Maps\SF1.dbf** and **C:\LearningAndUsingGISPristine\Project1\ProcessedFiles\SF3.dbf** to the map document.

2. Join **SF3.dbf** to a copy of **tgr04013trt00** using **STFID** in both tables as the join column.

3. Symbolize the joined copy of **tgr04013trt00.shp** using **PUBTRANS** as the Value field and **Workers16P** as the Normalization field with graduated colors and manual break points of **0.05, 0.10, 0.15, 0.20,** and **0.3503** with a **blue monochromatic** color ramp. Change the layer name to **Percent Workers Using Public Transportation**.

4. In the Symbology tab of the Layer Properties window, click the **Label** heading in the lower-right panel, click **Format Labels**, click **Percentage**, click the option button for **The number represents a fraction**, and click **Numeric Options** to select 0 decimal places.

5. Join **SF1.dbf** to the other copy of **tgr04013trt00** using **STFID** in both tables as the join column.

6. Symbolize this copy of **tgr04013trt00.shp** using **Graduated Symbols** with **FHH_CHILD** as the Value field and **HOUSEHOLDS** as the Normalization field with break points of **0.05, 0.10, 0.15, 0.20,** and **0.60** and a **red monochromatic** scale. Change the layer name to **Percent Female Headed Households with Children**.

7. Zoom in to the portion of Phoenix with high percentages of **Percent Female Headed Households with Children**, and select tracts that have high **Percent Female Headed Households with Children** and low **Percent Workers Using Public Transportation**.

Build a Map Layout

1. Go to **Layout view** in ArcMap, and create a layout.

    a.   Use Landscape orientation for 8.5 x 11 page size.

    b.   Add a legend for **Percent Female Headed Households with Children** and **Percent Workers Using Public Transportation**.

    c.   Right-click the **legend**, click **Convert to Graphics**, and click **Ungroup**.

    d.   Click the frame for **SF1.FHH_CHILD/SF1.HOUSEHOLDS** and delete it. Do the same for **SF3.PUBTRANS / SF3.WORKER16P**.

    e.   Double-click the **long headings**, and split them into two lines each.

    f.   Rearrange elements of the legend to eliminate extra space.

    g.   Select **all elements of the legend**, right-click the **legend**, and click **Group**.

    h.   Rearrange the map and legend. (Note: Instead of including a title in the layout, we'll type it into the Word document of our report, for more flexibility.)

2. Export a *.tif* image of the layout called **Figure1.tif** to
   C:\LearningAndUsingGISPristine\Project1\ProcessedFiles.
3. Create an inset map by drawing a **rectangle** around the zoomed-in map,
   extracting a **Phoenix map** from the cities map, symbolizing, and exporting the
   resulting *.tif* file as **InsetPhoenix.tif**. I added the drawing to a PowerPoint slide
   that has the layout of *Figure1.tif*.
4. Zoom in to a small area of interest, turn on and label **Streets**, and export the
   results as **Figure2.tif** to **C:\LearningAndUsingGISPristine\Project1\
   ProcessedFiles**.

Report

[The report is the most visible and portable deliverable that you produce. It is a stand-alone
document that covers all phases of the project and its results. It brings together several
parts of the proposal and process log along with new materials such as map layouts.]

Introduction

[The report in *C:\LearningAndUsingGIS\Project1\Documents\FinalReport.doc* includes an
introduction that just restates material found in the proposal. We do not repeat that material here to save space. See the electronic version of the report, which is complete.]

Data Sources and Processing

I obtained map layers for this project from the ESRI Tiger/Line 2000 Web site at *www.esri.
com/data/download/census2000_tigerline/index.html*. These consisted of three layers for
Maricopa County, Arizona: Minor Civil Divisions or Cities, so I could display the boundary of Phoenix; 2000 census tract boundaries, so I could prepare maps displaying variables representing the need for and utilization of public transportation; and streets for
context when zoomed in to problem areas that have potential gaps in providing public
transportation.

Census data is from two sources. Variables from Census 2000 Summary File 1 (SF1) are
from the ESRI Web site and include FHH_CHILD (the number of female-headed households with children) and HOUSEHOLDS (the total number of households).

The second data source is the U.S. Census Bureau's American FactFinder Web site at
http://factfinder.census.gov/. I downloaded table P30 from Census 2000 Summary File 3
(SF3). The variables needed from this table are P030001 = Workers 16 years and
over: Total, which I renamed WORKER16P, and P030005 = Workers 16 years and
over: Means of transportation to work: Public transportation, which I renamed
PUBTRANS.

Results

Figure 9-1 is a map for the central portion of Phoenix, Arizona, depicting the need for and utilization of public transportation. This figure shows the percentage of female-headed households with children by 2000 census tract as graduated point markers: the larger the area of the
circular point markers, the larger the percentage of such households. Also shown as a choropleth map of census tracts is the percentage of workers, ages 16 and older, who use public

transportation to get to work. Potential problem areas, where there might be inadequate public transportation, are census tracts with large percentages of female-headed households with children and low percentages of public transportation use for journeys to work. I have highlighted such areas with a cyan border color for tract boundaries in Figure 9-1.

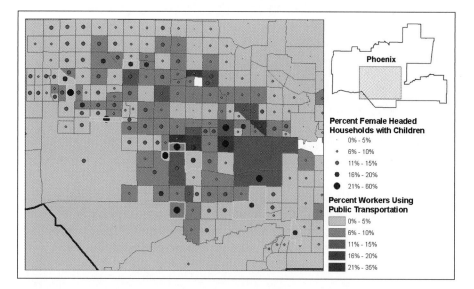

FIGURE 9-1 Map showing the distributions of percent female-headed households with children and percent workers using public transportation

Figure 9-2 zooms in to the highlighted rectangular tract shown in the northwest of Figure 9-1. Also shown in Figure 9-2 are streets. Clearly, a future study needs to include bus routes to see if areas, such as those in Figure 9-2, have adequate bus service.

Summary

This report has analyzed the need for and utilization of public transportation in Phoenix, Arizona. To represent need, I have used the percentage of households by census tract that have female-headed households with children. For the utilization of public transportation, I have used the percentage of workers, ages 16 and older, who use public transportation to get to work. There are clear gaps, as shown in Figure 9-1, with high percentages of female-headed households and low percentages of workers using public transportation.

Two major extensions are possible for future work. One is to use measures of poverty, such as the number of households that have poverty status, in addition to female-headed households with children. The second extension is to obtain a map layer, if possible, with bus routes. Then I could start analyzing potential new bus routes in areas with supply gaps.

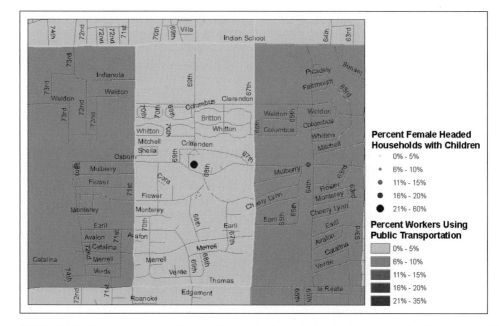

FIGURE 9-2   Zoomed-in map showing the distributions of percent female-headed households with children and percent workers using public transportation

PROJECT 2: ENVIRONMENT

The material we present on this project, like that of the first project, is in the form of project deliverables—a proposal, a process log, and a report—as if they were written by a student. This project is more advanced than the first project; it has more specialized map layers and a more advanced spatial analysis.

Proposal

The major issue on the feasibility of this project is data availability. The project needs data for point sources of pollution. Fortunately, environmental protection laws have led to the collection and public access of detailed pollution data.

Background

Air and water pollutants, toxic chemical releases, and other environmental hazards are of great interest to many persons, ranging from healthcare professionals to average citizens who want to learn more about the communities in which they live.

The Environmental Protection Agency (EPA), Environmental Defense (a leading non-profit organization representing more than 400,000 members), and others track and make available pollution data across the United States. For example, through its Envirofacts Data Warehouse, the EPA provides access to several databases for air, water, and land pollution anywhere in the United States. The EPA also makes its Toxics Release Inventory database available, with data on toxic chemical releases and other waste management activities reported annually by various industry groups and federal facilities. You can learn more about the EPA at its Web site, *www.epa.gov*.

Environmental Defense is another great source of environmental data. Established in 1967, Environmental Defense has combined approaches from science, economics, and law to create innovative, equitable, and cost-effective solutions to society's most urgent environmental problems. You can learn more about the Environmental Defense at their Web site, *www.environmentaldefense.org/home.cfm*.

The Problem and Approach to Solution

The problem to be addressed concerns the proximity of environmental hazards to the black population and highly populated areas in Minneapolis, Minnesota. I propose to compare maps displaying companies releasing the most pollutants in Minneapolis compared to locations of the black population in that city. I will use buffers to identify populations likely at risk because of proximity to large-volume toxic air releases.

Scope

Minorities tend to live in communities with high levels of pollution. There are many reasons why this is so, but the underlying causes are economic and political. Poverty is concentrated in minority populations, although, of course, not all people in minority groups are poor. The low-cost housing that poor persons can afford is often undesirable in many ways, including being in polluted environments. On the political side, poor people generally have little political clout and generally have been underrepresented in decisions impacting pollution in their areas. The field of environmental justice is concerned with redressing such inequities (see *www.epa.gov/compliance/environmentaljustice*). Clearly, minorities need increased protection from environmental pollution.

Generally, there are many polluters in an urban area, but for an exploratory study on environmental pollution in Minneapolis, I will restrict attention to the top 20 companies with toxic air releases in Hennepin County, Minnesota, based on how many pounds per year of pollution they emit.

Data and Map Layer Sources

Data for this project includes census layers for Hennepin County, Minnesota, which has the city of Minneapolis within its boundaries. These layers are Minor Civil Divisions and Census Tracts. Census tract data is also included.

I will download these map layers from the ESRI Tiger/Line 2000 Web site, *www.esri. com/data/download/census2000_tigerline/index.html*. I will download toxic release data from a Web site sponsored by the Environmental Defense organization at *www.scorecard. org*. The latitude and longitude of polluters is included in the data. Lastly, I will download latitude and longitude locations for schools in Hennepin County, Minnesota, from *www.hometownlocator.com*.

Folder and File Structure

The proposed folder and file structure for the project is as follows, where the Project2<MyName> folder is a subfolder of the LearningAndUsingGIS folder.

- *Project2<MyName>* : This folder will be the overall project folder. It will contain *Project2<MyName>.mxd*, the final ArcMap document.
- *Project2<MyName>\DownloadedFiles* : This folder will contain original map and data files as downloaded. Some of the files expanded from zipped files will be saved in other folders.
- *Project2<MyName>\ProcessedFiles* : This folder will contain files that were intermediate steps along the way to producing finished map layers. Any explanations needed about these files will be in *ReadMe.doc* files. This folder will also contain any images exported from ArcMap before they are inserted into the final report.
- *Project2<MyName>\Maps* : This folder will have the finished map layers used in the GIS. They will have the original map layer names as downloaded. Again, *Readme.Doc* files might be included for documentation.
- *Project2<MyName>\Documents* : This folder will contain the final report.

Process Log

This section has the list of major steps that I took to complete my project. Further details are in steps identified by lower case letter (a, b, c, and so forth).

Download Files

1. Open **http://www.esri.com/data/download/census2000_tigerline/index.html**, and download map layers for Hennepin County, Minnesota, **census tracts**, **census SF1 data**, and **municipalities**.
   a. Click **Preview and Download Data**.
   b. Click **Minnesota** and click **Submit Selection**.
   c. Click the list arrow for **Select a County**, click **Hennepin** and click **Submit Selection**.
   d. Click **Census Tracts 2000, Census Tract Demographics (SF1)**, and **County Census Divisions 2000 (Municipalities)**.
   e. Click **Proceed to Download**.
   f. Click **Download File**, and the PKZIP Plug-In window opens.
   g. Click **Extract** and browse to the **C:\LearningAndUsingGIS\Project2\DownloadedFiles** folder.
   h. Start **My Computer** and browse to the **C:\LearningAndUsingGIS\Project2\DownloadedFiles**.
   i. Unzip **trt0027053.zip**, **sf1trt27000.zip**, and **ccd00227053.zip** to the **C:\LearningAndUsingGIS\Project2\Maps** folder.

2. Open **http://www.scorecard.org**, and download data for the top 20 polluters in Hennepin County, Minnesota.

    a. From the **Pollution in Your Community** section, type in zip code **55401**, and click **Get Report**. (The program uses any zip code in the county to identify the county.)

    b. Under Toxic Chemicals Released by Factories, Power Plants and Other Industrial Companies, click the Top Polluters in Your County link. The top 20 polluters are listed.

    c. Click the top polluter, **Ritrama, Inc.**, to see its location (the top polluter might be different when data is revised on this Web site).

    d. Toward the bottom of the list, click **Facility Information**. In addition to the address and contact information, it lists the latitude and longitude data for the site.

    e. Start **Excel**, and build a spreadsheet for attributes: **Name**, **City**, **SIC_CODE**, **Latitude**, **Longitude**, and **Pounds** that you will copy and paste from the scorecard facility data site. Include all companies that are the top 20 polluters in Hennepin County.

    f. Before saving the file, select the cells in the latitude and longitude columns and change their format to **Number** and **5 Decimal places**.

    g. Repeat the cell format change for **Pounds**, but change the decimal places to **0**.

    h. Save the file as a DBF IV file called **HennepinCountyPolluters.DBF** in the **C:\LearningAndUsingGIS\Project2\Maps** folder.

Build an ArcMap Document

1. Start **ArcMap** and add **tgr27053trt00.shp**, **227053ccd00.shp**, and **tgr27000sf1trt.dbf**.

2. Change the layer projection to **state plane, 1983 NAD (feet)**, and **Minnesota South**.

3. Symbolize **ccd00227053.shp** with a **transparent fill** and **dark blue** outline **1.5** pixels wide. Change its name to **Municipalities**, and label the municipalities by **name**.

4. Join **tgr27000sf1trt.dbf** to the attribute table of **tgr27053trt00.shp** using **STFID** in both tables as the join column.

5. Symbolize **tgr27053trt00.shp** using the field **BLACK** and manual break points of **500**, **1000**, **1500**, **2000**, and **2519** with a **gray monochromatic scale**. Change its name to **Black Population**.

6. Add the **HennepinCountyPolluters.dbf** as an XY theme using **X field = LONGTUDE** and **Y field = LATITUDE**, and symbolize it using **red graduated circles** sizes 4-14 with **3** manual classifications of **less than 25,000**, **25,000 to 50,000**, and **50,000 and greater**. Change its name to **Hazardous Emissions (Pounds per Year)**.

7. Convert the **XY theme** to a **shapefile**, using the coordinate system of the data frame, by right-clicking the **XY theme**, and clicking **Data**, then **Export**, and so on. Call the new theme **TopPolluters.shp**.

8. Select the **top four polluters in Hennepin County** (those over 50,000 pounds per year of emissions) and create a **2-mile buffer** around these companies. Note: Because the polluter point layer is projected into rectangular coordinates, the buffers will be circular as desired. If left to latitude and longitude coordinates, they would be ellipses when viewed in state plane coordinates.
9. For all tracts in Hennepin County, get statistics for the population of blacks and whites. Then select the census tracts that have their centers within the 2-mile buffer. From the selected tracts, get statistics on the number of blacks and whites living within 2 miles of the polluters. Then calculate the percentage of blacks and the percentage of whites living within 2 miles of the largest polluters.

Build Map Layout

1. Go to Layout view in ArcMap and create a layout.
    a. Use Landscape orientation for 8.5 x 11 page size.
    b. Add a legend for **Top Polluters** and **Black Population**.
    c. Right-click the **legend**, click **Convert to Graphics**, and click **Ungroup**.
    d. Modify the text and placement of elements as desired.
    e. Select all elements of the legend, right-click the **legend**, and click **Group**.
    f. Rearrange the map and legend. (Note: Instead of including a title in the layout, we'll type it into the Word document of our report, for more flexibility.)
2. Export a *.tif* image of the layout called **Figure9-3.tif** to **C:\LearningAndUsingGISPristine\Project2\ProcessedFiles**.

Report

The report draws attention to a potential environmental hazard: toxic pollutant emissions emitted into the air near black and white populations. The results show what is happening, but they cannot show effects of potentially related ill health.

Introduction

[The report in *C:\LearningAndUsingGIS\Project2\Documents\FinalReport.doc* includes an introduction that restates material found in the proposal's background, problem and approach to solution, and rationale for scope sections. To save space, we do not repeat that material here. See the electronic version of the report for the introduction.]

Data Sources and Processing

I obtained map layers for this project from the ESRI Tiger/Line 2000 Web site at *www.esri.com/data/download/census2000_tigerline/index.html*. These consisted of two map layers for Hennepin County, Minneapolis: Minor Civil Divisions so I could display the boundary of Minneapolis and the 2000 census tract boundaries so I could prepare maps displaying the black population.

The second data source is the Environmental Defense Agency's Web site at *www. scorecard.org.* I downloaded data on the top 20 polluters in Hennepin County and compiled a table describing the company name, type of company, latitude and longitude location, and the amount of toxic emissions in pounds per year.

Results

Figure 9-3 displays the top 20 polluting companies in Hennepin County, Minnesota, by the amount of hazardous emissions in pounds per year compared to the black population by census tract. Also shown on the map are 2-mile buffers of the top four polluters, each emitting over 50,000 pounds per year (25 tons per year) of toxic pollutants.

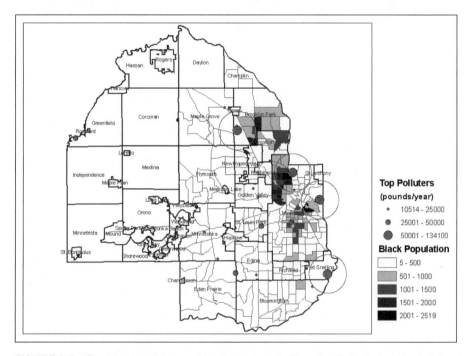

FIGURE 9-3 Top 20 air pollution sources for toxic emissions, 2-mile buffers of the top four polluters, and black population by 2000 census tract: Hennepin County, Minnesota

From Figure 9-3, we can draw the conclusion that a higher percentage of the black population lives near top pollution sources than the white population. To further make this point, Table 9-1 provides statistics derived from the GIS that produced Figure 9-3. The first row of the table provides the number of blacks and whites living within 2 miles of the top four toxic air pollution sources. I obtained these populations by selecting all census tracts that have their centers within two miles of one of the four major pollution sources. The second row provides the total population of blacks and whites living in Hennepin County. Finally, the third row uses the first two rows to calculate the percentage of blacks and percentage of whites living within 2 miles of the top four polluters. We see that 26 percent of blacks are so located, whereas only 9 percent of whites are near the pollution sources. This is an indication of an environmental justice problem.

TABLE 9-1 Population within a 2-mile buffer of top polluters: Hennepin County, Minnesota, 2000 census tracts

	Blacks	Whites
Residing within 2 miles of the top four toxic air pollution sources	25,844	85,599
Residing with Hennepin County	99,943	898,921
Percentage of population residing within 2 miles of the top four toxic air pollution sources	25.9%	8.6%

Conclusion

This report has analyzed the black and white populations in close proximity to environmental hazards in Hennepin County, Minnesota. For data on environmental hazards, I have used the top 20 polluters in Hennepin County and their toxic emissions (pounds per year). For population statistics, I have used U.S. Census data for black and white populations. Clearly, a higher percentage of the black population lives within the vicinity of toxic air emissions than the white population: 26 percent for blacks versus 9 percent for whites. There appears to be the potential for exposure to environmental hazards around the top polluters; however, actual risks would need to be determined through in-depth studies.

There are two major extensions possible for future work. One would be to consider other at-risk populations, such as very old or very young persons. Another would be to obtain data on prevailing wind directions and to study populations downwind of polluters.

Chapter 9 Summary

Project management is a field concerned with the phases, components, and deliverables of project work. Project phases are organized into systems development life cycles. The most common such cycle is called the waterfall model because of the assumption that after a phase is completed, the project flows on to the next stage, never to return to earlier phases. Real-life projects often violate this assumption because (1) later phases uncover new information that affect earlier decisions, (2) the nature of the problem changes because of external influences, such as enactment of a new law, or (3) the client—if there is one—changes his mind about some aspect of the project.

Project phases include problem identification, analysis, design, and implementation. In simple GIS projects, we combine analysis with problem identification and introduce some special components for GIS. The deliverable for problem identification and analysis is a project proposal that includes problem-area background, problem identification, project scope, and a rationale for the scope. For GIS project proposals, we also include identification of GIS resources and the design of a folder structure for all project files.

The process log records major steps and some detailed steps used to build the GIS. The deliverable for implementation is the folder structure with completed GIS and other files and a written report that includes an introduction, data sources and processing, and results sections.

We presented deliverables for two completed projects: one on public transportation in Phoenix, Arizona, and the second on environmental pollution in Minneapolis, Minnesota. Exercises 1 and 2 of this chapter have you use these projects as templates for replicating the projects for your own county and city. Exercise 3 compiles and finishes the Swimming Pool Case Study. If time permits, you could work on an entirely new project, as suggested in Exercise 4.

Key Terms

Analysis phase A phase of project management that transforms a problem statement into a solution on paper. This phase requires much creative work to forge a solution approach and results in a description, diagrams, or other paper-based representations of the end product.

Deliverable Documents or computer-based components that are the result of a phase of project management. Generally, the client or instructor reviews and approves deliverables at the end of each project phase.

Design phase A phase of project management during which the solution gets built. It is here that the ArcGIS map document gets built.

Implementation phase A phase of project management in which the client or instructor starts using the completed system. Deliverables might be limited to reports and presentations, or in some cases, might include a working GIS along with documentation for its use.

Problem identification phase The first phase of project management in which the problem is stated along with a solution approach that includes project scope and limitations.

Scope A statement of what a project will and will not accomplish. Generally, some rationale is desirable for choices and limitations, such as limiting work to high-priority, feasible, or important objectives.

Systems development life cycle The collection of all project phases and deliverables.

Waterfall model The most common systems development life cycle, in which a project's phases are linear rather than recursive. In reality, project development usually requires cycling back through previous phases; however, the simplicity of this model makes it desirable.

Work-breakdown structure A list of tasks, generally organized by project phase, with who is assigned to do each item and when each item is due.

Short-Answer Questions

1. What is the purpose of project management? Would a GIS staff person need project management for daily tasks, such as adding new points to a map layer for events that occur regularly (an example is a crime analyst who adds yesterday's crimes to a point map layer every day)? Why or why not?

336

2. Two options for describing the problem to be addressed in a computer-based project are as follows: (1) to state the solution, including appropriate use of information technologies, or (2) to state symptoms of a gap between current and desired states of affairs. One of these options is right and the other wrong. Which is which? Explain your answer.

3. The systems development life cycle has two major parts: conceptual work (problem identification and analysis) and hands-on work (design and implementation). What are the benefits of doing the conceptual work before starting hands-on work?

4. Scope is a critical aspect of project management. What is scope, and why is it important?

5. What purposes does the work-breakdown structure serve? If you were the manager of a project team, how would you go about creating the work-breakdown structure?

6. A simple option for storing the files of a computer project is to create a folder with a good, descriptive name and then place all files directly in that folder. Is this a good idea for GIS projects? Why or why not?

7. On a team project, it is desirable to store project files on a shared network server. Why? What rules would you establish for team members and their project work in regard to use of the shared storage site?

8. What is a process log? Why is it valuable to project members, the project manager (if there is one), and the client?

9. If you were to make a PowerPoint presentation of a GIS project, what would the major sections of the presentation be? State them in order of presentation.

10. Should project reports include a "future work" section? What is the value of such a section to team members? To the client?

Exercises

1. **Public Transportation Project.** Replicate the public transportation project of this chapter for the county or city of your choice. Create a folder called **C:\LearningAndUsingGIS\ProjectPublicTransportation<YourName>** that includes all subfolders and files comparable to C:\LearningAndUsingGIS\Project1\. You can simply reuse certain parts of the deliverables, if applicable, such as the background of the proposal. As an option, carry out one of the future work suggestions that we provided in the project's solution, or pursue an additional issue that you identify on your own. Make arrangements

to compress C:\LearningAndUsingGIS\ProjectPublicTransportation<YourName>\ and its subfolders and files to turn in to your instructor. Call your compressed file **ProjectPublicTransportation<YourName>.zip.**

2. **Environmental Pollution Project.** Replicate the environmental pollution project of this chapter for the county of your choice. Create a folder called **C:\LearningAndUsingGIS\ProjectEnvironmentalPollution<YourName>** that includes all subfolders and files comparable to C:\LearningAndUsingGIS\Project2\. You can simply reuse certain parts of the deliverables if applicable, such as the background in the proposal. As an option, carry out one of the future work suggestions that we provided in the project's solution, or pursue an additional issue that you identify on your own. Make arrangements to compress C:\LearningAndUsingGIS\ProjectEnvironmentalPollution<YourName>\ and its subfolders and files to turn in to your instructor. Call your compressed file **ProjectEnvironmentalPollution<YourName>.zip**.

3. **Swimming Pool Case Study.** The objective of this project is to conduct a proximity analysis of open Pittsburgh Pools.

   In addition to *pooltags.shp* data previously analyzed, use new data sets *JackStackVisits.dbf* and *PhillipsVisits.dbf* provided in C:\LearningAndUsingGIS\Data\. These data sets are random samples of actual pool visits made by pool tag holders to one of two pools—Jack Stack and Phillips—for the same summer season as other data that you have analyzed for this case study.

   In the summer season of the data sample, there were 16,878 visits by 4412 unique pool tag holders to Jack Stack Pool. The random sample of these visits in *JackStackProtected.dbf* has size 761 and includes a "sanitized" street address (we moved each street number to the center of the block-long street segment to protect identity of pool tag holders), zip code, whether the pool tag holder is a resident of Pittsburgh, the number of persons at the pool-tag-holder's residence in total who had pool tags, the age of the person making the visit, and the number of visits that the person made to the pool during the summer season. For the Phillips data, there were 14,214 pool tag visits made by 3651 unique pool tags holders with a random sample size of 740. This data set has the same schema as the Jack Stack data. You need to geocode (address match) this data. Then you can conduct an analysis of use rates based on travel distance, similar to that of Exercise 3-3.

   Hints for the use rate analysis include the following:

   - Use State Plane coordinates for your ArcMap data frame, and project the pools shapefile permanently to State Plane coordinates. Otherwise, pool buffers will not be circular when displayed in rectangular coordinates but will be elliptical.

   - Be sure that ArcCatalog is closed when building buffers because it will put a lock on files and not allow you to process them.

   - Reanalyze the intended use rate patterns using several buffer radiuses with the Multiple Ring Buffer tool. Start with a small buffer radius and increase buffer increments as the buffers become larger; for example, start with 0.25 miles and further out have a 2- to 3-mile radius—use patterns change quickly as one moves away from pools. Use the dissolve option of All to get polygons that are rings, useful for spatial joins. Be sure to set buffer unit to miles for convenience. Summarize counts of pool tag holders and sums of youths of ages 5 to 17 for the use rate analysis.

- For the Phillips and Jack Stack data, select one pool at a time and, again, use several buffer radiuses with the Multiple Ring Buffer tool with increasing buffer increments. Use the dissolve option of All to get polygons that are rings, and be sure to set buffer units to miles. One attribute to analyze is average number of visits per summer per pool tag holder as a function of distance.

Produce Excel scatter plots of various measures versus buffer radius or average distance within a buffer. Produce one or more map documents to do your analytical work and one or more map documents for presentation. What buffer radius do you recommend that defines the boundary between served and underserved areas in Pittsburgh in regard to pool access? Which closed pools, if any, would plug gaps in coverage if opened?

Place your results in your C:\LearningAndUsingGIS\ProjectSwimmingPools<YourName>\ folder. Make arrangements to compress the folder and its subfolders and files to turn in to your instructor. Call your compressed file **ProjectSwimmingPools<YourName>.zip**.

4. **Independent Project.** Carry out a project that you or your instructor identify. If you have an instructor, write the proposal, turn it in, and get feedback from your instructor before proceeding too far in building the GIS. Often, the feedback will be that you should narrow the scope of your project to make it feasible within time limits. Finally, build the GIS and produce all deliverables. Name your project folder **C:\LearningAndUsingGIS\ProjectIndependent<YourName>**, compress it, and turn it in to your instructor.

References

ESRI Census 2000 Tiger/Line Data, Internet URL:
   http://www.esri.com/data/download/census2000_tigerline/index.html (accessed
   April 26, 2005)
Hometown Locator, Internet URL: http://www.hometownlocator.com/ (accessed April 26, 2005)
Kendall, K. E. and J. E. Kendall. *Systems Analysis and Design*, 3rd Ed., Prentice Hall,
   Englewood Cliffs, 1995, pp. 7-11.
Public Transportation Partnership for Tomorrow, Internet URL:
   http://www.publictransportation.org/pt2/ (accessed April 26, 2005)
Scorecard, The Pollution Information Site, Internet URL: http://www.scorecard.org/ (accessed
   April 26, 2005)
U.S. Census Bureau, American FactFinder: Internet URL:
   http://factfinder.census.gov/servlet/DatasetMainPageServlet?_program=DEC&_lang=en
   (accessed April 26, 2005)
U.S. Environmental Protection Agency, Internet URL: http://www.epa.gov/ (accessed
   April 25, 2005)

APPENDIX **A**

INSTALLING THE LEARNINGANDUSINGGIS DATA FILES AND OBTAINING THE ARCGIS, ARCVIEW SOFTWARE

INSTALLING DATA FILES

The CD included with this book has the Data Files necessary to complete its step-by-step tutorials and exercises. You will need 627 MB of free space on a hard drive. We recommend that you install the data on your C drive, but you can use any drive that has sufficient space.

1. Insert the **Learning And Using GIS** CD into your CD-ROM or DVD-ROM drive.
2. If the CD does not automatically open in a My Computer window, open **My Computer** and double-click your **CD** or **DVD** drive.
3. Right-click the **LearningAndUsingGIS** folder, and click **Copy**.
4. Click the **Up** button in My Computer so that you can see the icon for your C drive or other target drive for copying.
5. Right-click the **C:** or other drive, and click **Paste**. (*This creates the C:\LearningAndUsingGIS\ folder, all of its subfolders, and files.*)

OBTAINING ARCGIS, ARCVIEW SOFTWARE

If you are a matriculated student at a school, college, or university that has a site license for ArcGIS Desktop software, you can obtain a copy of ArcView for use on your own Windows XP or Windows 2000 computer from your instructor or computer center. See *www.esri.com/industries/university/education/sitelic.html* for more information.

Alternatively, you can obtain a copy of the ArcView Student One-Year License for $100 directly from ESRI by calling (800) 447-9778, with delivery within one week. You will have to fax or otherwise send proof that you are a student, such as a student ID photocopy or transcript. This is a full version of the software that will function for one year.

If you are not a student, but an individual studying on your own, you can obtain a 60-day evaluation version of ArcView for Windows XP and Windows 2000 from *www.esri.com/software/arcgis/arcview/eval/evalcd.html*. This is also a full version of the software. Instructors can contact their regional salesperson (see *www.esri.com/company/contactusa.html*) and often obtain trial copies for a class of students in a single order. It takes two weeks or longer to obtain trial copies.

INDEX

Numbers in **bold** indicate where a key term has been defined in the text.

personal geodatabase, 204
point centroids, 236–238
spatial bookmarks, 47–48
world map documents, 67
current extent, 40, **71**

D

data
cleaning, 256, 280, **281**
dictionary, 80–83, 196–198
downloading point, 188–190
files, installing, 339
frames, creating, 164–166
geocoding location, 253–254
mapping with polygon identifiers, 255
mapping zip code, 259–262
spatial reference, 45, 64
spatial referenced, 178
data tables
converting, 207
joining to map layers, 200–202
data types, common, 80
databases
described, **123**
vector map formats, 80
date data type, **122**
dBase format, 196–198
decimal data type, **122**
degrees of longitude, 42
deliverables, 319, **335**
demographic analysis, conducting, 28–29
design phase, project management, 319, **335**
designing
maps, 125–137
maps using ArcGIS, 137–157
diagrams, spider, 220, **248**
dichromatic color scale, 131, **171**
differential corrections, 290, **310**
digital ortho quadrangles (DOQs), 191
digitizing
heads-up, **281**
map features generally, 287–288, 310
photographs, 85–86

stream, 291, **311**
tablets, 290–291, **310**
ways of, 290–291
Dim statements, 219
discrete variables, **172**
dissolve function, 214, 218–219, 227–231, **247**
documents
See also map documents
creating world map, 67
map, described, 3, **34**
DOQs (digital ortho quadrangles), 191
dot density maps, 156–157
downloading
data for maps, 10
map boundary files, 183–184
point data, 188–190
raster maps, 191–192
Draw toolbar, 107–109

E

E00 export format, 80, **122**
editing
line features, 299
polygon features, 301–309
emergency medical services (EMS) zones, 227, 271–272
enlarging
Magnification window, ArcMap, 56–59
with zooming tools, 48–53
equivalent projections, 46, **71**
ESRI Web site, 186–188, 207, 220
event themes, 80, **122**
Excel, cleaning data using, 196–98
expert systems, **281**
exponential scale, 134, **172**
exporting map layouts to PowerPoint, 161–162
extent, map, full, 40, **71**
extracting
features from base maps, 247
features from map layers, 215–220, 221–227
information from information system, 76–77